CLAUSEWITZ AND MODERN STRATEGY

Carl von Clausewitz (from *BBC Hulton Picture Library*)

CLAUSEWITZ
AND
MODERN STRATEGY

Edited by
MICHAEL I. HANDEL

FRANK CASS

First published 1986 in Great Britain by
FRANK CASS AND COMPANY LIMITED
Gainsborough House, 11 Gainsborough Road,
London E11 1RS, England

and in the United States of America by
FRANK CASS AND COMPANY LIMITED
c/o Biblio Distribution Centre
81 Adams Drive, P.O. Box 327, Totowa, NJ 07511

British Library Cataloguing in Publication Data

Clausewitz and modern strategy — (journal
  of strategic studies, ISSN 0140 - 2390; 9,
  No. 2 & 3)
  1. Clausewitz, Carl von. 2. Military art
  and science — History — 19th century
  I. Handel, Michael I. II. Series
355'.02'0924   U21.2

  ISBN 0-7146-3294-5 (cased)
  ISBN 0-7146-4053-0 (paperback)

Library of Congress Cataloging-in-Publication Data

Clausewitz and modern strategy.

Published also as v. 9, no. 2–3 of the Journal of
strategic studies.
Includes index.
1. Clausewitz, Carl von, 1780–1831. Vom Kriege.
2. Military art and science—History—19th century.
3. Military art and science—History—20th century.
4. War. I. Handel, Michael I.
U102.C6643C54 1986   355'.02'0924   86–4166
ISBN 0-7146-3294-5 (cased)
ISBN 0-7146-4053-0 (paperback)
This group of studies first appeared in a Special Issue on
Clausewitz and Modern Strategy of *The Journal of Strategic
Studies* Vol. 9, Nos. 2 and 3 published by Frank Cass & Co.
Ltd.

Printed and bound in Great Britain by
Robert Hartnoll Ltd, Bodmin, Cornwall

TO MY FRIEND
RICHARD K. BETTS

CONTENTS

NOTES ON CONTRIBUTORS

Michael I. Handel is Professor of National Security Affairs at the US Army War College, Carlisle, Pennsylvania. He is the author of several monographs and books including *Israel's Political-Military Doctrine* (Harvard University Center for International Affairs), *The Diplomacy of Surprise: Hitler, Nixon, Sadat* (Harvard University Center for International Affairs, 1981), and *Weak States in the International System* (Frank Cass, 1981).

Martin van Creveld is Associate Professor of History at The Hebrew University, Jerusalem, and among his publications are *Hitler's Strategy 1940–41: The Balkan Clue* (Cambridge University Press, 1977); *Supplying War: Logistics from Wallenstein to Patton* (Cambridge University Press, 1977); *Fighting Power: German and U.S. Military Performance, 1939–1945* (Greenwood Press, 1982) and *Command in War* (Harvard University Press, 1985).

Katherine L. Herbig is Adjunct Research Professor at the Naval Post-graduate School, Monterey, California. Her research has been on intelligence issues, particularly on strategic deception, and a recent monograph, *American Strategic Deception in the Pacific 1942–1945*, is on the US deception campaign against the Japanese in the Second World War. She is also author of several books and articles.

David Kahn is Assistant Viewpoints Editor of *Newsday* (the Long Island daily) and the author of *The Codebreakers, Hitler's Spies* and *Kahn on Codes* (all published by Macmillan), and of many magazine, journal and newspaper articles on cryptology and military intelligence.

Werner Hahlweg is Professor of Military History and Military Sciences at the University of Munster and includes among his publications *Die Heeresreform der Oranier: Das Kriegsbuch des Grafen Johann von Nassau-Siegen* (Wiesbaden, 1973), *Carl von Clausewitz, Vom Kriege* (Bonn, 1980). In preparation is a second volume of *Carl von Clause-witz, Schriften-Aufsatze-Studien-Briefe*.

Colonel Harold W. Nelson, US Army is Director of Military Strategy at US Army War College, Carlisle Barracks, Pennsylvania, and has taught history and strategy at the US Military Academy and the US Army Command and General Staff College, besides serving in various troop assignments in the United States, Vietnam, Korea, and Germany and working in the Office of the Defense Advisor at the US Mission to NATO. He is the author of a forthcoming book, *Leon Trotsky and the Art of Insurrection, 1905–1917.*

Jay Luvaas is currently Professor of Military History at the US Army War College, Carlisle Barracks, Pennsylvania, and lists among his publications *The Military Legacy of the Civil War: The European Inheritance* (Chicago, 1959) and *The Education of an Army: British Military Thought 1915–1940* (Chicago and London, 1964). He has completed a basic translation of Napoleon's selected thoughts on war and is currently working on a title 'The Lure of Old Battlefields', a study of the evolution of the generalship of Frederick the Great, and a series of interpretative essays on the evolution of the art of war during the American Civil War.

Wallace P. Franz is presently theater combined arms analyst for the Boeing Aerospace Co. in Seattle, Washington. He is author of several articles in *Military Review* and is currently working on a book about large unit maneuvers. While at the US Army War College, he conducted courses on Clausewitz, large unit operation and war gaming.

Jehuda L. Wallach is Professor for Military History at the Aranne School of History, Tel-Aviv University. Among his published works are *The Dogma and the Battle of Annihilation: Theories of Clausewitz and Schlieffen and their Impact on the German Conduct of Two World Wars* (German and American editions) and *Kriegstheorien. Ihre Entwicklung im 19 and 20* (German and Hebrew editions).

Klaus-Jürgen Müller is Professor of Modern and Contemporary History at the University of the Bundeswehr and the University of Hamburg, and lists among his publications *Das Heer und Hitler. Armee und National-sozialismus 1933–1940* (1969), *Armee, Politik und Gesellschaft in Deutschland* (1979), and *General Ludwig Beck – Generalstabschef des deutschen Heeres 1933–38* (1980).

Williamson Murray is currently Visiting Professor of Strategy at the Naval War College, Rhode Island and Associate Professor of History at Ohio State University. He is author of *The Change in the Euro-*

pean Balance of Power, 1938–1939: The Path to Ruin (Princeton University Press, 1984) and *Luftwaffe* (Nautical and Aviation Press/ Allen & Unwin, 1985).

Douglas Porch is presently Mark Clark Professor of History at The Citadel, The Military College of South Carolina and has published several books including *Army and Revolution, France 1815–1848* (Routledge & Kegan Paul, 1974) and *The March to the Marne: The French Army 1871–1914* (Cambridge University Press, 1981).

John Gooch teaches history at the University of Lancaster and is co-editor of *The Journal of Strategic Studies*. Among his books are *The Plans of War: The General Staff and British Military Strategy c. 1900–1916* (Routledge & Kegan Paul, 1974), *Armies in Europe* (Routledge & Kegan Paul, 1980) and *The Prospect of War: British Defence Policy 1847–1942* (Frank Cass, 1981).

PREFACE

The essays in this book were presented at an international conference 'On Clausewitz' held at the US Army War College in Carlisle Barracks, Pennsylvania in April 1985. The conference could not have taken place without the active support and encouragement of Major General William F. Burns. While preparing the essays for publication, the editor received the support of Major General James E. Thompson and Brigadier General Richard L. Reynard, Colonel Charles H. Beitz, Jr., Colonel Keith A. Barlow, the Director of Academic Affairs, Dr Charles M. Hersh, Colonel Robert L. Oliver, Colonel Dave Johnson, all of the US Army War College. In the final analysis it is the enthusiasm and intellectual contribution of each of the authors which made the conference such an unusual learning experience for both the participants and audience. I wish to thank them all and hope that this book will convey to the reader some of the intellectual excitement of the conference.

Michael I. Handel

HOW TO READ CLAUSEWITZ

I wish to guard myself carefully against even the appearance of recommending Clausewitz as if he were an inspired author to question whom is presumption. For infallibility is not given to mortal man. On the contrary, the best way to read any author, however great and famous, is in the spirit of resistance, to deny the truth of everything one does not clearly see, to wrestle it out, and to admit nothing till one is convinced that it really is so. Thus with Clausewitz. What one acquires in this way becomes part of one's own mental possessions for every afterwards.

It is true that Clausewitz' work 'On War' is bulky, which frightens away many people. But, owing to the form of his writings, it is not necessary to read him straight through, as one would an ordinary text-book. He is far too bulky and concentrated for that kind of rapid reading. First of all, buy Clausewitz and keep it in your room; then read it when, and only when, the spirit moves you, and mark with blue pencil the most important passages that strike you, so that you can easily find or refer to them again, which otherwise in so large a book is difficult. Any question you are engaged upon, strategical or tactical, look in Clausewitz to see what he has to say, deny it if you can, and compare it with what the most recent writers on the subject say. Of course, I know that each man has only got a limited amount of time and a limited amount of reading energy, on both of which there are many other demands. But I submit that if you keep Clausewitz as a 'book of reference', he won't interfere at all with other necessary reading, and that you will then gradually and quietly saturate your mind with his practical way of looking at things, and, further, that you will in the end come to look upon him as a guide, philosopher, and friend, whom you would not for worlds be without. As Clausewitz himself would say, 'On this we stand firm, and look upon it as a fact to be depended on'.

Major Stewart L. Murray, The Reality of War:
An Introduction to Clausewitz
(London: Hugh Rees 1909) pp. 14–15.

INTRODUCTION

The *magnum opus* of Carl von Clausewitz, *On War*, is a work frequently quoted (usually the one famous quotation) but often superficially read. This is not surprising. *On War* is a rather lengthy book that requires careful and repeated reading, in part because of its highly theoretical and abstract nature, and in part because sections of it are tedious, boring, or outdated.

In developing his comprehensive theory of war, Clausewitz relied on a number of different approaches and disciplines. *On War* is, at one and the same time, a text dealing with the philosophy, epistemology, and methodology of the social sciences, as well as with history, political theory, psychology and, of course, military strategy and tactics. This interdisciplinary, eclectic approach to the study of war is natural since the conduct of war is a complex phenomenon that cuts across every type of human activity. The fact that, by definition, the study of war cannot be as narrowly focused as is that of some other disciplines in the social sciences (for example, economics or psychology) enables us to understand the monumental difficulty of the task Clausewitz accomplished. The broad scope of his work also explains the book's failure to become popular in any one of the aforementioned disciplines despite its importance and originality.

For philosophers, *On War* always has been too much of a practical book and therefore not sufficiently challenging. For political theorists, on the other hand, it has dealt too much with purely military affairs and too little with political theory as such. Although *On War* is dedicated to the theme of international politics and politics in general (that is, by addressing the use and application of force among independent political units), it has nevertheless been regarded as a text on military – not political – affairs because of its emphasis on war itself and not on the causes, origins, or aftermath of war. Furthermore, *On War* does not include a detailed discussion of the state or the law of nature; nor does it provide a utopian solution to the problems of conflict and war.

To professional historians, who have traditionally been more interested in the detailed reconstruction of history than in theories concerning war, Clausewitz' narrower approach seemed far too theoretical. Clausewitz did indeed make extensive and accurate use of historical examples in his work, but his writing was not sufficiently detailed to pique the interest of historians. This stands in contrast to the approach of Thucydides (with whom Clausewitz shares many ideas), who clearly and meticulously recounted the history of the Peloponnesian Wars, including a detailed and perceptive discussion of the origins and causes of the war, its political and military development, and its aftermath. In addition, while the fact that there is little other historical evidence on the Peloponnesian Wars makes Thucydides an indispensable source, the plethora of detailed historical accounts on both Frederick the Great and Napoleon means that reading *On War* is definitely not crucial for strictly historical purposes.

Above all, philosophers, historians, political scientists, and other members of the academic community were never enthusiastic about introducing the study of military affairs into the Olympian heights of academia. Unlike Clemenceau, who believed that the conduct of war was too important to be left in the hands of the military, academics (particularly those in liberal Western society) were convinced that such a primitive and inferior activity did not merit their attention. The reluctance of academics to study war might also explain why no one, as yet, has written a book on the subject that even remotely surpasses that of Clausewitz. While Adam Smith can be said to have laid the foundation for the study of modern economics, his theories, over the years, have been further developed and refined by scholars who produced additional theories at least as original and creative as his own. In comparison, Clausewitz' theories on war have not been yet matched; in fact, most modern efforts are less creative, perhaps even regressive, in comparison to his original achievement.

Although professional soldiers obviously have not suffered from a reluctance to study war, Clausewitz was never very popular in the military community either. In this sense, he did not fit wholly into either the academic or military category. Whereas for the scholar, *On War* lacked adequate discussion of the causes or aftermath of war, for the military man it was too theoretical.

Well aware of the military mindset, Clausewitz must have realized only too well that his book was unlikely to be appreciated by the average military mind. The typical military professional, often intolerant of ambiguity and complexity, would probably have sought a manual with detailed rules to provide him with guidance for action. He would *not* have looked for a treatise describing war as unpredictable, ambiguous, and intuitive rather than clear, precise, and manageable. To Clausewitz, war was a messy affair that could not be reduced to a set of lessons or laws. Its uniqueness lay in its complexity, which could only be comprehended by the military genius. It is for this reason that Jomini's work, as well as that of other theorists who attempted to reduce war to a set of 'principles' that would guarantee success, was more popular than that of *On War*.

Moreover, when military professionals did make the effort to read *On War*, they tended to use (or rather misuse) it as a manual, and not as a work intended to impart a general grasp of the unique problems generated by war and its management. Instead, they quoted only those chapters or passages justifying their own choices of military doctrines or preferred courses of action. In view of the fact that Clausewitz' approach – more so than that of most other works on war – must be taken as a whole and should not be read out of context, such selective reading has frequently proven to be more dangerous than no reading at all. This may explain why those military men or armies that *did* read Clausewitz (for example, the French) did not perform better militarily. It must also be remembered that many military professionals seldom have the time or inclination to read and re-read a complex tome the direct utility of which is not always clear to them.

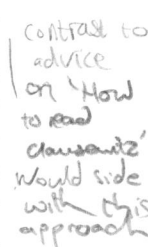

contrast to advice on 'How to read Clausewitz'? Would side with this approach

Despite its emphasis on theory, *On War* is as eminently practical a work as Machiavelli's *The Prince*, although it has always attracted much less attention than the latter book. This is attributable to the clarity and brevity of *The Prince* and also perhaps to Machiavelli's brutal realism and honesty, which so many philosophers, political theorists and moralists loved to hate but did not have to invest too much time and effort to read. There is no doubt, however, that Machiavelli's contribution to the understanding of politics is matched by Clausewitz' insights into the conduct of war. Of the two, Clausewitz seems to be the more creative and intellectually challenging. Both, however, managed to write 'simple' books on enormously complicated subjects without trying to reduce politics or war into scientifically precise enterprises. Yet, although *The Prince* and *On War* are certainly capable of enlightening new political or military leaders, in each instance the political or military genius could arrive intuitively at the same conclusions without ever having read Machiavelli or Clausewitz. This is true because both works present theories based on common sense and observations distilled from the astute observation of reality. Ironically enough, in a sense it is on this level of applied wisdom or common sense that Clausewitz has been understood the least. For example, his seemingly simple observations – that politicians should never relinquish control over the conduct of war; that a doctrinaire approach to war should be avoided; that every war is highly unpredictable and uncertain; and that every attack has its culminating point – have been continuously ignored or misunderstood.

Perhaps this was always the case, not only because military leaders tended to read selectively, but also because they were more likely, as a result, to concentrate on his 'positive' observations rather than on the 'negative' caveats. It is easier to accept that the defense is stronger than the offense; that there is a need to be strongest at the decisive point; or that the tendency in war is toward the extreme rather than to heed the warnings that war is a highly uncertain affair; that friction will interfere with every plan; or that means and goals should undergo constant re-evaluation as the war progresses. *Possible. Equally possible that soldiers aren't always as stupid as this passage makes out.*

Great works in political theory and philosophy should be analyzed in light of the following four questions:

    a. How does the work reflect the spirit of a given time and its problems?
    b. What is the theory (or theories) it advances to explain or solve specific contemporary problems?
    c. How was the work interpreted in different periods and circumstances?
    d. In what ways has the theory become obsolete?

(a) No theory or great work can be understood without a close look at the historical conditions or *Zeitgeist* prevailing at the time it was written. For example, Hobbes' *Leviathan* was conceived in an era of political turmoil and anarchy in Great Britain and, consequently, was concerned with the problem of restoring political order and stability. Marx's *Das Kapital*, as well as other works written with Engels, reflected the search for economic understanding and economic and political justice in resolving problems created by the Industrial Revolution.

Similarly, Clausewitz' study *On War* outlined his reflections on changes in the nature of war brought about by the French Revolution and the Napoleonic Wars. In contradistinction to the long-standing eighteenth-century rules of war, changes such as the establishment of the levee *en masse*, the political ideology which motivated adversaries, and the lack of moderation brought about a revolution in the shape of war which, in turn, prompted Clausewitz to make his observations on the tendency of war to become absolute. His work, then, was in the first place an attempt to comprehend changes that had recently occurred in war as well as to formulate a more general theory of war. In other words, Clausewitz could not have written his theories as we know them *before* the French Revolution.

(b) The second question addresses the theoretical explanation and practical solution offered for the problems of the specific era under consideration. In order to be intellectually attractive, the theory must have explanatory power and be of heuristic value. It must be succinct in the sense that it employs the minimal number of variables necessary to provide a framework for analysis and establish the criteria by which it can be tested or which lead to its transformation or substitution by another theory.

Hence, Hobbes' solution to the political anarchy and disorder prevailing in the England of his time was the surrender of all freedom to the Leviathan in order to attain security and stability. Marx and Engels proffered the Communist ideology in order to cure the ills of society through a new form of government and the economic redistribution of wealth.

To the contemporary reader, the most powerful appeal of *On War* lies in the elegance and explanatory value of Clausewitz' theories. In developing a theoretical ideal type linked to reality by intervening variables, Clausewitz managed to construct a concise framework incorporating all elements necessary for the study of war. On the one hand he developed the ideal type of war, that is, the absolute war that represented the way war ought to be from a purely logical point of view. Aspiring to the extreme, this type of war is a zero-sum game in which the fighting continues uninterruptedly until one side has won. This ideal war was undoubtedly inspired by the experience of the French Revolution and, in particular, war as initiated and waged by Napoleon. Clausewitz understood that war in reality did not strictly follow the logic of his theory, yet its explanatory power could not be denied. How could he then account for the fact that his theory did not correspond to reality? Not unlike Newton, Clausewitz' need to square his theory with reality inevitably led to the formulation of his most creative concepts. He found that war deviated from reality as a result of certain 'intervening variables' such as (1) the political guidance which rationally relates ends to means in war; (2) the asymmetry of the superiority of the defense over the offense; (3) the lack of information as well as the uncertainty and friction; (4) the tendency of human nature to make worst case assumptions about the enemy, and play it safe in the absence of clarity and sufficient information; (5) the fact that all military forces cannot be concentrated in space and time simultaneously; and (6) the fact that results in war are rarely final. This conceptual framework is timeless; regardless of the changes wrought by material and economic developments, it will remain all-encompassing and relevant.

Closely related to his ideal type method is the dialectical method of contrasting and/or synthesizing many of his concepts (see Raymond Aron, *Clausewitz: Philosopher of War* (London: Routledge & Kegan Paul, 1983), Part II, pp.89–173). By contrasting theory and practice (*praxis*), means and ends, the attack and defense, action and inaction, tension and rest, reason and uncontrolled emotions, the physical and

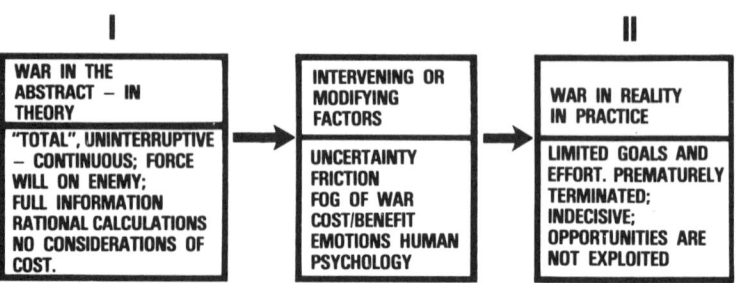

moral, he forces the reader to develop his own ideas on the meaning and interrelationship of each of these subjects. His argument by polarities, as Martin Van Creveld suggests (see his essay below), is the second method which allows him to reduce a subject of infinite complexity and size to manageable proportions.

Another explanation for the timelessness of Clausewitz' analytical method is to be found in the equal weight he gave to both the rational and non-rational elements in the study of war. Like so many other German intellectuals of his time, he combined the best of two worlds – the tradition of the Enlightenment, which emphasized rational objective analysis and the search for clarity, with the German romantic tradition (formulated in part as a reaction to the French as representative of the Enlightenment), which focused on the psychological, emotional, intuitive, and subjective dimensions in the interpretation of the surrounding world. The dialectical relationship between the Enlightenment on the one hand and German romanticism on the other – the two elements complementing rather than contradicting one another – created a synthesis on a higher level. Representing the duality of human nature, his theory is as successful in presenting the calculating and rational side of war as in analyzing its non-rational and unpredictable qualities. While war is waged primarily to achieve rational ends, it is not a rational process. Hence, his emphasis on the role of uncertainty, chance, friction, and luck in war owes as much to German romantic perceptions of the human condition as to Newtonian rationality.

In addition to the general theories from which his basic concepts were derived, Clausewitz produced other brilliant theoretical insights that will remain valid as long as wars are fought (for example, his observations on learning and the role of doctrines, the role of the military genius, the place of friction in war, the culminating point of victory, and human behavior in the face of battle).

What makes Clausewitzian theory so challenging even today is that

while his conceptual framework is fundamentally so simple, it nevertheless requires considerable hard thinking and deciphering to comprehend.
It may even be argued that had his ideas been presented more clearly, they
would have appeared so obvious that much of the learning process
involved in teaching them and trying to understand what he meant would
have been lost. At the same time, it is doubtful that the enormous complexity of the subject could have been presented in a better way.

Clausewitz' greatest contribution to the study of war – his Copernican
revolution – was his emphasis on the centrality of politics in war. Before
the advent of this deceptively simple concept, war was studied as an
independent or discrete activity (what Clausewitz referred to as 'the
purely military view of war') (p. 609).* Clausewitz demonstrated that war
makes sense only as an extension of the logic of political action. 'The only
source of war is politics' (p. 605). War divorced from political life is
pointless, for ideally, politics itself pursues a rational goal by enhancing
the welfare and interests of the state. This is the axiomatic foundation of
his theory of war. Like so many other great ideas, this one is so obvious
that it appears to be trival. Yet, as straightforward as the idea of the
primacy of politics in war is, it is also the most difficult to accept and
implement in time of war.

His second most important group of ideas pertains to the uncertain
nature of war. For Clausewitz, the essence of war was uncertainty,
chance, friction, and ambiguity. While the majority of those writing on
the subject of war seek clarity and positive guidance for action, Clausewitz concluded that the best way to succeed in war was through compre-
hension of its uncertain nature. The majority of his principal analytical
concepts cannot therefore provide the reader with more than a clue to
success, ('Rules', Clausewitz stated, 'are not only made for idiots, but are
idiotic in themselves') (p. 184). For example, while his suggestion that one
must 'be very strong first in general, and than at the decisive point'
(p. 204) may be the key to success in war, it offers the reader no specific
advice regarding its implementation. Likewise, although the analytical
concept of 'the culminating point of victory' was important enough to be
chosen as the subject of three complete chapters, it is as uncertain in its
practical application as everything else in war. In fact, these concepts
cannot be said to guarantee success in the long run and can be correctly
implemented only according to the intuition of the military genius, which
in turn cannot be identified with any degree of certainty.

Unlike Liddell Hart, who thought that he had found the recipe for
military success in his indirect approach, Clausewitz did not present his

* All quotations from On War are from: Carl von Clausewitz On War, edited and translated by
Michael Howard and Peter Paret (Princeton, NJ: Princeton University Press, 1986).

key ideas as a panacea, but instead treated them as important problems or questions. According to Clausewitz, there are no laws or rules that can serve as guidance for action because in war '... many roads lead to success' (p. 94). '... Different ways of reaching the objective are *possible* and they are neither *inconsistent, absurd,* nor even *mistaken*' (p. 93) (emphasis in the original).

(c) Regardless of an author's original intention, his work is destined to be interpreted in different ways at different times. Many renowned works are as well-known for what they did not say as for what they said (that is, there are a variety of highly influential interpretations that have little to do with the original ideas of the writer). The way in which a theory is interpreted depends upon many factors such as the clarity of the text, the distance in time and circumstances, the expectations and experience of the reader, and the nature of the subject. At times, the author is better understood in later periods because he is ahead of the thinking in his own era. For some, Machiavelli's *The Prince* is the epitome of cruelty, cynicism, immoral politics and brutality, while for others it represents the commendable efforts of a patriot aspiring to unite Italy. In the same way, admirers touted Rousseau's *Social Contract* as one of the greatest works espousing the causes of democracy, human dignity and human rights, while critics in later years viewed it as one of the sources of what has been referred to as 'totalitarian democracy'. Certainly Darwin's *The Origins of Species* has been denounced repeatedly as a blasphemous denial of God's creation of the universe, although for most it has emerged as one of the greatest scientific works of all time.

Clausewitz, as we shall see below, suffered a similar fate, perhaps even more so than most authors, because he was less carefully read than he was frequently quoted. To some he was a source of inspiration (for example, for Moltke the Elder or Foch presumably), while to others he was a closed-minded Prussian lusting for blood and destruction. Liddell Hart referred to him as the 'Mahdi of Mass' although Clausewitz did not propose anything different from Liddell Hart. The Germans, who should have known better, read Clausewitz even more selectively than others and chose to dogmatize the idea of the decisive battle while completely ignoring his emphasis on the control and guidance of the political leadership, not to mention his caveats regarding the uncertainties and dangers inherent in war or the superiority of the defense over the offense. The results were disastrous.

The appeal of Clausewitz for the contemporary American military reader is exactly the opposite of that which he had for the German military reader. In the aftermath of the Vietnam War, it is natural for American readers to stress the unpredictability of war as well as the primacy of politics over the military. Significantly, the US military's high expectations that American technology would be able to perform miracles were rudely disappointed when this panacea failed to deliver victory or success in Vietnam or elsewhere for that matter. It was realized that war cannot be reduced to simple formulas, nor can the infinitely complex problems that it generates be solved by modern computer technology. This disillusionment, in turn, led to the rediscovery of the non-material qualitative dimensions of war that Clausewitz emphasized. The American military experience of the past 25 years clearly demonstrates the need for the senior military leadership to move away from the concept of war as a problem in management and organization, back to the study of war on its higher levels as an art and a problem of leadership in which the role of intuition is paramount.

(d) The final question that must be asked about every theory or work of great importance is not only in which way it is still relevant – but also in what ways it has become obsolete. The scholar should try to ascertain which aspects of a theory can be accepted as originally written; which aspects need to be modified; and which have become irrelevant. The Leviathan may be an excellent alternative to political chaos, but is not directly relevant to the problems of a modern politically and economically stable society. In like manner, the direct participation of all citizens in a marketplace democracy may have been a wonderful and perhaps even practical idea in the ancient Greek city-state or in eighteenth- or nineteenth-century Switzerland and thus have great appeal for Rousseau, but it is definitely less suited to the complexities of the modern world.

Clausewitz recognized the changing nature of war in the selection of historial examples to illustrate his theoretical observations.

> Once one accepts the difficulties of using historical examples, one will come to the most obvious conclusion that examples should be drawn from modern military history, insofar as it is properly known and evaluated.
>
> Not only were conditions different in more distant times, with different ways of waging war, so that earlier wars have fewer practical lessons for us; ...
>
> If we examine the conditions of modern warfare, we shall find that the wars that bear a considerable resemblance to those of the present day, especially with respect to armaments, are primarily campaigns beginning with the War of the Austrian Succession. Even though many major and minor circumstances have changed considerably, these are close enough to modern warfare to be instructive. The situation is different with the War of the Spanish Succession; the use of firearms was much less advanced, and cavalry

Handwritten margin notes: ((1740 - 1748)) ↘ 7 yrs war 1756-63 * Eastern conflict - Rev & Nap wars I. 1792 - 1815. See P17 notes for more detail.

Handwritten note bottom left: ending 1713.

was still the most important arm. The further back one goes, the less useful military history becomes, growing poorer and barer at the same time ....

The uselessness is of course not absolute; it refers only to matters that depend on a precise knowledge of the actual circumstances, or on details in which warfare has changed. (p. 173)

We wanted to show how every age had its own kind of war, its own limiting conditions, and its own peculiar preconceptions. Each period, therefore, would have held to its own theory of war, even if the urge had always and universally existed to work things out on scientific principles. It follows that the events of every age must be judged in the light of its own peculiarities. (p. 593)

Certainly technological and material innovations have changed the nature and conditions of warfare since Clausewitz' death much more than they did in the time span between the Austrian War of Succession and Clausewitz' own time.

Although Clausewitz' basic and most important theories are as valid today as they were when first set down on paper, the growing political, economic, and technological complexities of the modern world require the updating of his theories. More than any other human activity, war has been heavily influenced by material and technological changes. Civil–military relations, modern government and policy-making, the role of public opinion, economic constraints, the input of intelligence into the strategic-tactical decision-making process, the relative strength of the defense and offense, the incredible array of modern weapons systems, radio communication and developments in C^3I, the new dimensions of air power, firepower, mobility and range in general, not to mention nuclear weapons – have all transformed war as Clausewitz observed it. Clausewitzian statements such as the contention that most, if not all, intelligence on the battlefield is unreliable, or that strategic surprise is a good idea in principle but is unlikely to be achieved in reality, need to undergo critical re-examination. Furthermore, few contemporary scholars would endorse wholeheartedly and uncritically the statement that the defense is always stronger than the offense, or the idea that material developments cannot be expected to cause radical changes on the battlefield. No text or theory should be elevated to the point where it is considered immune from criticism. A detailed discussion of how On War can be examined in the modern environment is contained in my own essay below.

The essays presented in this book are grouped into three general categories. The first category is concerned with Clausewitz' relevance to our own time, the second is devoted to a detailed examination of some of his principal theoretical concepts, and the third takes a look at the interpretation, or even more frequently the misinterpretation, of his work throughout various historical periods and in different nations.

In his essay, 'The Eternal Clausewitz', Martin van Creveld argues that *On War* has always remained relevant precisely because of the author's refusal to fall into the trap that caught many military thinkers; namely, that of trying to discover the existence of constants in a field of human activity where no scientific laws can exist. Clausewitz approached the study of war as objectively and systematically as possible, but he also recognized that it always involves clashing purposes and free creative choices. Unlike the physical world in which experiments can be repeated under controlled conditions and measured against objective criteria, 'every war is rich in unique episodes' (p. 120) that is, each interaction between adversaries is a unique event from which it is dangerous to make universally applicable generalizations. Reflecting the lack of objective criteria by which to satisfactorily measure success or failure in war, Clausewitz' emphasis on moral forces and the psychological dimensions of war as well as its political essence transcends rational objective analysis.

Thus, Clausewitz' greatness stems from his willingness to accept ambiguity and uncertainty as the essence of war while resisting the temptation to impose a false sense of clarity. *On War* is a consistent and deliberate effort to reject the manual-like approach to war which implies that the ambiguities and uncertainties can be reduced or eliminated and positive results guaranteed if only certain principles were followed. Paradoxically, this unwillingness to write such a practical handbook is the main reason for the considerable practical value of his work today.

While it is easy to accept all of Martin van Creveld's arguments on Clausewitz' eternal relevance, my article, 'Clausewitz in the Age of Technology', focuses on those dimensions of *On War* that have become obsolete or need to be modified. No book on war written a century and a half ago can satisfactorily explain all facets of modern warfare. Clausewitz' work must therefore be read critically in light of at least three considerations: (1) the enormous changes that have taken place in the material environment of war since the beinning of the nineteenth century; (2) new dimensions that are now considered relevant to the study of war either did not concern, or could not have concerned, Clausewitz; (3) *On War* must be read in view of the ideas and explanations presented in other works written on war before and after Clausewitz' time.

The first consideration is also the most important one. Modern weapons technologies as they have developed since the nineteenth century have revolutionized every facet of war. The impact of the technological revolution on warfare is not simply quantitative or environmental – it is indicative of a much deeper qualitative and psychological change as well. Although the fundamental explanation and definition of war as discussed by Clausewitz in *On War* has remained relevant, almost everything else has changed. In view of the pace at which technological changes take place, the material and technological dimension itself must assume a much more important part in the study of war. Nor is technology merely an environmental 'given' as Clausewitz assumed, in which changes tend to cancel each other out; it is an autonomous dimension of war with its own dynamics that in turn have a decisive impact on all other aspects of war. For this reason, I suggested adding a fourth material dimension to Clausewitz' triad, which is based on the three human, political, and organizational dimensions.

On the most obvious level, technological-material changes have added the new dimension of war in the air and revolutionized firepower to the extent that there are no more winners or losers as Clausewitz understood the terms. In fact, the development of nuclear weapons has led to a paradigm shift in the theory of war. What was for Clausewitz possible only in theory – the idea that war could be decided in a single, concentrated blow – was made possible in practice by the development of nuclear weapons. War can now be decided in a single, short blow which could be delivered by both antagonists at approximately the same time. Since there can only be losers in such a conflict, war can no longer be considered a logical political activity. Through the development of greater speeds combined with increased firepower, modern weapons technologies have made strategic surprise possible, increased the rate of cyclical change between the relative strength of the offense and defense, improved communication and control on the battlefield, and revolutionized the role of modern intelligence from mere noise and instant obsolescence of information in Clausewitz' time to perhaps the only way to reduce (although certainly not eliminate) the fog of war, friction and uncertainty. Whereas the nineteenth-century military genius had to learn how to make the best decision in the absence of almost any real time information concerning events on the battlefield, the modern military genius must learn how to make the best decision amidst an overabundance of information.

Furthermore, modern technology led to greater specialization in the structure of military forces and hence to the increased bureaucratization of war. Decisive victories that, according to Clausewitz, were won primarily on the battlefield can now almost as often be won in the laboratory, testing grounds, or factories, far from the actual point of contact between opposing forces.

The second point has to do with the changing perspective on war in modern times – a perspective which was determined to a large extent by the technological revolution. Clausewitz dedicated most of the discussion in *On War* to fighting on the battlefield itself ('pure strategy'). Although he emphasized the primacy of politics in all decisions preceding as well as during war, details of the political and economic background of war did not concern him. In this sense, what must be taken into consideration are not the dimensions of war that have changed since Clausewitz' time as much as the many war-related subjects that Clausewitz simply did not address but which are of far greater interest to the modern reader. These include discussions of the origins and causes of war; problems of deterrence or how to avoid war through the use of military threats; the impact of arms races (another problem created primarily by the technological revolution); the economic dimension of war and the study of war potential; the military-industrial complex and the acquisition of weapons for war; and the problem of war termination. This comment does not suggest that *On War* is obsolete, but rather that its scope is too narrow for the modern non-military student of warfare.

The third consideration concerns the comparison of Clausewitz' work with that of other strategists, whose writings can either deepen our understanding of *On War* or indicate a number of directions in which it might be modified. One such example is Sun Tzu's much greater emphasis on the desirability of achieving a bloodless victory. While Clausewitz stressed the necessity of searching for a military decision as well as the idea that, in war, the battle itself is the ultimate, and to a large extent, the unavoidable goal, Sun Tzu believed that the battle should be avoided if possible, for it essentially represents a failure to win by other means. Perhaps this is why Sun Tzu also gave much greater priority to deception in war than did Clausewitz.

Another example which provides ideas in light of which *On War* can be studied is Hans Delbrück's distinction between two modes of war: the strategy of attrition (*Ermattungsstrategie*) and the strategy of annihilation (*Niederwerfungsstrategie*) as applied on the strategic and tactical levels and in various combinations between the two modes of war on the two levels.

To be sure, Clausewitz' theory does not contradict or negate any of the examples mentioned above. He would probably have agreed that winning without bloodshed is preferable to winning with it, yet he did not explore in detail the possible ways of doing so. Similarly, the idea of attrition was not unknown to Clausewitz, yet he did not develop it in depth or compare it directly with the other alternatives. A look at these examples reveals that Clausewitz' theories on the whole require not so much modification as refinement. The validity and relevance of his conceptual framework for the study of war lies in the fact that it is flexible enough to incorporate quite a few changes and refinements without having to alter its basic structure (with the possible exception of the technological dimension as mentioned above).

The idea that uncertainty is the essence of war is not new. In Thucydides' *The History of the Peloponnesian War*, the Athenians warn the Lacedaemonians prior to their decision to support the Corinthians:

> Take time then in forming your resolution, as the matter is of great importance and do not be persuaded by the opinions and complaints of others to bring trouble on yourselves, but consider the influence of accident in war, before you are engaged in it. As it continues, it generally becomes an affair of chances, chances from which neither of us is exempt and whose event we must risk in the dark. It is a common mistake in going to war to begin at the wrong end, to act first, and wait for disaster to discuss the matter. (Thucydides, Book I:78)

Yet in no work other than *On War* are the roles of uncertainty, chance, friction, risk, and other related concepts brought into such a clear focus. Other than the primacy of politics, chance and uncertainty are the concepts most crucial for an understanding of Clausewitz' theory on war. These are the concepts that led him from the abstract level of theory and the ideal type of war to the ambiguous realities of war. This view of war as an activity in which even the true probabilities are unknown must have been the central element in his decision not to write a scientific study of the subject.

In 'Chance and Uncertainty in War', Katherine Herbig discusses the foregoing concepts in connection with four interrelated clusters of issues: (1) the nature of war in general; (2) the military genius; (3) the link between chance and uncertainty; and (4) the alternatives for action. In the first section, she argues that unlike most other military thinkers, Clausewitz discerned in the uncertain nature of war not only a negative element, but also a positive one that could be exploited to the benefit of a creative commander. Thus, under certain circumstances, the fog of war, friction and uncertainty can constitute a force multiplier for the military commander even as they confuse the uncreative commander.

In the second cluster Herbig discusses the qualities that Clausewitz considered necessary for a military commander to be able to deal successfully with uncertainty. These are *coup d'oeil* or his ablity to perceive events correctly despite the surrounding confusion, *determination*, and *presence of mind* or the gift of quick thinking.

The third and fourth clusters concentrate on the interrelationship between chance and uncertainty and a variety of related concepts such as friction, the fog of war, exertion and danger, lack of determination and, finally, the existence of blind fate (similar to Machiavelli's 'fortuna'). The prospect of uncertainty could also have a deleterious effect on the attitude of a commander, who might suffer a serious loss of self-confidence which in turn leads to hesitation and therefore greater vulnerability to chance. Finally, a discussion of the connections between uncertainty, chance and surprise is presented.

David Kahn's essay, 'Clausewitz on Intelligence' is, in a way, a direct continuation of Herbig's essay on chance and uncertainty because, as Kahn points out, Clausewitz viewed intelligence not only as ineffective but as another form of uncertainty. Although Clausewitz occasionally mentions some examples of intelligence successes in his analysis of the role of intelligence in war, his overall assessment of its utility is very negative. The causes for intelligence failures, as classified by Kahn, are on the *collection* side. To begin with, the role of chance reduces the accuracy and predictive value of information. This is compounded by the growing complexity of estimating the resources available for war, a task which has been increasing in difficulty since the French Revolution released the full potential of an entire nation. Then one must consider the natural limits to observation of the battlefield as well as the fact that no one can penetrate the mind of the enemy's commander. Analytically speaking, the infinite number of variables involved makes the synergistic evaluation of a battle's future outcome highly unreliable. These drawbacks are further exacerbated by the dominance of preconceived perceptions and wishful thinking over fact. Poor intelligence results in incomplete knowledge of the enemy's actual physical strength; this allows the enemy to achieve surprise and the unexpected superior concentration of power at his point of choice while causing the opposing commander to lose confidence and underestimate his own strength (as also discussed by Herbig). A shortage of information will lead most generals to paralysis. The compensating factors for inadequate intelligence are, on the physical level, extra strength to rectify initial errors in judgment and, on the psychological level, the will power and determination of the commanders. Kahn concludes that Clausewitz' skeptical attitude can no longer be justified in view of the state of modern technology.

Werner Hahlweg explores Clausewitz' study of guerrilla warfare. The only chapter in *On War* devoted to this subject is 'The People In Arms', found, appropriately enough, in Book VI, the section concerned with various aspects of the defense. As in the rest of the book, Clausewitz is not interested in discussing the political and economic conditions necessary for waging a successful guerrilla campaign, but deals almost exclusively with the purely military aspects of such a war. This is unfortunate not only because the political, economic and social conditions are so significant, but also because Clausewitz himself must have devoted a considerable amount of thought to these factors, as he indicates in the text. This subject was certainly of great import for Prussian military reformers who, following the defeat in Jena, realized that the only way to prevail over Napoleon was through full mobilization of the German masses.

As the first modern Western strategist to discuss guerrilla warfare, Clausewitz seems to have been successful in capturing its essence. Much of what he has to say, including his caveats, resembles the observations of Mao Tse-tung a century later. For Clausewitz, guerrilla warfare was a strategy to be employed only if the regular armed forces were defeated. Furthermore, it should be executed in close coordination with the regular armed forces. Clausewitz named five conditions essential to the success of guerrilla warfare: (1) it must be fought in the interior of the country; (2) it must not be decided by a single stroke; (3) the theater of operations must be fairly large; (4) the national character must be suited to that type of war; (5) the country must be rough and inaccessible (p. 490). Of these conditions, three (1, 3, and 5) are geographical or topographical, while the second deals with strategy and operations and the fourth is psychological. Most of the discussion therefore is dedicated to the second and fourth points.

From an operational point of view, guerrilla forces should be strategically on the defensive and tactically on the offensive, operate in relatively small units supported by regular military forces, and avoid concentration. As Mao also warned, they should be extremely careful to avoid a premature move from the level of dispersed guerrilla operations to the level of concentrated conventional operations. It is worth noting that although Clausewitz was aware of the importance of attrition in guerrilla warfare, he did not expand his remarks on this dimension. The need to avoid concentrated large-scale operations, which meant risking a major defeat, is also important from a psychological perspective, for Clausewitz believed that an armed people might not be strong enough to endure a series of defeats and would quickly lose their enthusiasm for war.

On the role of space and time in guerrilla warfare, Clausewitz states:

> By its very nature, such scattered resistance will lend itself to major actions, closely compressed in time and space. Its effect is like that of the process of evaporation: it depends on how much surface is exposed. The greater the surface and the area of contact between it and the enemy forces, the thinner the latter have to be spread, the greater the effect of a general uprising. Like smoldering embers, it consumes the basic foundations of the enemy forces. Since it needs time to be effective, a state of tension will develop while the two elements interact. This tension will either gradually relax, if the insurgency is suppressed in some places and slowly burns itself out

* Ref Afghanistan

[margin note: This might mean that Taliban guerilla resistance ongoing in Afghanistan now (2006) might be designed to remain a serious hindrance (rather than ultimately successful mile) it is not linked to a reg force assuming NATO political will holds out & withstands casualties.]

[margin note: which as at 2012 it doesn't look like it will! 2014 - pull out date (regardless of whether?). A con cope economic imperative.]

in others, or else it will build up to a crisis: a general conflagration closes in on the enemy, driving him out of the country before he is faced with total destruction. (p.480)

Despite the numerous references in *On War* to space and time, Clausewitz dedicates only two relatively short chapters to each. Harold Nelson's essay, 'Space and Time in War', is based on a comprehensive survey of Clausewitz' references to these two interrelated variables.

Nelson throws light on Clausewitz' deliberate effort not to over-emphasize the role of space and time. Reluctant to give too much weight to the quantifiable elements of war, Clausewitz felt that devoting a special longer section of *On War* to space and time might lead many of his readers astray by creating the impression that such variables could form the basis for a scientific approach to the study of war. Instead, he was interested in drawing attention to the more elusive psychological and moral factors. In accordance with this goal, Clausewitz refused to reduce his observations on space and time to formulas of points, lines, and angles as many of his contemporaries did. Furthermore, he specifically warned that the relationship between these two elements (or their combination as velocity) is *not* transitive (that is, he rejected the notion, as Nelson points out, that a small force applied over a longer time could have the same effect as a large force over a short time). No scientific or linear regularities can be discerned in the relationship between space and time although they are clearly connected.

Nelson first discusses Clausewitz' observations on space, then time, and finally explores their interaction. Clausewitz saw *space*, or even more so terrain, as a constant source of friction for the commander, particularly in an era when much larger formations had to be moved across greater distances while the means of transportation remained unchanged. He also related space to the offense and defense by arguing that while the attacker could concentrate his troops in space, the defender was forced to disperse his own. This is, of course, one of the very few inherent advantages of the offense. The difference between the offense and defense is discussed again in the context of *time*. While space is contested, time is shared between the opponents. Time elapses at the same rate for both adversaries, but its effect varies. Time favors the defender, who must merely gain time by delaying action as long as possible. It works against the attacker, who must arrive at a decision as fast as possible before he passes the culmi-nating point of the attack and begins to weaken. The side making rela-tively better use of this critical dimension of war will gain a major advantage. The skilful manipulation of time and space is an important art that has often been neglected in the teaching of strategy. Nelson also comments upon the place occupied by these two concepts in military doctrine since Clausewitz' time and then concludes his survey with a summary of space and time as they appear in contemporary US Army doctrine.

A question that Nelson has avoided, perhaps deliberately, pertains to the impact of modern technology on the factors of space and time and their interrelationship. Is it necessary to modify Clausewitz' observations on this subject? The ranges of modern weapons have certainly expanded the space involved as modern technology has made the projection of force over greater distances much more rapid, if not always easier. Terrain and space, as Nelson points out, were a major source of friction in the past but, for the modern commander, these problems have been magnified by the pressure of time and the necessity of making instant decisions. Conversely, it can be argued that while contemporary commanders must make decisions more rapidly and therefore under greater pressure, they also have access to more reliable information than in the past. Have the relationships of time and space to the defense and offense changed, or have they remained more or less constant except on higher or different levels? These and other questions require further elaboration, although Clausewitz already has created the framework within which they could be discussed.

As Jay Luvaas shows, Clausewitz rested his study and teaching of war on two foundations: the detailed study of military history and the military campaigns of his own era, combined with theoretical observations on its nature and conduct. His approach to teaching shunned neatly packaged sets of rules or principles; instead it gave students the tools with which to teach themselves so that they could learn by understanding rather than through the mechanical application of pseudo-scientific laws.

Clausewitz' teaching was based on two methodological principles: the first can be called *the vicarious experience method* (Max Weber's *Verstehen*) and the second is what he termed *critical analysis*. The vicarious experience method, as the name suggests, involved a conscious attempt on the part of Clausewitz to 'put himself at the side of the commander' making the critical decisions, to 'get inside his skin'. This 'imaginative insight' into the military leader's thought processes is what Luvaas calls 'the dialogue between Clausewitz and his two great captains'. The two great captains were, of course, Frederick the Great and Napoleon.

Luvaas demonstrates just how successful Clausewitz was in applying the first method to gain insight into Napoleon's ideas on war. 'So close were their ideas on fundamental points ... that had Napoleon's correspondence been published at the time Clausewitz wrote his treatise and historical studies, readers might well have concluded that Napoleon furnished him with many of the ideas advanced in *On War*' (Luvaas, p. 167).

Again it is interesting to note the use of contradicting poles in Clause-witz' work. In a sense the lessons learned from Frederick the Great and Napoleon are not so much contradictory as complementary. From Frederick the Great, Clausewitz learned about limited war, the value of complete political control over the conduct of war, the importance of matching ends and means and, as a result, the need to limit goals in war. He also learned when to stop fighting as well as how to fight, how to avoid becoming intoxicated by initial victories, when to switch from the offense to the defense and, perhaps above all, how the political-military leader must pay as much attention to political maneuvering and the balance of power as to the art of maneuvering on the battlefield.

From Napoleon he acquired knowledge of the nature of *absolute war* and the critical importance of logistics. While Frederick the Great had taught him 'the virtues of an active defense', Napoleon taught him the necessity of a 'relentless offensive', the benefits to be reaped from bold-ness and persistance in the attack and in the search for decision, and the advantages of flexibility. Napoleon was also instructive in the character, temperament, and qualities of the military genius.

Clausewitz' second methodological approach is his *critical analysis*, by which he meant 'the application of theoretical truths to actual events' (p. 196). As a method by which the student attempts to reconstruct the thinking processes that preceded a given action, critical analysis demands a consideration of the decisions and actions of a commander and how they affected subsequent events. By examining all possible options that a commander could have selected (given the information *actually* avail-able at the time of his decision), the student can explore the outcome of alternative courses of action (pp. 156–69). In refusing to rely on the wisdom of hindsight, Clausewitz stressed a more positive and con-structive approach to the study of the decision-making process in war. Although 'judgment by *results*' (p. 166) is usually inevitable, its impor-tance should not be exaggerated. As Clausewitz shows, success may even mask a poor decision (that is, where an even better decision could have been made) while at other times, failure is not necessarily proof of poor judgment (for example, see his brief discussion of Napoleon's decision to invade Russia on p. 166 and p. 628). Above all, Clausewitz wanted to force the student to think his way as objectively as possible through a military situation. His dialectic method becomes evident in his approach to the study of war. Luvaas quotes Peter Paret's perceptive observation that Clausewitz' *critical analysis* 'is neither history nor theory, but forms the transition between the two'.

Luvaas then goes on to explain the connection between the critical analysis method and the teaching of the operational art. Clausewitz' personal application of this method as a teaching technique is the subject of Wallace P. Franz' essay, 'Two Letters on Strategy: Clausewitz' Contribution to the Operational Art of War'. Through an interesting discussion of the French and German misinterpretation of Napoleon's and Clausewitz' writing on war as a result of distorted national perspectives and different military doctrines, Luvaas also leads the reader to the third section of the book – Clausewitz misperceived.

Wallace Franz contends that Clausewitz used the term strategy primarily to mean the conduct of war on what is now referred to in the US Army as the operational level. For Clausewitz, 'pure strategy' always involved direct contact (that is, fighting with the enemy). Today the term strategy is used more broadly to describe activities on numerous levels. Most often it refers to the highest political-military level, which does not necessarily involve decisions directly related to combat; instead, the decision might relate to giving one theater of war priority over another, opening new fronts, and allocating resources among those fronts.

Franz' interpretation needs to be applied with caution. Nevertheless, the much greater scope of war, as in the First and Second World Wars in which the war is simultaneously fought by independent commands, may require a more precise definition of the term strategy and perhaps the interposition of the operational level between the strategic and tactical levels. Franz then defines this level of operations according to Clausewitz by the criteria of *space* (a well-defined sector of war that is not directly related to other sectors); *mass* (the force concentrated under one commander in one sector); and *time* (the duration of an operation by a given mass in a given space).

The somewhat more technical analysis that follows discusses other terms related to the conduct of military operations and explores some of Clausewitz' ideas on military operations as recorded in two letters he wrote in 1827 in reply to Major von Roeder's questions on a military exercise. (For the text of the two letters and a commentary by Peter Paret, see *Carl von Clausewitz: Two Letters On Strategy*, edited and translated by Peter Paret and Daniel Moran and published as a monograph in the Art of War colloquium by the US Army War College, Carlisle Barracks, Pennsylvania, November 1984.)

'Neither Fuller nor Liddell Hart appear to have been influenced by Clausewitz in formulating their own theories – quite to the contrary. As original thinkers they regarded him as a part of history and not as a source of fresh ideas', concludes Jay Luvaas in his chapter 'Clausewitz, Fuller and Liddell Hart'. This is indeed a fair assessment of their generally negative predisposition toward Clausewitz' work, one with which their biographers are in full agreement. (Anthony John Trythall, *Bonney Fuller* (London: Cassell, 1977); and Brian Bond, *Liddell-Hart* (New Brunswick, NJ: Rutgers University Press, 1977.)

Neither of these British strategists took the time to read *On War* very carefully let alone study Clausewitz' other works on military operations. As British students of war and former soldiers, they had little patience with the German metaphysical and philosophical approach to the study of war. Liddell Hart never really altered his views on this subject, although Fuller did so toward the end of his life. In his book, *The Conduct of War 1789–1961*, Fuller designates his chapter on Clausewitz as the most important one, yet a perusal of that chapter indicates that even at that time he read Clausewitz superficially.

Liddell Hart and Fuller misunderstood and misperceived Clausewitz for numerous, interrelated reasons. The more pragmatic, less theoretical English approach to the study of history and politics was the milieu in which they began their work. Furthermore, this was during the First World War, a period in which Germany's responsibility for the most disastrous and senseless war in history was not in doubt. Thus it was difficult for them to view any German work on war in a positive light. Other explanations may be found, as Luvaas shows, in their respective searches to discover the true science of war. An ambition to be the true prophets of the science of war very likely rendered them less receptive to the possibility that someone else had already founded the systematic study of war, particularly since Clausewitz regarded war as more of an art than a science. (Again, it was Fuller, not Liddell Hart, who, after a lifetime of searching for the principles of this science ended up stating in the first sentence of his later work, *The Conduct of War*, that 'The conduct of war, like the practice of medicine, is an art ...' (p. 1).)

Fuller characterized *On War* as 'little more than a mass of notes, a cloud of flame and smoke' and Clausewitz as 'a general of the agricultural age'. In *The Conduct of War*, he still viewed *On War* as '... largely a jumble of essays, memoranda, and notes set together in a very precise form. It is prolix, repetitive, full of platitudes and truisms, and in places contradictory and highly involved. Instead it is a pseudo-philosophical exposition of war ... the bulk [of which] ... is only remotely related to the higher conduct of war, and is now obsolete ...' (pp. 60–61). He criticizes Clausewitz for 'indulging in philosophy' (p. 64) while his assessment of *On War* leaves little doubt that he was still reading it chiefly in search of scientific principles.

Liddell Hart referred to Clausewitz in somewhat more dramatic terms: the German strategist was labelled 'a false prophet', 'the Mahdi of Mass', and 'the Evil Genius' whose theories led to wholesale destruction and total war. Like Fuller, Liddell Hart confused style and substance. 'The ponderous tomes of Clausewitz are so solid as to cause mental indigestion to any student who swallows them without a long course of preparation. Only a mind developed by years of study and reflection can dissolve the solid lump into digestible particles') quoted in Luvaas, p. 208–9). Liddell Hart never took the time to read and properly digest these 'ponderous tomes'.

Perhaps Fuller and Liddell Hart were, after all, not as original as they had thought. A careful reading of *On War* may have revealed that Clausewitz frequently developed similar ideas without the pretense of inventing a positive science capable of making accurate predictions. In many instances, the two British strategists may have created a new jargon to describe old concepts.

For example, as Luvaas explains, Fuller thought that Clausewitz did not understand that the true aim of every war is peace and not victory and that therefore 'peace should be the ruling idea of policy, and victory only the means toward its achievements'. (Luvaas quotes a similar criticism by Liddell Hart suggesting that Clausewitz 'looked only to the end of a war, not beyond war to the subsequent peace'; see p. 209). Although Clausewitz admittedly wrote a book entitled *On War* and not *On Peace*, his approach makes it very clear that war is only a means of achieving a better peace. In the first place, he put politics in control of war and its goals more than any other military theorist before or after his time. Clausewitz modifies war in the abstract because 'in war the results are never final' (p. 80). If the result in war is not final, it must obviously be accompanied by something else, namely, diplomacy. But diplomacy was not the subject of Clausewitz' book. Furthermore, Clausewitz states: '... we must always consider that with the conclusion of peace the purpose of war has been achieved and its business is at an end' (p. 91). 'In many cases, particularly those involving great and decisive actions, the analysis must extend to the *ultimate objective*, which is to bring about peace' (p. 159, emphasis in the original!). Fuller also contradicts his own statement about Clausewitz' disregard for peace as the ultimate goal in war when he quotes in the same chapter: 'No war should be commenced ... without first seeing a reply to the question, what is to be attained by and in the same' (*The Conduct of War*, p. 66). (See also *On War*, Book VIII, pp. 579 and 584 for other similar points.)

Although Liddell Hart believed that he discovered the 'scientific principle' of indirect approach as the rule guaranteeing the greatest degree of success, there is nothing in *On War* to contradict that principle as Liddell Hart liked to think. In effect, much of what Clausewitz says about the conduct of war is very similar except that it does not claim to be a formula for victory.

First of all, Clausewitz' short chapter on the Economy of Force (Book III, Chapter 14, p. 213) includes the essence of many of Liddell Hart's ideas on the indirect approach. *On War* abounds with phrases such as 'The commander and the army who have come closest to conducting an engagement with the utmost economy of force and the maximum psychological effect of strong reserves are on the surest road to victory' (p. 241), and 'Battle ... is rather a killing of the enemy's spirit than of his men ...' (p. 259).

Certainly Clausewitz would be the last one to deny the utility of the indirect approach whenever possible. (On this see also Brian Bond, *Liddell-Hart*, p. 35.) The only difference is that Clausewitz did not shy away from describing the bloody battle that often occurs at the culmination of the indirect approach, when maneuver must be translated into costly action.

Liddell Hart thought that Clausewitz' writings contributed to the deification of the Napoleonic method, which supported the structure of the 'nation in arms' (Luvaas, p. 208). This is a gross misperception, since Clausewitz did not advocate the 'nation in arms' or the 'absolute war' as much as he described them. Liddell Hart's logic is fallacious because both the nation in arms and the absolute war are actually more *political* than military phenomena. This was correctly recognized by Clausewitz:

> It is true that war itself has undergone significant changes in character and methods, changes that have brought it closer to its absolute form. But these changes did not come about because the French government freed itself, so to speak, from the harness of policy; they were caused by the new political conditions which the French Revolution created both in France and in Europe as a whole, conditions that set in motion new means and new forces, and have thus made possible a degree of energy in war that otherwise would have been inconceivable.
>
> It follows that the transformation of the art of war resulted from the transformation of politics. So far from suggesting that the two could be disassociated from each other, these changes are strong proof of their indissoluble connection.
>
> Once again: war is an instrument of policy. It must necessarily bear the character of policy and measure by its standards. The conduct of war, in its great outlines, is therefore policy itself, which takes up the sword in place of the pen, but does not on that account cease to think according to its own laws. (p. 610)

In accusing Clausewitz of having promoted absolute war, Liddell Hart confused cause and effect, thereby holding him responsible for the subsequent misinterpretations of self-proclaimed disciples. As the transition in *On War* from war in theory to war in reality and Book VIII reveal, Clausewitz was fully aware of the conditions under which goals can be limited.

To argue, as Liddell Hart did, that Clausewitz either suggested or implied that strategy takes precedence over policy runs counter to the major theme of Clausewitz' work, that is, the primacy of politics.

Where does Clausewitz stand in regard to religious wars? Is this why they are so dangerous?

That the political view should wholly cease to count on the outbreak of war is hardly conceivable unless pure hatred made all wars a struggle for life and death. In fact, as we have said, they are nothing but expressions of policy itself. Subordinating the political point of view to the military would be absurd, for it is policy that has created war. Policy is the guiding intelligence and war only the instrument, not vice versa. No other possibility exists, then, than to subordinate the military point of view to the political. (p. 607)

Again, not unlike Fuller's reading of Clausewitz, Liddell Hart's misinterpretation may have been caused by the fact that he 'concentrated almost exclusively on the operational sections of *On War*' (Bond, *Liddell Hart*, p. 63, note 29). It is ironic that both criticized him for over-emphasizing the importance of 'the battle' and the search for a decisive victory on the battlefield. After all, the word decisive appears more often in the titles of their own books than in the text of *On War*. After the traumatic experience of the First World War, they were probably more in search of methods to achieve decisive victory than Clausewitz ever was.

'The Copernican Revolution was a revolution in ideas, a transformation in man's conception of the universe and his own relation to it' (Thomas S. Kuhn, *The Copernican Revolution* (Cambridge, MA: Harvard University Press, 1971, p. 1). A revolution involves 'a break with continuity, the establishment of a new order that has severed its links to the past' (I. Bernard Cohen, *Revolution In Science* (Cambridge, MA: Harvard University Press, 1985, p. 6). Fuller and Liddell Hart may have hoped to do for war 'what Copernicus did for astronomy, Newton for physics, and Darwin for natural history' (Luvaas, p. 201), but their whole approach indicated that they failed to develop a comprehensive theory of war. Their quest for the elusive scientific principles of war led mainly to the study of practical questions and the operational level, much to the neglect of philosophical questions on the nature and essence of war, questions that must be considered in an attempt to impose order on such a vast and complex subject. Through his refusal to approach war as a scientific subject, Clausewitz brought about the 'Copernican revolution' by focusing on the essence of war, related philosophical issues, and movement from the highest political and strategic levels to the operational one.

It is even more surprising to discover that Clausewitz suffered a worse fate at the hands of his countrymen. As Jehuda Wallach, Klaus Jürgen Müller, and Williamson Murray illustrate in their articles, even on those occasions that he was understood, his ideas were flatly rejected by political and military leaders.

Again the source of all trouble from the vantage point of the German military was that Clausewitz wrote neither an easy book to understand nor a practical manual replete with concrete advice. According to Wallach, German officers regarded Clausewitz 'as a military philosopher, rather than a practical teacher' (Field Marshal von Kleist); 'a theoretician to be read by professors' (General Gayer von Schweppenburg). Von Seeckt referred to *On War* as 'difficult reading' and as 'rather obscure and clumsy ...'; not surprisingly he opined that 'the mentioning of his [Clausewitz'] name alone makes one feel sick'. Ludendorff felt that *On War* was an atavism: 'His work belongs to a past period of World History, and is mostly out of date. One may even get confused by reading it.' To the extent that the Germans read Clausewitz at all, they studied only the operational sections of *On War* and in the process took ideas out of context to satisfy an obsession with the search for a decisive victory. But as Wallach shows, such biases warped their understanding of Clausewitz' theories even on the operational level. A doctrinal emphasis on the offensive caused them to disregard Clausewitz' insistence on the inherent superiority of the defense over the offense. In both world wars, they obstinately refused (until they paid a very high price) to accept Clausewitz' ideas on the advantages of flexible defense operations or defensive retrograde movement, a topic which he had described in great detail. In other words, even those prescriptive measures that Clausewitz had to offer were rejected as heresy.

The German military also refused to accept his most fundamental idea on the primacy of political authorities in the guidance of war. In the West, political culture and tradition put political leaders at the helm without having to learn this basic principle from a German theorist. The position of the political leadership was never really questioned. But in Germany, where such a political culture did not exist, Clausewitz' emphasis on the importance of political guidance in war was a valuable, innovative concept.

As Wallach and Müller demonstrate, German military leaders always insisted that in wartime they must maintain some degree of control on the political level. The question was not who would be in control, but rather how much control they would actually demand. While politics could not vanish as they might have wished, it was militarized and subordinated to purely military considerations. Unfortunately for Germany, this demand for absolute military control over political issues during wartime was accepted without resistance by the civilian political leaders. As Kaiser Wilhelm II said, 'Policy keeps its mouth shut during war until strategy allows it to speak again.' It is ironic that Hitler, the first political leader to be in full control of the Germany military, accepted an almost purely militaristic view of the conduct of war and in effect waged the war as a military, not a political, leader.

The German military's reluctance to be subordinated to the civilian authorities is illustrated by the history of the publication of *On War*. In the original edition, Clausewitz argued that '... unless the statesman and soldier are combined in one person, the only sound expedient is to make the commander-in-chief a member of the cabinet, so that *the cabinet can share* in the major aspects of his activities' (my emphasis, *On War*, p. 608). In the second edition, which appeared in Germany in 1853, the last part of the sentence was changed to read: '... so that he *may take part* in its councils and decisions on important occasions' (my emphasis, *On War*, p. 608, n.1). This was a subtle reversal of Clausewitz' original suggestion that the commander report to or consult with the cabinet rather than actively participate in its decisions as a *primus inter pares*. (See also Werner Hahlweg's introduction to *Vom Kriege*, Bonn: Dummler, 1980, 19th edition, pp. 69–71; 169–70; note 378; pp. 1236–8.)

The general lack of familiarity with Clausewitz' work that Wallach found in the German officer corps is also borne out in Müller's exhaustive case study on the development of General Ludwig Beck's ideas on the relationship between the military high command and the political leadership. Clearly General Beck did not have the opportunity during his military career to study *On War* very carefully, while his interest in the theories of more contemporary strategists, in particular Ludendorff's ideas on the nature of total war, intellectually distanced him from Clausewitz. It also becomes apparent that as long as he was on active duty, he sought to bring about equal participation for military leaders in the political decision-making process during war. (In fact, Beck was one of the few German generals who demanded equality and not full political control for the military.) Once General Beck left the army and became involved in the political opposition to Hitler, he changed his mind. Now he read Clausewitz to obtain support for the idea of the primacy of politics, through which he hoped to avoid the total militarization of society as advocated by Ludendorff and subsequently realized by Hitler. By virtue of attacking Ludendorff's 'total war', he condemned Hitler's conduct of war for the sake of war.

Although General Beck did indeed find intellectual solace in *On War*, it cannot be said that he truly understood Clausewitz. His interpretation of the book was too narrow to embrace the wider political and social dimensions of war as Clausewitz saw them. Beck therefore failed to connect the political conduct of war with its social origins and the general political conditions prevailing in Germany at the time. As Müller explains, Clausewitz' perception of politics and policy in the direction of war transcends foreign policy; it must include 'all interests of the community' (that is, an understanding of domestic politics). 'Policy ... is nothing in itself; it is simply the trustee for all these interests against other states' (pp. 606–7). Accordingly, war is the reflection of a society's specific political character at a given point in time.

The articles of Müller and Wallach indicate that there is a need for further study concerning the impact of modern civil–military relations on Clausewitz' central idea – the primacy of politics. Clausewitz failed to delineate the specific form that relations between the military high command and the political leadership would assume; merely suggesting that the military commander must participate in cabinet meetings is too vague. Perhaps the unity of the military commander and political leader in one person simplified the problems involved in civil–military relations in his own mind (Handel, p. 58–61).

While Williamson Murray agrees with the argument that German officers were not really familiar with Clausewitz' work, he tries to prove that the German military nevertheless integrated much of Clausewitz' approach into their educational system and performance on the battle-field. Murray sets a difficult task for himself, since the link between Clausewitz' theory and the attitude and education of the German officer corps could at best be indirect. Yet even such an indirect link is not easy to verify. One could argue that the same qualities characterizing the German military were developed independently. Perhaps Clausewitz' writings embodied the essential German attitude toward war and thus summarized what was already there. In this respect, it might be said that instead of the Germans being Clausewitzian – Clausewitz was German!

Be that as it may, Murray establishes that many of the qualities Clause-witz emphasized were indeed adopted by the German military. Much like the philosophy of training in the German military academy in Berlin, Clausewitz did not believe in the so-called school's solution, but encouraged criticism, self-criticism, diversity, and the concept that more than one solution can be correct as long as it is chosen quickly and boldly executed. This type of education encourages the development of character and 'moral forces', independent thinking, flexibility, de-centralization, and the delegation of authority, all qualities that Clause-witz considered crucial to the success of an army. The indirect connection betwen Clausewitz' spirit and the education of the German military requires much more attention to examples concerning his 'moral ele-ments' and their adaptation to the German military educational system. There are also other important points of divergence between Clausewitz' work and the German military tradition. One not discussed by Murray is the vital role of the 'military genius' in Clausewitz' theory. Instead of identifying 'military geniuses', the Germans stressed the achievement of a higher average level for all officers, the development of efficient staff work, and less reliance on the brilliance of individuals.

Clausewitz was somewhat more popular in France than in Germany, but his work was not better understood. As Douglas Porch makes clear, the French 'nibbled' at his work in a highly selective way, using him, as Liddell Hart believed, to 'give a spurious appearance of rationality to what were little more than statements of faith' (that is, to justify the military doctrine and policy they would have chosen anyway). Porch presents the situation in France as it developed until the outbreak of the First World War, which helps to explain why the French favored specific aspects of Clausewitz' work and conveniently ignored others.

By the turn of the century, the French realized that they were hopelessly outmanned and outgunned by the Germans. They could not expect to catch up with the Germans in the quantitative dimension, so they desperately hoped to compensate for their numerical inferiority with the superior quality of their 'moral force'. As long as the French refused to accept the harsh implications of the realities of the balance of power, they inevitably slipped into a fantasy world by espousing a doctrine that emphasized quality over quantity.

Some consolation was at hand in Clausewitz' discussion of the critical role of moral forces in war. This choice coincided, as Porch explains, with the intellectual atmosphere in France at the time – that of the Bergsonian turning away from Positivism to the spirit of *élan vital*. Even if this trend had no direct influence on the military's choice of 'moral forces' as a key doctrinal element, it certainly fits nicely into the *Zeitgeist* of France in the early twentieth century.

The second key element of French military doctrine – the identification of the offense as the 'operational' manifestation of the 'moral forces' in action – did not, however, find any support in *On War*. Indeed, given the degree of French military inferiority, Clausewitz would have undoubtedly recommended the choice of a defensive military doctrine. Considering the inherent superiority of the defense over the offense as Clausewitz made clear, France's only realistic hope lay in the choice of an almost purely defensive military doctrine. This, as Porch shows, would have dovetailed nicely with developments in weapons technologies at that time. The French ignored such potentially helpful developments in the belief that superior 'moral forces' would cancel out any advantages that could be gained from better weapons.

Although a purely rational calculation would have convinced the French to adopt a defensive military doctrine, psychological pressures made it almost inevitable that they choose an offensive posture. The selection of a defensive doctrine would have required the admission of military inferiority *vis-à-vis* the Germans and acceptance of the fact that Alsace Lorraine could not be regained. The prospect of becoming a second-rate power was definitely not acceptable to their Gallic pride. The very choice of a defensive military doctrine implied inferiority, passivity, and the tacit acknowledgment that France could not emerge victorious. The psychology of weakness, as the case often is, forced the French to choose a highly irrational and risky offensive strategy which in their own minds closed the gap between reality and the historical perception of themselves as a nation. Only after the First World War with the building of the Maginot line and the adoption of a purely defensive strategy did the French accept, at least *de facto*, the realities of the balance of power in relation to Germany. The psychology of the French and their military predicament have little to do with Clausewitz, but certainly provide valuable insight into why the French read *On War* so selectively.

John Gooch's article, 'Clausewitz Disregarded: Italian Military Thought and Doctrine, 1815–1943', explains why the Italian Army was unable to develop a single coherent military doctrine to serve as the basis for strategic planning and military operations. The Italians were first plagued by too many competing lower-level military doctrines that changed in quick succession, then later were attracted to the wrong military doctrines for political or economic reasons. Their theorizing on war lacked 'a coherent philosophical and solid intellectual foundation'. Such a foundation could have been provided by the study of *On War*, but no translation of this work was available until 1942.

The overriding reason for this disinterest in Clausewitz was based on the ethnocentric Italian approach to strategy; that is, the belief that Italy's unique geographic location and economic conditions called for the creation of an original Italian military doctrine. Such a doctrine was never developed. The only truly original Italian military doctrine was that of Douhet, who advocated the central role of air power and strategic bombing. Although only a partial theory at best, Douhet's doctrine was embraced because the Italians perceived the war in the air as one that would put less pressure on their limited resources (which were not large enough to support powerful land forces). In addition, this doctrine seemed to enhance the dynamic, technologically-oriented image desired by the Fascist regime. The conviction that 'non-Italian ideas were irrelevant' or that the adoption of foreign military doctrines could do more harm than good was, of course, very provincial. Although the Italians insisted (as they should have) on developing an original military doctrine, they were not justified in foregoing the serious study of foreign military theories and doctrines. After all, even the most original doctrine must be designed to counter those of the adversary and therefore requires familiarity with his theories. In this sense, it can be said that the Italians developed their own military thought in a vacuum.

As Gooch argues, the Italians most certainly could have learned more from Clausewitz about the interrelationship between politics and strategy, the critical dimension in which their performance in both the First and Second World Wars 'proved to be a dismal failure'. Similarly, they could have benefited considerably in the development of their own ideas on the operational level of war from reading Clausewitz.

Most clearly, the preceding survey of the essays comprising this volume indicates that Clausewitz' work was grossly misunderstood in a variety of different times and places. Given the length and complexity of *On War* as well as some of its internal contradictions, this is not entirely unexpected.

Two central themes reappear in almost every essay. The first concerns the universal tendency of military men and strategists to focus on the operational sections of *On War* because they were easier to comprehend and satisfied a yearning for positive doctrines and rules. This phenomenon runs entirely against the spirit of Clausewitz' work. His non-doctrinaire approach to the study of war, his belief that war could never be studied as an accurate science, and his emphasis on the study of military history as a process of self-education rather than as a pragmatic search for concrete solutions to military problems, should have been sufficient to prevent such misinterpretation.

To some extent, however, this was Clausewitz' own fault. Concentration of his methodological discussion in a separate section, 'On the Theory of War' (Book II, pp. 127–77), made it easier for readers to ignore. Moreover, inasmuch as his methodological discussion is absolutely essential to a proper understanding of his whole approach, it could be argued that the serious reader should begin by reading Book II, 'On the Theory of War' before proceeding to the rest of the book. There is no doubt that many of Clausewitz' readers will continue to misread his work in pursuit of a 'scientific way to fight war', for his thesis is not much more popular today than in any other period of history.

The second common theme bears upon the deliberate distortion of Clausewitz' ideas ranging from the supremacy of the political over the military leadership in the guidance of war, to the inherent advantages of the defense over the offense, and his ideas on the absolute war. Unlike the first type of misunderstanding which is based on errors of perception or selective reading of the text, deliberate distortions are 'political in nature' and therefore also inevitable.

If a military organization has determined that its doctrine will be offensive in nature, then regardless of the truth or what Clausewitz observed, it will be conveniently ignored in the interest of that organization. Ironically enough, this is possible precisely because the fact that war is an art makes it impossible to prove that one doctrine is intrinsically superior to another. Moreover, as Clausewitz observed, even victory on the battlefield does not necessarily prove that the strategy chosen by the winner is better than that of the loser.

Similarly, his insistence on the supremacy of the political leadership over the military in war will always be challenged by military leaders who would naturally like to preserve their freedom of decision and believe that they better understand war in all of its aspects. The problem of responsibility of control over the conduct of war has no clear-cut answer. The question of what constitutes a political dimension and what is purely military defies precision as it depends to a large extent on the nature of a specific war (total or limited), and on such other factors as political culture and technological developments. The varying perspectives on war and tensions between the political and military leadership will never be satisfactorily resolved. And because politics will remain forever an art, so will war.

MICHAEL I. HANDEL

Clearly a largely dim view of the mental capacity of 'military men and strategists' who either avoid clausewitz altogether because it is too long and doesn't offer the clarity and unambiguous rules that minds like mine 'universally' crave, or misunderstand him by selectively reading the bits only most directly applicable to operations. How accurate an assessment is this? Not entirely satisfactory. See pp 3 & 4 in particular.

PART ONE
CLAUSEWITZ REVISITED

It was my ambition to write a book that would not be forgotten after two or three years, and that possibly might be picked up more than once by those who are interested in the subject.

Clausewitz on the genesis of his early manuscript
on the theory of war (1818), p. 63.

The Eternal Clausewitz

MARTIN VAN CREVELD

The problem which the present article seeks to address is why, among all the better-known writers on military theory within Western civilization, it is Clausewitz alone whose work appears able to withstand every kind of political, social, economic, and technological change since it was published, and seems to stand fair chance of remaining forever of more than purely historical interest.[1] It is a problem which would have intrigued Clausewitz himself, for he was an ambitious if frustrated man. Like Shakespeare ('so long as men can breathe or eyes can see/so long lives this and this gives life to thee') and Horace ('a monument I have built/ more durable than bronze') he fully intended his work to last. As he wrote in an introductory note, 'It was my purpose to write a book that would not be forgotten after two or three years and which would be consulted more than once by those interested in the subject.' The question that needs answering is why, of all those who tried, he was the only one to succeed.

To begin with, a few observations on what Clausewitz is not. His work is acutely relevant to the actual conduct of war and has been so for the century and a half since it was written; yet its popularity has nothing to do with the kind of 'usefulness' that causes good handbooks to sell, and indeed it is precisely those sections where he comes closest to offering advice of the how-to-do-it-variety – concerning fortress warfare, for example – which are most often regarded as hopelessly obsolete.

Nor can its continuing fame be attributed to its being readable in a literary or journalistic sense. True, many of Clausewitz' metaphors, such as the one comparing war to a game of cards (thus bringing out the role of chance), battle to cash payment in a business transaction (illustrating battle's role in war), and activity in war to walking in water (clarifying the nature of friction) are very well selected. *On War* also contains an occasional quotable sentence, such as 'War is the continuation of politics by other means' or 'The best strategy is always to be really strong, first in general and then at the decisive point.'

The work violates the rules of composition in that it offers no single, clear progression of thought, no well-defined 'culminating point' towards which everything strives, not even 'conclusions' succinctly summarizing the main points that it seeks to make. Instead, it moves about in a spiral-like way. It examines the same arguments from many different angles, sends the reader back and forth by means of innumerable cross references, and returns time and again to ram home the same fundamental points. Although the overall division of the work into eight books, each with its own title, is logical enough, the structure of the individual books is often complicated and always asymmetrical, the section-captions themselves being almost invariably dull and pedestrian. What would an editor of *Time* make of a caption that reads: 'Frequent periods of inaction remove war still further from the realm of the absolute and make it even more a matter of assessing probabilities'? How exciting is the announcement that 'The preceding chapter showed that the nature of war is complex and changeable. I now propose to inquire how its nature influences its purpose and its means'? Surely, anybody who wrote like this in a creative writing course would see his work thrown out the window.

Thus, Liddell Hart in *The Ghost of Napoleon* to the contrary, Clausewitz' writings are very far from constituting a kind of 'Prussian Marseillaise' which 'inflames the blood and intoxicates the mind';[3] in fact few writers have tried to make their influence felt so purely by means of the intellect alone. Both in his personal life and his work, Clausewitz deliberately avoided any appeal to the emotions. Although it probably *is* possible to sum up Clausewitz' doctrine in a few ringing phrases, to do so would represent a gross narrowing down and even distortion of the real significance of his work, and would often lead to mere banalities.[4] The greatest of all writers on war, in brief, makes for no easy bedside reading. If one is to benefit fully from his work – and if it is not to give rise to endless misunderstandings, as he himself feared it would – it has to be studied repeatedly, seriously, and in depth, taking into account both the immediate historical background against which it was written and its timeless eternal character. Thus, whatever the reasons behind Clausewitz' growing fame and continuing popularity, they do not include a facile pen making for easy reading and quick understanding.

I

Without a doubt, one reason why Clausewitz has succeeded in retaining his relevance through a century and a half of very rapid changes in warfare is the sheer comprehensiveness of his writings. Although he did not deal with economics (the entire problem of mobilizing the state's material resources for war) or with technology (which he regarded as constantly changing and therefore as essentially irrelevant to the unchanging verities he was concerned with)[5] for the rest there is practically no kind or element of war on which he does not have something sensible to say within the scope of a single book. The statesman and the politician may find in him a guide to war as one of their instruments and also to the way in which war ought to relate to policy. The warlord may find much to help clarify his thoughts concerning strategy, battle, attack, defense, surprise, external and internal lines, and a host of related matters. The tactician may find in him, besides a profound analysis of the nature of battle and the way it is decided, some of the best discussions ever of such subjects as mountain warfare and cordon defense. The historian will look to *On War* for guidance on the functions of military history and the way in which it ought to be studied and written, whereas the theoretician can find an immense amount of value in Clausewitz' discussion of the nature of military theory and the way in which it does and ought to relate to military practice. Although written mainly with conventional warfare in mind, the book is also relevant to guerrilla warfare,[6] and its definition of war as a rational instrument in the hands of politics puts it into the very center of the nuclear debate.[7] *On War*, in short, differs from other works in that it contains much more than occasional insights however trenchant or even brilliant. Nor does it commit another common error, that of trying to reduce war to a handful of 'nothing buts'. Instead it presents a systematic, comprehensive and well-rounded discussion that would, as was the author's explicit intention, have been even more complete had it not been for his untimely death. Consequently whatever the kind of armed conflict one plans, or is engaged in, or investigates, one is certain to find something relevant in Clausewitz.

The real problem, however, is not merely how to say something about everything; rather, it consists of compressing a subject of infinite complexity and size – war – into a book of finite length. It is a problem that confronts every great work of philosophy and art, and it is very largely by their success in solving it that the greatness of such works is measured. Clausewitz' solution is to argue by polarities. He always postulates a thing and its opposite. There is theory and there is practice. There is real war and there is absolute war. There is the moral and there is the physical. There is the genius of the individual and there is the spirit of the army. There is attack and there is defense. There is annihilation and there is attrition. There is regular war and people's, or guerrilla, warfare. There is a profound awareness of the individuality of each separate historical event, but there is also a grasp of 'history' as a whole. This method of argumentation makes certain that, whatever one's particular problem and selected course of action, it will always be possible to compare it with its opposite and thus clarify one's thoughts, which is the true objective of theory.

Moreover, the poles once they have been set up do not remain entirely distinct. While opposed to each other, they are also shown to merge into each other, complement each other, and contain elements of each other. It is in this way that Clausewitz – like, for instance, Sigmund Freud, who uses the same device in postulating such concepts as *eros* and *thanatos* – achieves that most difficult feat, compressing a multi-dimensional, kaleidoscopic, rich reality into the sequential order of language and thought.

Characteristic of Clausewitz' dualistic approach is his discussion of the phenomenon of genius on the one hand and its relationship with what might be called 'the rules of the game' on the other.[8] The question as to whether genius breaks the rules – in this case imposed by the total of the means available to the art of war at a given time and place – or merely grasps them more completely and applies them more successfully than anybody else is of course a very ancient one. Believing that genius breaks the rules leads to hero worship of the kind associated with Carlyle; whereas believing in the genius' complete understanding results in analyses of the 'objective' circumstances which made this or that action 'inevitable'. Typically, Clausewitz' solution to the problem combines the two approaches. Living after Napoleon but before Marx, he insists that they do not contradict but rather complement each other, that genius *both* makes its own rules *and* obeys existing ones, *both* makes the utmost use of the available means *and* combines them in new and unprecedented ways.[9] Thus genius without those means is nothing, but those means without genius will never rise above the mediocre.

Another good example of Clausewitz' dual approach is the way in which he approaches the question of rationality in war. Surely nobody has ever been more insistent than he that war is (or, at any rate, ought to be) a rational instrument in the hands of policy; at the same time, however, Clausewitz more than anybody else emphasizes that war is the domain of anger and fear, boldness and passion, in short, of the most violent emotions known to man, and that any analysis of it which does not take these emotions into account will be completely without value. In war as elsewhere reason and emotion stand poles apart, yet at the same time they must complement each other and interact with each other, indeed make use of each other. It is precisely his insistence that both these things are and should be present which sets Clausewitz apart from theoreticians such as Jomini or du Pic who have emphasized the one or the other.

When a work is able to look at both sides of the coin, to contrast them and yet at the same time bring out their relations and overlappings, that work may be described as profound. It moves on many different levels, captures many different meanings at once. Like Plato's *Republic* or Shakespeare's *Hamlet*, it is capable of evoking not a single interpretation – no work of philosophy capable of being understood in only one way will last for long – but many different ones.[10] And this Clausewitz does in language which, though not always simple, is neither abstruse, nor technical, nor pedantic, but readily understandable to specialist and layman alike. It is a remarkable achievement.

II

One way to understand why Clausewitz has lasted so well is to compare the study of war with the study of nature. War does not qualify as a natural event, but partly for that very reason, its study does offer some useful analogies and contrasts to the methods of natural science. As understood since the time of the 'scientific revolution' – that is, the days of Galileo and Descartes – natural science consists of examining physical nature and establishing the existence of regularities in it. For example, Newton's studies of nature led him to the conclusion that bodies move according to the formula $A = F/M$ (acceleration equals force divided by mass). Einstein found that energy equals mass times the square of the velocity of light ($E = MC^2$). Newton's conclusion was dubbed the Second Law of Mechanics; Einstein's, the General Law of Relativity. Both regularities are supposed to exist in nature regardless of whether or not they are observed or by whom; it is in this sense that they are said to be 'objective'.

Given that it is the business of science to discover regularities, 'scientific progress' may mean one of several things. It may mean the establishment of more and more regularities within a single field; their progressive extension to new fields (for example, from physics and astronomy, where the process began in the seventeenth century, to chemistry and biology, which became scientific two hundred years later); their progressive reduction, as far as possible, to ever broader, more comprehensive and fewer regularities (such as the attempt to combine the four basic forces known to us in a single formula); and the discovery, from time to time, that this or that regularity which was supposed to hold true does not in fact exist in nature. Conversely, a work on natural science may be said to be 'out of date' either because the regularities which it postulates are false, or because it does not regard them in their proper context, or because it does not take cognizance of additional regularities which were discovered after the time it was published.

In any case, once a work of this kind is 'out of date', once nature has been shown to obey regularities additional to or deeper than or different from those which it postulates, it generally ceases to be of any but historical interest – that is, as evidence of the way people thought about nature at a given time and place. Although it may still attract attention because of the historical importance of its thesis (a good example would be Charles Darwin's *Origins of Species*), or else because of the sheer elegance of its reasoning, it can no longer be regarded as a correct explanation of the way things work and, consequently, as a useful guide as to how they will work if tried.[11]

Understood in this sense, then, natural science presents a double face. It is concerned with explanation in the sense of discovering regularities in the way things actually happen; and, once this is done, it seeks to use those regularities to make them happen, to predict what will happen to factor A if factor B or C, or D, to which it is related in such and such a way, is altered. Science thus explains why things happen and, therefore, how to make them happen – knowledge is power, as Francis Bacon succinctly put it.[12]

Turning now from natural science towards war, it is remarkable how often the latter has been approached with a similar purpose in mind. That purpose was explicitly stated by Maurice de Saxe in the opening pages of his book, *Reveries*: 'Every science has its rules and maxims, except that of war where everything is enveloped in darkness.' This was a deficiency which he, the victorious commander anxious to impart his knowledge, set out to correct. A son of the enlightenment, Saxe assumed that war, like nature whose secrets had just been laid bare by Newton, operates in accordance with fixed regularities which are part of its essence if indeed they do not themselves constitute that essence. It was the task of the study of war to discover those regularities and, once it had discovered them, to encapsulate them in rules, principles, and maxims. To follow these rules would result in victory, whereas to violate them would lead to defeat.

Although not all of Saxe's successors (or his predecessors) have been as explicit as he is in prescribing the object of the study of war, it is neverthe-less remarkable how often the subject has been approached in this way. Starting from logic, or experience, or history, men have sought to define the 'objective' principles of war in the same way they discovered those of nature, reducing them to a single great principle if possible. Thus Heinrich von Bülow in *Der Geist des neueren Kriegssytem* (1799) found this great principle in the geometrical relationship between base and objective. Jomini, who is his *Precis de l'art de la guerre* (1838) explicitly states his belief that strategy is eternal and unchanging, found his answer in the principle of operation on internal lines. Moltke – or perhaps it was merely his successors and interpreters, since the master himself modestly called strategy 'nothing but a system of expedients' – claimed to have discovered an even more effective recipe for victory in the form of operations on external lines.[13] Schlieffen, a technician if ever there was one, replaced both principles by the simpler and more comprehensive one of always hitting the enemy's flank and rear, rather than his front.[14] Liddell Hart sought the secret of victory in the indirect approach and, as Schlieffen had done before him, next proceeded to cast this principle right back through history in an attempt to show that victory had always and everywhere been won only by its being followed.[15] Whatever the differences among these men, and also between them and the many others who have tried their hand at discovering and pronouncing the 'principles of war',[16] they all shared the belief that war, like physical nature, proceeds according to certain regularities. These regularities it was the task of military studies, and military history above all, to discover, explain, and elaborate, both by way of an explanation of past wars and as a guide to the conduct of future ones.

If we ask now why all these men, in spite of the many nuggets of wisdom contained in their writings, ultimately appear to have failed to produce anything of truly lasting value,[17] perhaps the real answer is that they tried to apply the scientific method to a field in which it is basically inapplicable. In nature regularities, whether or not they are known to science, are assumed to be fixed and immutable. The same cause will always produce the same effect, a single exception being considered sufficient, in principle at any rate, to invalidate any scientific law however well established. We must assume that an atom of hydrogen behaved in the same way a billion years ago as it does today (and will continue to display the same behavior a billion years hence), or else the concept of nature itself will disintegrate into sheer meaningless chaos. We must assume nature was governed by Newton's (or Einstein's, or whoever's) laws in the past and will continue so eternally, or else it simply does not make sense to speak of 'nature'. Nature, in short, is eternal precisely in the sense that it obeys eternal laws. It might even, in that very sense, be said to consist of those laws.

The case of war is different. War, though it does rest on certain regularities – a man struck by a given force at a given spot always dies, and a tank that has run out of fuel always stops – neither consists of these regularities nor always obeys the same ones. As the German Army Regulations *Truppenführung* of 1936 put it very well, 'War is a free creative activity resting upon scientific foundations'.[18] The form of war is very largely determined by the character, both individual and collective, of the people who wage it; by the instruments through which it is waged; the environment in which it is waged; and the circumstances under which it is waged. As Clausewitz himself points out in Book II of *On War*, each of these factors represents such tremendous variety and complexity as to render any attempt to establish universal 'maxims' or 'rules' according to which war proceeds and should be waged almost entirely without value. Put in other words, war differs from nature in that whatever regularities may exist in it are confirmed to the very lowest, in other words, purely technical, level. Valid, at best, only for their particular times and places, these regularities must be carefully attuned to those times and places. In no sense can they be compared with 'natural laws'; and indeed often victory is due precisely to the *absence* of their application.[19]

The essential difference between war and physical nature, however, goes deeper still. Unless one believes in the existence of an active god who regulates it (in which case its study should be regarded as a subdivision of theology, as was in fact the case during much of human history) nature is blind, its processes unfolding in accordance with the rules that define it. War, by contrast, is an activity with a purpose. That purpose, which is not inherent in the phenomenon itself but is laid down for it by the requirements of policy, does more than any other single factor to define its shape and direction and indeed to determine whether it makes any sense at all. Just as the thousands of components that go into, say, an urban transportation network will not in the absence of a directing hand combine into a purposeful system but rather collapse into a formless jumble, so the various elements that war comprises can make sense solely in terms of the purpose at hand. This purpose is in some ways related to, but by no means simply the outgrowth of, the means at hand and the environment in which they operate. Ultimately it is not a product of material factors at all, but rather of the free human will.

The fundamental point to grasp is that war differs from physical nature in that it unfolds according to a purpose; and that, consequently, the methods which science applies in order to study nature are, by definition, irrelevant or at any rate inadequate to it. The failure of virtually all writings on war to produce anything of truly lasting value therefore does not, as Liddell Hart believed,[20] derive from their authors' being unscientific (in the sense of not establishing enough regularities, or of setting up the wrong ones because of bias or inattention) but, on the contrary, from the fact that they were too much so. By trying to study war 'scientifically' the authors of these writings *ipso facto* denied themselves the right of asking not merely what war is, but also what it serves for; since these are questions which modern science, as it has been practiced since the beginning of the seventeenth century, simply does not admit.

Clausewitz' method is different. The very first paragraph of *On War* is concerned to find out what war is. The question of the purpose it serves is addressed in the most famous sentence he ever wrote. Had he lived to revise his work as planned, he would have given this sentence even greater prominence than it already possesses. Both questions are critically important to Clausewitz' thought since, as he himself points out,[21] it is from them that everything else derives; however, they are neither of them such as modern science would regard as legitimate. The question as to what things are forms the core of the Platonic philosophical tradition, just as the question as to what purpose they serve stands at the very root of the Aristotelian one. Among other things, the scientific revolution consisted precisely of discarding these two traditions: it was by abandoning the *what is* and the *what for* in favor of the *how* that modern science was able to embark upon its triumphal march of conquest.[22] By so doing, however, science as applied to the physical universe automatically disqualified itself from any claim to deal with the province of social life of which, in Clausewitz' own words, war forms a part.[23]

Thus, if the interpretation here presented is correct, perhaps the principal reason why Clausewitz was able to contribute so much to our understanding of war consists precisely in that he was not a scientist and did not approach history as if it were a science. Accordingly, his principal task was neither to ask 'how to' questions nor to answer them. He did not rest content in finding out how things work, but attempted to discover what purpose they serve and what their true nature is. This led him towards an understanding of war different from, and more profound than, anything that would have been permitted by science or that was actually permitted to anyone who chose to remain within a scientific framework.

Although Clausewitz was not a scientist and did not commit the error of regarding the study of war as a science, in another sense his work owes more to the scientific method than is commonly realized. Much has been written concerning Clausewitz' preference for ideal concepts, such as 'absolute war' or 'the best strategy' or 'the attack' which he establishes and examines with great care before proceeding to contrast them with reality, setting them up as useful points of reference even when, as is often and indeed normally the case, they cannot be fully applied in practice. What is seldom realized, however, is how much this method owes not to philosophy – Kant's influence is often mentioned in this connection, although there is no direct proof that Clausewitz read his work – but to natural science as practiced, say, between Newton and Einstein.

We have already defined science as understood since the seventeenth century in terms of the nature of the questions that it asks, and must now proceed to do the same in terms of the methods that it uses in order to arrive at the truth. As most textbooks, following in Francis Bacon's wake, describe the phenomenon, the shift from pre-modern to modern science consisted essentially of a change in the acknowledged source of truth. Instead of looking for it in books – whether sacred, such as the Bible, or secular, such as Aristotle – men moved towards experiment and observation of nature.[24] The story of Galileo dropping different weights from the top of the inclining tower of Pisa, though possibly apocryphal, represents a famous case in point; here is an attempt to use an experiment in order to discover how things actually work, instead of reading and interpreting some text on how they should work. What is less commonly realized, however, is that Galileo was much more than a practical experimenter.

Besides carrying out many actual experiments, in the laboratory that he built for himself, he also performed numerous so-called 'thought experiments'. In these he sought to clarify what would happen if this or that was tried under such and such circumstances.[25] Nor can it be said that this line of reasoning was unfruitful. Ultimately, it was not by experience – which in many ways tended to confirm the doctrines held by Aristotle – but by postulating an ideal world in which bodies are subjected to no external forces and are consequently able to move at a constant speed and in a straight line (no such body has ever existed since the world was created, and none ever will) that Newton came to formulate the three laws of mechanics named after him. The laws thus arrived at were purely theoretical; but they made it possible to extrapolate back from an ideal world to the actual one, which was the method that Newton followed.

We cannot be certain whether Clausewitz read or understood Newton deeply enough to appreciate the method on which his most famous discoveries were based; it appears, however, that towards the end of the eighteenth-century this method was fairly common among what we would nowadays call social scientists (Clausewitz, remember, defined war as belonging to the province of social life). For example, Adam Smith when he formulated his theory of supply and demand and the way they balanced each other and affected prices first postulated an imaginary world of perfect elasticity in which there were perfect substitutes for all commodities and no monopolists among unlimited numbers of both buyers and sellers, then proceeded to work back from this imaginary world toward the real one.[26] Thomas Malthus, when discussing the results of a population increasing at a geometrical ratio feeding on supplies increasing at an arithmetical one, did the same.[27]

A good example of the way in which Clausewitz' thought derives the real from the ideal is presented by his discussion of the relationship between offense and defense.[28] Contrary to what is often assumed, Clausewitz does not say that the latter is always stronger than the former; only that the defense as such is stronger than the offense as such, a relationship which derives from the nature of things rather than from actual observation. Once that relationship has been established, there is no reason why the ascendancy of the offensive over the defensive under certain circumstances should not be granted, just as Newton's First Law of Mechanics only refers to things as they would be in an ideal world rather than the way they are in the actual one. Clausewitz thus presents the relationship between offense and defense as an entirely imaginary exercise, a point of reference from which to start one's calculation rather than as an unalterable law.

Thus it might be said that Clausewitz, though he did not regard the study of war as akin to natural science, nevertheless made use of the scientific method; and did so, moreover, without falling into the all-too-common error of regarding the latter as arising solely from practical experience and observations supplied by military history. It was, on the contrary, precisely by leaving practical reality behind that he became the most practically realistic writer on war. This point will be further discussed in the next section.

III

War is a practical activity above all, and has always been regarded as such by the vast majority of those who engaged in it and reflected upon it. However much they might reflect upon its various aspects, ultimately their purpose was almost always the same, namely, to contribute towards a better understanding that might lead to victory; victory for themselves, their subordinates, their superiors, or their countrymen.

This being the case, the vast majority of existing works on the theory of war are ultimately nothing but glorified cookbooks. They are full of recipes, more or less well thought out, and justified with the aid of a smaller or greater number of examples taken from military history, as to how things ought to be done. Given such and such circumstances, according to Onasander's *The General*, one's phalanx should be made wider or narrower, thinner or thicker. Under such and such circumstances, according to Jomini, one should attack in such and such a formation, taking care that such and such points should be occupied and that such and such conditions should be met. According to the same author, cavalry is most useful in such and such terrain and ought to be deployed in such and such formation. The purpose of such works, ranging all the way from Maurice's *Strategicon* to the latest edition of the American FM 100-5, is always the same: namely, to instruct practical men engaged on a very practical pursuit how to go about their business. Often, indeed, this purpose is seen as the prime, if not the sole, reason why works of war should be written, or at any rate read by those responsible for waging and directing it.

In part, Clausewitz himself follows this tradition. He was a practical soldier writing primarily for other practical soldiers, passionately interested in his country's freedom and greatness, and actively involved in the effort to help secure both. His concern with the practical conduct of war is illustrated by the 'Summary of the instruction given by the author to His Royal Highness, the Crown Prince'. Opening with the declaration that 'the great object of the theory of war is to guide us to the way of obtaining a preponderance of physical force and advantages at the decisive points', this treatise suggests such measures as 'avoiding long, continuous lines of troops' and 'posting the cavalry behind the infantry' as means towards that end. To illustrate his meaning, Clausewitz even adorned his work with schematic diagrams of the kind that would have delighted Jomini and for which Jomini has so often been derided. All this was no doubt highly relevant at the time it was written; but has now been almost entirely forgotten, and deservedly so.

Clausewitz, however, was not only a practical soldier. He was that, but he was also a philosopher who asked, not merely how war ought to be made, but what its real nature is and what purpose it serves. By focusing on ideas and the logical connections between them he was able to answer. In this way he transcended mere practicality and also the limits of the here and the now. For, whereas the methods of warfare change, its true essence and purpose do not. War, regardless of how and where it is waged, is *always* a duel between two moral forces each of which is to some extent free to act in accordance with its will (where there is only one such force there can be no war, only a massacre). Whenever and wherever waged, the purpose of war by definition is to serve as a continuation of policy by other means. To return to the cookbook analogy, Clausewitz' unique relevance derives from the fact that he does more than provide recipes, however tasty or healthy. Instead he delves deeply into the question as to what cooking is and what purpose it serves, coming up with answers that are able to resist changes in both the foodstuffs employed and the utensils in use. He is less concerned with cooking than with thinking about it, less with making war than with reflecting about it, *penser la guerre* in Aron's admirable phrase. In the end, it is precisely this very lack of practicality as usually understood that makes him supremely practical, and able to survive change as well.

Attempting now, however cautiously, to say a few things about the circumstances that enabled Clausewitz and *On War* to attain the stature that they did and transcend their own age and place, it is essential to realize at the outset that it is possible only to identify some necessary conditions thereto. Unlike natural science, history can probably never establish sufficient conditions for anything; that is, it cannot explain why one event, rather than another, had to take place.

Perhaps the first clue may be found in Clausewitz' life.[29] He was born into one period, lived through another very different one, and died during a third which in some ways attempted to restore the spirit of the first but differed from it profoundly in others. Entering service in any army of powdered, periwigged robots, an army isolated from the people and directed by an absolute monarch whose plaything it was, he saw it quickly and decisively defeated by what one contemporary observer described as 'fifty thousand savage beasts, foaming at the mouth with rage and yelling like cannibals'.[30] Born and raised into one set of axioms, rules, theories, beliefs, he saw it abruptly shattered by defeat and replaced by another superior to it. It was this fact, however traumatic, which enabled him to compare both sets, contrast them and reflect on their relative merits, a method which he does in fact use through much of *On War*. By definition, the first condition for gaining eternity is somehow to wrench loose from the accidental, temporal circumstances into which one has been born and under which one spends one's life; a service which in Clausewitz' case was assisted by the sheer magnitude of the changes he lived through – changes that, since he was very involved in them, he may on occasion have exaggerated.[31]

Second, Clausewitz, though virtually an army brat – he was the son of an ex-officer and spent his entire life in the military from the age of eleven on – was not solely a practical soldier and master of his profession. He was an insider to war, but he was a lifelong outside as well. A Prussian through and through, he had lived sufficiently long in France and Russia to learn something about these very different civilizations. Although not perhaps a particularly deep student of the outstanding philosophers of the day, he had certainly reflected a lot on external and domestic politics, literature, art, and education, all topics he had occasionally written about and took an intelligent interest in. Although outstanding mainly as a theoretician, he was never solely a man of theory, having spent the first 35 years of his life actively trying to rise as high in his profession as possible. Before he was forty he had taken part in some of the most decisive battles of world history; unlike Prince Eugen's mule,[32] however, he had also profited from his experience by reflecting and writing about it. From all these different experiences and concerns there arose that mixture of profound thought and practical experience, theory and a sound understanding of the actual workings of war, which is characteristic of his work; from it too derives the ability to employ metaphors – those most powerful means of human expression – taken from economics, biology, navigation, and numerous other fields, all closely intertwined and used in order to shed light on each other. Clausewitz, in brief, was able to do so much better than any other writer on war precisely because, unlike the majority of them, he did not focus either his life or his thought on war alone.

Finally, a very important point which may easily be overlooked in these days of the 'up or out' system, the achievement-oriented society, Clausewitz had time on his hands. There was no question, for him, of publish or perish. He spent the last fifteen years of his life, from 1816 to 1830, almost incessantly working on his great book, revising it time after time, clarifying concepts, contrasting them with each other, and constantly adding new points of view. Financial security he possessed and his duties as administrative director of the war academy in Berlin were not onerous. All of which may perhaps help explain why he was able to think things out to the end; though of course it does not tell us why he actually succeeded in doing so.

In another sense, too, Clausewitz had time on his hands. There were no publisher's deadlines to meet, no advances to be returned if he failed to produce the stuff as promised, no editors who might feel that his work was not 'policy relevant' or that 'our readers' would regard the ideas as too profound and the style as too turgid. He probably realized almost from the beginning that his was not a work to be published in his lifetime, a fact which might have discouraged another man, but which in his case only acted as a spur to even greater efforts. All of which does of course demonstrate that, however useful the principle of 'selection of the fittest' may be in many or even in most cases, it is by no means applicable to all. Had Clausewitz lived under the 'can do' or 'zero fault' or constantly attempted to achieve an 'outstanding' efficiency report, had he been forced to apply for grants and to fill in quarterly progress reports in order to get them continued, surely *On War* would never have been written.

To conclude this article by referring back to the original problem which it raised, I am painfully aware of the limited nature of the explanations that have been attempted here. The fact that Clausewitz possessed leisure in which to think does not, of course, mean that thinking is the product of leisure as such. To produce a work of the stature of *On War* it is almost certainly necessary to be both soldier and scholar, but to be both of these things is in itself not sufficient thereto. While Clausewitz undoubtedly did live through a period of very great and wrenching change, so did every one of his contemporaries. To approach the study of war from a theoretical and philosophical point of view may be important, but it cannot explain why such an approach is successful. That Clausewitz used the scientific method but did not fall into the common error of regarding war as a science, and that he hit upon a stylistic device for compressing an infinite subject into a finite number of pages, formed indispensable prerequisites for his success but did not in themselves guarantee it. All the factors that we have listed amount to some of the necessary conditions that went into the writing of *On War*, and made it into the eternal treasure of the human spirit that it is; necessary conditions are not everything, however, and in fact without sufficient ones they alone are nothing and can explain nothing.

To realize that *On War*, like its subject matter, however much both are rooted in the objective circumstances surrounding them and the techniques of which they make use, are not finally the product solely of those circumstances and those techniques – that may well represent the only valid lesson to be learned from the present article, and it is one of which Clausewitz himself would surely have approved.

NOTES

1. Within thirty-five years of his death Clausewitz was being compared to Thucydides as 'a work for all times'; W. Rustow, *Feldherrnkunst des Neunzehnten Jahrhundert* (Leipzig: F. Schultheiss, 1867), 100–1. Since then he has been likened to Goethe (G. von der Goltz, *Das Volk in Waffen* [Berlin: Decker, 1883], p. 1), Shakespeare (S. L. Murray, *The Reality of War* [London: Hugh Rees, 1906], p. xiii), and Machiavelli (Bernard Brodie, *War and Politics* [New York: Macmillan, 1973], p. 436). A. Rapoport in his introduction to the Pelican edition of *On War* compares him with Bacon, Hobbes, Marx, and Adam Smith.
2. By repeatedly cutting sentences in half, the new English translation by Michael Howard and Peter Paret (Princeton: Princeton University Press, 1976) makes Clausewitz appear more straightforward, but also less profound, than he really is. This is a shortcoming not shared by Col. J. J. Graham's earlier translation. Nevertheless, all references in this article are to the later translation, henceforth referred to as *On War*.
3. Basil Henry Liddell Hart, *The Ghost of Napoleon* (New Haven: Yale University Press, 1933), p. 126.
4. A good example is presented by the Prussian commander in 1866, Prince Frederick Charles, who according to his biographer was 'a profound student of Clausewitz' from whom he learned that one should always keep one's forces concentrated. This doctrine he put into practice, with the result that his forces blundered about blindly for weeks before finally hitting the enemy by accident. See W. Foerster (ed.), *Friedrich Karl von Preussen: Denkwürdigkeiten aus seinem Leben* (Stuttgart: Deutsche Verlags-Anstalt, 1910), Vol. 2, pp. 40–41.
5. A good study of Clausewitz' attitude to military technology remains to be written. He did not completely ignore the subject, but has comparatively little to say about it because he did not regard it as an integral part of war. See *On War*, p. 127.
6. See for example H. G. Summers, Jr., *On Strategy, a Critical Analysis of the Vietnam War* (Novato, CA: Presidio Press, 1982), which applies Clausewitz to the American experience in Vietnam.
7. See, above all, Bernard Brodie, *War and Politics*, Ch. 1.
8. 'Bemerkungen über die Reine und angewandete Strategie des Herrn von Bülow', *Neue Bellona*, No. 9 (1805), 276.
9. For a good modern analysis of the way genius 'transforms' existing rules see I. Bernard Cohen, *The Newtonian Revolution* (Cambridge, MA: Harvard University Press, 1980).
10. Including, presumably, some that are false.
11. This interpretation of science generally follows that of Karl R. Popper, *The Logic of Scientific Discovery* (London: Hutchinson, 1959) rather than that of T.S. Kuhn, *The Structure of Scientific Revolutions* (Chicago: Chicago University Press, 1962).
12. In fact Bacon did not quite say this. In the *Novum Organum* (London, 1620; reprinted New York: American Home Library, 1902), 162, he wrote that 'knowledge and human power are synonymous, since the ignorance of the cause frustrates the effect'.
13. Moltke's claim to have invented a new principle of strategy rests on a letter to the historian Heinrich von Treitschke in 1891 ('The meeting of two hitherto separate armies on the battlefield I consider the highest goal than can be attained by strategy'), printed in Foerster, op. cit., Vol. 2, p. 67. It may, however, have been based on hindsight, and certainly Moltke's principle, if he held it during his first campaign in 1866, was not understood by any Prussian commander except himself.
14. Letter to Freytag Loringhoven, 14 Aug. 1912, printed in E. Kessel (ed.), *Schlieffen* (Gottingen: Musterschmidt, 1958), p. 317.
15. Liddell Hart explained the principle of the indirect approach for the first time in *The Decisive Wars of History* (London: G. Bell, 1929). Here (p. 4) he says that 'throughout the ages decisive results have only been achieved when the approach was indirect'.
16. For a list of those men and their principles see J. I. Alger, *The Quest for Victory* (Westport, CT: Greenwood Press, 1982).
17. Their works are 'likely to be sought by the curious and most of them are kept by some of the libraries'; Michael Carver, *The Apostles of Mobility*, the Lees Knowles Lectures, 1973 (New York: Holmes and Meier, 1979), p. 101.

18. Heeres-Dienstvorschriften, 300 (Berlin, 1969), Vol. 1, p. 1.
19. A good case in point is the Egyptian offensive across the Suez Canal in 1973, which violated the principle of 'concentration of forces'. Surely this is among the most ancient and well-established principles of war; and yet it was Egyptian disregard for it which kept the Israelis guessing for a few days and helped prevent them from mounting an effective counterattack. See Martin van Creveld, *Command in War* (Cambridge, MA: Harvard University Press, 1985), pp. 205–18.
20. Basil Henry Liddell Hart, *Why Don't We Learn from History?* (London: Allen & Unwin, 1944), pp. 24–6.
21. *On War*, p. 90.
22. The move from Platonism and Aristotelianism towards modern science and methods of inquiry is well analyzed in Hugh Kearney, *Science and Change 1500–1700* (New York: McGraw-Hill, 1971), Chs. 1–3; see also Richard F. Jones, *Ancients and Moderns*, 2nd ed., (Magnolia, MA: Peter Smith, 1961), Ch. 1.
23. For a searching discussion of the kinds of 'understanding' that modern science does and does not provide see Michael Polyani, *Science, Faith and Society* (Chicago: University of Chicago Press, 1946), Ch. 1.
24. For the role of experiment in modern science see Herbert Butterfield, *The Origins of Modern Science* (London: Macmillan, 1957), Ch. 5.
25. On Galileo's methods see Stillman Drake, *Galileo at Work* (Chicago: Chicago University Press, 1978), especially Chs. 3–7.
26. *The Wealth of Nations* (London: Penguin, 1982), Chs. 5–8.
27. *An Essay on the Principles of Population* (London: Pelican Classics, 1979), Ch. 2.
28. *On War*, pp. 357–69.
29. By far the best biography, from which much of what follows is taken, is Peter Paret, *Clausewitz and the State* (Oxford: Oxford University Press, 1976); but see also Michael Howard, *Clausewitz* (Oxford: Oxford University Press, 1983).
30. Mallet du Pan quoted in Hoffman Nickerson, *The Armed Horde, 1793–1939: A Study of the Rise, Survival and Decline of the Mass Army* (New York: G.P. Putnam's Sons, 1940), p. 91.
31. If anything, Clausewitz probably exaggerated the tactical and logistic changes brought about by the French Revolutionary Wars; see Robert S. Quimby, *The Background to Napoleonic Warfare* (New York: Columbia University Press, 1957), as regard tactics, and Martin van Creveld, *Supplying War: Logistics from Wallenstein to Patton* (Cambridge: Cambridge University Press, 1977), as regards logistics.
32. Which, according to Frederick the Great, had participated in fourteen campaigns without learning anything.

Clausewitz in the Age of Technology

MICHAEL I. HANDEL

As water has no constant form
there are in war no constant conditions.
– Sun Tzu, *The Art of War* (*c.* 500 BC)

I. CLAUSEWITZ AND THE STUDY OF WAR

Any early nineteenth-century textbook or theoretical work in chemistry, physics, or geology would be of little more than anecdotal value for the same profession's contemporary practitioners. It would certainly not be looked to as a source of important relevant insights, nor would it have value for the instruction of modern students, let alone be expected to represent the state of the art in an important profession. In many fields, in fact, the pace of change is so rapid that a major theoretical work can become obsolete within a generation or a decade, and textbooks must be updated or replaced every few years. Yet in the study of war – a subject of the utmost importance for the survival of modern civilization, and an area in which even one mistake can be disastrous for a whole society or generation – no theoretical work has yet surpassed Carl von Clausewitz' unfinished study, *On War* (1832), in its richness of wisdom and heuristic value.

This situation stems from the extremely complex nature of modern warfare with its seemingly infinite number of variables, ranging from the quantifiable to the intuitive, from the moral to the material. Since modern warfare therefore is not readily subject to scientific analysis, complete mastery of this subject is extremely difficult for a single scholar. Who can study, in depth, even a fraction of the topics considered relevant today for the understanding of modern war? Under the rubric of modern warfare, one can study psychology; anthropology; politics; political, military and economic history; the extremely wide variety of modern military technologies; measures and countermeasures of all sorts; intelligence;

arms control; civil–military relations; military–industrial potential; the
origins and terminations of wars; bureaucratic behavior; management;
leadership; and decisionmaking processes – to mention only a few.

Modern studies of war are often either specialized monographs (focusing on a particular, narrowly-defined subject area or historical period)
and abstract 'transhistorical' studies of less than general scope, [1] or very
broad encyclopedic surveys, such as Quincy Wright's *Study of War*,[2]
which include every detail but often explain very little.

Clausewitz was fortunate to live during the last era in which it was
still feasible for one person to create a comprehensive and *simplified*
framework for the study of war; that is, to incorporate almost all the
relevant knowledge existing in his time without being superficial. Consequently, he could reasonably limit his analysis of politics, strategy,
and the essence of war to the actual conduct of war. For the most part, he
ignored the origins of war, its moral and economic aspects, domestic or
internal politics, and many other subjects now indispensable to a comprehensive theory: war has become too complicated to be studied in the
methodological isolation of an *amoral, apolitical, 'non-economic', non-
technological* 'black box'.

It is, then, not surprising to find that all recent attempts to capture the
'essence' of the conduct of war in a comprehensive and succinct form
have not been entirely satisfactory. They have oscillated between contrived *simple* generalized formulas on the one hand and *encyclopedic
surveys* on the other. Clausewitz avoided both extremes. He succeeded in
being abstract without going theoretically overboard; in developing
powerful concepts while avoiding the temptation to develop 'laws',
'rules', and 'practical' recommendations for action;[3] in providing apt
examples to demonstrate his points while avoiding the quagmire of
excessive trivial detail, including too many case studies. In his work there
is not a single cliché to be found on a subject about which others cannot
write without clichés.

One hundred and fifty years after his death, Clausewitz' contribution
to the study and understanding of war remains unsurpassed. Still relevant
today are his ideas on the primacy of political control in war; on the
roles of friction, uncertainty, and chance; on danger and boldness; on
historical examples; on war as an art; on the need to avoid dogmatic and
positive theories, given the existence of several correct solutions to any
military problem; and on the nature of war in general. Concepts such as
tension and rest, the culminating point of victory, his critical discussion of
maneuver, and the psychology of the defense and offense are perhaps even
more relevant today than when they were written. Like that of other great
men who were ahead of their time, Clausewitz' genius was not recognized
by his contemporaries, although he had indeed, as he suggested in his note

of 10 July 1827, '[brought] about a revolution in the theory of war' (p. 70).[4]

Despite the wealth of original ideas and concepts that make the most important aspects of Clausewitz' theory applicable today, many other facets of his theory have grown obsolete or remain valid only by virtue of modification and revision. Other dimensions that are important today, but which remained nascent during his lifetime, are simply not addressed in his writings.

Clausewitz' theories and observations on war that require modification can be classified in four major categories:

First, the differences in modern warfare resulting from technological innovations he could not have foreseen and therefore could not take into account;

Second, problems that existed in a relatively simple form in the nineteenth century but which are manifested today in a much more complicated form as a result of technological changes: for example, problems in strategic policy-making and in civil–military relations, and in improving the reliability of military intelligence (in which he had little confidence);

Third, topics such as the causes of war, moral/ethical questions related to war, and war's economic dimension. Clausewitz did not focus on these areas because he was concerned exclusively with the conduct of war itself. These topics are, however, of great interest to today's student of warfare, and are essential to any modern theory of war.

The fourth category consists of theories or observations that were wrong or inaccurate even for his own time. But my purpose is not to look for flaws in Clausewitz; rather, I will focus on those modifications required by the passage of time, primarily as a function of material changes, in order to give Clausewitz his proper place in the Age of Technology.

II. THE IMPACT OF THE INDUSTRIAL-TECHNOLOGICAL REVOLUTION ON WAR

With the benefit of hindsight it is apparent that Clausewitz lived and created during one of the most decisive transitional periods in the evolution of warfare — at the crossroads of two of the greatest revolutions in history, the French and Industrial Revolutions. The first revolution radically changed the nature of war from its formerly rather limited and moderate scope — in terms of both means and aims — into a matter of total mobilization and immoderate goals. After the powers of nationalism and revolutionary ideology were unleashed, war became, for the first time, not only the business of kings and the military, but also that of every citizen in the state. Democracy and nationalism released a large amount of heretofore latent energy for the pursuit of war. Although Clausewitz

clearly identified this new trend in warfare, he was not completely sure
that the change it had wrought was irreversible:

> Very few of the new manifestations in war can be ascribed to new
> inventions or new departures in ideas. They result mainly from the
> transformation of society and new social conditions. But these, too,
> while they are in the crisis of fermentation, should not be accepted as
> permanent. There can therefore be little doubt that many previous
> ways of fighting will reappear. (p. 515)

Ironically, at approximately the same time as Clausewitz' death, a new
revolution which he could not have identified was in its formative stage:
in combination with the trends established by the French Revolution, the
Industrial and Technological Revolution changed the world in numerous
irreversible ways. Since Clausewitz' time the military/technological
environment has undergone at least two major revolutions, one in the
conventional realm, the other in the nuclear realm, which have caused a
paradigmatic shift in the nature of war. Numerous smaller military-
technological and organizational revolutions have occurred as well (for
example, the revolution in mobility, the revolution in firepower, the
creation of war in the air as a third dimension of warfare, the revolution in
communication from the invention of the radio and telegraph to that of
'smart weapons', computers and satellites).

Whereas in Napoleon's era, geography, time, and space were major
environmental constraints on strategy, technology has to a large extent
modified the imperatives of environment. The radio made distance
irrelevant for the transmission of information; the submarine destroyed
the British sense of geographic isolation; and ICBMs have threatened the
security of 'Fortress America'. Technology has liberated the military
strategist from some concerns of the past, while posing new problems in
other areas.

The 'element of uncertainty' which – according to Clausewitz – dominates warfare has now been compounded by the introduction of a new
dynamic variable. Many factors, including: the performance of new and
untested weapons systems on the battlefield; these systems' interaction;
their impact on military doctrines, tactics, strategy, as well as on the
development of measures and countermeasures and on the military (and
political) decision-making process – all have caused a quantum jump in
the complexity of warfare.[5]

In war and its preparation, every technological change touches off
a chain reaction that is not only technological, but also social, political,
bureaucratic, managerial, and psychological. Such changes can be clear
or subtle, short term or long term, critical or marginal – but they will
occur with each technological innovation. When hundreds or thousands

of changes occur simultaneously there is a corresponding increase in the uncertainty involved in predicting the shape of modern warfare and of the battlefield of the future.

Within less than a year following Clausewitz' death (16 November 1831), a major new element in warfare was introduced to Europe in the form of the first railways ('... the accelerator of nineteenth century warfare').[6] No sooner had the ink dried on the first edition of his *magnum opus, On War*, than the appearance of this new element of military technology began to render some dimensions of his theory obsolete.[7]

As early as 1833, a German by the name of Friedrich Wilhelm Harkort made 'the first definite proposals for the use of railways for strategical purposes'.[8] The first actual use of railways for a military operation occurred in 1846 when the Sixth Prussian Corps of 12,000 men with their horses, weapons, and ammunition, was dispatched by rail to subdue the independent Republic of Cracow.[9] By the time of the French campaign in Italy, the American Civil War, and the wars of German unification, railways constituted a major element of military mobility and were of decisive importance in warfare.

Clausewitz could still justifiably argue that 'today, armies are *so much alike* in weapons, training, and equipment that there is little difference in such matters between the best and worst of them' (p. 282) [my emphasis]. But the wars of the 1860s irrefutably demonstrated that a new force multiplier – to resort to modern jargon – had been introduced. Technological innovation could now, when all other things were equal, make a decisive difference, a fact that could hardly have been recognized in Clausewitz' time. For instance, the battle of Koniggratz proved the superiority of the Prussian Dreyse rifle over the Austrian rifle, when 'the rate of fire of the Dreyse rifles inflicted appalling losses on the advancing Austrians: they suffered 45,000 casualties to the Prussians' 9,000'.[10]

The advent of the new technological age was unmistakable when European military observers during the American Civil War focused their interest not on the study of military doctrines or new tactics, but on the performance of new weapons.[11] This new emphasis on the study of weaponry would have made little sense to Clausewitz only fifty years earlier.

By the latter half of the nineteenth century, military technology was an autonomous force capable of influencing the shape of war in a decisive way. Man had created a Frankensteinian monster that could no longer be controlled. That battlefield decision, which Clausewitz made central to his theory, had rapidly shifted from the battlefield to the rear; from war to pre-war preparations in peacetime; from the soldier to the worker, inventor, and scientist. In the aftermath of the Industrial Revolution, the outcome of war was to be determined as much by the existence of an industrial base and war potential as by performance on the battlefield. As William James wrote: '... the intensely sharp competitive *preparation* for war by the nation *is the real war*, permanently increasing, so that the battles are only a sort of public verification of mastery gained during the "peace" intervals'.[12]

Correspondingly, for military leaders in the technological age, the destruction of the enemy's army – so central to Clausewitz' theory – became only as important as, or less important than, the destruction or occupation of the industrial centers necessary for the maintenance of enemy forces in the field.[13] In the American Civil War, the industrial superiority of the North, despite the equal or superior generalship of the Confederacy, was critical. Such a development would certainly have been strange to Clausewitz (unless of course industrial might could simply be translated to mean much larger armies, a quantitative advantage which his theory clearly recognized).

Although the foregoing changes took place rapidly after the 1860s, they were also difficult to perceive. The signals were still mixed. Prussia's rapid and clear victory over France in 1870 may have diverted attention from the growing importance of economic and industrial factors for performance on the battlefield. Even as late as the First and Second World Wars, the various general staffs and political leaders hoped to outflank material and economic imperatives by achieving quick and decisive results against the enemy's armed forces, as Clausewitz recommended. By devising brilliant new strategies, they hoped to escape the longer-term consequences of economic contraints.

Thus, although Clausewitz recommended a war of annihilation whenever possible, a strategy emphasizing the ultimate decisive clash between opponents, modern warfare is not only a clash between two armies, but also between the opponents' industries, economic resources, and entire populations. This situation has rendered the search for the decisive battle of annihilation futile – at least in the non-nuclear realm. In this respect Hans Delbrück's distinction between a strategy of annihilation (*Niederwerfungsstrategie*) and a strategy of attrition or exhaustion (*Ermattungsstrategie*) is an important theoretical addition to Clausewitz.

Modern conventional wars, when not decided in a single blow, tend to deteriorate into wars of attrition.[14] The German military which selectively extracted those passages in Clausewitz' work that emphasized the need for quick and decisive victories, thus misunderstood in two world wars the environment in which total modern warfare is conducted.[15]

As the two world wars demonstrated, the nature of war has altered irreversibly. While becoming more capital-intensive, war has changed materially at an ever-accelerating pace. Thus, while the modern student of warfare can certainly learn much from wars of the distant past, he will be better off concentrating on the immediate past and more so on the present. Clausewitz could still recommend, however, with much practical as well as theoretical benefit, that his readers study the eighteenth-century wars of Frederick the Great. Certainly, from the material and 'technological' points of view, these earlier wars resembled the wars of his own time. Until then, military-material and technological change had been slow and gradual. Continuity rather than change had been the norm. Because he expected all future wars to resemble these past wars, Clausewitz indeed had a good reason for drawing on the past to formulate his theories. He did recognize political, ideological, and social changes in his eras, but he viewed them as reversible.

Although Clausewitz could not and did not predict these imminent changes in the nature of war, his theory could accommodate change. After all, he did say that 'war is more than a true chameleon that slightly adapts its characteristics to the given case' (p. 89). The essence of war is change and adaptation to change.

Raymond Aron is unfair when he suggests that Clausewitz 'paints a fixed picture of the world'.[16] It was, in fact, Clausewitz' recognition of radical changes in the nature of warfare caused by the French Revolution which prompted him to develop a new theory of war:

> Clearly the tremendous effects of the French Revolution abroad were caused not so much by new military methods and concepts as by radical changes in policies and administration, by the new character of government, altered conditions of the French people, and the like .... It is true that war itself has undergone significant changes in character and methods, changes that have brought it closer to its absolute form .... They were caused by the new political conditions which the French Revolution created both in France and in Europe as a whole, conditions that set in motion new means and new forces, and have thus made possible a degree of energy in war that otherwise would have been inconceivable.
>
> It follows that the transformation of the art of war resulted from the transformation of politics. (pp. 609–10)

Clausewitz' theory emphasized the tendency of war to drive to extremes, to pursue immoderate unlimited goals. In fact, he developed an almost Marxist analysis in his sophisticated periodization of the history of warfare. He points out that warfare is conducted differently according to the

> nature of states and societies as they are determined by their times and prevailing conditions .... The semibarbarous Tartars, the republics of antiquity, the feudal lords and trading cities of the Middle Ages, the eighteenth century kings and the rulers and

> peoples of the nineteenth century – all conducted war in their own
> particular way, using different methods and pursuing different aims.
> (p.586)

Clausewitz' world was therefore far from fixed and unalterable. As we
have seen above, change for him even worked in reverse. His very
emphasis on uncertainty and dialectical method also implies change. But
the sort of change he recognized was primarily political and social – not
material. He also assumed a static world when he ignored the possibility
of material and military technological changes which he could not have
foreseen in detail but might have anticipated in a general way. His picture
of warfare is as accurate as it could have been for his own time. In
addition, those aspects of his theory which deal with human nature, with
uncertainty and friction, with the primacy of politics, and with the need to
conduct war in a calculated rational fashion, will remain eternally valid.
In all other respects technology has permeated and irreversibly changed
every aspect of warfare.

Technology has altered the nature of international politics by introducing destabilizing weapons systems and intense qualitative arms races;
it has continuously affected the relationship between the defense and
offense; it has transformed strategic surprise from a course of action
'highly attractive in theory' to an ever-present possibility. These developments in turn led to a rise in the importance of intelligence organizations
and have increased the likelihood of preemptive attacks. They multiplied
the number and types of special military branches and supportive
organizations, thus triggering the unprecedented growth of military
bureaucracies and the bureaucratization of military life, with all the
attendant consequences. Technological developments also created the
circumstances in which the 'military genius' may need to be replaced by a
'managerial genius'. Since greater professional knowledge and skills are
required to comprehend military affairs, technology has undermined
the capacity of political leaders to understand and control the military
and the course of warfare. Technology created new opportunities for
command and control and centralizing the conduct of war; it expanded
warfare from the battlefield to the civilian rear; it blurred the differences
between combatant and non-combatant – and it otherwise changed the
shape and nature of modern war. All of these changes will be discussed in
sections IV to XII below.

III. SQUARING THE TRIANGLE

In trying to construct the simplest possible analytical framework for the
study of war, Clausewitz *reduced* the infinite number of variables and

their complex interactions to the lowest common denominator. Thus he developed his famous triad – as he called it, his 'paradoxical trinity'. The three basic groups of variables were *the people* (or primordial violence, hate, and enmity – the blind natural forces); *the military* (the commander and his army who must manage the elements of chance and uncertainty and make the creative decisions and choices before and during a battle); and *the government* (which must introduce the rational calculus of war in order to protect the interests of the state, provide the goals for war, maximize and preserve the strength of the state relative to other states, and devise the overall strategic direction, including the matching of resources and expenditures to anticipated gains). Clausewitz sought 'to develop a theory that maintains a balance between these three tendencies, like an object suspended between three magnets' (p. 89). We have seen that, although complete for his time, Clausewitz' triad does not account for modern military technology, one of the most principal elements of contemporary warfare.

In fact all three elements of his trinity are non-material in nature. In view of the central importance of military technology to all aspects of contemporary warfare, we can assume that if Clausewitz were alive today, he might well propose a four-variable analytical framework with the material realm as the fourth dimension (see Figure 1).

Trying to reduce his argument to its essence, Clausewitz chose not to emphasize material considerations in the explanation of war. 'It is clear that weapons and equipment are not essential for the concept of fighting, since even wrestling is fighting of a kind' (p. 127). If he were solely interested in explaining the logic of conflict he may have been right, but in reality the philosophical and psychological explanation of war is not enough. Without going so far as to adopt a Marxist interpretation of

FIGURE 1
CLAUSEWITZ' DESCRIPTION OF WAR MODIFIED

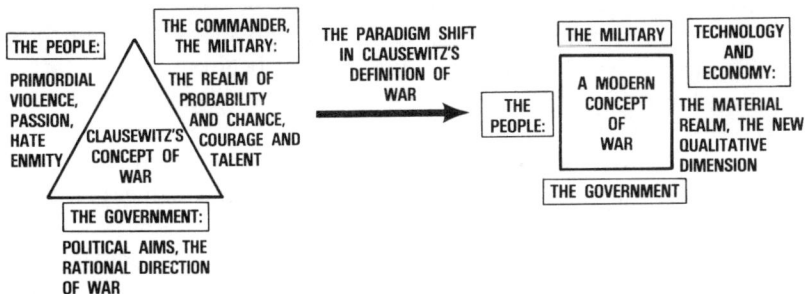

CLAUSEWITZ DESCRIPTION OF WAR MODIFIED

history or politics, we still must realize that the philosophical, political, psychological, social – not to mention the military – aspects of warfare are influenced by material circumstances and developments.

Thus, while the bare essence of war may be explained without resort to the material/technological environment in which wars are fought, any detailed discussion must take that environment into account. Clausewitz himself does, following Book I of *On War*, discuss many issues that cannot be properly understood outside the material context (for example, intelligence, strategic surprise, mobility, military organization, civil–military relations, and the relationship between the offense and defense). Living in an era of slow material progress, Clausewitz naturally viewed the material military environment as relatively static.

It could be argued that had he written *On War* fifty years before, following the wars of Frederick the Great and before the French Revolution, the rise of nationalism and democracy, and the *levée en masse*, he would not have developed his ideas on absolute war. He might not have discussed the differences between absolute war and limited war, for it was the French Revolution which revealed the possibility of a war in reality which approximated the absolute war in theory (p.593).

Similarly, it can be argued that if Clausewitz had written *On War* fifty or a hundred years later, he could not have ignored the forces released by the industrial/technological revolution. He would probably have adapted his theory to the radically changed material environment, probably dedicating special sections to the economic, technological, and material environment of war.[18]

Theory is meaningful, as Clausewitz has recognized, only in contrast to reality, and is no more important than reality. Clausewitz' most original concepts, such as friction and uncertainty, intervene between theory and reality. *On War* is not merely a philosophical treatise, but a book of practical heuristic value.

To simplistically project contemporary interpretations of certain concepts on the past is anachronistic. For example, we have a different understanding of the concept and role of intelligence in war from that of Clausewitz and his contemporaries (see section V below). We also have a different understanding of technology. Although in its basic purpose technology may have remained the same since the beginning of warfare, it has changed in many of its aspects. From a psychological point of view, technology has become the modern military's panacea, used to solve problems previously solved by non-material means. Modern technology has acquired a momentum, an importance of its own, which explains the changing nature of modern warfare.

Therefore, if Clausewitz' trinity is indeed both unchanged and changeless, technology must be the additional factor required for our understanding of contemporary and future warfare. Without it, we will fail to see the new problems and opportunities that it may present. After all, Clausewitz himself, by developing in Book VIII a historical periodization of warfare, does distinguish between the various environments in which war takes place. Thus, although the essence of war is unchanging, in many ways change is the essence of war.

In the final analysis, the decisive Clausewitzian factor in winning wars and battles was quantitative. True, the 'military genius', the leader who was better able to find a solution to the need 'always to be very strong; first in general and then at the decisive point' (p. 204), appears to be a qualitative element. But the qualitative superiority of a commander was aimed at acquiring a *quantitative* edge on the battlefield. In spite of the attention Clausewitz pays to moral and other qualitative factors directly altering the outcome on the battlefield, he basically believed that battles were won by larger armies. Technology has, however, introduced a new *qualitative* dimension – which is not based on the 'quantity idea', as J. F. C. Fuller called it – but instead concerns an element which could compensate for a disadvantage in numbers, serving as a 'force multiplier'.[19] When Clausewitz devised his theory he could still compare the different European armies of his time and assume that 'all other things could be held equal' and that the 'biggest battalions' led by the military genius would win. In today's world of high technology all things are not equal, and unexpected technological military innovations, technological surprises and breakthroughs may (among other elements) make the size of armies less critical for victory. A smaller but technologically more advanced army has frequently won against a larger army.

Having extended Clausewitz' trinity by adding technology and other economic and material considerations, we must recognize the importance of this fourth element as simply equal to that of the other three elements for the theoretical understanding of war. For under varying circumstances, one or more elements may gain in importance relative to others: for example, in guerrilla warfare the people will play a more critical role than will technology; while in modern conventional warfare weapons may be relatively more important than people. Clausewitz of course recognized this variability:

> These three tendencies are like three different codes of law, deep-rooted in their subject and yet *variable* in their relationship to one another. A theory that ignores any one of them or seeks to fix an arbitrary relationship between them would conflict with reality to such an extent that for this reason alone it would be totally useless. (p. 80, my emphasis)

Yet Clausewitz' caveat concerning the need to maintain a balance among all three (or in our case four) groups of variables has not always been heeded. Theorists or creators of military doctrines tend to overemphasize those elements which seem to support their particular biased perspective (for example, overemphasizing the people factor in guerrilla warfare can lead to what Mao has called 'guerrillism' and thus to serious defeats). The temptation is to exaggerate the importance of modern technology in technologically- and materially-oriented societies. Technology may be viewed as a panacea, as it was by the US in Vietnam. The very idea of a trinity or a 'square' is in the search for an equilibrium or a balance between all groups of variables. They exist only in relation to each other – not independently.

Exaggerating the importance of technology is as dangerous as ignoring it. For example, J. F. C. Fuller, author of one of the first and still one of the most interesting books on the role of technology in modern warfare, went too far when he stated that 'tools, or weapons, if only the right ones can be discovered, form 99 percent of victory .... Strategy, command, leadership, courage, discipline, supply, organization and all the moral and physical paraphernalia of war are nothing to a high superiority of weapons – at most they go to form the one percent which makes the whole possible'.[20] According to this logic the United States should never have lost the war in Vietnam, nor would any type of guerrilla warfare ever succeed. Fuller ought to have read Clausewitz more carefully.[21] To be put in its proper context, military technology must be studied in juxtaposition to the other three elements of Clausewitz' theory. Having examined the logic of adding another dimension to Clausewitz' triad, we should consider the impact of military technology and *other* material factors on some of Clausewitz' basic theoretical assumptions.

IV. MOBILITY AND STRATEGIC SURPRISE

Perhaps the greatest revolutionary change in warfare was the tremendous increase in mobility with, first, the introduction of the railway and, later the combustion engine and aviation. Increased mobility compressed time and space, quickened the movement of supplies, altered the relationship between offense and defense on the strategic level, and created a need for much better intelligence and faster mobilization. It did all this by increasing the possibility for strategic surprise. Thus, increased mobility introduced a major destabilizing element into the international system.

Although Clausewitz believed that surprise was a very important element of warfare, he was also convinced that its use was largely confined to the tactical level seldom feasible. For him, therefore, strategic surprise was of greater theoretical interest than practical value:

> While the wish to achieve surprise is common and, indeed, indis-

pensable, and while it is true that it will never be completely ineffective, it is equally true that by its very nature surprise can rarely be
outstandingly successful. It would be a mistake, therefore, to regard
surprise as a key element of success in war. The principle is highly
attractive in theory, but in practice it is often held up by the friction
of the whole machine .... Basically, surprise is a tactical device,
simply because in tactics, time and space are limited in scale. Therefore in strategy surprise becomes more feasible the closer it occurs to
the tactical realm, and more difficult, the more it approaches the
higher levels of policy .... Preparations for war usually take months.
Concentrating troops at their main assembly points generally
requires the installation of supply dumps and depots, as well as
considerable troop movements, whose purpose can be assessed soon
enough.

It is very rare therefore that one state surprises another, either by
an attack or by preparation for war. (pp. 198–9)

Indeed, Clausewitz was certain that strategic surprise lacked the power
to overcome the inherent advantages of the defense.

The immediate object of an attack is victory. Only by means of his
superior strength can the attacker make up for all the advantages
that accrue to the defender by virtue of his position, and possibly by
the modest advantage that this army derives from the knowledge
that it is on the attacking, the advancing side. Usually this latter is
much overrated: it is short-lived and will not stand the test of serious
trouble. Naturally we assume that the defender will act as sensibly
and correctly as the attacker. We say this in order to exclude certain
vague notions about sudden assaults and surprise attacks, which are
commonly thought of as bountiful sources of victory. They will only
be under exceptional circumstances. (p. 545)[22]

Initially, the development of railway networks, particularly in
Germany, seemed to enhance the strategic capabilities of the defense.
Gradually, however, it became evident that a secret or even open concentration of large numbers of troops could, under the guise of conducting maneuvers, employ railway networks and, later on, combustion
engine mobility and air power, to launch a strategic surprise of decisive
impact. Under certain circumstances the aggressor could overwhelm
the defender who would be unable to mobilize his troops in time. As
mobility increased, the warning time available for counter-mobilization
decreased: from months or weeks in the early nineteenth century, to
weeks and days in the railway and combustion engine days, to days and
hours in the age of air power, and finally to hours and minutes in the
nuclear age (see Figure 2).

Modern states and alliance systems had therefore to develop intricate hair-trigger mobilization systems. By 1914 those systems became so complex and difficult to control that mobilization also meant war.[23]

Technological change has thus made a major contribution (not for the last time) to the destabilization of the international system. The possibility of a strategic surprise has become one of the most worrisome problems facing heads of state and general staffs.[24]

Clausewitz could not have anticipated the development of this *reciprocal fear of strategic surprise* into a crucial if not dominant factor in international politics. Now the side which possesses a unilateral advantage is tempted to achieve a quick and decisive victory, while the side with inferior technology could launch a preemptive strike in order to acquire a decisive advantage over its better-armed adversary.[25] For example, when the Japanese attacked the Russians in 1904, they disrupted the construction of the Trans-Siberian railway – the completion of which would have been catastrophic for the Japanese.[26]

Whereas in the past surprise was confined to the tactical and grand tactical levels, and was thus a relatively simple phenomenon, the advent of strategic surprise introduces many complexities: The choice of one's time, place, mode and speed of movement, as well as of the particular weapon or weapons system to be deployed, must be made quickly and simultaneously on several levels. New weapons produce fresh opportunities, new doctrines, as well as new problems for the strategist and military planner.

FIGURE 2
STRATEGIC SURPRISE IN HISTORICAL PERSPECTIVE
– THE DECLINE OF WARNING TIME

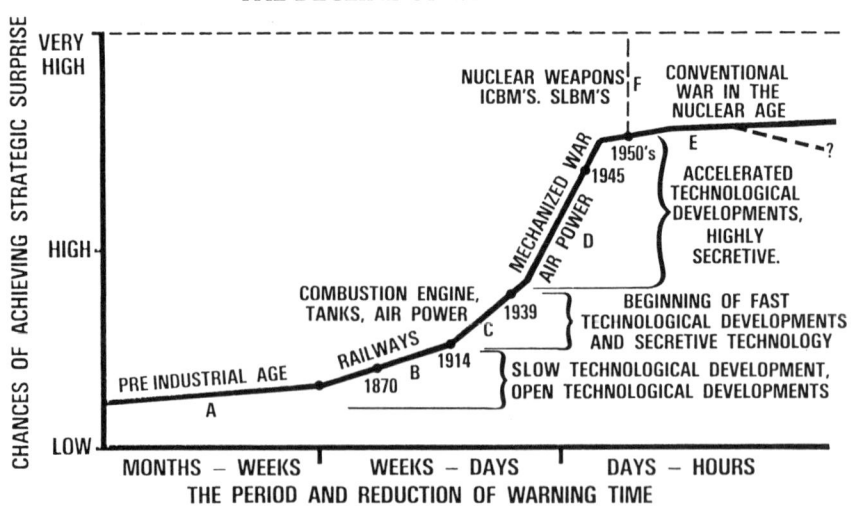

The fact that strategic surprise has now become an integral part of warfare contributes in yet another way to the need to modify Clausewitz' theory. Clausewitz emphasized the superiority of the defense over the offense on both the strategic and tactical levels. He viewed the inherent advantages of the defense as a permanent feature of warfare. One of the few offensive advantages that Clausewitz recognized was on the *strategic* level: the holding of the initiative, that is, the attacker's ability to exploit the element of surprise in the initial phase of the attack to his advantage:[27]

> As regards surprise and initiative, it must be noted that they are infinitely more important and effective in strategy than in tactics. Tactical initiative can rarely be expanded into a major victory, but a strategic one has often brought the whole war to an end at a stroke.

He qualifies this observation by adding that, 'On the other hand, the use of this device [that is, surprise] assumes *major, obvious and exceptional* mistakes on the enemy's part. Consequently it will not do much to tip the scales in favor of attack' (pp. 363–4, his emphasis).[28] He also remarks that:

> ... an aggressor often decides on war before the innocent defender does, and if he contrives to keep his preparations sufficiently secret, he may well take his victim unawares. Yet such surprise has nothing to do with war itself [that is, it is a political decision preceding war], and *should not be possible*. (p. 370, my emphasis)

As we have seen, revolutionary changes in mobility made possible surprise on the strategic level and therefore also contributed to a change in the relationship between the *strategic* defense and offense. The offense gained a unilateral advantage, which has expanded with the concomitant growth in mobility, range, speed, and firepower of modern weaponry. This is especially true in the opening phase of any modern war. The attacker can decide the *time, place, and method* of the attack, concentrate superior forces at the point chosen for the attack, and at least temporarily paralyze and overwhelm the defender. Strategic surprise in the opening phases of war is therefore the most powerful force multiplier in conventional war.

Clausewitz could not have foreseen the unmistakable evidence of modern military history, which affirms that regardless of the defender's excellent intelligence capabilities, it is almost impossible for him to prevent a strategic surprise (that is, to receive a timely warning).[29] If the attacker can learn to exploit fully the initial impact achieved by strategic surprise and to calculate carefully the culminating point of the attack, he can then move over to enjoy the benefits of the defense; thus the attack becomes, on the strategic level, the more powerful form of warfare. (For

more regarding the impact of technological change on the relation
between the defense and attack, see section VI below.)

V. INTELLIGENCE: FROM FRICTION TO PANACEA

The transformation of strategic surprise from a theoretical possibility
to a practical reality necessitated the establishment of better military
intelligence organizations. Since military intelligence is a key factor in the
discovery of the adversary's mobilization plans and procedures, actual
preparations for war, and troop concentrations, its increasing importance
– as evidenced by the fact that European general staffs in the last quarter
of the nineteenth century began to establish special sections for the
collection and analysis of intelligence – was closely linked to the emergence
of modern military technology. Thus, the development of military intelligence was related not only to the need to warn against strategic surprise,
but also to the need to gather information about the development and
production of new weapons systems, their effectiveness and performance,
their integration into the military doctrine and so on. The independence
of intelligence as a military activity was one aspect of the growing professional specialization and differentiation of military organizations
created in response to the technological revolution.

Like surprise, intelligence interested Clausewitz primarily on the tactical and grand tactical levels as a command and control problem. He wrote
little that was relevant to intelligence on the strategic level. Nevertheless,
although his observations on intelligence must be understood in the
tactical context, they can also be seen as part of his general discussion of
the problems of warfare, primarily in the context of the key concepts of
friction and uncertainty.

Clausewitz had little appreciation of the potential contribution of
intelligence for the commander in charge of the conduct of war and to his
decisions on the battlefield. Instead of viewing intelligence as we do today
– as an element that could potentially reduce the degree of uncertainty,
chance, and friction in war – *Clausewitz actually saw intelligence as a
source of friction*, and a possible cause of failure:

> By 'intelligence' we mean every sort of information about the
> enemy and his country – the basis, in short, of our own plans and
> operations. If we consider the actual basis of this information, how
> unreliable and transient it is, we soon realize that war is a flimsy
> structure that can easily collapse and bury us in its ruins. The
> textbooks agree, of course, that we should only believe reliable
> intelligence, and should never cease to be suspicious, but what is the
> use of such feeble maxims? They belong to that wisdom which for

want of anything better scribblers of systems and compendia resort to when they run out of ideas.

Many intelligence reports in war are contradictory; even more are false, and most are uncertain .... One report tallies with another, confirms it, magnifies it, lends it color, till [the officer] has to make a quick decision – which is soon recognized to be mistaken, just as the reports turn out to be lies, exaggerations, errors, and so on. In short, most intelligence is false, and the effect of fear is to multiply lies and inaccuracies (p. 117) .... The general unreliability of all information presents a special problem in war: all action takes place, so to speak, in a kind of twilight, which like fog or moonlight, often tends to make things seem grotesque and larger than they really are.

Whatever is hidden from full view in this feeble light has to be guessed at by talent, or simply left to chance. So once again for lack of objective knowledge one has to trust to talent or to luck (p. 140) .... Consider the unreliable and fragmentary nature of all intelligence in war. Remember that both sides fumble in the dark at all times (p. 462) ....

The unreliability of most intelligence or what he calls 'imperfect knowledge' plays a central role in the Clausewitzian theoretical construction by providing one of the most important explanations for the 'interruption of military activity', or the 'suspension of action' (pp. 81–5). This in turn explains the need to modify the definition of war in theory to that of war in reality.

In general Clausewitz' pessimistic views on the value of intelligence to command and control and on the availability of reliable information and intelligence were correct, reflecting the objective conditions of his own time. Modern technology, however, while far from providing us with any panacea for the problems of uncertainty and imperfect information in war, has nevertheless radically altered our views on intelligence. Despite its flaws, intelligence is viewed today as an indispensable source of support in warfare, providing hope for the reduction of friction and for better control by both political and military leaders over events as they unfold.

The development of the telegraph had an immediate influence on the command and control of troops moving about on the battlefield. (Prussian military field telegraph units were established as early as 1856.) The telephone and radio further improved the transmission of information, and most recently the introduction of electro-optical sensors on mini-RPVs allows the transmission of real-time visual information on the battlefield.[30]

The development of such technological means of communication has in turn led to the establishment of special organizations to deal with them, as well as to the need to monitor the adversary's transmission and reception of this voluminous information. This in turn accelerated the growth of the intelligence bureaucracy, just one aspect of the continuous differentiation of the military bureaucracy.

Undoubtedly, the invention of these varied means of communication revolutionized the ability of commanders to receive information from and on the battlefield, allowing them to dispatch their orders and decisions much more effectively than in Napoleon's time. Clausewitz' (and even more so Tolstoy's) pessimistic view of the commanders' lack of effective control over the course of events on the battlefield is no longer justified – certainly not from the technical point of view.[31] While the difficulties in receiving and transmitting information on the battlefield have not been completely eliminated, they have been considerably reduced. Today almost all failures of command and control and inappropriate uses of intelligence do not stem from a lack of adequate communication instruments or information, as was the case earlier in history, but instead from human error and problems of perception. Similarly, technological developments including radio interception, computer-assisted crypto-analysis, high-altitude photographic aircraft reconnaissance, and satellite intelligence-gathering have all contributed to the tremendous progress in the collection of intelligence. Yet despite these improvements on both the tactical and strategic levels, many of the problems inherent in intelligence procedures as pointed out by Clausewitz have found no satisfactory solution. As he put it, 'We now know more, but this makes us more, not less uncertain' (p. 102). In the final analysis, intelligence problems are human – problems of perception, subjectivity, and wishful thinking – and thus are not likely to disappear no matter how much the technological means of intelligence improve.[32] Therefore the suggestion that war since the time of Napoleon and Clausewitz has lost much of its 'friction' is baseless.[33]

Were Clausewitz to rewrite *On War* today, he might identify different problems. While continuing to emphasize the complexities and uncertainties of the human factor in intelligence, he would probably acknowledge that technological means have changed the nature of friction and the command and control problems on the tactical level. But today's commander may suffer from psychological overdependence on the availability of intelligence, and hesitate to take action without it even when necessary. Modern intelligence may have become an addictive disincentive to the development of the 'military genius' intuition and readiness to accept risks, the qualities of great commanders.

While a lack of intelligence can create indecision and delays in action, the 'overdevelopment' of the technological means of intelligence and its increased availability may cause other serious problems. The modern commander will be so deluged with intelligence that he may become paralyzed trying to sift the relevant data from the trivial information. Such an overabundance of intelligence, like its absence, may cause serious delays in decisions. If a dearth of information was the major cause for friction in the past, the surplus of information in the present has given rise to a new form of friction. Thus while friction and uncertainty continue to exist, their causes and origin have changed with time. Another modern danger is that less-important decisions will be made at higher echelons as political and military leaders attempts to *centralize* the management of war by removing authority from lower-level commanders on the battle-field. Field commanders will thus become agents inspecting the imple-mentation of orders from the rear, rather than military decision-makers grappling with the dangers and uncertainties of war. Technology has changed the nature of intelligence by eliminating some problems while creating others.

VI. THE DYNAMICS OF THE OFFENSE–DEFENSE RELATIONSHIP

For Clausewitz, unlike most military writers of his time, the superiority of the defense over the offense was axiomatic on both the tactical and the strategic levels.[34] This assumption is central to his theory. The inherent asymmetry between the strength of the defense and that of the attack is one of the most important intervening variables between war in theory and war in practice.

Even had Clausewitz been convinced of the perfect equality between the defense and attack, he might still have been tempted to present them as inherently unequal as a 'methodological trick' necessary to make this transition from theoretical to real war. Such a 'methodological trick' was not essential to the development of Clausewitz' argument, however, for he made a very convincing case *for his time* that the defense is stronger:

> It is easier to hold ground than take it. It follows that defense is easier than attack, assuming both sides have equal means. Just what is it that makes preservation and protection so much easier? It is the fact that time which is allowed to pass unused accumulates to the credit of the defender. He reaps where he did not sow. Any omission of attack – accrues to the defender's benefit .... Another benefit, one that arises solely from the nature of war, derives from the advantage of position, which tends to favor the defense. (pp. 357–8)

As mentioned earlier, Clausewitz was also convinced that on the *tacti-cal* level the defender could make better use of the element of surprise.

The attack, unlike the defense, also suffers from its very success, which may contain the seeds of its defeat:

> By initiating the campaign, the attacking army cuts itself off from
> its own theater of operations, and suffers by having to leave its
> fortresses and depots behind. The larger the area of operations that
> it must traverse, the more it is weakened – by the effect of marches
> and by the detachment of garrisons. The defending army, on the
> other hand, remains intact. It benefits from its fortresses, nothing
> depletes its strength, and it is closer to its sources of supply. (p. 365)

In the majority of cases the defense will also benefit from the support of
the population. Furthermore, frequently the defender will benefit from
the support of friendly states, interested in maintaining the balance of
power and the stability of the system. In a paragraph that could easily
have been taken from any modern textbook on the systems theory
approach to the study of international relations, Clausewitz wrote:

> It may be objected, of course, that history offers examples of single
> states effecting radical changes that benefit themselves alone, with-
> out the slightest effort by the rest to hinder them. There have been
> cases in which a single state has managed to become so powerful
> that it could virtually dictate to the rest. We would reply that this
> does not disprove the tendency on the part of common interests to
> support the existing order .... We therefore argue that a state of
> balance tends to keep the existing order intact – always assuming
> that the original condition was one of calm, of equilibrium. Once
> there has been a disturbance and tension has developed it is certainly
> possible that the tendency toward equilibrium will shift direction
> .... [But] such a change can affect only a few states, never the
> majority. (p. 374)

Clausewitz concludes that this 'common effort toward maintenance of
the status quo' explains 'the fact that Europe, as we know it, has existed
for over a thousand years' (p. 374).

Finally, Clausewitz even went so far as to deny the possibility of a
change in the relationship between the defense and attack when he
argued:

> If the offensive were to invent some major new expedient – which
> is unlikely in view of the simplicity and inherent necessity that
> makes everything today – the defensive will also have to change its
> methods. But it will always be certain of having the benefit of
> terrain, and this will generally ensure its natural superiority; for
> today the peculiarities of the topography and the ground have a
> greater effect on military action than ever. (p. 362)

This static view of the relationship between the defense and offense has been modified in contemporary history. Many contemporary analysts have argued that Clausewitz' emphasis on the superiority of the defense was wrong even for his own day, in light of Napoleon's military successes based primarily on offensive tactics and strategy. Inasmuch as Clausewitz was a great admirer of Napoleon, on this point he may seem inconsistent. This apparent inconsistency resolves itself if we compare his argument for the superior strength of the defense to his concept of the culminating point of victory. The attacker (that is, the offense) can have the best of two worlds. He can enjoy the advantages of the attack (for example, the time, the place, the method, the element of surprise), and at the point where the attack exhausts itself he can move over to the defense and benefit from its inherent advantages. Of course, his success hinges upon his moving over to the defense at the optimum point in time, that is, at the culminating point of victory. On how to identify this point, unfortunately, Clausewitz gives no clues. (But see text, pp. 527, 528, 566–73.) Paradoxically, then, one of the major advantages of the attack lies in its ability to move over to the defense.

It is still true that when all other things are equal, the defense is the stronger form of warfare. In reality, however, things can never be kept equal. Modern military technology, even more so than in the past, causes frequent changes in the relative strength between the defense and offense. The relationship between the two forms of war is cyclical – not static as Clausewitz assumed. Such cyclical changes add to the uncertainty as to which of the two modes of war is stronger, both on the strategic and tactical levels.

Clausewitz cited the influence of imperfect knowledge to explain the frequent suspension of action in war – mentioning especially the human tendency to make worst-case, over-cautious estimates under conditions of uncertainty (p. 117). Yet, even if there was full knowledge as to the relative strengths of both sides, certainty regarding the inherent superiority of the defense was by itself enough to cause inaction. Today inaction may result from another cause: namely, the *uncertainty* of the relationship between the offense and defense.

The cycle of modern weapons development, of weapons and counter-weapons, measures and counter-measures, has shifted the advantage from the defense to the offense, and back, a number of times since the start of the technological revolution. Such changes are not always perceived before the outbreak of war. For example, despite numerous indications from the Boer War and Russo-Japanese War, in which the growing advantage of defensive over offensive weapons was clearly demonstrated, most European armies before the First World War emphasized the development of exclusively offensive doctrines; similarly, the Israeli army before the 1973 war misread the technological trends favoring the defense in anti-tank and anti-aircraft weapons and consequently relied on an exclusively offensive doctrine. Conversely the French, before the Second World War, learned the lessons of the First World War so well that they overestimated the power of defense.

Despite the critical importance of technology in military affairs, very little theoretical work has dealt with this subject. J. F. C. Fuller developed two important analytical concepts that help us to describe and understand the cyclical nature of the relationship between the offense, defense, and technology in modern warfare. The first is the *dominant weapon*, the second the *constant tactical factor*.[35] The first concept suggests there is always a more effective type of weapon (that is, better protected, and/or with greater firepower and/or greater speed, etc.) which dominates (that is, has a greater impact on) the battlefield. Most other weapons as well as the tactical doctrine will therefore have to be organized around that weapon, as will the counter-weapons and counter-doctrine. (The dominant weapon need not be a single weapon excluding all others.) His second concept, that of the *constant tactical factor*, suggests that in the age of rapid technological change (as in earlier times) *no* dominant weapon will remain dominant for too long. This is the concept of change, to a large extent absent from Clausewitz' work. While Fuller's concepts are of great heuristic and analytical value, they usually have little or no predictive value. Thus the importance of uncertainty, an element emphasized by Clausewitz and further complicated by technology, remains unchanged.

VIII. TECHNOLOGY AND DOCTRINE: THE GAP WIDENS

As the rate of technological progress accelerates, resulting in a larger variety of weapons whose synergistic or systemic interaction is unclear, the gap between military technology and strategic/tactical military doctrines is constantly widening. Military organizations adapt even more slowly to change than individuals. Therefore, the gap that has opened up between the birth of a new technology and its proper absorption into military doctrine and practice is likely to be permanent.

Even those armies which are more open to change, frequently as a result of a defeat or a sense of vulnerability, still never completely succeed in matching technology's potential with its actual use on the battlefield. Thus, for instance, Nazi Germany's offensive blitzkrieg represented the culmination of an evolutionary trial-and-error process rather than an inspired flash from the mind of some military genius. The blitzkrieg took a considerable time to perfect in the face of resistance and lack of understanding – a lack clearly demonstrated in the war against Poland and the attack on the West in May 1940.

Another interesting example is the development of naval and air strategy between the two world wars – an excellent case study of the uncertainty involved in the development of new technologies. A comparative analysis of the major navies of the world (those of the US, Great Britain, Germany, Italy and Japan) in the 1920s and 1930s indicates that all committed similar errors in the perception of technology. Although all parties recognized the importance of air power, they had no realistic way of testing aircraft against battleships. The result was that all major powers conservatively chose to invest by 1939 in approximately a 2:1 ratio of battleships to aircraft carriers. The Second World War quickly proved the superiority of air power over traditional sea power, so that by the end of the war the procurement ratio of battleships to carriers had been reversed.

Likewise, although submarines were the only First World War weapon to come close to being decisive, they were neglected between the wars. No major technological improvements occurred in the design of submarines or their main weapons, the torpedoes. Assuming the technological success of British counter-measures, both Germans and British grossly underestimated the full potential of the submarine. The initial German success in U-Boat warfare against Great Britain was not attributable to any new weapons or technology, but rather to new submarine deployment tactics (for example, night attacks on the surface and later wolf pack tactics).

In regard to the blitzkrieg, air power, and the submarine, the strategists of the Great Powers failed to perceive the trends in military technology, developed inappropriate military doctrines, and were, once the Second World War started, slow to modify these doctrines even when they proved inadequate. In many cases, the weapons and the doctrines were mismatched. At times, well-tested weapons such as the submarine or tank could have been better used by the application of more innovative doctrines. Then again, sometimes new weapons rendered older ones obsolete, requiring the invention of completely new doctrines. In any event, weapons and doctrines, technology and its intellectual understanding, were rarely in harmony.

The reason for the gap between technology and doctrine is obvious. It has never been possible in modern times to test the full effectiveness of newly-developed weapons/counterweapons under realistic conditions in peacetime. Frequently the answer as to who is superior, the defense or the attack, is given only on the battlefield when it is too late.

VIII. THE UNITY OF COMMAND IS BROKEN

Although Clausewitz made a clear distinction in his trinity between the political and military direction of war, elsewhere, particularly when he describes his models of 'military genius' (for example, Frederick the Great and Napoleon), he seems to prefer the unity of the two types of leadership in one person:

> A prince or a general can best demonstrate his genius by managing a campaign exactly to suit his objectives and his resources doing neither too much nor too little (p. 177) .... To bring a war, or one of its campaigns, to a successful close requires a thorough grasp of national policy. On that level strategy and policy coalesce: the commander-in-chief is simultaneously a statesman. (p. 111)

Furthermore, he asserted that

> In the highest realms of strategy ... there is little or no difference between strategy, policy and statesmanship (p. 178) .... We argue that a commander-in-chief must also be a statesman, but he must not cease to be a general. On the one hand he is aware of the entire political situation. On the other, he knows exactly how much he can achieve with the means at his disposal. (pp. 111–12)[36]

The growing complexities of modern warfare caused not only by technological but also by political developments, make it increasingly difficult to find a leader who possesses a high degree of both political and military skills. There are two reasons for this difficulty:

First, modern warfare requires a much higher level of professional education (for example, general staff work) and familiarity with military technology than can usually be claimed by any political leader – unless, of course, he had a military career before entering politics. Then, too, the growing demands of military expertise create a universal tendency in all military establishments, to claim a monopoly on military knowledge in order to minimize the participation of civilian leaders in the actual conduct of war. This tendency runs counter to the most important of all Clausewitz' theoretical assumptions: the primacy of politics in the conduct of war. In his work on total war, Ludendorff developed an opposing theory emphasizing the primacy of the military leadership over the political in war:

> All the theories of Clausewitz should be thrown overboard. Both warfare and politics are meant to serve the preservation of the people, but warfare is the highest expression of the national 'will to live', and politics must, therefore, be subservient to the conduct of war.[37]

He continues,

> The World War has already removed any possible doubts as to the necessity of the nation's armed forces to be subordinated to the

Commander-in-Chief, and his standing above the war minister as the chief of military administration and *above the political chiefs*. In a word, the position of the Commander-in-Chief must be as high and as unlimited in war as was that of King Frederick the Great.[38]

The second reason that political and military leadership are rarely combined is that in the era of modern total war the political leader must direct almost all his energies to the mobilization of political, economic, and popular support for fighting the war. This activity leaves him less time and energy to deal with the conduct of military operations.

Reflecting upon the bygone era of political and military unity of leadership in war, General Sir Archibald Wavell stated:

> The friction between civil and military is, comparatively speaking, a new factor in war, and is a feature of democracy, not of autocracy .... The interchangeability between the statesman and the soldier passed forever, I fear, in the last century. The Germans professionalized the trade of war, and modern inventions, by increasing its technicalities, have specialized it. It is much the same with politics, professionalized by democracy. No longer can one man hope to exercise both callings, though both are branches of the same craft, the governance of men and the ordering of human affairs.[39]

The friction between the political and military professions to which Wavell refers has increased in the age of technology, when many military leaders feel that 'amateur' civilians are not qualified to deal with the growing complexities of modern warfare. Defeat, or simple lack of success, has led military leaders to pin the blame on 'interfering' politicians. Such accusations, ranging from suspicion of 'a stab in the back' to the notion that 'there is no substitute for victory', appear during and following every modern war. This universal problem has prompted other military leaders to express views similar to those of Ludendorff and opposed to those of Clausewitz. For example, after the First World War Lieutenant General Sir Gerald Ellison wrote that Churchill was wrong in asserting, 'At the summit true politics and strategy are one'. 'Ergo, quite obviously', says Ellison, 'the politician is fully qualified to deal with strategy?

> Hence Amateur Strategy?
> Hence Gallipolli!'

He continues, with heavy irony, to explode the popular belief that

> every politician is a heaven-born naval and military strategist, that the man who produces a weapon is necessarily the right man to use

it, that the administrator automatically becomes the commander
.... The politician, unfortunately, either cannot, or will not, recognize limitations in the scope of politics which ordinary common
sense would seem to dictate.[40]

The good general then concludes that '*Politics and strategy are radically
and fundamentally things apart from one another. Strategy begins where
politics end*' (his emphasis).

The record of modern warfare makes one thing very clear: the need to
keep the two types of military leadership separate, *not united*. Many
cases in which the civilian leaders tried either to control or to intervene
excessively in the conduct of military operations (for example, Kaiser
Wilhelm, Hitler, Mussolini, Stalin and at times Churchill) ended in
disaster. Attempts on the part of the military to control the political and
grand strategic goals of wars ended equally badly (for example, the
Schlieffen plan, the decision to launch unrestricted submarine warfare,
and the German high command's literally taking over the political conduct of the First World War).

Clausewitz did not go into detail concerning the problems of coordination between the political and military leadership in war. Given the
frequent unity of the two during his lifetime and the relative simplicity of
both political and military affairs, this is not altogether surprising. Nevertheless, the technological and political complexities of the modern world
have necessitated a degree of 'fine tuning' unthought of by Clausewitz
in order to achieve a workable balance between the civilian and military leadership in modern war. Clausewitz offers few insights into the
problem, beyond his brief comment in Book VIII that

> If war is to be fully consonant with political objectives, and policy
> suited to the means available for war, then unless statesman and
> soldier are combined in one person, the only sound expedient is to
> make the commander-in-chief a member of the cabinet, so that the
> cabinet can share in the major aspects of his activities. But this, in
> turn, is only feasible if the cabinet – that is the government – is near
> the theater of operations, so that decisions can be taken without
> serious loss of time .... What is highly dangerous is to let any soldier
> but the commander-in-chief exert influence in the cabinet. It very
> seldom leads to sound vigorous action. (pp. 608–9)

Although in emphasizing the primacy of politics Clausewitz was ahead
of his time, he could not foresee the complications of civil–military
relations and their impact on the political supremacy necessary to the
conduct of war.

IX. THE DIFFERENTIATION AND BUREAUCRATIZATION OF THE MILITARY

When Clausewitz discussed friction in war he was primarily referring to the uncertainties generated by the collision of two opposing armies on the battlefield. His 'friction' was chiefly the result of the adversary's unexpected actions and their impact on one's own forces and on the outcome of battle. Friction was thus created by *external* causes. He tacitly assumed that one's own army and leader behave as what is called a 'uni-actor', that is, a single unit making decisions *vis-à-vis* other such units. While this may have approximated reality in the days when the king was also the commander-in-chief, it certainly does not describe current reality. In today's military environment it is useful to make a distinction between *external friction*, created as a result of conflict between two opposing sides, and *internal friction*, generated by the growing specialization and compartmentation of the military.

Clausewitz did not think it was important for military leaders to deal with issues of management and organization: 'One would not want to consider the whole business of maintenance and administration as part of the *actual conduct of war*. While it may be in constant interaction with the utilization of troops, the two are essentially very different' (p. 129, his emphasis). The distinction between leading troops to war and administration would appear even more pronounced today. Just as the political leader and military leader are now separate individuals, the military leader may be a manager or even a technocrat, rather than a warrior.

Coordinating many military and civilian organizations requires careful calculation and diplomatic skill, rather than the courage, daring, and acceptance of risks required on the battlefield. In all likelihood the optimal temperament and character required for managing and fighting cannot be found in one military genius, as Clausewitz proposed. The requirements are contradictory. Frederick the Great and Napoleon, the models for Clausewitz' military genius, were very different from Carnot (whom Clausewitz never mentions), Marshall and Eisenhower. Were Clausewitz alive today, he would recognize the need to describe, besides the 'military genius', the 'military-organizational genius'.[41]

Just as there are now several different types of military leader, there are also many different military organizations, set up to maximize the utility of the multiple dimensions of military technology. The military management of technology (for example, organizational decisions concerning the research, design, and choice of weapons; the procurement cycle; the relationship with the scientific and industrial communities; the inspection of production; the testing and maintenance of equipment; the writing of instruction manuals; and training) has created a military bureaucracy of immense proportions that continues to grow with technology.

Furthermore, the basically simple structure of the Napoleonic armies (that is, primarily infantry, cavalry, and artillery) has been greatly complicated, and can no longer be controlled by a single leader.[42] Far more specialized, today's armies are made up of numerous organizations — infantry, artillery, signal, armor, engineers, anti-aircraft, transportation, intelligence, etc. — each having its own weapons, doctrines, school, and unique expertise. Each one of these military organizations enjoys a certain degree of autonomy, and fights to protect its own parochial-professional interests, including its share of the military budget. Thus, although all of these organizations exist in order to contribute to the achievement of the same goal and support each other in the process, they also have many conflicting interests that separate them. The desire to maintain their autonomy and articulate their various perceptions has generated considerable friction within each military organization.

The anonymous, capital-intensive character of modern war led J. F. C. Fuller (with his usual knack for bringing things *ad absurdum*) to reverse Clausewitz' emphasis on the importance of the military genius in war.

> The outstanding lesson of the [Franco-Prussian War of 1870] was that a conflict of masses is a war of conflicts in which genius is out of place. Though the general can still plot and plan, and increasingly must do so, he can no longer lead or command because the masses are too vast to grasp. Command now passes to the General Staff, its foremost problem being the development of firepower.[43]

The truth obviously lies somewhere in between Clausewitz and Fuller. Fuller, like Adam Smith and the Marxists, tends to move the focus to the invisible hand of economic forces or the role of the masses in war. Ultimately, however, much depends upon what Michels has termed 'the Iron Law of the Oligarchy', that is, that a single individual inevitably exists at the top of the decision-making ladder, who, whether a political, military, or managerial-organizational leader, must make the final choice.

Meanwhile, important decisions concerning both peace and war require greater efforts at political compromise and a more intensive search for consensus than they did in Clausewitz' time. Such complications of coordination between different organizational perceptions and interests have offset the advantages gained from great technological advances in command and control. Thus while friction has been reduced in some ways since Clausewitz' time it has increased in others.

X. THE DEMOCRATIZATION OF WAR AND THE NEW PROMINENCE OF DOMESTIC POLICY

Today, both historians and military strategists are concerned about the causes of war and the extent to which war can be waged without popular consent. Clausewitz, however, wrote the greatest book on the logic and conduct of war without devoting much attention to its causes. He does mention two important causes, but fails to develop them in any depth. The first is human nature, or what he refers to as 'hostile feelings and hostile intentions', the 'primordial violence, hatred and enmity, which are to be regarded as a blind natural force ... passions ... inherent in the people' (pp. 76, 89). The second cause of war is the need to restore the 'balance of power', to return the international system to equilibrium (p. 374). The transition from peace to war, international crises, mobilization as a destabilizing factor, preventive and preemptive war, ideological and economic causes of war – all of these did not really concern him. This lack of interest can be explained, but not justified, by two factors. The first is that Clausewitz, as a military man who accepted war as a 'fact of life', focused on the specific task of bringing war, once begun – for whatever reason – to a successful conclusion.[44] The second is that, since his time, the technological revolution and political/ideological changes have made the causes of war inherently more interesting and important. In modern times mobility and the accelerated pace of war have made the specific circumstances under which war breaks out much more relevant to military planning, the preparation of contingency plans, the choice of weapons, and the design of a strategic doctrine.

Nevertheless, even for his own time, the absence of a discussion of the causes of war in a general treatise on war is quite striking. It was, after all, Clausewitz who first emphasized the primacy of political control in war – and the outbreak of war and the decision to go to war are indeed political decisions that bear directly on military planning. Thucydides, for example, devoted considerable space to a discussion of the origins and causes of the Peloponnesian wars.[45] Clausewitz' attitude is all the more puzzling given the unique circumstances that preceded the outbreak of the French Revolution and the Napoleonic Wars.

Clausewitz' attitude to war was amoral. For him, war was an inevitable, legal, and acceptable part of the relationship between states. He felt that 'wars are the willful creation of the state, that wars are made and that they do not "break out"'.[46] He believed in 'the absolute priority of foreign affairs over domestic considerations'.[47] For him, therefore, the decision to go to war was a rational choice made exclusively on the basis of external considerations and was intended to maximize the power and interests of the state *vis-à-vis* all others in the international system. The decision itself,

the last resort of kings, was taken by the head of state who knew (presumably) what he wanted and could prepare his army, while largely
disregarding domestic considerations.

This simplified *raison d'état* model may have been realistic during the
ancien regime, but it is less than adequate in an age of democracy and
mass mobilization. In fact, it was also Germans like Ludendorff and
Eckhart Kehr who emphasized the primacy of domestic politics (*Der
Primat der Innern Politik*) over foreign policy.[48] In addition, of course, the
Marxists emphasized even earlier the need to examine domestic economic
(and political) considerations when seeking the major causes for war.[49]

Thus, starting with Marxist theories, very powerful explanations for
the causes of war were shifted from the international system to the
domestic environment. This is not the context in which to discuss Lenin's
theory of imperialism, Schumpeter's criticism of his theory, the 'military-
industrial complex' explanation, or numerous other relevant theories. It
is, however, necessary to discuss briefly the contemporary domestic
environment in which the decisions concerning the initiation and conduct
of war are made. Certainly in a modern democratic society, but in fact in
any society, there is a need to explain and justify a war to the people to be
mobilized for the supreme effort and the sacrifices it entails. Ludendorff
has recognized, for example, that in fighting the modern total war it is
essential to mobilize the moral support of the masses:

> It is a mistaken assumption that a war must begin with a declaration
> of war .... The declarations óf war of the Imperial Chancellor Von
> Bethman-Hollweg on Russia and France in August 1914, are still in
> everybody's memory. They gave the enemy propaganda a useful
> start in strengthening the morale of their peoples, and weakened the
> morale of our people .... The supreme Commander-in-Chief has to
> see to it that such damage should not be done to the conduct of war
> and the people alike at the very beginning by war declarations, and
> also by deficient instruction of the nation, such as the German
> people and the German Army were destined to suffer in 1914, and in
> the following years, through the German declarations of war in
> particular. This is the more necessary as a nation and every indi-
> vidual within it can only help the war leaders with their whole
> strength when they are firmly convinced that their very existence is
> at stake.[50]

The task of convincing one's own population of the need to go to war
and to continue fighting until the war is won is even more arduous in an
era when television brings the images of war and its atrocities into every
home. Every military leader must therefore plan his strategy and execution of the war while continuously looking over his shoulder at his own

people. Certainly in recent history several wars have been lost through miscalculating the people's willingness to continue fighting a war of attrition. The wars fought by the French in Algeria and Vietnam; by the US in Korea, Vietnam, and Lebanon; by the Israelis in Lebanon; have revealed that the key to winning modern wars may not be on the battle-field but on the home front. The need to maintain a consensus at home demonstrates that, once the domestic scene becomes as important as the external one, many of the assumptions supporting the *raison d'état* model collapse. In modern democracies there is no definitive central source of influence where critical decisions can easily be made, nor is there necessarily an agreement concerning the goals of a war or at what price it should be fought. The fiction of the 'uni-actor' making national decisions collapses very quickly. Thus, the military-cum-political genius cannot make all the decisions by himself as Clausewitz maintains, but must, in order to implement his policies, persevere in his search for an operational consensus.

The dilemma is that the conduct of war by consensus does not necessarily create the best conditions for waging a decisive war. For example, during the war in Vietnam, Presidents Johnson and Nixon had to maintain a delicate and carefully calculated balance between the opposing pressures of doves and hawks – a balance which resulted in a prolonged and indecisive, limited war.[51] The military leader of today is often forced to wage a limited war and to find acceptable substitutes for victory. In this manner, another dimension of internal friction has been added to warfare, for a leader must consider not only the costs and benefits of war but also the need to adjust the burden of war to a level acceptable to his own population.

While Clausewitz in *On War* appears to take domestic support for granted, the modern political leader cannot.[52] Indeed this dimension represents one of the greatest problems in modern warfare for the political leadership (and hence also for the military). Friction, uncertainty, and chance may prevail in the calculation of obtaining domestic public support as much as in gauging the performance and moves of the enemy. Leaders often seem to take the initial domestic consensus to go to war for granted – yet the longer the war, the less decisive and the more costly, the more problematic the domestic support becomes.

XI. IS VICTORY OBSOLETE?

Unlike Sun Tzu who thought that 'to subdue the enemy without fighting is the acme of skill',[53] Clausewitz ridiculed the idea of winning without fighting:

> Kind-hearted people might of course think there was some ingenious way to disarm or defeat an enemy without too much bloodshed, and might imagine this is the true goal of the art of war. Pleasant as it sounds, it is a fallacy .... It would be an obvious fallacy to imagine war between civilized peoples as resulting merely from a rational act on the part of their governments and to conceive of war as gradually ridding itself of passion, so that in the end one would never really need to use the physical impact of the fighting forces – comparative figures of their strength would be enough. That would be a kind of war by algebra. (pp. 75–6)

Quite to the contrary, he defined war as 'an act of force to compel our enemy to do our will' (p. 75). Since the aim of war is to disarm the enemy, this must be done by force. In order to 'impose our will on the enemy', we must also win. Achieving a military victory was thus a necessary condition to achieving the political goals of war. The more ambitious the political goals, the more desirable the victory. Conversely, if military victory is unattainable we cannot impose our will on the enemy and hence cannot achieve our political goals.

Clausewitz' repeated emphasis on the necessity of victory on the battlefield is the epitome of Western means/ends rationality, which posits a direct correlation between military and political achievements. Modern wars, in particular guerrilla wars of attrition fought not only against the enemy's army but also against his domestic public opinion front, have demonstrated beyond any doubt that it is possible to lose a war militarily and yet win it politically. In such a war it is enough to play for time. The Algerians in the French War in Algeria, and the Vietnamese against the French and US in Vietnam, are good examples. Perhaps another example was the decision of Egypt's President Sadat to launch a limited war against Israel in 1973. Sadat knew he could not win militarily, but he (correctly) believed that the war would allow Egypt to attain many of its political goals. The Israelis, whose military thinking is typically Western, failed to anticipate the war, despite the many warning signals, because they could not understand why any state would launch a war it could not win. (Here, of course, the Israelis also projected their own attitude, since for them a military defeat would mean political disaster.) Arguably, then, Clausewitz' idea of the primacy of politics has been carried one step farther in the non-Western world, to the point where military victory is no longer a prerequisite for political success.

Nuclear weapons, which also added a revolutionary new dimension to military strategy, are not merely increased firepower, as Curtis LeMay is rumored to have believed, but actually represent a quantum jump in the destructiveness of war. War has undergone a metamorphosis, or, in

Kuhn's term, a paradigm shift. If strategy in Clausewitz' time was the art of using force on the battlefield to achieve political ends, nuclear strategy (that is, deterrence) is precisely the opposite: It is the art not of using force but of avoiding war. In a nuclear war – which resembles Clausewitz' war in the abstract – victory has become a meaningless concept. We would resort to Clausewitz' authority in vain regarding a subject that he could not have anticipated. One should be very cautious about applying Clausewitz to the realm of nuclear strategy.

Nevertheless, the emergence of nuclear weapons has, if anything, even further accentuated Clausewitz' insistence on the primacy of politics in warfare. The awesome destructive power of nuclear weapons and the speed with which a nuclear war can be launched and decided have shifted the center of strategic-operational decision-making from the military to the political leadership.

> Today, therefore, nuclear arms have wrought a drastic transformation by promoting strategy to the policy level, the level of deterrence. No one thinking in terms of deterrence can any longer be satisfied with the military level of thought, but must ascend to the conceptual heights of policymakers.[54]

The swiftness with which nuclear attack can be carried out, its lack of historical precedent, its simplicity compared with conventional warfare, and the need for *absolute* political control, have made the military genius and the whole military establishment redundant in an all-out nuclear war:

> War had aspects of an art in the past. Commanders took pride in their tactical skill, in the degree of imagination and ingenuity required to deploy their forces, in qualities of character, courage and daring, and in the capacity of leadership to implant confidence and enthusiasm in the troops. A man's qualities and character found expression in battle. In all-out nuclear war, the human factor is disappearing and alienation between man and war has been created. This is machine warfare, increasingly transformed into a province of science and technology. All-out nuclear war is a war of covering targets by calculating probabilities of hits, a war of azimuths and computers. War is becoming mathematical, and from many standpoints simpler and more amenable to advance planning ....[55]

> Due to the revolutionary change implicit in nuclear warfare, historical experience from previous wars has ceased serving as a guide for such a war. Military experience, therefore, no longer affords an advantage in analyzing the course and results of a future war, and the primacy of the officer corps has ended. Those divining

the uncertainties of the next war are all 'arm-chair strategists', without exception, and all are submerged in an area of guess-work and conjecture, whether they are military or civilian. No one possesses experience in the question of how man will behave in the nightmare conditions of nuclear war. Military experience is less helpful in dealing with these questions than some familiarity with scientific problems, an acquaintance with political and psycho-logical reality, and the ability to weigh logical considerations.[56]

Strategic nuclear war has therefore eliminated *the military* from Clause-witz' triad. A Clausewitzian definition of nuclear warfare consists of a new triad: *the people, the government*, and *technology* – perhaps even only the last two elements.

XII. WARFARE AND THE ECONOMIC IMPERATIVE

Thucydides said that 'war is a matter not so much of arms as of money, which makes arms of use'.[57] The Austrian general Montecuculi is quoted by Ludendorff as saying that 'for the conduct of war money, and again money and thirdly and last money is needed'.[58] To be sure the economic dimension of modern warfare includes much more than financial support – it involves industrial capacity, research and development, the availa-bility and distribution of raw materials, and the organization and management of the war economy.

   Clausewitz never really discusses the financial and economic aspects of war. He seems to take for granted that all the resources necessary for waging war will be made available by the political to the military leader-ship.

> The conduct of war has nothing to do with making guns and powder out of coal, sulphur, saltpeter, copper and tin; its given quantities are weapons that are ready for use and their effectiveness. Strategy uses maps without worrying about trigonometric surveys; it does not inquire how a country should be organized and a people trained and ruled in order to produce the best military results. It takes these matters as it finds them in the European community of nations, and calls attention only to unusual circumstances that exert a marked influence on war. (p. 144)

   This is certainly a narrow view of war even for the nineteenth century. After all, economic and financial considerations or the cost of war have always been a key element in the decision to launch a war and have played a vital role in the course of war itself. Although Clausewitz frequently followed an economic way of thinking (for example, his numerous references to the need to calculate the means/ends cost/benefit relationship in war) he never directly addressed economic issues. He may have not done so deliberately, as Michael Howard suggests, but by this omission he conveniently ignored a crucial dimension of war that was extremely important even in his own time.[59] Although he studied the Napoleonic campaigns in minute detail, he completely ignored the '... part played in Napoleon's strategy, and perhaps his downfall, by the Continental System – his attempt to use economic as well as military instruments to consolidate and extend his conquests'.[60]

That Clausewitz ignored the economic dimension of warfare is of particular interest for two reasons. The first is that the economic dimension of warfare is closely related to the political dimension, whose primacy he always emphasized. Decisions on the allocation of economic resources for the buildup of the military forces before war, as well as their allocation to different purposes, fronts, and divisions during war itself, are an important link between the political and military authorities. Clausewitz' tacit assumption that all the resources necessary for war will be made available to the commander-in-chief is too simple. Who will decide how much of a nation's resources should be devoted to war and who should decide how and by what priority to allocate such resources to the armed forces are questions which Clausewitz left unanswered.

Clausewitz' omission of the economic dimension of war is interesting for yet another important reason. It seems to be missing from his discussion of the transition from war in the abstract to war in practice. Yet it provides another excellent explanation why absolute war must be modified by reality, for absolute war would require the use of *all* the economic resources of a nation at war. In reality, economic constraints dictate the amount of resources that can be invested in war and related activities, thereby playing a major part in limiting the tendency toward absolute war.

Of course, the industrial/technological revolution has increased the importance of economic considerations. Although many technological developments have forced the consideration of economic calculations on the tactical level, such calculations are of even greater importance on the strategic level. On the strategic level knowledge of economic factors in a prolonged war can considerably reduce the uncertainty of the final results. For the outcome of such modern wars is determined not so much by the inspired military genius as by more subtle factors such as gross national product, industrial and research and development capacities, the organization and management of the wartime economy, and the mobilization of resources. The 'economic' nature of modern warfare has spawned more wars of attrition and fewer of decision. This is perhaps the reason why in the past two World Wars the weapons that came the closest to being decisive, for example, the U-Boat as used against Great Britain in the First and Second World War, and perhaps the Allied blockade on Germany in the First World War, were all directed against the economy of the targeted nation.

In fact, Clausewitz does recognize the need to measure the war potential of nations, which he discusses very briefly in Book VIII, Chapter 9. Here he demonstrates that a simple calculation of the availability of manpower indicates that France cannot be expected to win against a coalition of Austria, Prussia, the rest of Germany, the Netherlands, and England. Nevertheless, this is a very simple measurement of war potential using only one criterion (population) for prediction. Modern warfare requires the use of more variables to evaluate the balance of power and the most likely outcome of war. Such an evaluation could have clearly indicated the disastrous outcome of a German decision to declare war on the US as well as the USSR. In two world wars, German leaders thought that a successful war of annihilation or blitzkrieg could avoid the long-range consequences of economic inferiority – a disastrous illusion. One can only wonder if this neglect of the economic dimensions of war is somehow related to the absence of the same dimension in Clausewitz' study *On War*.[61]

Our material environment has radically changed since the early nineteenth century. Wars, which simultaneously depend upon material change and promote material change more than any other human activity, have therefore been radically transformed as well. For that reason any book written on war before the industrial/technological revolution must be subect to modification. This, as we have seen, is the case with Clausewitz' work. Much of what he wrote is timeless, but some aspects of his thoughts and theories on war have been overtaken by the march of history. Although Clausewitz is the least dogmatic and the most flexible of all military theorists, in some respects his views of war are inevitably static and difficult to apply to a different material environment.

Military-technological developments permeate every facet of war: its destructiveness, its expansion in space and compression (or acceleration) in time, the relationship between the offense and defense, the role of intelligence and the possibility of achieving strategic surprise, the shifting emphasis from the front to the rear in the conduct of war, and the correlation between economic and military strength. The accelerated development of military technology has increased the complexity of war in innumerable ways since Clausewitz' time. Furthermore, material change is always followed by nonmaterial changes no less important than the material changes themselves. Nonmaterial changes such as the bureaucratization of military organizations, the creation of a permanent gap between technological innovation and the development of a complementary military doctrine, and the new relationship between the military and civilian authorities must be included in our modern calculus. All of these problems could not have been foreseen by Clausewitz and therefore could not be addressed by him.

Theories, like weapons, are replaced in the course of time by other, better ones. As Clausewitz himself suggested: 'Perhaps a greater mind will soon appear to replace these individual nuggets with a single whole, cast in solid metal free from all impurity' (p. 67). It is a tribute to the greatness of Clausewitz that 150 years after his death there has yet appeared no better theory on war.

NOTES

1. Raymond Aron uses this infelicitous neologism – 'transhistorical' – to describe the relevance of Clausewitz theory to any period in history. *Clausewitz: Philosopher of War* (London: Routledge & Kegan Paul, 1983) is an abbreviated translation of *Penser la guerre: Clausewitz* (Paris: Editions Gallimard, 1976). This is a very disappointing book.

2. Quincy Wright, *A Study of War* (Chicago: University of Chicago Press, 1971).

3. See John I. Alger, *The Quest for Victory* (Westport, CT: Greenwood Press, 1982).

4. Unless otherwise stated, all quotations from Clausewitz are from Carl von Clausewitz, *On War*, ed. and trans. Michael Howard and Peter Paret (Princeton, NJ: Princeton University Press, 1976). Page number given in text.

5. Changes on the tactical level do not necessarily occur at a faster rate than those on the strategic level, since the two levels are closely linked. The appearance of the tank, a weapons platform invented to solve a tactical problem, had of course very important implications for strategy in both the First and Second World Wars. Similarly the use of radar or PGMs primarily on the tactical level had critical and cumulative influences on the strategic level. Any important shift in the balance of strength between the offense and defense on the tactical level will have a decisive impact on the strategic level. In this sense strategy and tactics have come much closer than they were in Clausewitz' time.

   It is interesting to note that Ludendorff quoted Moltke as saying, 'Mistakes made in the beginning of war cannot be made good in the later stages of war'. General Erich Ludendorff, *The Nation at War* (London: Hutchinson, 1936), p. 155. Clausewitz, on the other hand, felt that tactical mistakes could always be retrieved on the strategic level (pp. 182, 243, 582). While this remains basically true in today's world, it might be more difficult given the speed of developments on the battlefield and the slowness of the redesign-replacement process for faulty weapons systems. In the age of modern technology, the most important decisions in war are often taken during the period of peace preceding it. The idea that the 'battlefield decision' is to a large extent now made in peacetime would certainly have sounded strange to Clausewitz.

6. The phrase is from Alfred Vagts, *Defense and Diplomacy: The Soldier and the Conduct of Foreign Relations* (New York: Kings Crown Press, 1956), p. 379.

7. This was also the opinion of Hans Delbrück who wrote: 'With the appearance of Clausewitz' works after his death in 1831, the Napoleonic period of history of the art of war comes to a close .... It leads into the new period .... The new period is defined in its content by the new technology, not only of weapons but also of transportation and all the resources of life, from the railroads and telegraph to the foodstuffs, which increased in such unlimited proportions in the course of the nineteenth century.' *History of the Art of War Within the Framework of Political History*, Vol. 4, *The Modern Era* (Westport, CT: Greenwood Press, 1985), pp. 454–5.

   Among the more interesting works covering the accelerated development of military technology since the beginning of the nineteenth century are: J. F. C. Fuller, *Armament and*

History (New York: Scribners, 1945), Chs. 5–7; J.F.C. Fuller, *The Conduct of War 1789–1961* (London: Eyre & Spottiswood, 1972, Ch. 5); Michael Howard, *War in European History* (Oxford: Oxford University Press, 1976), Chs. 5–7; Maurice Pearton, *The Knowledgeable State: Diplomacy, War and Technology Since 1830* (London: Burnett Books, 1982); Hew Strachan, *European Armies and the Conduct of War* (London: George Allen & Unwin, 1983), Ch. 8. For an excellent brief survey of contemporary military technological developments see *The Economist*, 'Marching Forward: A Survey of Defense Technology', 21 May 1983, 5–32.

The surge in the number of inventions in general during the nineteenth century is demonstrated by the following table:

Period	Number of Inventions
1755–1799	680
1800–1824	1,034
1825–1849	1,885
1850–1874	2,468
1875–1879	2,880

(Based on Appendix 17, Table 20, Quincy Wright, *A Study of War*, p. 163.) The military technological revolution had started earlier, at sea, with Robert Fulton's steamship (1803), the first iron steamship (1820), screw propulsion instead of the paddle wheel (between 1843–45), the complete replacement of sail by steam power (1850), and the all-iron warships HMS Warrior (1861) and Whitehead Torpedo (1864).

The military revolution on land was not far behind. Important new 'civilian technologies' relevant for military application, as well as purely military technologies, started to appear by the early nineteenth century and to accelerate in a cycle of invention, adaption, proliferation, mass production, and obsolescence from about the time of the American Civil War onward. Among the major inventions were:

Shrapnel's shell (1803), Appert's canning technique (1810), Forsyth's percussion lock (in place of a flintlock (1807), and in the 1830s the copper cap that made Forsyth's invention of practical military use (the principal attribute of the percussion cap was the certainty of firing in all weathers).

George Stephenson constructed the first practical steam locomotive (1814), and with the advent of the Stockton–Darlington railway line (1815), the Liverpool–Manchester (1830), and the first trains and railway lines in Europe (1832), military technology moved to land warfare.

The breech-loading Dreyse needle gun was invented (1829), ordered by the Prussian government (1840), accepted as regular issue (1851), and finally fully demonstrated at the battle of Koniggratz (1866). This cycle would later be compressed from a whole generation to a few years.

Communication was revolutionized by Morse's telegraph (1832), the opening of the Baltimore–Washington telegraph line (1844), the telephone (1877), Marconi's radio (1895), and the first transatlantic radio call (1901). From here we leap to the teleprinter radar computers, satellite communications, and the microchip.

Colt's automatic revolver (1835) was being mass-produced by 1853. New explosives included nitroglycerine (1846), dynamite (1866), lyddite (1880s), cordite (adopted by the British army in 1890), and melanite (1880s). There was a tremendous increase in firepower with the invention of the Gatling gun (1862) and Maxim's machine gun (1882).

The first oil well was drilled near Titusville, PA, in 1859; Diesel invented the combustion engine (1892); the first cars (Ford and Benz) appeared in 1893; and the first powered flight took place in 1903. From here we advance to rocket propulsion and, finally, nuclear weapons.

Clausewitz certainly should not be expected to have noticed the early signs of the technological-industrial revolution. Although they can be clearly identified in retrospect, they were not demonstrated on the battlefields of Europe during his lifetime. Not long after his death, the gates of technology were opened and the flood of military inventions began, never to cease again.

Michael Howard in his book *Clausewitz* (New York: Oxford University Press, 1983) suggests that Clausewitz ignored technology unconsciously (p.3). This is incorrect. Clause-witz could not ignore something that did not exist as we know it today.

8. Edwin A. Pratt, *The Rise of Rail Power in War and Conquest, 1833–1914* (Philadelphia: J.B. Lippincott, 1916), p.2. See also John Westwood, *Railways at War* (London: Osprey, 1980); Dennis Showalter, *Railroads and Rifles: Soldiers, Technology and the Unification of Germany* (Hamden, CT: Archon Books, 1975), Part I; also Pearton, *The Knowledgeable State*; George E. Turner, *Victori Rode the Rails: The Strategic Place of the Railroads in the Civil War* (New York: Bobbs Merrill, 1953).

9. Pearton, *The Knowledgeable State*, pp.64–9; also Pratt, *The Rise of Rail Power*, pp. 1–14; Showalter, *Railroads and Rifles*, pp.17–75.

10. Strachan, *European Armies and the Conduct of War*, 115; Showalter, *Railroads and Rifles*, pp.75–190. In Part 3 of this book Showalter discusses the development of modern cannons. Gordon A. Craig, *The Battle of Koniggratz: Prussia's Victory over Austria, 1866* (Phila-delphia: J.B. Lippincott, 1964).

11. Jay Luvaas, *The Military Legacy of the Civil War: The European Inheritance* (Chicago: University of Chicago Press, 1950), p.226.

12. William James, quoted in Grant T. Hammond, 'Plowshares into Swords: Arms Races in International Politics 1840–1941' (Ph.D. dissertation, Johns Hopkins University, 1975), p.26.

13. J.F.C. Fuller in *Armament and History*, pp.115–16, writes: 'The nation which makes the greatest use of peace intervals to advance its mechanical and engineering potentials for war, and which possesses the greatest number of skilled workers as well as trained soldiers, and the most abundant supply of raw materials, as well as of arms, is the nation upon which victory smiles.'

14. For Delbrück's theories, see Hans Delbrück, *Geschichte der Kriegskunst im Rahmen der politischen Geschichte* (Berlin: Georg Stilke, 1900–20). Also, Gordon A. Craig, 'Delbrück the Military Historian' in E. M. Earle (ed.), *Makers of Modern Strategy* (Princton, NJ: Princeton University Press, 1943), pp.260–87; Richard H. Bauer, 'Hans Delbrück' in Bernadotte Schmitt (ed.), *Some Historians of Modern Europe* (Chicago: University of Chicago Press, 1942).

15. See Arden Bucholz, *Hans Delbrück and the German Military Establishment: War Images in Conflict* (Iowa City: University of Iowa Press, 1985).

16. Aron, *Philosopher of War*, p.xiii, also pp.92–3.

17. Some scholars may argue that technology and economics are simply part of the environment in which war is carried out. This interpretation – which may be represented by Clausewitz' triangle enclosed by a circle (environment) – minimizes the *qualitative* differences which result from the accumulation of *quantitative* changes.

18. Similarly, the timing and development by Marx and Engels of their theories on communism and dialectical materialism is not a mere historical coincidence. Marx could not have developed his specific form of communist theory before the industrial revolution. That revolution, in fact, made the appearance of a theory like his almost inevitable.

19. J.F.C. Fuller, *Armament and History*, pp.108, 121.

20. Ibid., p.18. Although Fuller is far from being a Marxist, it is interesting to note how close he comes to adopting a Marxist analysis of war. It is not surprising, therefore, to find that Fuller's theories on war were favorably commented on and adopted by the British Marxist and military analyst T.H. Wintringham. See, for example, his *Weapons and Tactics* (Harmondsworth, England: Penguin, 1973).

21. Fuller read Clausewitz carelessly, but not as carelessly as Liddell Hart. See J.F.C. Fuller, *The Conduct of War 1789–1861*, Ch. 4, 'The Theories of Clausewitz', pp.59–77. For Liddell Hart's misperceptions of Clausewitz see Jay Luvaas' essay in this volume.

22. Clausewitz claimed that the successful achievement of surprise (on any level) depends on secrecy and speed. The tremendous changes in mobility (that is, speed) since his time have thus considerably improved the chances of obtaining strategic surprise even by his own criteria. The second variable, secrecy, has not changed in any radical way since his own time but is easier to counter.

23. Pearton, *The Knowledgeable State*, pp.22–4. For the loss of control, deterioration to war, and mobilization on the eve of World War, see Luigi Albertini, *The Origins of the War of*

1914, Vol. 3 (Oxford: Oxford University Press, 1967); Lawrence Lafore, *The Longest Fuse* (Philadelphia: J.B. Lippincott, 1965); Ludwig Reiners, *The Lamps Went Out in Europe* (Cleveland: World Publishing Co., 1966); Alfred Vagts, *Defense and Diplomacy*, Ch. 10, 'Mobilization and Diplomacy', pp. 377–437; Paul M. Kennedy (ed.), *The War Plans of the Great Powers 1880–1919* (Boston: Allen & Unwin, 1985).

24. See Thomas C. Schelling, *The Strategy of Conflict* (Cambridge: Harvard University Press, 1965) and *Arms and Influence* (New Haven: Yale University Press, 1966).
25. Pearton, *The Knowledgeable State*, p. 25.
26. Ibid., pp. 25–6.
27. 'The enemy force can never assemble and advance so secretly that the defender's first news of it would come from his outposts. If that were to happen, one could only feel very sorry for him.' *On War*, p. 454; see also pp. 544 and 557.
28. Also pp. 200–1. On the tactical level Clausewitz saw the element of surprise as favoring the defender not the attacker:

    It is self-evident that it is the defender who primarily benefits from the terrain. His superior ability to produce surprise by virtue of the strength and direction of his own attacks stems from the fact that the attack has to approach on roads and paths on which it can be observed; the defender's position, on the other hand, is concealed and virtually invisible to his opponent until the decisive moment arrives. *On War*, p. 361.

29. For a summary of the causes of strategic surprise and why it actually comes close to being inevitable, see Michael I. Handel, 'Intelligence and the Problem of Strategic Surprise', *Journal of Strategic Studies*, 7 (Sept. 1984), 229–82. Also Richard K. Betts, 'Analysis of War and Decision: Why Intelligence Failures are Inevitable', *World Politics*, 31 (Oct. 1978), 61–89.
30. There is no comprehensive historical study of the impact on war of the development of modern means of communication, from the telegraph and telephone through the radio and television.
31. Tolstoy's view on the value of intelligence and the ability of military commanders to obtain relevant information in time to control the course of events is even more pessimistic than that of Clausewitz, though influenced no doubt by the same events.
    See in particular Leo Tolstoy, *War and Peace* (New York: Simon & Schuster, 1954); W.B. Gallie, *Philosophies of Peace and War: Kant, Clausewitz, Marx, Engels, and Tolstoy* (Cambridge: Cambridge University Press, 1978).
32. See Handel, 'Intelligence and the Problem of Strategic Surprise', 229–82.
33. As suggested by Peter R. Moody, in 'Clausewitz and the Fading Dialectic of War', *World Politics*, 31 (April 1979), 417–33. The meaning of this statement is as empty as the title of the article (that is, dialectics by definition cannot fade away). The author admits to having read an inadequate 'compilation' of Clausewitz' *On War*.) Even had intelligence been perfect, friction would still exist on the battlefield in other, numerous, and unavoidable ways. The physical world has not lost any of its friction since the days of Newton: nor has the world of war since Napoleon.
34. Strachan, *European Armies and the Conduct of War*, p. 96.
35. J.F.C. Fuller, *Armament and History*; T.H. Wintringham, *Weapons and Tactics*.
36. See also Gerhard Ritter's discussion in *The Sword and the Scepter*, Vol. 1, 'The Prussian Tradition 1790–1890' (Coral Gables, FL: University of Miami Press, 1969), p. 57. Ch. 3 is on Clausewitz and Napoleon.
37. Ludendorff, *The Nation at War*, p. 24.
38. Ibid., p. 175.
39. General Sir Archibald Wavell, *Generals and Generalship* (London: Macmillan, 1941), pp. 27; 33–4.
40. Sir Gerald Ellison, *The Perils of Amateur Strategy* (London: Longmans, 1926), pp. 99–100.
41. Wavell, p. 23. Wavell emphasizes the modern general's need for administrative-organizational skills – a dimension neglected by Clausewitz in the study of military leadership. (See section IX below.)
42. During Napoleon's time, the French Army had already become much too large to be effectively commanded by Napoleon himself, who consistently refused to delegate authority

to his subordinates. Given the size of the army, the scope of the problems, and the absence both of adequate technology and of the organizational support a general staff provides – Napoleon's insistence on maintaining centralized control inevitably led to his defeat. For example, until 1812 Napoleon directed the military operations in Spain although he had not been there since 1809. Strachan, *European Armies and the Conduct of War*, p. 53.

43. Fuller, *Armament and History*, p. 118.
44. As W. B. Gallie points out, Clausewitz' concentration on the conduct of war itself, on its management, prevents him from being seen as a political theorist in the mold of Hobbes, Machiavelli, Locke, Montesquieu, and Rousseau:

> ... A common ground of criticism of Clausewitz ... is that he takes war so entirely for granted ... that he shows no positive interest in the particular kinds of social and political situation that are liable to give rise to or prolong or intensify it; still less does he ask how war might be contained or limited or eventually removed from the scene. In sum, Clausewitz can be criticized, with some cause although not with real justice, for having provided an enlightening anatomy of war – of its action as a whole and of the possible movements of the separate parts – but without adding anything to our understanding of its physiology – the vital forces that call it out and keep it in operation. *Philosophy of Peace and War*, p. 62.

While Gallie correctly analyzes Clausewitz' limitations, the reader must recognize that many of Clausewitz' ideas, particularly in Book I, Ch. 1; Book II, and Book VIII, are closely related to major issues of political theory and would merit attention by political theorists, most of whom have unfortunately ignored Clausewitz' work.

45. Donald Kagan, *The Outbreak of the Peloponnesian War* (Ithaca: Cornell University Press, 1969).
46. Jurg Martin Gabriel, 'Clausewitz Revisited' (Ph.D. dissertation, American University, 1971), 233.
47. Ritter, *The Sword and the Scepter*, Vol. 1, p. 52.
48. See, for example, in this context Ludendorff, *The Nation at War* (in particular, Ch. 7, 'The Nature of Totalitarian War', pp. 12–24); Eckart Kehr, *Economic Interest, Militarism and Foreign Policy* (Berkeley: University of California Press, 1977); Arthur Lloyd Skop, 'The Primacy of Domestic Politics: Eckart Kehr and the Intellectual Development of Charles E. Beard', *History and Theory*, Vol. 13 (Middletown, CT: Wesleyan University Press, 1974), pp. 119–32; James J. Sheehan, 'The Primacy of Domestic Politics: Eckart Kehr's Essays on Modern German History', in *Central European History*, 1 (June 1968), 166–75.
49. The Marxists and hence Soviet military analysts seem to have a great deal of respect for Clausewitz – among other reasons, because of his emphasis on the primacy of politics, his dialectical method, the fact that Lenin read and favorably commented on *On War*, and the connection Clausewitz makes in Book VIII, Ch. 36, between different economic and social infrastructures and different military systems. See Donald E. Davis and Walter S. G. Kohn, 'Lenin's Notebook on Clausewitz', in David R. Jones (ed.), *Soviet Arms Forces Review Annual* (Gulf Breeze, FL: Academic International Press, 1977), Vol. 1, pp. 188–229.
50. Ludendorff, *Nation at War*, pp. 143–4.
51. See, for example, Lesley Gelb and Richard K. Betts, *The Irony of Vietnam* (Washington: The Brookings Institution, 1979).
52. This is at least the tacit and often the explicit assumption that Clausewitz makes in *On War*. Clausewitz did recognize the changed role of the people in warfare since the outbreak of the French Revolution:

> In the eighteenth century, in the days of the Silesian campaigns, war was still an affair for governments alone, and the people's role was simply that of an instrument. At the onset of the nineteenth century, peoples themselves were in the scale on either side. The generals opposing Frederick the Great were acting on instructions – which implied that caution was one of their distinguishing characteristics. But now the opponent of the Austrians and Prussians was – to put it bluntly – the God of War himself.
> Such a transformation of war might have led to new ways of thinking about it. (p. 583)
> We will hardly find a more erroneous standard of measurement in history than that

applied in 1792. It was expected that a moderate auxiliary corps would be enough to end a civil war; but the colossal weight of the whole French people, unhinged by political fanaticism, came crashing down on us. (p.518)

Since Bonaparte, then, war, first among the French and subsequently among their enemies, again became the concern of the people as a whole, took on an entirely different character, or rather closely approached its true character, its absolute perfection. There seemed no end to the resources mobilized: all limits disappeared in the vigor and enthusiasm shown by governments and their subjects. (pp.592–3)

While he recognized the new role of the people and *levée en masse* in war he did not address the question of how the mobilization and increased participation and interest of the people in war came about. (At least not in his study *On War.*) This in reality, was one of the major problems the Prussian military reformers had to address after their decisive defeats by Napoleon at Jena and Auerstadt was how to mobilize the support of the German masses. This was by no means a simple task since it involved an extensive political reform of the autocratic Kingdom of Prussia. Peter Paret, *Clausewitz and the State* (Oxford: Clarendon Press, 1976); Peter Paret, *Yorck and the Era of Prussian Reform, 1807–1815* (Princeton: Princeton University Press, 1966); W. Shanahan, *Prussian Military Reforms* (New York: Columbia University Press, 1945); W. Simon, *The Failure of the Prussian Reform Movement, 1807–1819* (Ithaca: Cornell University Press, 1955); Gordon A. Craig, *The Politics of the Prussian Army, 1640–1945* (Oxford: Oxford University Press, 1955); Ritter, *The Sword and the Scepter*, Vol. 1.

53. Sun Tzu, *The Art of War* (Oxford: Oxford University Press, 1982), p.77. For an interesting discussion of the meaning of victory in modern warfare, see Richard Hobbs, *The Myth of Victory: What is Victory in War?* (Boulder, CO: Westview Press, 1979).
54. Harkabi, *Nuclear War and Nuclear Peace* (Jerusalem: Israel Program for Scientific Translations, 1966), p.2.
55. Ibid., p.4.
56. Ibid., pp.5–6.
57. Thucydides, *The History of the Peloponnesian War*, trans. Richard Crawley, Rev. R. Feetham (Chicago: Encyclopedia Britannica, 1971), Bk. I, Ch. 3, p.370.
58. Quoted in Ludendorff, *The Nation at War*, p.67.
59. Michael Howard, *Clausewitz*, p.3.
60. Ibid.; see also Strachan, *European Armies and the Conduct of War*, p.52.
61. See Arden Bucholz, *Hans Delbrück and the German Military Establishment*.

PART TWO
ON WAR:
THEORETICAL DIMENSIONS

A theory need not be a positive doctrine, a sort of *manual* for action. Whenever an activity deals primarily with the same things again and again – with the same ends and the same means, even though there may be minor variations and an infinite diversity of combinations – these things are susceptible of national study. It is precisely that inquiry which is the most essential part of any *theory*, and which may quite appropriately claim that title. It is an analytical investigation leading to a close *acquaintance* with the subject; applied to experience – in our case, to military history – it leads to thorough *familiarity* with it. The closer it comes to that goal, the more it proceeds from the objective form of a science to the subjective form of a skill, the more effective it will prove in areas where the nature of the case admits no arbiter but talent. It will, in fact, become an active ingredient of talent. Theory will have fulfilled its main task when it is used to analyze the constituent elements of war, to distinguish precisely what at first sight seems fused, to explain in full the properties of the means employed and to show their probable effects, to define clearly the nature of the ends in view, and to illuminate all phases of warfare in a thorough critical inquiry. Theory then becomes a guide to anyone who want to learn about war from books; it will light his way, ease his progress, train his judgment, and help him to avoid pitfalls.

Theory exists so that one need not start afresh each time sorting out the material and plowing through it, but will find it ready to hand and in good order. It is meant to educate the mind of the future commander, or, more accurately, to guide him in his self-education, not to accompany him to the battlefield; just as a wise teacher guides and stimulate a young man's intellectual development, but is careful not to lead him by the hand for the rest of his life.

On War, p.141.

Theory cannot equip the mind with formulas for solving problems, nor can it mark the narrow path on which the sole solution is supposed to lie by planting a hedge of principles on either side. But it can give the mind insight into the great mass of phenomena and of their relationships, then leave it free to rise into the higher realms of action. There the mind can use its innate talents to capacity, combining them all so as to seize on what is *right* and *true* as though this were a single idea formed by their concentrated pressure – as though it were a response to the immediate challenge rather than a product of thought.

On War, p.578'

While history may yield no formula, it does provide an *exercise for judgment*.

On War, p.517.

Chance and Uncertainty in
On War[1]

KATHERINE L. HERBIG

An operation of war cannot be thought out like building
a bridge; certainty is not demanded, but genius,
improvisation and energy of mind must have their parts.
— Winston Churchill[2]

In 1943, as Great Britain's war leader, Winston Churchill could indulge in some acid impatience when his military commanders vacillated in the face of the Second World War's uncertainties. A century earlier the Prussian military theorist and historian Carl von Clausewitz showed a similar impatience with such behavior, but he also showed more understanding of it. Clausewitz' treatise, *On War*, is distinctive in part because it explores so persistently the effects of chance and uncertainty on warfare. The book returns to these factors repeatedly, and Clausewitz gives them a compelling prominence in his theory of war. 'No other human activity', he writes, 'is so continuously or universally bound up with chance. And through the element of chance, guesswork and luck come to play a great part in war.' 'War', he says, 'is the realm of uncertainty; three quarters of the factors on which action in war is based are wrapped in a fog of greater or lesser uncertainty.' Indeed, he goes on, war is a 'gamble .... In the whole range of human activities, war most closely resembles a game of cards.'[3]

For several reasons a close reading of *On War* that traces the theme of chance and uncertainty can be rewarding. First, Clausewitz linked chance and uncertainty with other important concepts in his theory of war. Following one thread quickly leads into the larger pattern of his thinking, and thus helps us analyze the relationships between his ideas.

Second, chance and uncertainty in war are not obsolete. Dealing with the constraints and opportunities chance provides is as relevant to solving today's military problems as it was to solving those of early nineteenth-century Prussia when Clausewitz thought about them. Unlike some of the ideas in *On War* whose relevance is now merely heuristic, understanding what Clausewitz says about chance and uncertainty in war can be applied directly to illuminate current military dilemmas.

Finally, chance and uncertainty in war are instances of the more general human predicament. Everyone lives with uncertainty, everyone is subject to the whims of chance. These elements may be intensified and made distinctive in war, but they are still recognizable, still the same forces of chance and uncertainty which bedevil all human activities. How to understand and prevail against what cannot be fully known or controlled has been a problem philosophers, theologians, and historians have considered for centuries. Like any serious inquiry into a complex problem, thinking – here with Clausewitz as our guide – about chance and uncertainty offers personal insights, as well as the certainty of some rigorous intellectual exercise.

Clausewitz looks at how chance affects the planning, implementing, and the very thinking about wars; at what qualities commanders must have to surmount chance and uncertainty; at how chance shapes interactions between adversaries. He mulls over uncertainty's sources and its distortion of the environment. He focuses on chance in his theories of the nature of war and of friction, considering even how the realities of chance affect the possibility of arriving at a theory.

Yet although he studies chance and uncertainty from many angles in *On War*, Clausewitz does not spell out the basis for his claim that war is the human activity *most* susceptible to the 'intruder' chance. Why is 'no other human activity' so uncertain, or so contingent (pp. 85, 101)? Why is war 'chancier' than business or commerce, competitive endeavors to which Clausewitz often refers for illustrations and analogies of war? Why is it 'chancier' than the legal competition of the courtroom, or the political competition of government which, Clausewitz insists, is the very context and grounding for war?

To infer his reasons for insisting that war is the most contingent of human enterprises, we must study the particular questions about chance and uncertainty he does address. These questions arise here and there in *On War*. Sometimes Clausewitz separates chance and uncertainty, sometimes he confounds them, and he often imbeds them in the context of other issues. Our task is to retrieve and order his arguments without twisting the ideas or their context. There are four clusters of ideas which, because Clausewitz interlaces his concepts so thoroughly, are just loosely structured enough to allow us to draw more informed inferences. The clusters are on the nature of war, on the personal qualities and ideas of the commander, on the relationship of chance and uncertainty, and on the options for action in the face of these contingencies.

I. CHANCE AND THE NATURE OF WAR

At the end of the magisterial first chapter, the only chapter he lived to revise, Clausewitz creates a remarkable metaphor for the nature of war which gives chance due weight and importance. He writes:

> As a total phenomenon its dominant tendencies always make war a remarkable trinity – composed of primordial violence, hatred, and enmity, which are to be regarded as a blind natural force; of the play of chance and probability within which the creative spirit is free to roam; and of its element of subordination, as an instrument of policy, which makes it subject to reason alone. (p. 89)

The three elements of this 'remarkable trinity' form a triangle held together less by harmony than by tension. Its elements are always found in war, but their proportions change and their relationships vary with particular circumstances. 'Our task', Clausewitz writes, 'therefore is to develop a theory that maintains a balance between these three tendencies, like an object suspended between three magnets' (p. 89).

One pole of the tripartite metaphor is passion, terrible when unleashed, a 'blind natural force' which fuels war with motives. These passions must arise, in Clausewitz' view, from feelings the public has when war starts. This element thus mostly concerns the people; it is their contribution to the nature of war.

The second pole is reason. It is exercised in Clausewitz' figure by the government in its policies governing the goals and direction of the war. Because war is by nature 'subordinate' to policy, only the reasonableness of the government's policies exert the necessary control over war. The element of reason is the particular responsibility and concern of the government, he says; those less sanguine than Clausewitz about the rational abilities of governments may doubt the possibility of control from that quarter.

The third pole is chance, described in this metaphor in a light, playful, give-and-take mood. It is the bearer of options and possibilities here, shown in its sunniest colors, not the betrayer of hopes and plans. The character of the commander and his army determines the 'scope which the play of courage and talent will enjoy in the realm of probability and chance,' and thus chance is the element of special concern to the commander. He must gauge the 'play of chance and probability within which the creative spirit is free to roam'.

If war is one part passion, one part chance, and one part reason, then two of the three elements in its nature are by definition wanton, even uncontrollable. The 'primordial violence, hatred, and enmity' of the public, which feeds on itself as it grows, and the interventions of chance, unpredictable and unexpected, make two wild cards in a hand of three. Only reason, given form in the political aims of government, exerts a counterforce against passion and chance. The political leadership weighs the nation's interests and its means, plans its goals, and responds to shifts of circumstance. Nevertheless, the first thing one notices about Clausewitz' trifold analysis of the nature of war is how the deck is stacked against war's being a rational endeavor.

Clausewitz portrays chance in this metaphor in an unusually positive light. He stops short of implying that chance itself is ever positive, as personified in the goddess Fortuna, Lady Luck, the comforter of anxious men. Chance remains neutral and out of human reach in *On War*, but in his first chapter Clausewitz does emphasize the possibilities chance offers. They challenge the commander's creativity to seize and turn them to advantage. Although one may feel ambivalent about its disruptions, Clausewitz suggests people often welcome chance. 'Although our intellect always longs for clarity and certainty, our nature often finds uncertainty fascinating. It prefers to day-dream in the realms of chance and luck rather than accompany the intellect on its narrow and tortuous path of philosophical inquiry and logical deduction ....' (p. 86). Pursuing this romantic idealization of chance and uncertainty a bit further, he claims they can be the source of imagination and inspiration. 'Unconfined by narrow necessity', he writes, '[human nature] can revel in a wealth of possibilities; which inspire courage to take wing and dive into the element of daring and danger like a fearless swimmer into the current' (p. 86).

His argument presents both objective and subjective reasons for welcoming chance and uncertainties. Chance rearranges opportunities and thereby allows human creativity scope, while its open-endedness inspires courage, which is indispensable in war. The varieties of courage that are bold, dashing, and risk-seeking are stimulated by the free-wheeling possibilities chance affords; they are dampened by dull certainties. If war were a more cut-and-dried affair, men's courage could not 'take wing' so readily or so often.

The development of a positive side of chance in war was one of Clausewitz' special contributions to military theory, according to Clausewitz scholars Peter Paret and Michael Howard. Clausewitz' predecessors and contemporaries treated chance quite differently. Most assumed it was unwelcome and strove to minimize it with rules and systems as, for example, in the works of Heinrich von Bulow or Antoine Henri Jomini.[4] Others, such as Georg Heinrich von Berenhorst, threw up their hands at the expanded scope for chance generated by new technologies and declared that all war was chaos.[5] Clausewitz took neither of these paths because he was determined to frame a theory that could teach about real war. In real war he found that chance was inescapable but that regularities in war still existed that could be intelligently applied. In his decision to give chance the central place in theory which he had seen it play in actuality, Clausewitz focused on the creativity it calls forth, also ensuring that his theory could remain relevant to changing variants of warfare.

One senses from the exalted prose in these passages that Clausewitz was attracted to his vision of freedom and creativity provided by chance in the midst of war's destruction. The dichotomy he notes between the logical, rational side of human nature, confined on a 'narrow and tortuous path', and the playful, emotional, creating side is one many observers before and since Clausewitz have also described. A basic physical duality in the human mind has in the last several decades been confirmed by psychologists whose 'split brain' experiments have suggested that the two hemispheres of the brain specialize in their functions: the left appears to handle language and logic, the right patterns, spatial relationships, and aesthetics.[6] While it is not remarkable that Clausewitz perceived this duality, his insistence that the massive complexities of war demand the combined power of both dimensions of the human mind does suggest a particular sensitivity to human psychology. What made war so involving to Clausewitz, and made it worth his thinking and writing about for decades, was in part that it engaged the whole range of human abilities, and it was chance that tapped the right hemisphere's creativity – in theorizing about war as well as in fighting it.

If Clausewitz had lived to revise the later chapters of On War, perhaps he would have treated chance more positively throughout the book, carrying through the tone of Chapter One. Perhaps he would have rated the quality of imagination as more useful to the commander, instead of complaining about imagination that '[visualizing the landscape] is about the only service that war can demand from this frivolous goddess, who in most military affairs is liable to do more harm than good' (p. 110). As it stands, the positive side of chance appears mostly in Chapter One and the rest of the book shows us its negative side. Chance becomes the 'intruder ... [who] interferes with the whole course of events' (p. 101). The commander engages in a 'relentless struggle with the unforeseen' (p. 102). In the balance of the book Clausewitz concentrates on arming the commander for this struggle. To do battle with the negative effects of chance he prescribes sturdy virtues: staunchness and determination. The flexibility and creativity envisioned in the first, but latest, chapter are not developed further.

II. UNCERTAINTY AND THE COMMANDER: GENIUS, FRICTION AND
    THEORY

In his metaphor for the nature of war Clausewitz describes an inter-
locking system. The people stoke the passionate engine of hate, the
government lays down the track of national interest, but the commander
must decide how to drive the train of war. His responsibilities make the
impact of chance his particular concern. Chance affects them all, of
course, turning the public's attention willy-nilly to this atrocity or that
triumph, laying open some unexpected options for the government's
policies while blocking others. While these chance effects do help shape
the history of wars, to advance the theory of warfare one must grasp the
effects of chance on the commander. How he fares against the 'intruder'
will determine the military outcome, and that will determine the fate of
the people and government as well. Clausewitz was writing for the commander, not for the popular or academic audience of his day. The success
of his theories lay, in Clausewitz' view, in how well each commander
could apply the ideas – not the specific solutions – in *On War* to his own
unique problems.

The fact of chance and its attendant uncertainties imposes two demands
on the commander: he must have special qualities to deal with adversity,
and he must have intellectual flexibility to take advantage of chance
whenever possible. Two of Clausewitz' major ideas in *On War* address
these demands: the qualities of military genius, and the formulation of a
proper theory for war.

Clausewitz begins his discussion of military genius, a term he uses to
mean exceptional talent, by defining four basic characteristics of war.
These four facets are the context, or 'climate', of war; they are its essence.
War, he says, is always danger, physical exertion, uncertainty, and
chance. For danger he prescribes courage; for exertion, steadfastness; but
we do not focus on these aspects here.

Deftly Clausewitz sketches the commander's dilemma as the battle
begins to unfold:

> Since all information and assumptions are open to doubt, and with
> chance at work everywhere, the commander continually finds that
> things are not as he expected. This is bound to influence his plans, or
> at least the assumptions underlying them. If this influence is
> sufficiently powerful to cause a change in his plans, he must usually
> work out new ones; but for these the necessary information may not
> be immediately available. During an operation decisions have
> usually to be made at once: there may be no time to review the
> situation or even to think it through. Usually, of course, new infor-

mation and reevaluation are not enough to make us give up our intentions: they only call them in question. We now know more, but this makes us more, not less uncertain. The latest reports do not arrive all at once: they merely trickle in. They continually impinge on our decisions, and our mind must be permanently armed, so to speak, to deal with them. (p. 102)

In such a situation the qualities of genius needed are determination to master 'the agonies of doubt and the perils of hesitation,' and an elusive faculty he calls, after the French, *coup d'oeil*, to perceive correctly despite distracting confusion. The commander with *coup d'oeil* can in a glance take in the general view and rapidly scan a position or plan, evaluating its good and bad points. Clausewitz stresses mental insight over purely physical visualization: 'the quick recognition of a truth that the mind would ordinarily miss or would perceive only after long study and reflection' (p. 102). With this skill the commander can sort through the rapidly accumulating unexpected impressions, without being panicked by their unfamiliarity or the pressure of time passing.

Insight should be married to determination in the military genius. Determination is what provokes the commander to act on his best estimates despite good reasons for hesitation and doubt. It is a quality called up by intelligence, which sees the need for boldness, but determination is also rooted in a temperament that despises waivering above all else. It is not thoughtless, impulsive heroics. The determined commander evaluates the risks facing him, yet does not let their enormity prevent him from acting decisively on his best judgment (pp. 102–3).

A third quality mingles advantageously with *coup d'oeil* and determination in a military genius: presence of mind. An 'increased capacity of dealing with the unexpected', presence of mind, as defined by Clausewitz, is the gift of responding immediately with a proper response when facing a crisis, the gift of 'quick thinking'.

Together these three qualities will carry the commander through the morass of distractions and conflicting information which threatens to paralyze him. They allow him to hold fast to the essence of his plans despite necessary changes or improvisations.

Circumstances vary so enormously in war, and are so indefinable, that a vast array of factors has to be appreciated – mostly in the light of probabilities alone. The man responsible for evaluating the whole must bring to his task the quality of intuition that perceives the truth at every point. (p. 112)

We may glance at some other qualities that go into Clausewitz' concept of military genius: intelligence, strength of mind and character, energy, even political acumen. Throughout his discussion of genius, however, Clausewitz emphasizes one trait of the military commander: can he 'intuit' how to accomplish his goals when chance circumstances and uncertainties mount up? If he cannot, Clausewitz implies, war will defeat him.

Despite having the necessary personal qualities to face down chance and uncertainty, a commander may still fail if he has inadequate ideas or if he applies misguided theories of warfare. Clausewitz dismisses as worse than useless efforts to systematize warfare with rules and formulas. Such systems are falsely comforting, he says, because they reduce the imponderables of war to a few meagre certainties about minor matters, ignoring the important issues which by their nature evade systems. Rules about the benefits of interior lines or secure bases or numerical superiority do not, Clausewitz scoffs, touch on what is permanent and universal in war, and so they cannot be the components of a true theory, one that would hold true in the future as well as for the past. He raises three objections to rigid systems of warfare:

> They aim at fixed values; but in war everything is uncertain, and calculations have to be made with variable quantities.
> They direct the inquiry exclusively toward physical quantities, whereas all military action is intertwined with psychological forces and effects.
> They consider only unilateral action, whereas war consists of a continuous interaction of opposites. (p. 136)

All three of these objections have at their core Clausewitz' perception of the pervasiveness of chance and uncertainty in war.

The uncertainty in war defies simplistic attempts to apply mathematical techniques, at least any as limited as mere geometry which, he writes in a slap at contemporaries like Baron Jomini, does illuminate tactics but not higher levels of strategy (pp. 214–15). His notion of making 'calculations ... with variable quantities' suggests that Clausewitz might have been intrigued with the twentieth century's computer-assisted decision-aids, with their multiple regressions and other statistical manipulations that build into information awareness of variations and gradations in validity. Yet he would have questioned over-reliance on mechanical means of even this brilliance. To him the 'general unreliability of all information presents a special problem in war', one not met by the strategists who approach their subject mathematically (p. 140). By over-simplifying war, they mislead commanders with the false security of tidy but irrelevant formulas.

Overlaid on uncertainty stemming from unreliable information is a second 'variable quantity', human psychology. The act of fighting itself stirs volatile emotions, and warfare's constant danger must be mastered with courage that ensures one's 'moral survival' by refusing to act on fear. The diversity in human intellects further complicates the equation of war, for it means that there is seldom only one 'best' way to proceed. Creative leaders will apply theories in different ways and reach unique but effective solutions, for, as Clausewitz notes, genius *'rises above all rules'*. 'What genius does is the best rule, and theory can do no better than show how and why this should be the case' (p. 136). Subject to unpredictable emotional responses under stress, diverse in combinations of talent and creativity, men do not fit into tidy schemes either.

His third objection to the rule-making school of strategy is that it ignores the interactive nature of warfare. By definition warfare is a system in which action provokes reaction and counter-reaction. To study only what one side could and should do to optimize success in war, thus overlooking the serial complexities of the system, further over-simplifies war; 'the very nature of interaction is bound to make it unpredictable', Clausewitz warns. '[T]heoretical *directives* tend to be less useful here than in any other sphere' (pp. 139, 140).

If not with directives, how should the commander prepare himself for his task? Although war defies rigid prescriptions, Clausewitz believes that theories aimed at describing war, when analytically rigorous, can still be useful. Theory can break down phenomena of war into their parts, distinguish between and define the parts, trace probable effects, define the goals – however, the result is not doctrine, but education, not directives to be acted on, but frameworks for further thought in the light of personal experience. '[Theory] is meant to educate the mind of the future commander, or, more accurately, to guide him in his self-education, not to accompany him to the battlefield' (p. 141).

When applied to military history, the laboratory of past experience, properly limited theory helps the commander to broaden his familiarity with war and to experience vicariously the challenges and solutions of other commanders. Because of the pace of warfare, its stress, the multi-plicity of impressions and information it presents, but, most of all, because of war's 'continual change and the need to respond to it', commanders cannot rely on abstract or external means for decision-making (p. 147). Their knowledge must be absorbed into their very personalities, so that they are ready to respond on demand. Clausewitz' ambitious goal for *On War* was that it help educate the next generation of military leaders by providing a theory of war expressive of war's complex reality, not ignoring but indeed emphasizing the uncontrollable elements in that reality.

III. THE RELATIONSHIP OF CHANCE AND UNCERTAINTY

To further explore the various themes in *On War* that sharpen the commander's perceptions of chance and uncertainty, we need to consider more closely how chance and uncertainty are related. Thus far it has been sufficient to treat them as intertwined or coexistent, since this is a common way to experience them. Something happens by chance, that is, an inexplicable or random event takes place whose cause is either inapparent or unconnected to its effects. This provokes uncertainty, the psychological state of discomfort from confusion or lack of information. The two are not necessarily linked, of course; one may feel uncertain for many reasons other than in response to chance, and chance does not always lead to uncertainty. If by chance one receives a windfall or some other pleasant surprise, one feels happy and 'lucky', not uncertain. Indeed, good fortune tends to increase self-confidence, since the temptation to attribute one's luck to one's own worth or actions is very persuasive. Nevertheless, the fact that people are subject to chance and therefore never securely in control does build uncertainty into human life.

Clausewitz considered chance and uncertainty both separately and together in *On War*. He aggregated their effects in one of his most famous concepts, friction. This was his metaphor for those factors 'that distinguish real war from war on paper' (p. 119). Friction is the decremental loss of effort and intention caused by human fallibility, compounded by danger and exhaustion. Like the mechanical phenomenon of friction that reduces the efficiency of machinery with moving parts, Clausewitz' friction reduces the efficiency of the war machine. It sums up all the little things that always go wrong to keep things from being done as easily and quickly as intended. The moving parts in a war machine are individuals, each of whom contributes his quotient of potential for error, misunderstanding, and volatility. One never knows when any one of these people will 'chance to delay things or somehow make them go wrong', so the only certainty is that one or more of them will do so (p. 119).

What makes friction more than a minor annoyance in war is its confounding with chance, which multiplies friction in random, unpredictable ways. 'This tremendous friction', Clausewitz writes, 'which cannot, as in mechanics, be reduced to a few points, is everywhere in contact with chance, and brings about effects that cannot be measured, just because they are largely due to chance' (p. 120). When chance intervenes it can instantly transform normal levels of performance into potential catastrophes. Fog prevents the observations that would otherwise reveal the enemy's movements, for example; or the plan for tomorrow's attack, wrapped around three good cigars, falls from the general's pocket onto a trail and, rather than being lost, ignored, or discounted, correctly informs the opponent.[7] Suddenly what was a trivial mistake or random annoyance can become a major crisis.

Such mischances cannot be prevented or forestalled, and Clausewitz notes that commanders of genius do not wear themselves out anxiously trying to eliminate the inevitable. Instead they understand that friction sets limits on what is possible and what is not, and they make their plans accordingly, standing ready to deal vigorously with any crises that occur. Chance is thus doubly implicated in the concept of friction: first, it governs the type and timing of those 'countless minor incidents' that may became major accidents; second, it goes beyond friction to multiply the severity with which any particular accident may affect the evolving war. In friction uncertainty and chance are knotted together, each overlapping and reinforcing the other.

A second theme in *On War* which juxtaposes uncertainty and chance concerns the dangerous effects of hesitation and loss of momentum. In several contexts Clausewitz associates an uncertain state of mind with increased vulnerability to the effects of chance. These situations befall the commander ostensibly on the offensive who gives in to his very human longing for certainty.

Clausewitz argues that 'an offensive war requires above all a quick, irresistible decision' (p. 598). He dismisses counter-arguments in favor of slow, methodical offensives on grounds that 'they usually camouflage misgivings on the part of the general or vacillation on the part of the government' (p. 599). Indeed, delay and vacillation are typical responses to uncertainty because they allow more time to seek information, clarify alternatives, or grasp the context of the immediate event. But to allow the chronic uncertainty of war to dictate the pace of an offensive is, in Clausewitz' view, to invite disaster.

This theme arises, for example, in Clausewitz' discussion of an offensive which assumes the limited goal of merely occupying territory, not destroying the opponent's ability to resist. The goal, occupation, burdens the offensive with ever-increasing amounts of territory to defend as it proceeds; strongpoints must be garrisoned, and resistance in the rear subdued before progress can continue. The demands burgeon alarmingly; action cannot be resolved into the essential 'single, massive blow, aimed in accordance with our major interest'. Too often the result of this type of offensive, Clausewitz warns, is that 'effort is increasingly dispersed, friction everywhere increases and greater scope is left for chance' (p. 612).

Why should an offensive which is scattered, overstrained, and lacking in concentrated momentum be more vulnerable to chance? We may infer that on the one hand, more friction generates more opportunities for accidents to flare into real crises and, on the other hand, distracting multiple objectives dissipate the commander's vision of the campaign's goals. '[T]he greater his self-confidence ...', Clausewitz says of such a commander, 'the more he will seek to break loose from this tendency [of trying to be strong everywhere at once] in order to give some one point a preponderant importance, even if this should be possible only by running greater risks' (p. 612). Chance, a neutral and random phenomenon, is as likely to interfere with a concentrated offensive as it is with those that are bogged down and distracted, but the latter are more open to severe effects and repercussions from chance interventions. Clausewitz here links uncertainty, circumspection, and reduced confidence with a resultant greater vulnerability to chance.

Another example of this association is found in his discussion of how main and supporting lines of advance should be related to one another. Clausewitz much prefers the concentrated advance with its greater momentum, even if to achieve it some sectors are temporarily left behind. To hold back the main force until all sub-units can advance with it 'would impose such sluggishness on movement, such paralysis on the attack, create such opportunities for chance and waste so much time', as to undermine the whole operation (p. 622). An offensive should 'drive like an arrow'; for to hesitate, to equivocate, to give in to uncertainty by prudently covering one's bets abdicates initiative and leaves one open to buffetings by chance. In trying prudently to reduce risk, one actually increases it.

Friction and offensive momentum are topics in which Clausewitz connects both uncertainty and chance. In other contexts he disconnects the two concepts and explores them separately. His discussion of information and intelligence, for example, shows the unique effects uncertainty alone can have on the commander's perceptions and judgments.

A primary reason for uncertainty – in war and elsewhere in life – is inadequate information. When Clausewitz lists the four factors that define the climate of warfare (danger, exertion, uncertainty, and chance), it appears from his examples that he has in mind the uncertainty caused by inadequate intelligence. Intelligence, that is, information of all sorts about the enemy, is seldom complete and reliable enough to allay uncertainty in war. Other writers on warfare prescribed that the commander suspect all intelligence as likely to be flawed and continually seek reliable information. Clausewitz recognized that such counsels of perfection are correct but, in real war, also irrelevant.

How should the commander proceed when he knows his intelligence will be contradictory, sometimes false and, above all, uncertain? Clausewitz recommends applying a 'standard of judgment', based on the commander's knowledge, experience, and common sense. He should be 'guided by the laws of probability'. Although sympathetic to the commander facing the difficulties inherent in intelligence, Clausewitz offers him little more specific guidance than do the 'scribblers of systems and compendia' he criticizes (p. 117).

Which 'laws of probability' does Clausewitz have in mind in this passage? One may infer that he does not mean what in his day was called the Doctrine of Chances, now usually called the mathematical or statistical theory of probability. This theory seeks to calculate the relative frequency with which a particular event, within a given class of events, will occur, but this calculation requires large numbers of events to be valid.[8] Clausewitz' emphasis in *On War* is at the opposite pole, on the distinctive and the unique events, and he rejects as too facile the search for mathematical certainty in war. He applies a more commonsensical notion of probability which is based on experience and intuition. He claims it is characteristic for commanders of military genius to consider methodically what is most likely to happen. One does not proceed by 'defying the natural order of things [or] in crudely offending the laws of probability ...'. Instead he commends 'that higher form of analysis by which genius arrives at a decision: rapid, only partly conscious weighing of the possibilities' (p. 192). This is intuitive, not statistical, probability.[9]

It is the psychological consequences of chronic uncertainty that interest Clausewitz more than the problems of intelligence *per se*. Despite the limitations of the psychological theory available to him in the early nineteenth century, when psychology remained close to its parent philosophy and was still descriptive and typological, he often derives insightful psychological patterns from observations and speculation.[10] So he notes, for example, that when confronted with contradictory bits of sequential information, the intelligence officer yields to the human preference for confirmation of initial impressions and fails to entertain alternative plausible explanations, thus reaching a hasty and ill-founded decision:

> [One] is lucky if [the reports'] contradictions cancel each other out, and leave a kind of balance to be critically assessed. It is much worse for the novice if chance does not help him out in that way, and on the contrary one report tallies with another, confirms it, magnifies it, lends it color, till he has to make a quick decision – which is soon recognized to be mistaken .... (p. 117)

In several other places in *On War* Clausewitz associates the uncertainty caused by flawed information with a tendency '[to] rather believe bad news than good, and ... to exaggerate the bad news' (p. 117). Reports of reverses and imminent disaster are disproportionately salient to the commander when he cannot disconfirm them with reliable information. Repeated arrival of bad news, some true, some false, tends to break down the confidence the commander feels in his plans. Prey to anxiety he cannot

usually allay, he is further undermined, says Clausewitz, by the disagree-
able shock of seeing the situation develop in ways he had not visualized or
expected. The immediate undigested evidence of his senses overwhelms
the earlier systematic thought that went into framing his plans. Debili-
tating misgivings increase.

Clausewitz is not recommending that the commander ignore evidence
that something is very wrong or at least unexpected about a projected
operation. He is emphasizing a human tendency to pay close, often too
close, attention to reports of danger in an uncertain and stressful setting.
When reinforced by chimerical appearances, this tendency can, unless
resisted, panic the commander into changing or abandoning his plans.
'The general unreliability of information', Clausewitz writes, '[creates] a
kind of twilight, which, like fog or moonlight, often tends to make things
seem grotesque and larger than they really are' (p. 140).

The anxieties and exaggerations caused by uncertainty in war cannot
be eliminated although, Clausewitz admits, the commander will always
aim to reduce them. He will be more effective, however, if he realizes that
'whatever is hidden from full view in this feeble light has to be guessed at
by talent, or simply left to chance' (p. 140). These bleak alternatives,
guessing and leaving things to chance, are among the options for action
Clausewitz grants to the commander. We next turn to these and other
aspects of how to act given the chance and uncertainty characteristic of
war.

IV. GUESSING, GAMBLING, AND GAMES

In situations where 'everything will be left very much to fate', Clausewitz
writes, 'no commander, not even the most audacious, will find this to his
liking' (p. 265). Leaving things to chance, thereby relinquishing the sense
of control and purposefulness, is especially unpleasant for military
leaders because it implies passivity, even helplessness, rather than the
boldness their calling typically requires. Clausewitz despises passivity and
distrusts prudence, yet he acknowledges that after a point the complexities
of war force the commander to depend on chance. He implies that, like
Napoleon Bonaparte, who was quoted as saying 'Engage the enemy, and
see what happens', the commander is stronger for having deliberately put
aside concern for what cannot be controlled. The mental act of leaving the
inevitable contingencies to chance frees his energies to concentrate on
what he *can* initiate and control.

Clausewitz further develops this point about the necessity of leaving
some things to chance in a discussion aimed at critics of warfare, theorists,
or historians, rather than at those actively fighting. To be accurate, he
says, critics must recognize the important part chance plays in the out-

come of any military encounter. Their accounts will be oversimplified if they credit or blame an outcome only on the skill of the commander and his armies. 'It would seem that a commander's personal merits, and thus also his responsibility, become irrelevant to all questions that have to be left to chance ...' (p. 167) and yet there is a strong human tendency to ignore the role of chance. We vicariously enjoy another's success and feel disappointed by his failures, even when we see that chance intervened to cause them. The pleasure derived from identifying with a successful commander Clausewitz links to the high value placed on a man's good fortune in war, a value that good fortune at gambling does not enjoy. Being lucky at gambling implies no special talent or merit. Being lucky at war, a more complicated, demanding, and much more serious endeavor, seems to us a sign of favor, a proof not only of the commander's talent but also of his worth. That even successful commanders leave to chance what cannot be controlled is the ultimate acknowledgement of chance's centrality in the nature of war, of 'that part whose deep, mysterious operation is never visible' (p. 167).

Nevertheless, the commander will wish to leave as little as possible to chance. How does he bring himself to act boldly despite the inherent uncertainties of war? Clausewitz suggests that he make an educated guess and then gamble that he guessed correctly. Often in *On War* Clausewitz compares the commander to a gambler and warfare to games of chance. Napoleon Bonaparte, 'the most daring of gamblers', is the best example, a man of phenomenal good fortune who was the beneficiary par excellence of the association of success with personal reputation noted above.[11]

Bonaparte transformed European warfare in part because he was willing to risk much to 'win big'. While his success held he ruthlessly pressed his advantage, betting his 'winnings', resources, morale, and the momentum of victory, to seek total victory over a beaten adversary. Like a gambler riding a 'run' of good luck, at such moments Bonaparte seemed unstoppable; as his opponents disintegrated, he swelled in power and everything conspired to favor him. Clausewitz sees a reciprocity in the momentum of victory and defeat. 'At such a time of good fortune, the victor must not be afraid to divide his forces in order to envelop every-thing within reach of his army .... He may do whatever he wants until the situation changes; the more liberties he takes, the later that moment will come' (p. 270). When things go badly and luck is 'running' in reverse, like the gambler the commander seems unable to get ahead of the momentum now favoring his opponent. 'The beaten army's loss from sickness and fatigue is grossly disproportionate, and its whole morale is weakened and depressed by constant fear of imminent disaster, until, in the end, organized resistance is inconceivable' (p. 270).

Commanders may also fall prey to the 'gambler's fallacy' of expecting chance to be fair as well as random. Chance produces 'runs' of events which in the course of time even out; gamblers prefer to believe that this 'evening out' will occur in the next play. Thus a losing commander feels compelled to keep playing, that is, fighting, by his hope that 'he will be able to reverse his fortunes just once more, and he will keep at it for as long as his courage and his judgment allow' (p. 250). Facing defeat, the commander who gambled and lost struggles over whether to fight on and risk annihilation or decide 'against spending all one has, against gambling away one's last resources' (p. 251). Napoleon provides the most memorable image. 'In that most famous of all battles, Belle-Alliance', Clausewitz writes, 'Bonaparte staked his last remaining strength on an effort to retrieve a battle that was beyond retrieving; he spent every last penny, and then fled like a beggar from the battlefield and the Empire' (p. 252).

Can the commander ever expect that chance will turn things around and save the battle or the war for him? Clausewitz discourages this expectation. Yet in elaborating his reasons in several places in *On War*, he seems of two minds about the implications of this position.

He takes one line of argument in his detailed consideration of the battle. He claims that the balance between the opposing forces shifts slowly in most battles, slowly and usually inexorably from early tendencies which accelerate as they grow. As the trend gathers force it becomes obvious to both sides. 'Battles in which one unexpected factor has a major effect on the course of the whole usually exist only in the stories told by people who want to explain away their defeats' (p. 249), Clausewitz says sternly.

He admits there are occasional exceptions where some accident reversed the course of a battle. These exceptions are the illusive hope of the commander who fights on 'to reverse his fortunes just once more' (p. 250). In general, though, battles are composites of many actions and effects and it is the sum of these which ultimately fix the outcome. The implication is that, despite the workings of chance, battles have regularities which can be described and analyzed and on which theoretical precepts may be based.

On the other hand, when Clausewitz takes up issues of grand strategy and asks what exactly it means to defeat an opponent, he accords much more weight to what a single accident may produce. He lists instances where a victory here or a different kind of defeat there would have changed the impact of whole campaigns; often merely overcoming the opponent's military forces proved insufficient to achieve his actual defeat. He writes:

> These events are proof that success is not due simply to general causes. Particular factors can often be decisive – details only known

to those who were on the spot. There can also be moral factors which never come to light; while issues can be decided by chances and incidents so minute as to figure in histories simply as anecdotes. (p.595)

He then considers the different vulnerabilities an opponent may have; only by focusing on the opponent's particular 'center of gravity' can defeat be assured. Clausewitz' point is that battle victories are means to the larger ends of grand strategy. If not fought with those larger ends in view, battles, even if victorious, may be wasted.

'Chances and incidents so minute' may snatch real success from a military victory, yet 'one unexpected factor' almost never reverses the course of a battle. Either he means to imply that there is a dynamic unique to the battle which denies the usually powerful role of chance events, or Clausewitz was thinking along contradictory lines in these two contexts. Whether the stray accident can reverse the course of events in a battle or in a campaign would seem of considerable theoretical importance, and in *On War* Clausewitz apparently supports both sides of the question.

War is like gambling and other games of chance in another sense which is also relevant to this discussion of Clausewitz' ideas of chance and uncertainty. War is a conflict between adversaries over time. The actions of one side elicit reactions from the other which provoke reactions in turn. The interdependence of opponents in war, in the midst of their hostilities, has often prompted a comparison of warfare with games. Games now have more respectability as analytical constructs than they did for Clausewitz. Over the last forty years whole theoretical empires have been built on mathematical game theory, on theories of negotiating behavior, and on decision theory. These theoretical approaches are devoted among other things to producing insights for military applications. While *On War* is not a proto-game theory, Clausewitz' insights into the subtle relationship and interaction between adversaries reveal parallels to the strategic games studied in game theory. Particularly relevant here is Clausewitz' emphasis on how this interaction generates a major source of uncertainty. 'The second attribute of military action is that it must expect positive reactions, and the process of interaction that results .... The very nature of interaction is bound to make it unpredictable. The effect that any measure will have on the enemy is the most singular factor among all the particulars of action'[12] (p.139).

Not only are the intentions and reactions of one's opponent a perennial source of uncertainty, but the opponent may by his secret dispositions or speed of movement or ability to do the seemingly impossible, achieve surprise. A military surprise is not simply an action which is surprising; given the uncertainties already enumerated, most developments in war are to some extent surprising. Instead it is an unexpected action for which the victim of the surprise had not prepared. He expected and prepared for something else. Because surprise demands that its victim 'shift gears' and respond to an unexpected situation it generates confusion, lowers morale, and increases stress. The disorganizing psychological impact, coupled with local superiority of force at the point a surprise occurs, make surprise a most tempting device. Indeed, surprise 'lies at the root of all operations without exception', Clausewitz argues (p. 198).

He is most sanguine about the efficacy of surprise in tactical situations, where the limited space and time concentrate the impact of a maneuver on an opponent. To steal a march, occupy a new position, or appear where not looked for can have considerable effect on a tactical level. The higher the level of strategy, however, the less likely Clausewitz sees effective surprises. At the grand strategic and diplomatic levels he virtually writes off surprise as impossible. In part this judgment is based on factors which were important in Clausewitz' time but are less so today: the length of time needed for war preparations and mobilization, for example, and the relative inability to hide tell-tale preparations in a period when counter-intelligence resources were primitive. But a second part of his skepticism about achieving major strategic results from surprise stems from his awareness that both sides in effect 'cooperate' in a surprise, the victim along with the surpriser. A clever commander may plan how he will surprise his opponent by moving suddenly, pressing his own forces hard, or using terrain or technology in new or different ways, but built into his plans are assumptions about how the opponent will act – that he will show up for the surprise as planned. Clausewitz presents examples of successful and unsuccessful surprises, but he focuses on cases where surprise was lost. He claims history is as replete with failed surprises as with brilliantly successful ones. It is chance and the unpredictable calculations of the opposing commander that intervene to keep a planned surprise from happening.

Even where surprise succeeds Clausewitz takes pains to point out that chance helped the surprise along and thus, by implication, that chance could just as likely have thwarted it. 'Major success in a surprise action therefore does not depend on the energy, forcefulness, and resolution of the commander: it must be favored by other circumstances' (p. 199). His examples demonstrate this: Bonaparte unexpectedly advances on Blucher in 1804 and defeats his forces in detail three times but, says Clausewitz, Napoleon's correct projection of how his opponent would proceed depended on a 'fortunate coincidence' between his and Blucher's views. When Frederick surprised Laudon in 1760 by suddenly changing position during the night, Clausewitz notes that Frederick simply disliked the position and moved to improve it. The opportunity this gained him to surprise Laudon was fortuitous. 'Here too chance played a large part, and the outcome would have been different had it not been for the difficult, hilly terrain, and the coincidence of Frederick's nocturnal shift of position with the preliminary phases of Laudon's attack' (p. 200).

'In war more than anywhere else things do not turn out as we expect', Clausewitz writes (p. 193). Chance may surprise us; the enemy may surprise us; or the enemy may surprise us because his own plans have been favored with the connivance of chance. This third level of complexity interests Clausewitz the most. In *On War* he stresses examples of the most contingent interactions between adversaries in order to stretch his theories of warfare to their limits.

Clausewitz wrote *On War*, along with his many other histories and essays, because he had been stimulated by the problems warfare posed in his own day. Ever since Napoleon Bonaparte had harnessed the French Revolution to his own ambitions and sent 'this juggernaut of war, based on the strength of the entire people, [on] its pulverizing course through Europe' (p. 592), war had entered a new era. Although Clausewitz strove for impartiality and acknowledged that styles of warfare in each age are shaped by social and political characteristics of the time and cannot be judged by the standards of later ages, he had his preferences. For example, he found the limited warfare of the eighteenth century unappealing. His reasons extend our basis for inferring that warfare is, for him, a strategic game.

Warfare in the eighteenth century was tamed, writes Clausewitz, because the economic base was too small to support open-ended aggressions. Absolutism, expensive mercenary armies divorced from the people for whom they fought, and the small size but large number of European states combined to limit severely the means for war, and thus limited the political uses to which war could be put. Bounded, made predictable, 'War was thus deprived of its most dangerous feature – its tendency toward the extreme, and of the whole chain of unknown possibilities which would follow' (p. 589). With no threat of ultimate exertions from one's enemies, there was no reason to risk one's own army, which was too expensive to replace, in ambitious or creative ways. So, Clausewitz remarks, 'The conduct of war thus became a true game, in which the cards were dealt by time and by accident' (p. 590).

There is something trivial to Clausewitz in this kind of playing at war. The interaction between opponents in this 'game' was determined by fixed rules: the time it took to amass, supply, march, and safely maneuver an army into the field, and by incidentals, not by the skills and character of the commander. Instead, the commander drifted between 'prudence and hesitation', a pawn to fortune, diminished to insignificance. It is not the interactive dimension itself, nor the managerial challenge of overcoming all the frictions in a large endeavor, which makes warfare worth thinking seriously about to Clausewitz. The games in which players break, challenge, even transform the rules, where they risk stakes comparable to the survival of the nation to achieve ultimate ambitions – the games Bonaparte taught Europe – these he feels are worthy comparisons for war. Such games are unpredictable. They come trailing their 'whole chain of unknown possibilities'. They create new conditions of life, which may be better or worse, or both, for their players. We may infer that it was this open-endedness which attracted Clausewitz and justified for him, and for us, the effort in a serious study of war. When he writes 'our nature often finds uncertainty fascinating', he writes about himself. In *On War* he explained this fascination, tracing the careers of uncertainty and chance in a game too important to always follow the rules.

V. WAR AND THE 'TENDENCY TOWARD THE EXTREME'

We may now be able to answer, by way of summary, the question raised at the outset of why Clausewitz claims war is the most uncertain and the chanciest of all human activities. In part it is because of the scale of warfare which, as Bonaparte demonstrated, can absorb the human and material resources of a people to no visible limit. On the one hand, total war is the largest and most complex exercise in coordination and direction that mankind attempts. Compounded on this scale, the friction caused by human failings and foibles raise war's quotient of uncertainty, while the unreliability of information undercuts efforts to find the truth. Large-scale enterprises are not just smaller-scale ones writ larger; they reach dimensions which suddenly transform them into new phenomena and warfare, above all, demonstrates this. On the other hand, a limited war fought for specific objectives with less-than-total resources can be more uncertain than a total war in which the issue comes down to which side has superior economic and material means. The degree of stress on the human body and psyche from war's threatening, often heart-rending environment adds to its burdens no matter what its scale. The eerie mutual dependence of adversaries locked in hostile interaction further complicates war. But finally, it is, in Clausewitz' words, the 'tendency toward the extreme' in war that makes it so uncertain.

War is life-and-death serious. There are no 'rules' that if successfully violated will still apply in such an interaction. The contingencies of warfare occur within a process which in theory has no limit, and thus the margins for chance and for uncertainty are greatly magnified.

Once begun, wars may take on a logic of their own and carry their participants in unexpected directions toward goals they had not dreamed of. Clausewitz looked over this precipice in *On War* and drew back from it.

> Were it a complete, untrammeled, absolute manifestation of violence, [he wrote] … war would of its own independent will usurp the place of policy the moment policy had brought it into being; it would then drive policy out of office and rule by the law of its own nature…. (p. 87)

Luckily, he thought, wars fall short of the absolute; counterforces sap their fury and contain them so that wars remain harnessed by the policies that created them.

Clausewitz, however, was unaware of the human potential, now realized, to build the means to destroy life itself. If we grant his argument for the pervasiveness of chance in war; if we agree with him that two-thirds of the basic nature of war is by definition uncontrollable and that we must assign to man's frail reason the remaining one-third, the task of controlling the whole; and if we take to heart his demonstrations of the human penchant for misjudgments under conditions of chronic, crushing uncertainty, this can but increase the disquiet with which we contemplate our future.

NOTES

1. The author gratefully acknowledges the generous assistance of Michael Handel, whose ideas and suggestions helped shape the result of this research.
2. Quoted in Michael Howard, *Grand Strategy*, August 1942–September 1943, in *History of the Second World War*, 7 vols. (London: Her Majesty's Stationery Office, 1972), Vol. 4, p. 295.
3. Carl von Clausewitz, *On War*, ed. and trans. Michael Howard and Peter Paret (Princeton: Princeton University Press, 1976), pp. 85, 101, 86. Subsequent page numbers given in text.
4. Peter Paret, 'The Genesis of *On War*', introductory essay in *On War*, p. 6; Michael Howard, 'Jomini and the Classical Tradition', *The Theory and Practice of War*, ed. Michael Howard (New York and Washington: Praeger 1965), p. 8.
5. Howard, 'Jomini', p. 9.
6. Robert E. Ornstein, *The Psychology of Consciousness* (New York: Viking, 1972), pp. 49–75. The typical figure for expressing the duality of human nature is the head and the heart. Thomas Jefferson wrote a now-famous dialogue in which the head and the heart debate one another, implying his struggle between the rational and the intuitive sides of his nature. 'Split-brain' experiments became possible after a surgical procedure was developed to help severely epileptic patients by cutting the physical linkage in the brain between the two hemispheres. Such patients did improve, and they demonstrated that the logical, verbal abilities of the left hemisphere contrast sharply with the abilities of spatial orientation, facial recognition, art and music, and body orientation of the right hemisphere. Because the right hemisphere 'is more holistic and relational, and more simultaneous in its mode of operations', according to Ornstein (pp. 52–3) than the left, which is sequential and analytic, it is the right brain's faculties Clausewitz has in mind when he describes the 'coup d'oeil' necessary to quickly take in and evaluate a complex situation. On Jefferson's dialogue see Garry Wills, *Inventing America* (Garden City, NY: Doubleday, 1978), pp. 275–80.

7. This accident happened to Confederate General Robert E. Lee during the preliminaries to the battle of Antietam in 1862. J.C. Randall and David Donald, *The Civil War and Reconstruction*, 2nd rev. ed. (Lexington, MA: D.C. Heath, 1969), pp. 220–21.

8. Maurice Kendall, 'Chance', *Dictionary of the History of Ideas*, ed. Philip P. Wiener (New York: Charles Scribner's Sons, 1973), Vol. 1, pp. 335–40, and Horace C. Levinson, *Chance, Luck and Statistics* (New York: Denver Publ., 1939), pp. 44–6.

9. For a parallel discussion of Clausewitz' use of the idea of probability, see Raymond Aron, *Clausewitz, Philosopher of War*, trans. Christine Booker and Norman Stone (Englewood Cliffs, NJ: Prentice-Hall, 1985), pp. 184–7.

10. Peter Paret, *Clausewitz and the State* (New York: Oxford University Press, 1976), pp. 158–9.

11. Quoted in ibid., p. 362; also see p. 153.

12. On game theory see M. Shubik (ed.), *Game Theory and Related Approaches to Social Behavior* (New York: Wiley, 1964); and Thomas C. Schelling, *The Strategy of Conflict* (New York: Oxford University Press, 1960).

Clausewitz and Intelligence

DAVID KAHN

Carl von Clausewitz disdained intelligence. His remarks about it are mostly pejorative. He classed it negatively among the major factors of military activity. He relegated it to a secondary role in all aspects of war.

Yet, today, commanders and military theoreticians value intelligence. They use it in their plans and battles. They emphasize it in their histories. They cite it as essential to military operations.

Of course, technology has effected this change. But technology has not outdated all Clausewitz' remarks: in the age of the ICBM, he is still cited as an authority.[1] Has he become obsolete only in intelligence? Has he become entirely obsolete in intelligence? Or have some of his views retained their validity?

I

In *On War*, Clausewitz rests his three-paragraph chapter on intelligence on a statement that illustrates his scorn for the activity: 'Many intelligence reports in war are contradictory; even more are false, and most are uncertain' (p. 117).[2] He summarizes his main paragraph with the lapidary 'In short, most intelligence is false' (p. 117). He expresses this view throughout the text. The third of his three major characteristics of military activity is the 'Uncertainty of All Information' (p. 140). In listing the factors that affect engagements – the psychological, physical, geographical, mathematical (lines of advance, for instance), and logistical – he excludes information about the enemy (p. 183). He says that 'The only situation a commander can know fully is his own; his opponent's he can know only from unreliable intelligence' (p. 140). In discussing the engagement, he states that 'At the moment of battle, information about the strength of the enemy is usually uncertain' (p. 233). Likewise, in strategy, decisions are based in part 'on uncertain reports' (p. 210). Indeed, *On War* contains not a single example of good intelligence ferreting out an enemy's plans, let alone an instance where such intelligence led to a victory.

Nevertheless, Clausewitz does not close his eyes to the need for information, nor does he dogmatically maintain that it can never serve. He admits, usually by implication, that it is sought and that sometimes it can help. Feints and fighting patrols have as a purpose 'making the enemy show himself' (p. 236). Advance guards and outposts are needed 'to detect and reconnoiter the enemy's approach before he comes into view' (p. 302). An army 'must use its vanguard as its strategic eyes, sending out individual detachments, spies, and so forth' (p. 259). An advanced corps 'is never intended to stop the enemy's movements, but rather, like the weight of a pendulum, to moderate and regulate them so as to make them calculable' (p. 352). An advantage of high ground is 'a wider view' (p. 352). In the politico-strategic area,

> to discover how much of our resources must be mobilized for war, we must first examine our own political aim and that of the enemy. We must gauge the strength and situation of the opposing state. We must gauge the character and abilities of its government and people and do the same in regard to our own. Finally, we must evaluate the political sympathies of other states, and the effect the war may have on them. (pp. 585–6)

In a more general sense of intelligence, he remarks 'Everyone gauges his opponent in the light of his reputed talents, his age, and his experience, and acts accordingly' (p. 137). One who did so was Frederick the Great, who, in his successful campaign of 1760, 'chose these positions and made these marches, confident in the knowledge that [Austrian Field Marshal Leopold Count von] Daun's methods, his dispositions, his sense of responsibility and his character would make such maneuvers risky but not reckless' (pp. 179–80). Clausewitz specifically lists among 'the true reasons' for victories not only of Frederick but of Napoleon 'the correct appraisal of the opposing generals (Daun, [German Field Marshal Prince Karl Philipp zu] Schwarzenberg)' (p. 196).

Nevertheless, these occasional acknowledgments of the usefulness of intelligence bow before his more fundamental disparagement of it. Examination of what he believes are the causes of the uselessness of information helps explain why he holds this negative view.

The most important ground for his suspicion of intelligence lies in the role of chance. This concept permeates his philosophy of war. Chance reduces the accuracy and predictive value of information.

> War is the realm of chance. No other human activity gives it greater scope. (p. 101) ... In war more than anywhere else things do not turn out as we expect .... Since all information and assumptions are open to doubt, and with chance at work everywhere, the commander constantly finds that things are not as he expected .... The very nature of interaction is bound to make it unpredictable. (p. 139)

Clausewitz makes many other comments in the same vein. And, although he nowhere says so, poor intelligence probably contributes to friction in war, which increases the effects of chance.

Another ground consists of the growth of imponderables in war. For governments in the eighteenth century, 'Their means of waging war came to consist of the money in their coffers and of such idle vagabonds as they could lay their hands on either at home or abroad. In consequence the means they had available were fairly well defined, and each could gauge the other side's potential in terms both of numbers and of time' (p. 589). But in the new wars of the French Revolution, in which not just a small professional army but the whole nation took part, 'there seemed no end to the resources mobilized; all limits disappeared in the vigor and enthusiasm shown by governments and their subjects' (pp. 592–3). Although Clausewitz does not say so explicitly, mass conscription had to lead to greater complexity in warmaking and so to greater difficulty in determining enemy potential. Support for such a view appears in his discussion of the tactical level. While Frederick did not maintain strong outposts, Napoleon 'almost always used a strong advance guard' (p. 303). One reason for this was 'the increased size of modern armies' (p. 303). Another was 'the change that had occurred in tactics ... with the old system of tactics and encampment it was far easier to find out the position of the enemy than it is today' (p. 273).

A third reason for Clausewitz' suspicion of intelligence is the limitation inherent in observation. 'After all, a troop's range of vision does not usually extend much beyond its range of fire' (p. 302). Enemy forces 'may be hidden by every wood and every fold of undulating terrain' (p. 210). Night, too, 'is a great source of protection' (p. 241). Lack of strength may constrain investigation of the enemy. A small detachment cannot satisfactorily observe the enemy, 'partly because it would be more easily driven back than a large one, and partly because its means, its tools of observation, would not be sufficiently powerful' (p. 308). To these restrictions must be added a temporal one.

> Unless the enemy is so close as to be in full view (as Frederick the Great was to the Austrians before the battle of Hochkirch), knowledge of his position will be incomplete. It will be acquired from reconnaissance, patrols, prisoners' statements and spies, and it can never really be reliable for the simple reason that all such reports are always a little out of date, and the enemy may in the meantime have changed his position. (p. 273)

Finally, not even the most energetic intelligence operation can penetrate an enemy's brain; he will succeed in keeping at least some of his secrets: 'He will not just shoot his guns off blindly' (p. 273). Some things will thus remain unknown until 'the final third of battle, when the defender has revealed his whole plan' (p. 391). Battle, Clausewitz is saying, is the ultimate reconnaissance – but then it is too late.

To the limitations of collection are added those of analysis. So numerous and so nebulous are the factors involved in determining what an enemy will do that they prohibit a scientific approach. So 'colossal' a task it is for a state to assess its own and an enemy's political aims, strength, character and abilities 'in all their ramifications and diversity' that 'Bonaparte was quite right when he said that Newton himself would quail before the algebraic problems it could pose' (p. 586; see also p. 112). During consideration of how much effort should be expended for a military objective,

> intellectual activity leaves the field of the exact sciences of logic and mathematics. It then becomes an art in the broadest meaning of the term – the faculty of using judgment to detect the most important and decisive elements in the vast array of facts and situations. Undoubtedly this power of judgment consists to a greater or lesser degree of the intuitive comparison of all the factors and attendant circumstances; what is remote and secondary is at once dismissed while the most pressing and important points are identified with greater speed than could be done by strictly logical deduction. (p. 585)

For Clausewitz, analysis is little more than intuition, and even that sometimes sinks to guesswork.

> In reviewing the whole array of factors a general must weigh before making his decision [on whether to press an attack], we must remember that he can gauge the direction and value of the most important ones only by considering numerous other possibilities – some immediate, some remote. He must *guess*, so to speak: guess whether the first shock of battle will steel the enemy's resolve and stiffen his resistance, or whether, like a Bologna flask, it will shatter as soon as its surface is scratched; guess the extent of debilitation and paralysis that the drying up of particular sources of supply and the severing of certain lines of communication will cause in the enemy ... guess whether the other powers will be frightened or indignant. (p. 572)

The fifth and final reason for Clausewitz' distrust of intelligence is the dominance – at least at times – of preconception over fact. He recognized the importance of a person's theories or emotions. In another context, he called courage, or the sense of one's own strength, 'the lens, so to speak, through which impressions pass through the brain' (p. 137). That and other lenses can also distort information about the enemy. 'One may have been aware of it [that the enemy is stronger] all along, but for the lack of more solid alternatives this awareness was countered by one's trust in chance, good luck, Providence, and in one's own audacity and courage. All this has now turned out to be insufficient, and one is harshly and inexorably confronted by the terrible truth' (p. 255) – that the enemy is more powerful and that one has been defeated.

For all these reasons, Clausewitz looked askance upon intelligence.

II

Fundamental to Clausewitz' thought is the existence of both a physical and a psychological component in war. The physical consists of men, guns, horses, works. It finds an expression in Clausewitz's dictum that 'In tactics, as in strategy, superiority of numbers is the most common element in victory' (p. 194). The psychological factors – which Clausewitz calls 'moral elements' – include the skill of the commander, the experience and courage of the troops, their patriotic spirit and will.

Intelligence affects both the physical and the psychological components of war. In the physical realm, intelligence (that is, good intelligence) magnifies strength. Knowing where an enemy will attack enables a commander to put more men there, taking them from where they are less needed. In the psychological domain, intelligence improves command. Knowing that a town ahead is empty of the enemy eases a commander's mind, freeing him to resolve other problems.

The contrary of these theses is that failures of intelligence reduce strength in the physical realm and impair command in the psychological.

In the physical domain, Clausewitz expresses this effect through the concept of surprise, which by definition constitutes a failure of (the victim's) intelligence. Superiority of numbers is 'hardly conceivable' without the desire 'to take the enemy by surprise .... Surprise therefore becomes the means to gain superiority' (p. 198). Among the main factors in strategic success is

> surprise – either by actual [unexpected] assault or by deploying unexpected strength at certain points. (p. 198) ... Surprising the enemy by concentrating superior strength at certain points is again comparable to the analogous case in tactics. If the defender were compelled to spread his forces over several points of access, the attacker would obviously reap the advantage of being able to throw his full strength against any one of them. (p. 364)

Clausewitz concedes that 'Even the higher, and highest, realms of strategy provide some examples of momentous surprises', as does tactics.

But he emphasizes that 'history has few such events to report' (p. 200) – because 'in practice it [surprise] is often held up by the friction of the whole machine .... It would be a mistake, therefore, to regard surprise as a key element of success in war' (p. 198).

In the psychological domain, poor intelligence harms command most commonly by leading a general to exaggerate the enemy's strength and consequently to lose confidence. 'Most intelligence is false, and the effect of fear is to multiply lies and inaccuracies (p. 117) .... Men are always more inclined to pitch their estimate of the enemy's strength too high than too low' (p. 85).[3] A general 'is exposed to countless impressions, most of them disturbing, few of them encouraging. With its mass of vivid impressions and the doubts which characterize all information and opinion, there is no activity like war to rob men of confidence in themselves and in others, and to divert them from their original course of action' (p. 108). In a strategic situation, lack of information will lead to 'most generals' being 'paralyzed by unnecessary doubts' (p. 179). The frequency of such references to psychological difficulties, and his couching them in general terms, suggests that Clausewitz believes that the impairment of command owing to poor intelligence is more common than the problems resulting from poor intelligence in the physical domain.

III

However, he would not have won a reputation as outstanding in his field had he not prescribed – though only by implication – what to do in the face of this inadequacy of intelligence.

In the physical field, Clausewitz made up for the reduction in strength occasioned by bad intelligence by adding men and guns. They usually take the form of a reserve. Clausewitz specifies that one of the purposes of a reserve is 'to counter unforeseen threats' (p. 210; see also p. 391). A reserve is necessary both in strategy and in tactics.

> In a tactical situation, where we frequently do not know the enemy's measures until we see them ... we must always be more or less prepared for unforeseen developments, so that positions that turn out to be weak can be reinforced, and so that we can in general adjust our dispositions to the enemy actions. Such cases also occur in strategy .... In strategy too decisions must often be based on direct observation, on uncertain reports arriving hour by hour and day by day, and finally on the actual outcome of battle. It is thus an essential condition of strategic leadership that forces should be held in reserve according to the degree of strategic uncertainty. (p. 210)

In discussing defense, Clausewitz gives another example of force replacing lack of knowledge: a defender's reserve of one fourth to one third of his strength acts in part 'to protect him against the unexpected' (p. 310).

Psychologically, what substitutes for the confusion caused by poor intelligence is will power. After iterating that 'most intelligence is false', Clausewitz declares that 'the commander must trust his judgment and stand like a rock on which the waves break in vain' (p. 117). He uses this image elsewhere as well, and also makes the same point in other words. 'The role of determination is to limit the agonies of doubt (pp. 102–3). ... With uncertainty in one scale, courage and self-confidence must be thrown into the other to correct the balance' (p. 86). Uncertainty is one of the four elements that make up the climate of war, the others being danger, exertion, and chance.

> If we consider them together, it becomes evident how much fortitude of mind and character are needed to make progress in these impending elements with safety and success. According to circumstance, reporters and historians of war use such terms as energy, firmness, staunchness, emotional balance, and strength of character. (p. 104)

Strength of will defends not only against external inadequacies but also against internal ones – incorrect presumptions. Thus Frederick's recognition during the daring maneuvers of his successful campaign of 1760 that Daun would not attack him called for 'boldness, resolution and strength of will to see things in this way, and not to be confused and intimidated by the danger that was still being talked and written about thirty years later' (p. 180)

IV

Clausewitz seems objective and sensible in his non-intelligence comments; we may presume he is the same in those dealing with intelligence. Contemporaries who wrote on war paid little attention, like him, to the subject. And up to his time history reports hardly any battles won as a consequence of good intelligence: of Edward S. Creasy's *Fifteen Decisive Battles of the World: From Marathon to Waterloo*,[4] only one – the battle of the Metaurus, in which the Romans defeated the Carthaginians – depended upon intelligence. So Clausewitz appears justified in viewing intelligence with skepticism.

In the century and a half since his death, however, whole new technologies have been created that can gather far more intelligence than was possible in his time.[5] Chief among them are the camera in an airplane or a satellite and the radio. Moreover, the establishment of intelligence agencies has given the field a permanent institutional existence. As a consequence, it has produced success after success. Satellite photography enables the United States and the Soviet Union to count with astonishing precision each other's missiles for delivering nuclear weapons.[6] Most dramatically in the First and Second World Wars, case after case attests to the power of intelligence – a power it did not have in the time of Clausewitz.

The defeat of czarist Russia, one of the most consequential events of modern times, owes not a little to intelligence. Intercepts of enemy radio messages all but enabled Generals Paul von Hindenburg and Erich Ludendorff to crush the Russians at Tannenberg.[7] Later intercepts paved the way to Brest-Litovsk. 'We were always warned by the wireless messages of the Russian staff of the position where troops were being concentrated for any new undertaking .... Only once during the whole war were we taken by surprise', wrote the chief of staff of the German armies on the eastern front.[8] Such methods which sprouted during the first of the total wars matured in the second. On the eastern front, the repeated tactical warnings of Russian moves, largely obtained through radio intercepts, gradually persuaded the conservative elite of the German general staff of the value of intelligence.[9] Allied intelligence was even more successful. Aerial photographs confirmed the existence and provided details of the German V-weapons.[10] Codebreaking led to the victories of Midway and the Battle of the Atlantic, to the cutting of Japan's lifelines by US submarines and the midair assassination of Admiral Isoroku Yamamoto,[11] to scores of tactical victories on the battlefields of Europe.[12] Moreover, by engendering an atmosphere of knowing what the enemy was doing, the codebreaking facilitated command decisions.[13]

Far from being the negative, harmful element that it was in Clausewitz' time, intelligence sped victory. It shortened the war by several months, according to one authority,[14] by three years, according to others.[15] Allied commanders of the Second World War extolled intelligence as neither Clausewitz nor any general of his time ever did. Midway was 'a victory of intelligence', declared Admiral Chester Nimitz.[16] General Dwight Eisenhower said that the codebreaking intelligence was 'of priceless value to me'.[17] General George Marshall acknowledged that the solutions 'contribute greatly to the victory'.[18]

But intelligence is not perfect. Sometimes it is wrong; sometimes it is inconclusive; sometimes it is lacking.

In Viewnam, despite the use of all sorts of information-gathering devices, including sensors to count the vehicles passing them, intelligence analysts disagreed over how many troops North Vietnam had in South Vietnam.[19] In Iran, despite a strong US intelligence presence, despite the near-certainty that the telephone calls of the Ayatollah Ruhollah Khomeini from France were being monitored, US intelligence was surprised by the overthrow of the Shah. And military tactical surprises still take place: Pearl Harbor, the invasion of South Korea, the Yom Kippur War, the Falklands takeover. The causes of these intelligence failures are the same as Clausewitz' reasons for distrusting intelligence: chance, imponderables, limitations of observation and of analysis, preconceptions. Limitations of observations enabled the Japanese to pounce undetected on Pearl Harbor, for example,[20] and Israel's preconceptions played a major role in the failure of its intelligence at the start of the Yom Kippur War.[21]

Thus, although technology has invalidated Clausewitz' derision of intelligence, and although generals accept it where he rejected it, in the larger picture his views prevail. Intelligence can indeed magnify strength and improve command, but leaders do not always have it. Clausewitz, concerned less with the technological changes in war, such as intelligence's increased capabilities, than with the permanent aspects, such as the inevitability of uncertainty, found the solution to this perpetual problem. It consists of military strength and firmness of purpose.

NOTES

1. I have found only scattered items on intelligence in skimming two other published Clausewitz works. Werner Hahlweg (ed.), *Schriften–Aufsatze–Studien–Briefe*, Deutsche Geschichtsquellen des 19. and 20. Jahrhunderts, 45 (Göttingen: Vandenhoek & Ruprecht, 1966), gives advice, in the lecture notes on irregular warfare, on how to use outposts and advanced guards. But, unlike the passages on the same topics in *On War*, this shorter, earlier work does not connect the activities of these units with any larger considerations of intelligence. Werner Hahlweg (ed.), *Verstreute kleine Schriften*, Bibliotheca Rerum Militarium, XLV (Osnabrück: Biblio Verlag, 1979), offers occasional comments on intelligence. But these items add nothing significant to the material in *On War*, which, in fact, often repeats them in more refined form. For example, one of the selections in *Verstreute kleine Schriften* says, at p. 80, 'It is certainly a basis of the art [of war]: that one may count upon an enemy's erroneous conduct only insofar as it can be presumed probable.' *On War* says, at p. 117, that, in assessing information about the enemy, a commander 'should be guided by the laws of probability'.

Two recent studies of Clausewitz do not touch on intelligence: Raymond Aron's *Penser la guerre, Clausewitz* (Paris: Editions Gallimard, 1976) and Michael Howard's *Clausewitz* (New York: Oxford University Press, 1983). Ulrich Marwedel excludes intelligence in his discussion of the military philosopher's main statements on pp. 78–90 of his *Carl von Clausewitz: Personlichkeit und Wirkungsgeschichte seines Werkes bis 1918*, Militärgeschichtliches Studien, 25 (Boppard am Rhein: Harald Boldt Verlag, 1978). An index to Clausewitz' main ideas, *Clausewitz Casyndekan*, A Staff Project of Casyndekan, Inc. (Colorado Springs: Casyndekan, 1969), likewise omits intelligence.

In seeking the application of Clausewitz' ideas on intelligence to the use of intelligence in the Vietnam War, I received responses from four Vietnam veterans. I would like to thank them for their time: Lt. Eric Kronen, formerly in charge of enemy infiltration assessment, Joint Intelligence Command, US Military Assistance Command, Vietnam; Col. Jean K. Joyce, chief of the current intelligence and indications branch, Joint Intelligence Command;

Col. Edward H. Caton, former chief, Joint Intelligence Command; and Air Force Maj.-Gen. Grover C. Brown, former assistant director for intelligence production, Defense Intelligence Agency.

2. All page references to *On War* are included in the text. The edition used is the English translation by Michael Howard and Peter Paret (Princeton, NJ: Princeton University Press, 1976).

3. Shakespeare said it more graphically: 'In the night, imagining some fear,/How easy is a bush supposed a bear!' (*Midsummer Night's Dream*, V:i:22).

4. (London, 1851).

5. On p.102, Clausewitz says, 'We now know more, but this makes us more, not less, uncertain'. But the intelligence experience of the Allies in the Second World War disproves this view.

6. John Prados, *The Soviet Estimate* (New York: Dial Press, 1982), pp.203, 205, 284.

7. Max Hoffmann, *War Diaries and Other Papers*, trans. Eric Sutton (London: Martin Secker, 1929), Vol. 1, pp.41, 18.

8. Max Hoffmann, *The War of Lost Opportunities* (London: Kegan Paul, Trench, Trubner & Co., 1924), p.132.

9. Gen. Adolf Heusinger (head of the operations branch, German general staff), interview, 8 Oct. 1973.

10. F.H. Hinsley *et al., British Intelligence in the Second World War* (London: Her Majesty's Stationery Office, 1984), Vol. 3, pp.1, 368, 372, 403–4.

11. David Kahn, *The Codebreakers: The Story of Secret Writing* (New York: Macmillan, 1967), pp.561–613 passim.

12. Ronald Lewin, *Ultra Goes to War* (New York: McGraw Hill, 1978), passim.

13. Peter Calvocoressi, *Top Secret Ultra* (New York: Pantheon, 1980), pp.110–11.

14. Jürgen Rohwer, 'Der Einfluss der Alliierten Funkaufklärung auf den Verlauf des Zweiten Weltkrieges', *Vierteljahrshefte für Zeitgeschichte*, 27 (1979), 335–69 especially 361.

15. F.H. Hinsley, quoted in Christopher Andrew and David Dilks (eds.), *The Missing Dimension: Governments and Intelligence Communities in the Twentieth Century* (Urbana, IL: University of Illinois Press, 1984), pp.1–2. Major General Stephen A. Chamberlain, operations officer of the Southwest Pacific Area, quoted in Harold C. Deutsch, 'Clients of Ultra: American Captains', *Parameters: Journal of the U.S. Army War College*, 15 (Summer, 1985), 55–62 especially 61.

16. Chester W. Nimitz and E.B. Potter (eds.), *The Great Sea War: The Story of Naval Action in World War II* (Englewood Cliffs, NJ: Prentice-Hall, 1960), p.245.

17. Eisenhower to Menzies, 12 July 1945, Eisenhower Library, Abilene, Kansas.

18. In a letter printed in United States, Congress, Joint Committee on the Investigation of the Pearl Harbor Attack, *Pearl Harbor Attack*, Hearings, 79th Congress, 1st and 2nd Sessions (Washington: Government Printing Office, 1946), Vol. 3, p.1133.

19. United States District Court for the Southern District of New York, *General William C. Westmoreland, plaintiff, vs. CBS Inc. et al. defendants*, 82 Civ. 7913 (PNL), Memorandum in Support of Defendant CBS's Motion to Dismiss and for Summary Judgment (23 May 1984), especially pp.42–3, 60–72; Plaintiff General William C. Westmoreland's Memorandum of Law in Opposition to Defendant CBS's Motion to Dismiss and for Summary Judgment (20 July 1984), especially pp.31–3 and Plates 11–A, -B, -C, and -D.

20. David Kahn, 'The United States Views Germany and Japan in 1941' in Ernest R. May (ed.), *Knowing One's Enemies: Intelligence Assessment Before the Two World Wars* (Princeton, NJ: Princeton University Press, 1984), pp.476–501 especially at pp.500–1.

21. Michael Handel, *Perception, Deception and Surprise: The Case of The Yom Kippur War*, Jerusalem Papers on Peace Problems, 19 (The Hebrew University of Jerusalem: The Leonard Davis Institute for International Relations, 1976).

[Handwritten annotation at top:] Is guerrilla warfare an exception to idea that war always continuation of policy? See Afghanistan, or Spain 1807⊕. these are fights for survival? Look also to French Resistance against Nazis. Gives it/history its particularly fierce nature. Where too does 'holy war' fit in? Far more connected with fighting for inherent beliefs so presumably affects morale, intentions, etc.

Clausewitz and Guerrilla Warfare

WERNER HAHLWEG

[Handwritten annotation right margin:] Conflict engendered by 'War on Terror' has led to kind of ideological warfare not seen since C16/C17. C18, 19 & 20 largely territorial, political, C21 return to relig, ideological. Particularly brutal kind of warfare. Implications for Clausewitz's own theory?

I. GUERRILLA WARFARE IN CLAUSEWITZ' TIME

Whoever occupies himself with the theory and practice of modern guerrilla warfare will observe that Clausewitz finds ever-increasing attention among the advocates of this form of armed conflict. Mao Tse-Tung or Che Guevara may serve as examples of this fact. The introduction to the recent Cuban edition of *On War* also mentions guerrilla warfare.[1]

Clausewitz lived during a time when guerrilla warfare took on new dimensions, particularly during the American Revolution (1776–83) and the age of the French Revolution and Napoleon I (1789–1815). The first was a war for independence in the form of a people's war (*Volkskrieg*). The second was an era of socio-political transformation; the French Revolution and the later counter-revolutionary reaction led the masses to guerrilla warfare. In the course of this process, guerrilla war – then known as 'Kleinkrieg' or 'petite guerre', and conducted chiefly by special units of the regular forces – achieved an effectiveness previously unknown both as a means of territorial expansion and as a form of combat.[2] As a result of the new forms in which it appeared amid the almost overwhelming intensity of the revolutionary and Napoleonic wars, guerrilla war, the 'people's war', gained increasing importance. Ultimately it became a weighty component of warfare in general that could even make its contribution to the 'absolute' character of war.

Clausewitz experienced the collapse of Prussia in 1806–7, the following period of French occupation, and the subsequent wars of independence, as well as the campaign of 1812 in Russia. These experiences introduced him to the new guerrilla warfare, the 'people's war'. He closely observed the practice of this form of armed conflict in Europe, for example, as it appeared in the fighting at Vendee, the Tyrolean uprising of 1809, and particularly the events of the Spanish insurrection from 1808 on. Clausewitz lectured on small-scale warfare at the *Allgemeine Kriegsschule* (War College) during the years 1810 and 1811; in these lectures, he sought to draw a realistic picture of the practice of guerrilla warfare, both to instruct his listeners and to clarify its principles for himself.[3] In addition, during the campaign of 1812, Clausewitz became an eyewitness to partisan warfare as it was conducted by the Russian population against Napoleon's Grande Armee.

Writing as a Prussian patriot and reformer, he produced the well-known 'Bekenntnisdenkschrift' – statement of conviction or memorial of confession – in the spring of 1812. Here he thoroughly dealt with the topic of the people's war against the French occupational forces, addressing this topic thematically as well as with reference to its combat-technical aspects.[4]

Thus it became apparent to Clausewitz that in his work *On War* he had to consider guerrilla warfare ('the people in arms'): he had to analyze it, determine its relationship to other types of warfare and, from this perspective, determine its actual importance in the modern system of war.

II. GUERRILLA WARFARE IN CLAUSEWITZ' WRITINGS

(1) Clausewitz' Conception and Description of Guerrilla War

Since it cannot be determined exactly when Clausewitz began his study of guerrilla warfare, the academy lectures on small-scale warfare present a starting-point. These lectures must be understood in their relation to the especially urgent situation in Prussia. Guerrilla warfare was at that time the focus for hopes of liberation from French rule. To both government and military reformers, a people's war in the form of guerrilla war appeared more important than the so-called large-scale war.[5] They viewed the guerrilla war eventually to be conducted as springing from the same political and social roots as military and governmental reform. (So Gneisenau indicates in his studies of the popular uprisings of 1808 and 1811.)[6]

In his 'Lectures on Small-scale Warfare',[7] Clausewitz gives an overview of this form of warfare which he distinguishes from large-scale warfare by the sheer number of operating troop units: 'Small-scale warfare is to be defined', he wrote, 'as the use of small troop units in the field. Engagements of 20, 50, 100 or 300, 400 men, if they are not part of a greater action, belong to the small-scale war'.[8] Clausewitz develops a tactical-organizational description of small-scale war in detail, basing it upon historical as well as contemporary examples. One recent example is the outpost skirmish in north-western Germany (in the territory of Gronau-Bentheim-Schuttorf-Gildehaus) as conducted by Scharnhorst's together with allied troops against the French.[9] Clausewitz also analyzes the writings of leading small-scale warfare theorists and practitioners of the eighteenth century and revolutionary era, such as Johann von Ewald, Andreas Emmerich, and Scharnhorst.

When Clausewitz depicts the combat form of the small-scale war, in light of specific military aspects, he does not consider political and social impulses and pre-conditions. It is precisely the subject matter of the *Kriegsschule*, a military technical establishment, with which he deals. By systematically discussing all essential technical forms of combat in this area (outpost duty, surprise attack, reconnaissance, retreat, defense, and other activities), he presents the tactics of guerrilla warfare didactically, so that members of the regular armed forces can assimilate them. At the same time, Clausewitz, with this analysis of 'Kleinkrieg', laid some groundwork for his discussion of 'Volkskrieg' in the later work *On War*.

(2) Guerrilla War in Clausewitz' 'Bekenntnisdenkschrift'

In his 'Bekenntnisdenkschrift' (statement of conviction or memorial of confession) from the spring of 1812, Clausewitz goes beyond his lectures, perceiving guerrilla war as a general uprising, as a people's war of liberation or resistance. From this standpoint, he establishes what is more important, the *context* of this form of combat. The 'Bekenntnisdenkschrift' considers the will to liberate Prussia from the French occupational forces as the foundation and pre-condition for armed resistance. It goes on to develop the suitable form of armed conflict based on these political circumstances and objectives: that is, a general uprising (*Volkskrieg*) using the techniques of guerrilla war (*Kleinkrieg*).

Specially, Clausewitz gives concrete directions for organizing and deploying the militia in the Mittelmark. In this context, he also speaks of the possibilities and limitations of terror, arguing that, if one believes 'the enemy would, through the inhuman treatment of the captive insurgents with the death penalty, etc', demoralize the rebels, we must consider 'repaying atrocity with atrocity, violence with violence! It will be a simple matter for us to outdo the enemy and lead him back into the boundaries of self-control and humanity'.[10]

The use of guerrilla tactics in a war which is a general uprising is discussed quite practically in the 'Bekenntnisdenkschrift', which, moreover, Clausewitz first gave to Gneisau for appraisal.[11] Almost in the form of field-service regulations, Clausewitz outlines the combat forms of guerrilla warfare, its diverse possibilities, and its forms of appearance; he also regards the territorial reserve and militia as popular contingents that reinforce the regular military forces.[12] Finally, Clausewitz presents some theoretical reflections on the nature of defense (tactical and strategical) and thereby introduces guerrilla warfare into the general theory of war. In conclusion, he calls the popular uprising (using the means of guerrilla warfare) a major means of salvation ('Rettungsmittel'). As a 'natural expression of national forces melded together',[13] guerrilla war is, for Clausewitz, 'the last and desperate resort'.

Thus, it is clear that Clausewitz, before his final work *On War* was completed, had achieved virtually clear ideas of the organization, combat technique, possibilities and limits, socio-political importance, and military-theoretical assessment of modern guerrilla war. He viewed it as an essential manifestation of comprehensive and effective resistance by the people.

(3) Clausewitz' view of Guerrilla War ('The People in Arms') in On War

Clausewitz dedicated a short chapter, entitled 'The People in Arms', to guerrilla war. He placed this chapter under 'Defense' in the larger scheme of the sixth book.[14] In this chapter, Clausewitz deals with both the practical and the theoretical aspects of a popular uprising. He considers its many forms and conditions and simultaneously incorporates it into his general theory of war as a particular and effective element; thus he was the first to include guerrilla warfare in the context of modern military theory. In this discussion, Clausewitz established new criteria for this type of armed conflict, using critical-realistic analysis and systematization. These criteria extend beyond the merely pragmatic, instructional treatment of the subject by illuminating the phenomenon of guerrilla war as well as its structures.[15] Modestly Clausewitz emphasizes that in his exposition he is merely 'groping for the truth', rather than making 'an objective analysis, because this sort of warfare is not as yet very common; those who have been able to observe it for any length of time have not reported enough about it'.[16]

In his examination of guerrilla war, Clausewitz does not proceed from political, economic, or social pre-conditions; rather, as he expressly emphasizes, he wants to shed light on it 'simply as a means to combat, thus in its relationship to the enemy'. At the same time, he perceptively recognizes the broader context; that is, he sees this form of war 'in general as an outgrowth of the way in which the conventional barriers have been swept away in our lifetime by the elemental violence of war. It is in fact a broadening and intensification of the fermentation process known as war. The system of requisitioning, the enormous growth of armies resulting from it and from universal conscription, the employment of the militia' would all lead in the direction of the general uprising.[17] Clausewitz is unconcerned with ethical judgments of this type of warfare; he does not know 'whether mankind at large will gain by this further expansion of the element of war; a question to which the answer should be the same as to the question of war itself. We shall leave both to the philosophers.'[18]

Under the topic of arming the people, Clausewitz first pinpoints the moral impulse of the guerrilla fighters as essential to the general uprising. He also establishes the conditions surrounding the resistance of an entire armed population. The resistance itself should be divided; the greater the surface area of the country the greater will be the contact with enemy forces, and, thus, the greater the potential effect of a guerrilla war. This could, in time, destroy the 'basic foundations of the enemy forces'. Furthermore, the guerrilla bands would have to work together with regular forces towards a unifying, all-encompassing plan – a necessity which Frederick Engels also was to advocate.

Clausewitz then lists five conditions required for the effectiveness of a general uprising:

1. the war must be fought in the interior of the country;
2. it must not be decided by a single stroke of the enemy ('Katastrophe');
3. the theater of operations must constitute a 'considerable region';
4. the national character must be suited to this type of armed confrontation;
5. the terrain must be rough and inaccessible because of mountains, forests, swamps, or 'the local methods of cultivation'.

The operations of the guerrilla units, whether militia or bands of inhabitants, should always take place just outside the theater of war where the enemy forces do not appear in strength. On the 'edges', as Clausewitz writes, the popular contingents would function the most effectively and would carry the remaining population along with them: 'The flames will spread like a brush fire, until they reach the area on which the enemy is based, threatening his lines of communication and his very existence.'[19]

A popular uprising is, in Clausewitz' eyes, certainly not an all-powerful, 'inexhaustible, invincible' element; on the other hand, armed forces could not command armed peasants to surrender as they would an opposing division of regular soldiers. These peasants would easily scatter and get in position to renew their attacks on marching columns at any time. (Here Clausewitz compares the reaction of regular troops to the actions of guerrilla fighters with that of a robot to a human being.) In the end, the flame of the guerrilla war will be fanned by fights conducted by small, at first rather weak, bands who will in time gain strength to destroy the enemy. Clausewitz describes the nature of guerrilla war with words that are in some aspects still applicable today: A general uprising should be 'nebulous and elusive; its resistance should never materialize as a concrete body, otherwise the enemy can direct sufficient force at its core, crush it, and take many prisoners. When that happens, the people will lose heart and, believing that the issue has been decided and further efforts would be useless, drop their weapons.' Nevertheless, the guerrilla units must assemble themselves in certain positions and deal effective blows. Moreover, the commander should not distribute too many regular combat forces along the guerrilla units; this would lead to an extended defense line that would be vulnerable at all points. In addition, the presence of too many regular troops would not be conducive to the fighting morale of the inhabitants.

Clausewitz emphasizes that although a general uprising should certainly be regarded as an important strategic means of defense, guerrilla units must not turn into a fixed defense. Rather, their commander must remain flexible and, according to circumstances, defend points of access to a mountain area, or the dikes across a marsh, or points at which a river can be crossed, as long as this appears possible. In order to escape destruction at the hands of a superior enemy, the popular contingents should plan to scatter early enough to continue their resistance by means of surprise attacks from another position.

Finally Clausewitz incorporates guerrilla warfare (arming the people) into the general plan of strategic defense: it could be either the last resort after a defeat or the natural auxiliary before a decisive battle. In this context, he speaks of a retreat into the interior of the country and concludes the following: No matter how decisive the defeat experienced by a government, arming the people will remain the last means of salvation. 'The people's war' will become actively effective precisely upon the invasion of the victors – a thought that indeed finds verification in the events of the Second World War (for example, the German invasions of Yugoslavia and the USSR).

III. CLAUSEWITZ' VIEWS ON GUERRILLA WAR ASSESSED

Clausewitz' studies of guerrilla warfare, 'the people's war', show that he appropriately incorporated this form of armed conflict into military theory. In his treatment of the subject, he developed certain structures through analyzing the relationships between theory and practice. In other words, Clausewitz did not write a textbook or practical instructions for action in guerrilla war. He did, however, through his purely observational methods, make an assessment of the decisive value of this combat form that is still relevant today.[20]

As is true throughout *On War*, Clausewitz' philosophical-logical-dialectical method, leads to a balanced, many-sided, and realistic assessment of the phenomenon of guerrilla war. It is characteristic of Clausewitz' approach that he gives guerrilla war its own profile, its own specific dimensions, but never makes it an absolute in itself by viewing it as an isolated phenomenon. Rather, guerrilla war can only be understood in the larger political-strategic context. As part of a general strategy, it will fully develop its potential strength.

An investigation of the nature, function, possibilities, and limitations of guerrilla warfare – either in history or in the present day – cannot ignore Clausewitz. His work *On War* may contribute to the further development of a modern, comprehensive, and philosophically-founded theory of guerrilla warfare.

NOTES

1. See Carl von Clausewitz, *De la Guerra* (Havana: Ciencias Politicas, 1975): 'La concepcion dialectica de Clausewitz hace De la Guerra un libro clasico de constante actualidad .... En sus paginas discurren no solamente las concepciones convencionales de la guerra, sino, tambien la luche en las montanas, el germen de la guerrilla.' ('The dialectical conception of Clausewitz makes *On War* a classic book with contemporary appeal. In his pages one finds not only the conceptions of conventional war, but also, warfare as it takes place in the mountains, guerrilla warfare.')
2. In this context, see, among others, Werner Hahlweg, 'Preussische Reformzeit und revolutionarer Krieg', Supplement 18d. *Wehrwissenschaftliche Rundschau* (1962), 9ff.
3. 'Meine Vorlesungen uber den kleinem Krieg, gehalten auf der Kriegs-Schule 1810 und 1811', in Werner Hahlweg (ed.), *Carl von Clausewitz, Schriften–Aufsatze–Studien–Briefe* (Göttingen: Vandenhoeck & Ruprecht, 1966), Vol. 1, pp. 205–588.
4. 'Bekenntnisdenkschrift', in Hahlweg, op. cit., pp. 682–750.
5. Hahlweg, 'Preussische Reformzeit', 53ff.
6. Neidhard von Gneisenau, in Fritz Lange (ed.), *Schriften von und uber Gneisenau* (Berlin: Rutten & Loening, 1954), pp. 31ff, 233ff., 'Gneisenau – der Freischarler'.
7. See note 3.
8. 'Meine Vorlesungen uber den kleinem Krieg', op. cit., p. 231.
9. See also Hemann Buschleb, *Scharnhorst in Westfalen. Politik, Administration und Kommando im Schicksalsjahr 1795* (Herford: Mittler, 1979).
10. 'Bekenntnisdenkschrift', pp. 133ff.
11. Ibid., pp. 681f.
12. See in this context also M. Blumental, *Der Preussische Landsturm von 1913* (Berlin: R. Schroeder, 1900).
13. 'Bekenntnisdenkschrift', p. 750.
14. Hahlweg, *Clausewitz*, Vol. 2, pp. 799–806. The English version appears as Ch. 26 of Book VI, *On War*, ed. and trans. Michael Howard and Peter Paret (Princeton: Princeton University Press, 1976), pp. 479–83. Citations below are to the German version.
15. See also Vol. 2, p. 356.
16. Ibid., Vol. 2, p. 805.
17. Ibid., Vol. 2, p. 799.
18. Ibid., Vol. 2, p. 800.
19. Ibid., Vol. 2, p. 802.
20. Ibid., Vol. 1, p. 350.

Space and Time in *On War*

HAROLD W. NELSON

While considerations of space and time in Carl von Clausewitz' *On War* are sophisticated and filled with implications for modern soldiers, Clausewitz did not see these factors as the central elements in his theory of war: '... [A]lthough the equation of time and space does underlie everything else, and is, so to speak, the daily bread of strategy, it is neither the most difficult nor the decisive factor.'[1] Clausewitz asserted that the truly decisive factor was the personality of a commander in his interaction with the enemy – that commander's ability to appraise the opponent accurately, to energize his own force for rapid movement and bold attack, and to risk that force in the uncertainties of decisive battle.

> Let us admit that boldness in war even has its own prerogatives. It must be granted a certain power over and above successful calculations involving space, time, and magnitude of forces, for wherever it is superior, it will take advantage of its opponent's weakness. In other words, it is a genuinely creative force. (p. 190)

In fact, his contemporaries' tendency to focus upon such easily-measured factors as space and time and to formulate universal dicta based upon the geometric relationships resulting from this focus inspired Clausewitz' contempt:

> ... critics usually exclude all moral factors from strategic theory, and only examine material factors. They reduce everything to a few mathematical formulas of equilibrium and superiority, of time and space, limited by a few angles and lines. If they were really all, it would hardly provide a scientific problem for a schoolboy.'[2] (p. 178)

We would be justified if we read *On War* as an antidote to such simple-mindedness.

But it is not an antidote that rejects the calculation of space and time in military endeavors. Instead, these factors become important foundation stones in a theory of war that transcends them, and when we study Clausewitz' treatment of space and time in *On War*, we soon discover that he had mastered these fundamentals. Both that mastery and the subordinate role played by space and time in his theory can be illustrated by considering one of his concrete examples. When Clausewitz introduces the concept of friction (Book I, Chapter 7), he uses the example of a traveler who, late in the day, decides to cover two more stages of his journey before stopping for the evening. The traveler is supplied with poor horses, and he encounters hilly country and bad roads. Night falls and darkness further impedes his progress. Time passes quickly, and space cannot be conquered (p. 119). But Clausewitz is not interested in calculating the number of stages one ought to travel in a day or the time at which a traveler should make his final decision to proceed. He transcends the space–time relationship to discuss friction, a notion central to his theory of war that provides insight into far more than space–time considerations.

Whether using space–time combinations to illustrate a point, or writing of time in the absolute or relative sense, or considering space as the commander's friend or foe, Clausewitz was careful in his definitions, astute in his observations, and provocative in his generalizations. Since Clausewitz treated space and time as foundation stones, he set them in place wherever they would help support his theory, and thus he scattered references to them throughout the text. This article gathers those foundation stones together, examines their structure and use in *On War*, and contemplates their utility for today's military theorist.

I. CONSIDERATIONS OF SPACE AS A FACTOR IN WAR

Clausewitz accepted the abstract definition of space as an array of single undifferentiated points (p. 514) and showed no interest in philosophical discussions of the abstraction. Throughout his work he moves away from this generalized abstraction toward the relationship between warfare and *terrain*:

> The relationship, to begin with, is *a permanent factor* – so much so that one cannot conceive of a regular army operating except in a definite space. Second, its importance is *decisive in the highest degree*, for it affects the operations of all forces, and at times entirely alters them. Third, its influence may be felt in the *very smallest feature of the ground*, but it can also dominate *enormous areas*. (p. 109; his emphasis)

This emphasis on space as terrain rather than mere undifferentiated area is fundamental to Clausewitz' approach. He recognized that war in the Napoleonic era had stretched into terrain that would have rendered large-scale combat impossible in earlier times, but he also recognized that the increased flexibility of armies which had allowed this development had placed increased demands on commanders.[3] According to Clausewitz the commander's space-related problems were compounded by the increased size of the armies that could be brought to bear in all sorts of terrain. The lengthening line of battle that resulted would stretch the command abilities of the most gifted general to the limit. Increased scale, flexibility, and versatility of armies combined to place a greater premium on the commander's skill in decision '... at those points where strategy and tactics meet – in other words, where general deployment of armies passes into actual disposition for battle' (p. 293).

The relationship between the commander and the space in which he must operate was generally a hostile one, in Clausewitz' view. At one point Clausewitz called space the commander's 'partner', but a partner that could never be fully known (p. 109). More often, space must be overcome. It is at best a puzzle to be solved and at worst an insuperable obstacle to success. Conquering space through rapid movement will wear down an army, whether it moves to attack or defend, and Clausewitz explicitly rejected

> ... bombastic theories that hold that the most overwhelming surprise, the fastest movement or the most restless activity cost nothing; that these are rich mines which lie unused because of the general's indulgence. The final product may indeed be compared to that of gold and silver mines: one looks at the end result and forgets to ask about the cost of the labor that went into it. (p. 322; see also p. 324)

The adversarial relationship between the commander and the space in which he must operate was even more clearly delineated when Clausewitz considered the problem facing the defender. According to Clausewitz, the simplest course of action for this commander would be to concentrate his army and then strike the decisive blow against the aggressor at the place and time of his choosing. Why is this so seldom done? 'Since one cannot concentrate land as one can an army, it will be necessary to divide the army in order to defend the land' (p. 485). The need to adjust the army to the space to be defended while conforming with the enemy's actions resulted in conflicting interests: 'One, *possession of the country*, tends to disperse the fighting forces; the other, *a stroke at the center of gravity of the enemy's forces*, tends, in some degree, to keep them concentrated' (p. 486; his emphasis).

Because Clausewitz did not abstract space but appreciated it as terrain with intrinsic value to the political authorities as well as their military defenders, he was able to analyze that value clearly. From the military perspective, the broadest definition of space was the 'base of operations ... the local resources, depots at various points, and the area from which supplies are drawn. These [last] three factors are spatially distinct: they cannot be reduced to one' (p. 342). This complex formulation, which he

later calls 'the three tiers of the infrastructure' (p. 342), obviously was
developed in opposition to the reductionist approaches of some of
Clausewitz' contemporaries who would have abstracted the concept of
the base of operations into a set of points, lines, and angles. Since the
local resources are scattered unevenly throughout the area in which
the army operates, they can neither be concentrated nor represented
by a simple abstraction. Depots are truly 'spatially distinct' from these
local resources, because they can be represented as points and analyzed
separately or collectively within the context of terrain and forces available. The area from which supplies are drawn (today we might say 'the
rear' or 'the zone of the interior') is also 'spatially distinct', separated from
the area occupied by the army by some distance but connected by the lines
of communication. If, for a given army, these lines are short, the depots
are numerous and full, and the local area is richly-provisioned, that army
will enjoy the best possible arrangement. But Clausewitz obviously
understood something that other students of war often overlooked –
variation in each of these spatial relationships had to be considered
separately in each instance. This requirement could not be met by
reductionist geometricians.

Once the 'base of operations' concept is understood, Clausewitz' other
spatial concepts follow naturally. The first of these is the 'theater of
operations', which, in his interpretation, flows directly from the conflicting interests described above (possess the country *vs* strike the enemy's
center of gravity). As a result of this tension,

> A country and the forces stationed there are divided in such a way
> that any decision obtained by the main force in a particular theater
> directly affects the whole and carries everything along with it ... [A]
> theater of war, be it large or small, and the forces stationed there, no
> matter what their size, represent the sort of unity in which a *single*
> center of gravity can be identified. That is the place where the
> decision should be reached; a victory at that point is in its fullest
> sense identical with the theater of operations.[4] (pp. 486–873; his
> emphasis)

Combining this definition of the theater with the definition of the base
allows us to discern the ideal relationship Clausewitz saw between the use
of force at the national (or coalition) level and the deployment of the
armies that composed that force. By analyzing the nature of the 'three
tiers of the infrastructure' the strategist could determine the size of the
armies that should operate in each area. These appropriately-sized armies
could then concentrate against the single center of gravity within the
theater. Viewed from the highest level, the forces would be fragmented to

defend the country. But at the theater level forces would be concentrated[5] (pp. 159–60).

Clausewitz' last spatial concept addresses the way in which the army occupies its theater of operations. Even though it is to be concentrated for action against the enemy's center of gravity, this does not mean that the army was to be packed into a small space. Battlefield experience had taught Clausewitz the importance of adequate reconnaissance and security, and he advocated using a vanguard as the army's 'strategic eyes' (p. 299). The remainder of the army, whether on the march or in camp, would remain within mutual supporting distance – to be calculated using considerations of both time and space and therefore considered in some detail in a subsequent section of this article.

All three of Clausewitz' spatial concepts are straightforward. His treatment of the base of operations included some novel approaches to that feature of warfare, reflecting his attempt to counter other theoreticians' approaches while trying to interpret the importance of the base in Napoleonic operations. The ideas he formulated work well for the warfare he described and, with the exception of the local supply aspect of his base of operations concept, can be applied to good purpose to modern warfare. Some might argue that the conflict between concentration and dispersion in the defense has changed radically with industrialization of warfare, but the appearance of large armies with longer-range weapons has changed only the tactical complexion of the battlefield – it has not resolved the conflict facing the strategist that Clausewitz described.

II. CONSIDERATIONS OF TIME AS A FACTOR IN WAR

In war, space is contested but time is shared. The same minutes tick away for both adversaries. Clausewitz' ability to analyze the implication of this simple truth is one of his enduring contribution to our understanding of war. While his discussions of space were straightforward and seldom abstract, his thoughts on time are more challenging. In his simplest considerations of time, for example, the notion of the vanguard trading space for time, he manages to interject more sophisticated allusions to time: '[The advanced corps] is never intended to stop the enemy's movements, but rather, like the weight of a pendulum, to moderate and regulate them so as to make them calculable' (p. 311). This is not meant to suggest that Clausewitz sought to reduce military problems to clockwork precision or simplicity. But he saw time as a factor in virtually every problem set for a commander, and he advocated appreciation of this time factor as an important part of the solution. In the simple example cited above, the essence of his general view on time can be discerned: the defender *must* delay the decisive moment – time favors him. If we keep time's bias before us, the twists and turns of Clausewitz' thoughts on time become less confusing.

Time's inherent bias in favor of the defender is one of the key factors which makes the defense stronger than the attack: '... time which is allowed to pass unused accumulates to the credit of the defender. He reaps where he did not sow. Any omission of attack – whether from bad judgment, fear, or indolence – accrues to the defender's benefit' (p. 357). The defender's use of time granted to him by the attacker's delay can include military preparations (which are inherently less time-consuming for the defender) (pp. 198, 489), but Clausewitz' primary emphasis on the advantage inherent in this passage of time is at the political level:

> ... the aim of the defense must embody the idea of waiting – which is after all its leading feature. The idea implies, moreover, that the situation can develop, that in itself it may improve, which is to say that if improvement cannot be effected from within – that is, by sheer resistance – it can only come from without; and an improvement from without implies a change in the political situation. Either additional allies come to the defender's help or allies begin to desert his enemy. (p. 613)

At the political level, Clausewitz explicitly ascribed the defender's advantages in the use of time to psychological forces that favor the weaker side. 'Envy, jealousy, anxiety, and sometimes even generosity are the natural advocates of the unsuccessful' (p. 597). These cause the aggressor's allies to reconsider their commitment while rallying other states to the side of the threatened power. Frederick the Great's good fortune in the Seven Years War (Russia's withdrawal upon Elizabeth's death) supported this view, as did the shifting allegiances of states in the Napoleonic period.

As he moved from the political level to the strategic/operational, Clausewitz used the psychological strengths of the leader as his transition to the mechanistic use of time in the conduct of military operations. He asserts that the natural state of war is tension and destruction while the natural state of man is indecision and repose. The leader must apply his energy to overcome these natural tendencies. (pp. 228–9; 571; 597) The imperfect energizing of the material and spiritual means of war helps to explain the way in which time is used (or wasted) in war.

In Clausewitz' ideal state of war, antagonists would move with utmost rapidity (because of the attacker's determination) to a single, decisive battle. With forces concentrated in time and space, all would be determined in a climactic clash of wills. If the attacker overextended in seeking victory, the defender would strike a mortal blow with his remaining forces. If not, the attacker would emerge victorious (pp. 84–7). But

Clausewitz recognized that warriors and their political masters did not pursue victory with such abandon: 'War moves on its goal with varying speeds; but it always lasts long enough for influence to be exerted on the goal and for its own course to be changed one way or another – long enough, in other words, to remain subject to the actions of a superior intelligence' (p. 87). By slowing the pace – using time more cautiously – decision-makers gained time necessary to interpret actions on the battle-field and to modify plans and objectives accordingly. Slowing the pace also gave the generals tactical leeway:

> The slower the progress and the more frequent the interruptions of military action the easier it is to retrieve a mistake, the bolder will be the general's assessments, and the more likely he will be to avoid theoretical extremes and base his plans on probability and inference. Any given situation requires that probabilities be calculated in the light of circumstances, and the amount of time available for such calculations will depend on the pace with which operations are taking place. (p. 85)

Since the defense can afford to accept these natural tendencies to slow the pace while the offense *must* move with alacrity, this inherent relationship to the use of time is a part of the defense's relative strength in Clausewitz' interpretation of the offense/defense relationship (pp. 85–7).

Clausewitz explained the accelerated pace of war in his era by assert-ing that the periods of inaction would be inversely proportional to the tensions that led to war and the consequent war effort (p. 85). Thus Napoleonic warfare – in contrast to that of the early eighteenth century – had been characterized by extreme tension, maximum war effort, and short periods of inaction. Of course Napoleon's ability to exercise his will through large offensive operations kept this tension at unbearable levels: he maintained the accelerated pace by unleashing societal forces as well as through the actions of his armies.

As the consummate master of the military art, Napoleon seems to have been the inspiration for Clausewitz' thoughts on concentrating forces in time. In his short chapter on this subject, Clausewitz differentiated between the implications of prolonged action at the strategic and tactical level. A long engagement weakens the forces involved through simple physical exhaustion, and the wise commander offsets this natural course of events by feeding fresh forces into the fray at the appropriate moment[6] (p. 209). The modern battle array, whether offensive or defensive, gave the tactical commander the flexibility necessary to develop the situation, withstand the initial shock, and then make the decisive moves.[7] The master tactician would take advantage of this organizational flexibility, and array his forces so that he had time to act with maximum effect after his opponent was decisively engaged.

But to use the same approach toward the use of time at the strategic level would be folly, in Clausewitz' view:

> ... [I]t cannot be the intent of the strategist to make an ally of time *for its own sake*, by committing forces gradually, step by step ... all forces intended and available for a strategic purpose should be applied *simultaneously*; their employment will be the more effective the more everything can be concentrated [in] a single action at a single moment.[8] (p. 209; his emphasis)

Strategic advantage generally could not be achieved by gradual application of force designed to prolong the conflict. This fundamental difference in the use of time at the tactical and strategic/operational level is often overlooked in Clausewitz.

The relative use of time is another aspect that is somewhat elusive in *On War*. As indicated at the beginning of this section, time is shared by the antagonists in war. Since both are simultaneously trying to impose their wills upon the other, the one who can make better use of time gains the advantage. As we have seen, this apparently simple concept is complicated by the asymmetrical relationship between offense and defense and the differing force–time relationship at the tactical and strategic levels. But Clausewitz never lost sight of it, and his awareness of the relative use of time in plan and execution is one of the features of his approach to military theory that sets it apart from other efforts and contributes to its durable appeal. Unlike those who were fascinated by geometrical approaches to strategic problems, Clausewitz recalled that the enemy would be calculating odds, shifting forces, and implementing his own plans while the strategist put his scheme in operation. As a result, he cautioned that available time must always be considered, and complex plans that took too long to mature must be avoided. And 'too long' was measured in terms of the enemy's ability to act as well as react, a feature of military operations too often overlooked by the aspiring strategist (p. 228).

Developing plans that would bring force to bear faster than the enemy could react was not a sufficient condition for success, in Clausewitz' view. As he repeated so often, the force involved had to have adequate weight at the decisive point. He cautioned against simplistic analogies from physics, rejecting the notion that a small force applied over a longer time could have the same effect as a large force over a short time (p. 597). Mass and velocity were keys to success, but once we introduce the notion of velocity we are considering space and time together – a combination requiring a different perspective.

In the pure consideration of time, Clausewitz made wise use of a foundation stone that is usually overlooked. Time as the key to the strength of the defense runs through all of his discussion of the subject, but modern readers discussing the relative strength of the offense and defense usually couch their arguments in terms of technology and tactics. Neither of these considerations transcend time as a factor separating attacker and defender, and to miss this fundamental point in *On War* is to miss much of its continued relevance.

III. SPACE AND TIME CONSIDERED TOGETHER AS A FACTOR IN WAR

One of the durable images of Napoleon captures him hunched over his map, dividers in hand, considering the concentration of his armies and the movements of his foe. The day's march separating the points of his dividers is a space–time abstraction that he and his pupils had mastered. Simply knowing how far an infantry division or cavalry regiment could march in a day was nothing new, but synchronizing those movements to make the best possible use of all available roads to reach an agreed-upon point with full combat power at the ready was truly an art.[9] Clausewitz appreciated mastery of the art as one of the basic prerequisites for successful command, but he discerned changes in war that rendered application of that art more difficult. In the eighteenth century, the size of the force available to an enemy commander was relatively small and could be calculated with some assurance. In addition, the rate of movement of this known force was predictable. But the mobilizations of the Napoleonic era, together with the rapid movement of large armies, combined to introduce great uncertainty into the calculations (p. 589).

Given the uncertainty in calculations for general campaign situations, Clausewitz selected the special case of river-crossing calculation. These specialized operations provided the proper basis for illustrating this complex art, because one side of the time–space equation was reduced to relative mathematical certainty: the time necessary to bridge the river. Bridge building is engineering – overcoming obstacles in environment, materials, and human nature in order to execute a preconceived plan. This is an interactive, 'friction-filled' activity, but the bridgebuilders work to overcome agents subordinate to their will or natural elements. They do not try to impose their will on a thinking, acting enemy. By Clausewitz' definition then, what they do is not 'war' but one of those ancillary activities that more readily lends itself to definitive time–space prediction. The imponderables in bridge-building are formidable, but they pale compared to the imponderables of interacting forces.[10] (pp. 433–4).

So in this simplest case, the defender gauges the time necessary for his opponent to bridge the river as well as the forces he can push across the river by other means until the bridge can be built. Then the defender can position appropriately-sized units at intervals along the river. When the enemy attempts his assault crossing, the defensive force moves to the threatened point in sufficient number, defeats the assault crossing, and prevents completion of the bridge (p. 434).

All of these time–space–strength calculations are appropriate for the theoretician because the enemy's speed and strength can be predicted with some accuracy in this special situation; however, Clausewitz did not think that most situations were so straightforward. Even within this special case he noted that 'the slightest local variation often outweighs the most massive arguments in books' (p. 436), and after beginning a chapter with a mechanic's confidence, he eventually notes so many qualifying factors that he arrives at a generalization:

> It is enough to say that one should not extend one's forces too far, and that, in every case, one must be able to assemble one's troops by the end of the day on which the enemy has crossed. This principle will take the place of all further discussion about time, strength and space, which depend on a variety of local factors. (p. 440)

This 'principle' reminds us that Clausewitz thought of space as terrain, and 'local factors' helped him resist the temptation to develop abstract generalizations. But the other 'local factor' that seems to have deterred him in all situations other than river crossings was the size of the enemy force that might be encountered. His experience with Napoleon taught him that his force might be surprisingly large. He advocated deploying forces capable of independent action and keeping those forces within mutually-supporting disance as the proper method to deal with this potential for surprise. 'Mutually-supporting distance' was determined by simple time/space calculations: How long could a unit hold out against superior odds? How long would the supporting unit require to come to its aid? As long as the latter time was smaller than the former, the units were in mutual support, and tactical miscalculation or surprise could not result in strategic disaster (pp. 315–17).

Clausewitz' strategic consideration of time and space was primarily directed toward selection of the time and place for the decisive battle. The notion of trading space for time was nothing new, and his participation with the Russian army in the campaign of 1812 had given him first-hand experience in this technique. He recognized that fighting the main battle later, and deeper in enemy territory, increased its decisiveness (p. 624), but his fundamental theoretical approach stressed the difficulties the attacker would face as he tried to project adequate combat power deep into the enemy's country (pp. 93–5, 499). Allusions to this relationship between the decisive battle, time, and space are scattered throughout *On*

War, always reflecting the general notion of the 'culminating point' – the point of equilibrium reached by an attacker beyond which he lacks sufficient strength to continue offensive action against the defender. Aggressors who pass this point risk disaster, and defenders who await this moment to launch their counter-offensive enjoy the promise of great success (p. 572).

In this concept of the culminating point we see Clausewitz' fundamental attitude toward the role of time and space in modern war: these factors are important and must be calculated with the best possible precision. But a discerning commander is required who can translate calculations into action. The attacking commander who resists the forces that dissipate and erode his army will move the culminating point forward in time and space. The defender who can will his exhausted forces to counter-attack an even more exhausted attacker who has passed the culminating point should reap the fruits of decisive victory. In every case, space and time have different effects on the two sides, and the active use that each commander makes of them could tell in the outcome.

IV. SUBSEQUENT APPRECIATIONS OF SPACE AND TIME IN MILITARY THEORY

Considerations of space and time along the lines of Clausewitz' *On War* are relatively rare in subsequent theoretical writing. Mechanistic measurement of the parameters is not unusual, but one seldom finds them linked to the commander's will and differentiated with respect to the attacker and the defender.

Of course the elder Moltke considered time and space in the Clausewitzian manner. As early as 1860 (in his 'Memorial Number 3'), his calculations for a possible war with France reflect the same appreciation of time, space, and the commander's will that we encounter in *On War*. Calculating the time necessary to generate the forces necessary for defense in the vicinity of Frankfurt, he then posits the additional force necessary to assume the offensive and calculates the time necessary to concentrate those forces.

> If we once have our fighting forces together then we may expect to be equal, with God's help and our own means, to any French attack. Our only danger lies in *time* conditions. We must not hide the fact from ourselves that France can easily surprise us strategically. We must not await the enemy's initiative.[11]

We see echoes of Clausewitz in awareness of the importance of making active use of time on the offensive, and in the pervasive sense that the application of superior willpower should be the key to capitalizing on the time/space/force calculations.

The major application of the Clausewitzian approach to time/space appreciations in the nineteenth century was in the *Kriegsspiel*. Players were expected to make careful considerations of time and space in deploying and employing their forces. The inherent uncertainty in war was embodied in various Monte Carlo techniques, and fundamental emphasis was placed on the commander's will – his decisions and orders.[12] The relationship of time to outcome was especially close to Clausewitz' views, for the mechanistic system of moves made time naturally side with the defender and seriously penalized the attacker for inaction.

In 1877, when the war game was beginning to catch the attention of the faculty at the US Military Academy,[13] the Superintendent, Major-General Schofield, aligned himself with those 'impartial observers' who had concluded that war is a game of chance, and charged his audience of military professionals with reducing the chance in war to the lowest achievable level by learning to foresee and estimate all possible factors influencing outcomes. Drawing on his Civil War experience, and working in the theoretical framework of *Kriegsspiel*, he presented an operational narrative stressing the importance of time as the underlying factor against which staying power, marching speed, and coordinated action must be measured. Throughout, the will of the commander played a significant part in determining the outcome.[14] Like most others at West Point, he probably had not read Clausewitz, but the 'German Methods' had made him a Clausewitzian in this.

John Bigelow was another American who stumbled into a Clausewitzian appreciation of time and space – even though he applied it in a geometric framework that would make a von Bulow proud. He asserted, '... in war the all-important element is time', and he focused on the interactive nature of the use of both time and space:

> Every operation of strategy consists essentially in a movement upon an objective under one of the three following conditions:
> 1. The enemy is moving upon the same objective, in which case we have a race.
> 2. The enemy is covering the objective, in which case we have a maneuver.
> 3. The enemy is himself the objective, in which case we have a simple advance or pursuit, according as the enemy stands his ground or retires.[15]

But he ignored the importance of *will*, thus settling comfortably into lines, angles, and other arcane calculations that negate his mastery of the other features of Clausewitz' approach to time and space.

Writing in the same decade, an American who undoubtedly had read his Clausewitz put it correctly in his theoretical work:

> In modern war strategical combinations will generally depend for their successful execution upon questions of time. The army which can mobilize, concentrate and strike before the other is ready, can, usually, by keeping the initiative, push its strategical combinations to a successful issue, one after the other.[16]

He recognized the attacker's need to *push* against the impediments of space and the enemy to overcome the disadvantage of time. Few twentieth-century theoreticians have done much more with this aspect of Clausewitz' theory.[17]

V. CLAUSEWITZIAN CONCEPTS OF SPACE AND TIME IN CONTEMPORARY US ARMY DOCTRINE

While Clausewitz earns praise for particularizing space as terrain, current US Army doctrine must be faulted for not generalizing terrain into space. FM100-5, *Operations*,[18] provides detailed guidance on analyzing and using terrain, but it totally lacks Clausewitz' sense of the cumulative effect of terrain. What happens to an army that must spread its defense over large areas? That must attack an enemy willing to retire to the interior of his country? That must garrison occupied territory while continuing to operate against main force elements? If none of these things have changed since Clausewitz' time, we can find some answers in *On War*, but we will find no answers in current doctrine. Terrain is addressed at the tactical level, in a fashion suitable for an element fighting an engagement. Terrain remains important at the operational and strategic level, but at those levels we must also be able to think of it as 'space'. Because current US doctrine does not do this, it is basically static, depicting only a fixed image of forces and reflecting no awareness of the space implications of success-ful use of terrain. If the decisive deep battle succeeds, what are the spatial implications for the total force? What is the next step in offensive operations? If the defense is ruptured, what are the variations in com-mander's options imposed by spatial considerations? Appreciation of space in the Clausewitzian sense could be the source of valuable doctrinal insights in the context of modern campaign requirements.

The relationship of time to the offense and the defense posited by Clausewitz is also missing from current US Army doctrine. While the importance of speed in the attack is emphasized, and speed is properly defined relative to the actions of the defender,[19] the need to overcome time's bias in the attack is overlooked, and the need for the commander's will to be fully engaged in pressing the advantage receives only passing attention.[20] Similarly the time advantage in the defense lacks explicit coverage. While the use of the defense to gain time is recognized, the implications are not discussed.[21] As a result, considerations leading to the choice of offense or defense tend to be mechanistic, linked to the mission and forces available. While the doctrine states that offense and defense at the operational level will never be 'pure' because the operational offense will include elements of tactical defense, and vice versa, the dynamic relationship between attack and defense receives no attention. As a result, a reader gains virtually no enlightenment on the factors of time that might influence a commander in choosing the defense, and how time can be used to his benefit.

When we turn our search to considerations of space and time together, we are similarly disappointed. The time/space factor associated with unit deployment is discussed in a section entitled 'Depth', but it is not related to specific offensive or defensive situations.[22]

These missed opportunities to apply Clausewitzian concepts of space and time to current doctrine may stem from the fact that this key manual fails in its promise: 'FM100-5 explains how the Army must conduct campaigns and battles in order to win'.[23] In reality, the manual only discusses battles. The size of these battles, the frontages of the units involved, the distances between the units that would make them mutually supportive, and other key facts about battles that were included in old field service regulations are missing.

This lack of detailed explication of the elements of the battle weakens the text, but the manual's failure to link these generic battles into a campaign is the fatal weakness where space and time are concerned. As most students of modern war would agree, the decisive battle of Napoleon's day has been modified by technology into the linked engagements stretched over time and space that form the essence of a campaign. Clausewitz discerned this tendency, even though he wrote most of his theory with the decisive Napoleonic battle uppermost in his mind[24] (p. 358). Our modern doctrine writers have failed to transcend the battle to describe the campaign, and as a result they have no scope for considerations of time and space. But we can still profitably read Clausewitz alongside the manual, envision the campaign that modern weapons would impose, and flesh out the appropriate appreciations of space and time that we have reviewed here. Technology may have changed speeds and capabilities, but Clausewitz' theoretical considerations are still a valuable source of insight.

NOTES

1. Carl von Clausewitz, *On War*, ed. and trans. by Michael Howard and Peter Paret (Princton, NJ: Princeton University Press, 1976). Subsequent references given in text.
2. The most abstract discussion of spatial implications in *On War* is in Clausewitz' discussion of the nation in arms. He asserts that guerrilla resistance must, by its nature, be spread over a large area and compares its effect to evaporation, becoming more effective as larger surface area is exposed (p. 480). However, this abstract analogy is embedded in a chapter that explicitly recognizes the importance of difficult terrain to the conduct of partisan warfare.
3. 'Articulation', the way in which combatant arms of an army are organized and arrayed, was an important subject in Clausewitz' day and continues to deserve careful attention from the military professional. The subject is peripheral to this study, but Clausewitz asserted that late-eighteenth-century insights into the positioning of cavalry allowed the formation of balanced divisions within an army. Once these homogeneous units had been formed, 'the army ceased to be a monolith and became a many-jointed entity which was pliant and flexible' (p. 293). Given this inherent flexibility of the tool, commanders no longer needed to seek vast unobstructed planes for its application. But of course this proposition cut both ways: commanders who could not recognize and capitalize upon these implications of the new flexibility would be surprised by the ease with which their force could be attacked and destroyed on ground quite unlike the classical battlefield.
4. Elsewhere (p. 280), Clausewitz noted that the theater of operations is normally defined by 'protected boundaries'.
5. Clausewitz does not develop this argument explicitly in these pages, but his discussion of Napoleon's move against Archduke Charles in March 1797, is cast in precisely these terms.
6. The generalized statement on the tactical implications of the duration of an engagement is linked to Clausewitz' image of battle, which he sets forth most clearly on p. 226 with his graphic analogy, '... the battle slowly smolders away, like damp gunpowder'. At the tactical level, he thought in terms of small unit attrition: 'Gradually, the units engaged are burnt out, and when nothing is left but cinders, they are withdrawn and others take their place' (ibid.). This attritional image is reinforced by his comment that, 'Every engagement is a bloody and destructive test of physical and moral strength. ... Whoever has the greater sum of both left at the end is the victor' (p. 231). Similarly, 'losing an engagement is ... like the gradual sinking of a scale' (p. 240).
7. For Clausewitz' thoughts on the battlefield implications of organizational development of the late eighteenth century, see *On War*, pp. 231, 316.
8. See also p. 206: '... [I]n the tactical realm force can be used successively, while strategy knows only the simultaneous use of force'.
9. Modern students of time who comment on military history seem to be confused on this point. The ability to measure time with accurate, portable clocks is not the precondition for synchronized operations in the Napoleonic era. Diurnal measurement was adequate, since the purpose was to bring the army together at an appointed place. Once concentrated it could be fought by sound, voice, and message commands. Refinement of movement planning beyond an estimated day's march had no chance of success when terrain, poor road, and 'friction' made each march a series of obstacles that could consume far more time and energy than any commander might estimate. The brilliant generals could move their forces in marches that stretched capabilities without breaking units' wills. For Clausewitz' generalized calculations, see *On War*, p. 316. Modern students include David S. Landis. See his *Revolution in Time: Clocks and the Making of the Modern World* (Cambridge: Harvard University Press, 1983), pp. 95–6.
10. In this vein, we should note that *On War* does not systematically address siegecraft, where calculations of this type abound. As Jay Luvaas has demonstrated brilliantly (Lecture, U.S. Army War College, September 1984), it was the tendency of other theoreticians to derive their maneuver theory from siege theory that Clausewitz was rejecting. He sought to separate Military Art from Engineering.
11. Helmuth Karl Bernhard von Moltke, *Extracts From Moltke's Correspondence Pertaining to the War of 1870–71* (Ft. Leavenworth: The Army Service Schools Press, 1911), p. 38

(emphasis in the original).

12. Charles Walker Raymond, 'Kriegsspiel: A Paper Read Before the U.S. Military Service Institute' (Ft. Monroe: The Artillery School, 1881).

13. Captain Baring's *Rules for the War Game (Based on the German Model)* was introduced at West Point in 1873, and the first American game, Lieutenant Charles Totten's *Strategos* (New York: D. Appleton and Co., 1880), had been played by Cadets and faculty before it was published.

14. Major-General John M. Schofield, *Introductory Remarks upon the Study of the Science of War* (New York: D. Van Nostrand, 1877), pp. 6–21. Schofield saw technological developments rendering effective use of time more important in modern warfare. He advocated professional attention to the synchronized use of combined arms as a key to success on future battlefields. In this, he approaches the emphasis on 'timing' rather than 'timeliness' suggested in Landis (see note 9).

15. John Bigelow, *The Principles of Strategy Illustrated Mainly from American Campaigns* (Philadelphia: J.B. Lippincott Co., 1894), p. 81.

16. Brevet Major William A. Kobbe, *Notes on Strategy and Logistics* (Ft. Monroe: Artillery School Press, 1896), p. 17. The internal evidence for Kobbe's dependence on Clausewitz is overwhelming – war as an extension of policy, friction, 'in war all appears simple ...', etc.

17. Other contributions to this volume address key twentieth century theoreticians in some detail. Obscure thinkers close to Clausewitz in consideration of time and space include Captain George Meyers, *Strategy* (Washington, DC: Byron S. Adams, 1928); Captain J.E.A. Whitman, *How Wars are Fought: The Principles of Strategy and Tactics* (London: Oxford University Press, 1941); and Louis Bertiel, *De Clausewitz à la Guerre Froide* (Paris: Editions Berger-Levrault, 1958).

18. Field Manual No. 100-5, 'Operations' (Washington, DC: HQ, Department of the Army, 1982).

19. Ibid., pp. 8-5, 8-7.

20. Ibid., p. 2-9. Pressing soldiers to their utmost is addressed in a section entitled 'Sustain the Fight', related to neither attack nor defense. I can find no evidence that the increased importance of providing such pressure in the sustained attack was appreciated by the authors.

21. Ibid., p. 10-13.

22. Ibid., p. 2-2.

23. Ibid., p. i.

24. See also Michael Howard, *Clausewitz* (Oxford: Oxford University Press, 1983), p. 36 on the subtleties of translation associated with 'engagement', 'combat', and 'battle'.

Student as Teacher: Clausewitz on Frederick the Great and Napoleon

JAY LUVAAS

I. CLAUSEWITZ' INTEREST IN FREDERICK AND NAPOLEON

When Major Carl von Clausewitz, a Prussian general staff officer who had already spent more than half of his thirty years in the army, was appointed in 1810 to teach tactics in the newly established War School in Berlin, he was already on easy terms with history. He had read most of the basic works on military history and theory while on garrison duty at Neuruppin, where he enjoyed access to the excellent library of the deceased Prince Henry of Prussia, brother of Frederick the Great. Given the additional task of designing a course of instruction in the art of war for the Crown Prince (the future King Frederick William IV), Clausewitz based his scheme upon what he himself described as 'an assiduous study of military history'. A decade before Napoleon would advise his own son to read and meditate often about history, especially the campaigns of the Great Captains, as 'the only way to study war', Clausewitz pointed his young prince to the campaigns of Alexander, Hannibal, Caesar, Gustavus Adolphus, Wallenstein, and especially the Great Frederick. He also made pointed reference to Napoleon, but in the wake of the recent disaster at Jena he understandably displayed a light touch in treating the last of the Great Captains as a model.[1]

In the post-war writings Clausewitz focused by far the greatest part of his attention on Frederick and Napoleon. Earlier captains had fought under conditions so different from the 'new' era that it was not until Frederick the Great invaded Silesia in 1740 that circumstances, especially with respect to armaments, 'became close enough to modern warfare to be instructive'. Movement in battle 'began to rank as an autonomous principle of fighting'; armies acquired sufficient flexibility to force battle in difficult terrain and were more or less comparable in equipment, organization, and training. The ratio of cavalry to infantry had not changed significantly since Frederick's day, although there was a marked difference in the relationship between the two arms. In Clausewitz' view, the Prussians at Mollwitz 'reached a level of perfection in the use of firepower that still has not been surpassed'; the deployment of infantry in rough terrain and as skirmishes was a later development. The proportionate strength of artillery had also remained fairly constant.[2]

The general nature of war had undergone more sweeping changes. The transformation of politics occasioned by the French Revolution produced a corresponding transformation in the art of war. Rarely could armies in Frederick's day follow up a victory in the field beyond the next fortress or fortified position, and tents, baggage, food wagons, bake ovens, and other impedimenta likewise 'stopped the stream of victory'. But when Bonaparte, 'the most audacious of all dare devils', made his appearance 'and staked everything on one card – decisive battles of annihilation', the old restraints on movement disappeared. Since then all campaigns had produced 'such comet-like vibrations that they can scarcely be thought of as only military because they involve the whole of society'.[3] Modern war was thus governed by the imperial law of numbers, the first rule of which was to 'put the largest possible army into the field' (p. 195). Gone was the day when military men could argue that there was a certain optimum size for a field force and that any excess troops were more trouble than they were worth. In the future, Clausewitz argued, the aim of every government must be 'to take the field in the greatest possible strength' (p. 196).

There were other reasons why Clausewitz paid particular attention to Frederick and Napoleon. He himself was a product of the Frederickan army, and for the better – or perhaps the worse – part of a decade he had actively campaigned against the *Grande Armée* of Napoleon. There was a wealth of information available about the campaigns of both generals; each had discussed his plans and problems in extensive memoirs. Here, however, Clausewitz found it necessary to make distinctions. Frederick had written his memoirs 'with as much precision as was possible' that he might leave behind for his successor 'an authentic collection of the advantageous and disadvantageous situations' whenever Prussia 'may again have to contend with the house of Austria'.[4] The rationale for many of Frederick's decisions therefore was available to Clausewitz, although his particular perspective on strategy often cast Frederick's actions in a new light.

Napoleon's *Memoirs*, on the other hand, were compiled not so much to instruct as to impress posterity. While his restless mind during the years of captivity on St. Helena retained much of its sharpness, in his dictations to generals sharing his captivity Napoleon always presented himself in the most favourable light. While this was especially true of political matters, Napoleon also lacked Frederick's candor in acknowledging some of his own mistakes on campaign.[5] This is not to deny the value of Napoleon's reflections on generalship, the Great Captains, his own campaigns, and the art of war, but it is necessary to point out that Clausewitz, in explaining the reasons behind some of Napoleon's military decisions, was forced to rely upon memoirs that were blatantly self-serving. Not until Napoleon's *Correspondance* was published thirty years later could military historians probe deeper into Napoleon's mind.

One other point regarding Clausewitz' use of Frederick and Napoleon deserves mention. One might logically assume that *On War* is basically a synthesis arising from his earlier historical studies of both men. Such in fact was not the case. Even his first writings, particularly an analysis of the campaigns of Gustavus, reveal an interest in 'the timeless forces of politics and war' and other themes embodied in his major work. Similarly, the course of study that Clausewitz designed for the military education of the Crown Prince shows that his basic ideas on strategy were already well in place years before he devoted special attention to Frederick and Napoleon. According to Professor Paret the first stage of the manuscript eventually published under the title *On War* was written in the year immediately following the battle of Waterloo, when Clausewitz also composed his study of 'The Campaign of 1814 in France'. The first six books of his *magnum opus* were pretty much completed and the important Book VIII, entitled 'War Plans', was revised by 1827, by which time he had also written 'The Campaigns of Frederick the Great'. During the next three years, while working on revisions of *On War*, Clausewitz also produced detailed campaign studies of 1796 in Italy, 1799 in Italy and France, and 1815 in France.[6] From his work schedule alone it is easy to see that Frederick and Napoleon were never far from his thoughts as he reflected upon his own extensive military experiences and through historical analysis endeavored to develop a systematic and comprehensive approach to the study of war.

II. CLAUSEWITZ' PROCESS OF CRITICAL ANALYSIS

Clausewitz' approach enabled him to view the campaigns of Frederick and Napoleon in a different light from contemporary military theorists. They tended to think of theory in terms of certain and fixed principles variable only in their application (p. 136) – and here one thinks of Lloyd, Bülow, and to a lesser degree, Jomini. Clausewitz and Jomini had both derived their respective theories from the study of military history, but they disagreed sharply on the nature and purpose of theory. Jomini contended that military theory was prescriptive to the extent that it 'admits a certain number of regulating principles' that could not be deviated from without danger and which, when observed, 'almost invariably lead to success'. His own research had led to the discovery of these eternal principles, when he then applied in his extensive writings to the campaigns of Frederick and Napoleon. Manifestly he was able to demonstrate that 'all their successes or reverses were the result of the application, or of the neglect', of his principles, although he did acknowledge that 'natural genius will doubtless know how, by happy inspirations, to apply principles as well as the best studied theory could do it'. Although Jomini did not so specify, he certainly had Clausewitz in mind when he dismissed 'the metaphysical and skeptical works of a few writers who would have soldiers believe "that there exists no rule for war" '.[7]

In contrast, Clausewitz did not look to military history for any specific doctrine or 'manual for actions'. Rather he saw theory as providing the framework for a serious study of wars and campaigns, past as well as present. Theory, he wrote,

> will have fulfilled its main task when it is used to analyze the constituent elements of war, to distinguish precisely what at first sight seems fused, to explain in full the properties of the means employed and to show their probable effects, to define clearly the nature of the ends in view, and to illuminate all phases of warfare in a thorough critical inquiry.

Theory therefore should not be expected to provide rules or doctrine to accompany an officer in battle; it exists primarily to guide the future commander in his self-education (p. 141).

It is difficult to summarize Clausewitz' theory on war in one tidy paragraph, but the major ingredients are implicit in virtually everything that he wrote. War is an act of violence. It is also an act of policy, and strategy is the grand instrument of that policy. Strategy in turn is defined as the use of engagements – that is, of violence – for the object of the war.

Clausewitz saw war as a spectrum of conflict in which there is no *logical* limit to the application of force. In practice, however, there are many modifications. War is never an isolated act, nor are the results likely to be final. Once at war 'the world of reality takes over from the world of abstract thought' because of chance, human nature, and *friction* – which was Clausewitz' term for nearly every factor that causes things to go wrong. Clausewitz also stressed the paramount importance of moral factors:

> They constitute the spirit that permeates war as a whole, and at an early stage they establish a close affinity with the will that moves and leads the whole mass of force .... Unfortunately they will not yield to academic wisdom. They cannot be classified or counted. They have to be seen or felt .... If the theory of war did no more than remind us of these elements, demonstrating the need to reckon with and give full value to moral qualities, it would expand its horizon, and ... condemn in advance anyone who sought to base an analysis on material factors alone. (p. 184)

It follows that theory, to be valid, must not deal exclusively with any particular kind of war, or with war during a specific period in history. Theory must deal with each war and each age on its own terms, and Clausewitz did not even insist that war as it was experienced during the Napoleonic period, when it '*attained the absolute in violence*' (p.593; my emphasis), would necessarily recur. Theory must always accommodate itself to change.

In applying this theory to historical studies Clausewitz employed the methodology described in his chapter on 'Critical Analysis', by which he meant 'the application of theoretical truths to actual events'. If the purpose of theory is in fact to train a commander's mind, then critical analysis should enable the careful student to recreate, as far as is possible, the thinking of the commanders that preceded a given action.

> The man who means to move in such a medium as the element of war, should bring with him nothing from books but the general education of his understanding. If he extracts ... cut and dried ideas that are not derived from the impulse of the moment, the stream of events will dash his structure to the ground before it is finished. He will never be intelligible to ... men of natural genius; and least of all will he inspire confidence in the most distinguished among them, those who know their own wishes and intentions.[8]

Consequently Clausewitz, in his analysis of the generalship of Frederick and Napoleon, endeavored to get inside the skin of each while in the process of making decisions, for only when the modern soldier thus understands the motives, the apprehensions, and the problems confronting a successful commander is he able fully to develop his own talents. Experience alone, even with its wealth of lessons, 'will never produce a Newton or an Euler, but it may well bring forth the higher calculations of a Condé or a Frederick' (p.146).

III. FREDERICK, THE MASTER OF LIMITED WAR

As Clausewitz reconstructed Frederick's calculations, two central themes emerge – one that we would expect to find and the other coming as something of a surprise. As he studied the Silesian wars Clausewitz concluded that 'in no war was strategy so saturated with policy as this one'. Frederick's first four campaigns were dominated by his political plan, which was to seize Silesia and then to hold on for dear life. Better than most soldiers, Clausewitz, for example, would have understood the prolonged period of inactivity after the Prussian victory at Hohenfriedberg (4 June 1745), for it was Frederick's policy to end the war with his possession of Silesia confirmed by a peace treaty, and in the weeks following the battle political events occurred that seemed to be playing into his hands. His French allies had just won a convincing victory over the English at Fontenoy, which led to a reconquest of most of the important cities in the Low Countries. This blow to England was followed in August by the landing of Bonnie Prince Charlie in Scotland. With the greater part of their army on the Continent and faced with a rebellion in the north country, English statesmen were rapidly losing interest in Continental affairs, where they were tied to the fortunes of the House of Habsburg. Moreover, the new foreign minister was known to be more sympathetic to Frederick than his predecessor. Deserting his French allies for the third time in return for an English pledge to support him in retaining Silesia, Frederick remained in his fortified camp on the Austrian side of the mountains where he could consume enemy food and supplies while maintaining the diplomatic offensive. Thus goaded into action the Austrians eventually attacked him at Soor (30 September), where Frederick's superior mobility and great tactical sense enabled him to win another victory. If ever strategy was an instrument of policy it was in this campaign.

When his armies had invaded Silesia in December 1741 'almost without a stroke of the sword', Frederick had in fact achieved his objective, and in the ensuing campaigns he adopted a strategy that was largely defensive in order to hold it. Clausewitz interpreted Frederick's forays into Moravia in 1742 and Bohemia two years later as diversions to upset enemy plans and perhaps to gain time and strength. Frederick's early battles were similarly defensive in nature. At Mollwitz, Czaslau, and Soor, the Prussians, anticipating the Austrian advance, initially stood on the defensive; then, knowing retreat to be out of the question, Frederick ultimately went over to the offensive.[9]

Similarly, in the Seven Years' War Frederick 'had no thought of taking the offensive', at least not during the final three years, except as a 'better means of defense'. When Frederick perceived in 1756 that war was unavoidable and that he was lost unless he could forestall his enemies, it became necessity for him to initiate hostilities. He resumed the offensive in 1757, but after his defeat at Kolin he was forced to attack the French at Rossbach and the Austrians at Leuthen to prevent a dual invasion of his kingdom. Clausewitz summarized 1758 as a campaign of sieges, 1759–60 as campaigns of marches and maneuver, 1761 as a campaign of fortified positions, and the final year of the war as a campaign of diversions (pp. 191, 251). As in the Silesian Wars, Frederick thrust spearheads into Austrian territory in 1757 and again the following year, more to spoil enemy plans than to acquire additional territory. He remained true to his policy, which was 'to bring Silesia into the safe harbor of a fully guaranteed peace'. Clausewitz praised in particular the campaign of

1760, 'famous for its dazzling marches and maneuvers' and 'regarded by critics as a work of art':

> What is really admirable is the King's wisdom: pursuing a major objective with limited resources, he did not try to undertake anything beyond his strength, but always *just enough* to get him what he wanted .... His whole conduct of war ... shows an element of restrained strength, which was always in balance, never lacking in vigor, rising to remarkable heights in moments of crisis, but immediately afterward reverting to a state of calm oscillation, always ready to adjust to the smallest shift in the political situation .... That is the characteristic we admire in all his campaigns. (p. 179)

There can be little doubt that Frederick contributed directly to Clausewitz' understanding of limited war as the theme is developed in Book VIII. Noting that there are two kinds of limited war — 'offensive war with a limited aim, and defensive war' — Clausewitz pointed to Frederick's conquest of Silesia in 1740 and 1741 to show how, by extending the theater of war to a neighbouring state, it was possible to reduce the enemy's strength while at the same time augmenting one's own resources. And in his discussion of the limited aim of a defensive war, Clausewitz cited Frederick's campaign in 1758 when 'his one concern was to gain time, and to hold on to what he had'. Too weak to defeat Austria, Frederick had no choice but to husband his own strength. 'In war many roads lead to success', Clausewitz concluded,

> and ... they do not all involve the opponent's outright defeat. They range from *the destruction of the enemy's forces, the conquest of his territory, to a temporary occupation or invasion, to projects with an immediate political purpose, and finally to passively awaiting the enemy's attacks.* Any one of these may be used to overcome the enemy's will: the choice depends on circumstances. (pp. 94, 611–16)

Frederick's experience also influenced Clausewitz in his insistence that defense is the stronger form of war. According to Clausewitz there were four ways in which an army might elect to defend its theater of operations. 'It can attack the enemy the moment he invades', which Frederick did at Mollwitz and Hohenfriedberg. Alternatively an army 'can take up position near the frontier, wait until the enemy appears and is about to attack, and then attack him first'. Here Clausewitz cites specifically the battles of Czaslau, Soor, and Rossbach. A third choice is for an army 'to wait until the enemy actually attacks', which Frederick was prepared to do in his entrenched camp at Bunzelwitz. The fourth option, according to Clausewitz, is for an army to withdraw to the interior of the country and

CLAUSEWITZ: STUDENT AS TEACHER

resist there. This Frederick never attempted. Clausewitz also mentioned a number of occasions when Frederick, rather than worrying about fighting on better terms, occupied positions in front of some fortress where he would not have to fight at all – as at Glogau against the Russians and at Schweidnitz, Neisse, and Dresden against the Austrians (pp. 380–81, 504).

Even when forced on the defensive Frederick's army was almost always on the move, aiming to strike some enemy corps with his united force. Such maneuvers, even when they failed to lead to battle, were 'a most effective form of resistance', for the enemy commander was generally forced to take considerable pains to avoid unfavorable engagements and thus spend a portion of the strength necessary to maintain the offensive. Frederick on defense was habitually more aggressive than his opponents, in large measure because of the superior discipline, drill, and mobility of his army – qualities that were of greater value to him than intrenchments and natural obstacles (p. 513).

Had succeeding generations of German officers paid stricter attention to what Clausewitz actually wrote about the campaigns of Frederick, later in the century there would have been no reason for the controversy between the History Section of the General Staff and the celebrated academic military historian, Professor Hans Delbrück. General Staff officers, anxious to bring the national hero into line with contemporary doctrine, insisted that Frederick consistently pursued a strategy of annihilation ('*Niederwerfungsstrategie*'), aiming always at the decisive battle. Delbrück on the other hand argued that Frederick was an exponent of a strategy of exhaustion, ('*Ermattungsstrategie*'). Clausewitz, had he been alive while this debate was raging, probably would have pointed out that Frederick was not doctrinaire in his approach to strategy and that he did whatever his resources permitted in achieving his objective, of holding on to Silesia. Ironically Delbrück accused Clausewitz of 'insufficient historical understanding' in his 'failure' to comprehend the non-military reasons behind the two forms of strategy, while younger officers such as Major Friedrich von Bernhardi blamed Delbrück for reinterpreting Clausewitz![10] The debate lasted for years, and when the dust settled there stood Clausewitz, still holding the central position. Although a strategy of annihilation seems – in the eyes of many of his beholders – to be a predominant theme in his writings, Clausewitz did in fact maintain that sometimes wars could be won by attrition.

> Positions that have lost all value today could be effective then; and the enemy's general character was a factor as well. Methods which Frederick himself discounted could be the highest degree of wisdom when used against the Austrian and Russian forces under men like

Daun and Buturlin. This view was justified by success. By quietly waiting on events Frederick achieved his goal and avoided difficulties that would have shattered his forces. (p. 615)

Clausewitz was even more influenced by the Napoleonic concept of strategy, which was to bring superior forces, with strong reserves, to the decisive battle of annihilation and to exploit the smashing victory with relentless pursuit.

> A general such as Bonaparte could ruthlessly cut through all his enemies' strategic plans in search of battle, because he seldom doubted the battle's outcome. So whenever the strategists did not endeavor with all their might to crush him in battle with superior force, whenever they engaged in subtler (and weaker) machinations, their schemes were swept away like cobwebs .... Why? Because Bonaparte was well aware that everything turned on tactical results, and because he could rely on them .... *That is why* we think ... that all strategic planning rests on tactical success alone, and that ... only when one has no need to fear the outcome ... can one expect results from strategic combinations *alone*. (p. 386; his emphasis)

The difference between war in the old style and absolute war as it was waged by Napoleon was essentially political in nature: in Frederick's day war was still 'an affair for governments alone' – the people were merely an instrument. By the beginning of the nineteenth century the people themselves were 'in the scale' on either side and thus the degree of force necessary to achieve one's aims was inevitably higher.

IV. NAPOLEON'S APPROACH TO ABSOLUTE WAR

Clausewitz distinguished betweeen two forms of war. The first was derived from history, in which 'war consists of separate successes each unrelated to the next' with each separate result making its contribution toward the total score (pp. 94, 582). Frederick himself had written that there was 'more than one road to follow to the same goal', and that 'many small advantages ... taken together are the equivalent of great advantages'. Maneuver no less than battles led to successes: 'In war, as in everything else, a man does what he can and seldom what he desires'. 'Multiplied ... small successes are the equivalent of a battle won, and in the long run, they decide the superiority'.[11]

The second, or absolute, form of war introduced a different concept of success. Here 'war is indivisible', and its component parts – by which Clausewitz meant individual engagements – were of value 'only in their relation to the whole'. Successively and successfully linked together they led to the 'one result that counts' – final victory. This was perceived not so much by history as through theory, which demanded that at the outset of a war

> its character and scope should be determined on the basis of the political probabilities [and] the closer these ... drive war toward the absolute, the more the belligerent states are involved and drawn in to its vortex, the clearer appear the connections between its separate actions, and the more imperative the need not to take the first step without considering the last.

Although history did not reveal this concept of modern, absolute war until Napoleon's campaigns in 1805, 1806, and 1809, theory enabled Clausewitz to appreciate the interconnection between events when he analyzed Napoleon's first campaign in 1796. In a series of bold strokes Napoleon had separated the Sardinian forces from their Austrian allies. Only the strong fortress of Mantua prevented him from pushing on into the Alps to link up with other French armies advancing into Germany farther to the north. Although Napoleon won four victories against Austrian forces advancing to the relief of Mantua, these led to 'completely negative results', for Clausewitz speculated that a single enemy victory would have given the Austrians possession of Lombardy and perhaps even thrown Napoleon back upon the Maritime Alps. In this campaign, he noted, total success did *not* depend upon the sum of smaller successes, however brilliant, but really upon Napoleon's ability to capture Mantua. As long as this fortress remained in Austrian hands, his own force would be unable to penetrate into the Alps.

The solution was not, as those interested in elevating strategy into a science would assert, a matter of fixed lines and angles. According to Clausewitz, if Napoleon had 20,000 additional troops at his command he could have successfully besieged Mantua and simultaneously campaigned in the Alps while supposedly the lines and angles remained unchanged. As it was, however, Napoleon was forced by events to decide between raising the siege in order to deal with the enemy in the field, or to press the siege and at the same time endeavor to keep the relieving armies at arm's length. The first was superficially the bolder course – and Clausewitz no less than Napoleon considered boldness one of the premier qualities of a good commander – but it meant renouncing the hope of taking the city any time soon. It also meant the loss of his siege train. Clausewitz contended that this was a heavy price to pay for a few small victories in the field, and that had Napoleon stuck to his guns in the siege lines Mantua would have fallen within a week. Instead, at the price of a few spectacular but strategically insignificant victories, Mantua was able to hold out for another six months[12] (pp. 161–2).

Utilizing his distinctive method of critical analysis, which not only took into account the decisions and actions of a commander and how these impacted upon subsequent events but also examined all possible alternatives, Clausewitz in this instance concluded that Napoleon had not selected the wisest course. The center of gravity was Austria; the operations of the Army of Italy were expected to contribute to the overall strategical objectives, and there was no way that Napoleon could lead his army into the main theater as long as Mantua threatened his rear. With a larger amy at his command he could perhaps operate against both the enemy field army and the fortress at Mantua, but circumstances did not offer him that option.

The proper course, according to Clausewitz, would have been for Napoleon to protect his siege from any relieving army by throwing up lines of circumvallation – in other words, to revive a practice popular in the days of Louis XIV and construct works around Mantua that faced outwards, thus protecting the investing forces from Austrian enterprises in their rear. This is not mere second guessing: by comparing the strength of the forces at Napoleon's disposal with similar situations in history – and here Clausewitz included also Frederick's entrenched lines at Bunzelwitz – he was able to demonstrate that it would have been 'extremely improbable' for the Austrians to have actually attempted an assault. And once Mantua had fallen, Napoleon would then have been free to turn his undivided attention against the Austrian field armies. Napoleon, he contended, 'did not think the matter through to the point where he could assess the consequences as fully as we can in the light of experience'.

> In the study of means, the critic must naturally frequently refer to military history, for in the art of war experience counts more than any amount of abstract truths. Historical proof is subject to conditions of its own ... but unfortunately these conditions are so seldom met with that historical references usually only confuse matters more.[13] (p. 164)

Thus Clausewitz used both theory and history to analyze Napoleon's generalship and to weigh his options. If not all of these possibilities occurred to Napoleon, they nonetheless remained viable. History nearly always offered alternatives, and in this case Clausewitz decided that Napoleon had chosen 'a likelier but almost useless' victory in the field against the prospects of a pending surrender of Mantua, which was far more important to his future plans from the strategical point of view. True, he had won the plaudits of the military world for these brilliant victories, but nobody had appreciated that because of these proceedings the capture of Mantua was delayed for five months and the advance of the army into Germany had been neglected (p. 164).

V. CLAUSEWITZ' CRITIQUE OF NAPOLEON

Most contemporary military writers were content to describe Napoleon's maneuvers and battles and deduce general principles from his actions. Clausewitz, in contrast, insisted that the role of criticism was to assemble everything that the commander knew and all of the motives that had influenced his decision, and to ignore everything that he could not or did not know – especially the outcome. A major problem obviously was how to determine what had been in Napoleon's mind at the time, since the vast part of his correspondence was not yet published. Clausewitz does on occasion refer to specific letters that he had read, and he quickly learned that one could not always rely upon Napoleon's own version.

> For this reason we look so carefully for an explanation ... because we can not imagine that a general such as Bonaparte ordered the attack on Caldiero on the 12th (November, 1796) and on the 13th summoned his troops back to Verona without having determined to do this according to some other prepared plan or knowing what he wanted to do .... Neither the further content of his letter of 14 November or his later *Memoirs* give any information on the subject.

Elsewhere Clausewitz complained that Napoleon's *Memoirs* contained a cock and bull story to cover some of his mistakes. What had redeemed his strategical mistakes was the greater bravery of the French troops and his own persistance and daring.[14]

The notion that individual engagements were of value only in their relations to the operation was more clearly evident in Napoleon's subsequent operations. According to Clausewitz, Napoleon had basically one invariable formula for the conduct and termination of his wars – 'to begin with decisive battles, and to profit by their advantages; to gain others still more decisive, and thus to go on playing double or quits till he broke the bank'. It worked in 1805, 1806, 1807, and to a certain extent in 1809, but the impending campaign in Austria that year had diverted resources that Napoleon needed to corner and destroy British forces in Spain under Sir John Moore the previous autumn. Had Napoleon visited the Peninsula again in 1810 he might have succeeded in terminating the war in Portugal; Spain then would have been extinguished by degrees, since the Spanish insurrection and the Anglo-Portuguese struggles 'incontestably formented each other'. Even had he succeeded in driving the British from the Peninsula, however, Napoleon probably would have been forced to leave a considerable army in Spain, for as Clausewitz had been quick to recognize, the war there had already assumed the character of a People's War. 'To beat the enemy – to shatter him – to gain the capital – to drive the government into the last corner of the empire – and then while the confusion was fresh, to dictate a peace – had been ... the plan of operation in his wars'.[15]

It was the basis also of his plan for the invasion of Russia, as Clausewitz well understood. The campaign did not fail because Napoleon advanced too quickly and too far, as many critics have alleged. It failed because he was late in starting the campaign, because he squandered too many lives in the battles he fought before reaching Moscow, and because he did not pay adequate attention to logistics and his line of retreat. It failed also because the Russian leaders kept their nerve and the people remained loyal. The outcome certainly shows that he miscalculated, but if he had reached Moscow with 200,000 men instead of only 90,000 – 'which would have been possible if he had handled his army with more care and forbearance' – he might well have commanded a peace.

> To discover why a campaign failed is not the same thing as to criticize it .... Anyone who asserts that the campaign of 1812 was an absurdity because of its enormous failure but who would have called it a superb idea if it had worked shows complete lack of judgment. (p. 627)

During one stretch of the retreat from Moscow Napoleon was forced to fight six battles over a period of four days. The numbers were insignificant (many of the French casualties were victims of fatigue and straggling rather than Russian bullets), but the cumulative effect of these six actions was 'very influential' in the destruction of the French army and thus, seen in their relation to the whole, contributed materially to the success of Russian operations.[16]

The Russian campaign marks the turning point in the progress of Napoleon's 'juggernaut of war' which, as long as it had only to contend with armies of the traditional type, succeeded in 'its pulverizing course through Europe' (p. 592). The reaction was first apparent in Spain, where the People's War was a significant factor in the ultimate defeat of the French armies. In 1809 the Austrian government made 'an unprecedented effort' in the use of reserves and militia, foreshadowing on a modest scale the later achievements of the Prussians during the wars of liberation that followed the Russian debacle. Since Clausewitz had played an active role in this resurgence against Napoleon, first by being involved in the reorganization of the Prussian army after Jena, then as a general staff officer in the Russian army during the 1812 campaign and as the Russian general staff officer at Prussian headquarters in 1813 and 1814, and finally as chief of staff to the Third Prussian Corps during the Waterloo campaign, he had a keen appreciation for this transformation in war. War now had become the concern of the people as a whole, which gave it 'an entirely different character'. Indeed, Clausewitz would argue that war in 1812–15 'rather closely approached its true character, its absolute perfection', with the sole aim of overthrowing one's opponent. This, he suspected, would approximate the nature of war in the future: 'At least when major interests are at stake, mutual hostility will express itself in the same manner as it has in our day' (p.593).

In the summer of 1813 Clausewitz produced a brief study of that campaign to date, which he wrote at the request of General Gneisenau, who at the time was chief of staff to General Blucher. Since the purpose of this pamphlet was to justify the conduct of the war to the public and increase popular support for the war, it merits only a passing mention. Nor does space permit a discussion of his more detailed studies of the campaigns of 1814 and 1815. The first, written in the years immediately following the wars, was intended as a strategic critique of the war and, according to Professor Paret, 'is neither history nor theory, but forms a transition between the two'.[17] It was, however, of historical value to F.L. Petre, author of one of the few volumes dealing with the military events of 1814, for although Clausewitz had not seen Napoleon's letters and orders and hence could not document motives for many decisions, his thoughtful assessment of each military situation often provided imaginative insight of use to later historians. Although subsequent publication of Napoleon's correspondence occasionally revealed that Napoleon's intentions had not always been correctly appreciated – his decision to fight at Brienne would be a case in point – only once does Petre find fault with Clausewitz' estimate of a specific situation.

> Clausewitz has poured scorn on Napoleon's attempt to draw the allies from Paris by a march against Schwarzenberg's communications, treating it as a mere gambler's throw. On general principles, no doubt, the move should have proved ... futile. But, looking to the special circumstances of the case, and to the personality of Schwarzenberg, was it so bound to fail? ... Napoleon's move was, no doubt, a desperate one, but it was the last open to him, and looking to all the circumstances it may well be doubted whether it was quite so absurd as Clausewitz seems to think. For once, it looks as if the great critic had allowed his judgment to be warped by the actual result.[18]

Clausewitz' analysis of the Waterloo campaign was likewise sufficiently objective to be used as a basic source by historians of the campaign, although most English accounts seem to ignore him. This is somewhat surprising in view of the fact that Colonel Chesney makes frequent reference to Clausewitz in his critical study of the campaign. As a professor of military art and history at the Staff College, Chesney fought against those tendencies that seemed to blight so much of military literature of the period – and, one might add, a fair amount of the military literature of our own day as well. Critics, Chesney observed, are 'apt to build up theories upon inaccurate and superficial study of the facts'. Often 'the great strokes of strategy ... are apt to be lost, or greatly obscured, beneath a mass of pictorial details, interesting for the day ... but of little real importance to the general result'. Finally Chesney pointed to 'the more dangerous error of the so-called national historians, who skillfully pander to the passions of their countrymen at the expense of historical truth'. Clausewitz was guilty of none of these, which perhaps is why Chesney in 1868 maintained that 'the great reputation made for him by the genius his writings display deepens constantly with time'. In addition to Clausewitz' personal knowledge of the events, Chesney pointed to another reason why 'The Campaign of 1815' deserved particular attention: 'Wellington himself deemed this general's criticisms of sufficient importance to require an elaborate answer from his own pen, a compliment he paid no other of his censors.'[19]

This is not to say that all soldiers agreed with Clausewitz. One critic in particular deserves mention, if for no other reason than he wrote an entire volume to demonstrate that Clausewitz, the 'apostle of moral forces', had failed to appreciate 'the very simple procedure by which Napoleon obtained the demoralization of the enemy' – the enveloping attack. Colonel, later General, Camon, perhaps the leading authority on Napoleonic warfare in the French army at the turn of the century, disagreed with some of Clausewitz' specific criticisms of Napoleon in the 1796 campaign and claimed that he failed altogether to appreciate the essence of Napoleon's operational art, namely, the demoralization of the enemy by maneuvering against the rear of his army at the strategical level or turning his tactical flank. Camon suggested that one reason for this oversight was Clausewitz' lack of access to the published correspondence of Napoleon, which permitted French soldiers after 1870 to 'read his mind like an open book'.[20]

The date is significant. Prior to the defeat in 1870 at the hands of the Prussians – a victory, one might almost say, that represented a triumph for the pupils of Clausewitz over an army that had neglected Napoleon – a French mil'tary attaché in Berlin reported that in Prussia over the space of several months he had encountered more soldiers who had studied Napoleon's *Memoirs* than he had met in France during the previous twenty-five years.[21] The defeat stung the French army into the discovery of Clausewitz and a rediscovery of Napoleon. With the publication of Napoleon's *Military Correspondence* in 1876–77, a ten-volume set that had been extracted from the 32-volume work compiled during the Second Empire, French officers now had a rich source readily available for studying Napoleon's methods of war. One theme that emerged from this patriotic as well as professional activity was a strong emphasis on maneuver that can not be found in Clausewitz, an emphasis which prompts the comment, 'Selecting and combining as he pleases, each man reads his own peculiar lesson'.[22]

This is unquestionably true of Camon, who admired Clausewitz as a first-rate military critic but who none the less insisted that 'the Prussian military writer never understood Napoleon's favorite maneuver'. Camon wrote critically of the battle of Arcole, 'Ah well, the ingenuous combinations of Bonaparte, based upon the most precise calculations, have not found favor with Clausewitz'. Citing the published *Correspondance* Camon also claimed that Clausewitz had missed the object of the maneuver of Lodi, that Bonaparte was correct in abandoning the siege of Mantua to go after the Austrian field army, and that Clausewitz did not comprehend the maneuver of Villanova any more than he had understood that of Lodi.[23]

What is at issue here is not history so much as doctrine, and perhaps also a wounded national pride that refused to allow the foremost interpreter of a French national hero to be a German. Nor is it surprising that each generation of soldiers should write its own history. After Camon wrote an entire book on the subject, the difference between Napoleon and Clausewitz seems to boil down to this: 'whereas in tactics as well as strategy Napoleon made his plan *a priori*, seeking to subordinate the adversary to his own will, Clausewitz in contrast understands only the plan made *a posteriori*, after obtaining necessary information about the enemy.'[24] This is hardly fair to Clausewitz, and it may be relevant to point out that the Prussians themselves had been willing to depart from Napoleon's dictum that one should always concentrate *before* the battle, to embrace a doctrine that permitted concentration *during* the battle. French soldiers, it would appear, were obviously more concerned to keep theory close in line with their own interpretation of Napoleon.

VI. CLAUSEWITZ AND NAPOLEON COMPARED

Anyone familiar at first hand with Napoleon's published *Correspondance* should be impressed with the degree to which Clausewitz understood Napoleon – or perhaps it would be more accurate to say the similar ways in which the two understood war. Both agreed that good leadership was a blend of two kinds of qualities – qualities of the intellect, which are attained and cultivated, and qualities of temperament, which can be improved by determination and self-discipline. Both placed a high premium on boldness: Clausewitz asserted that 'a distinguished commander without boldness is unthinkable', while to Napoleon boldness was *the* common denominator among the Great Captains. Clausewitz observed that 'nearly every general known to us from history as mediocre, even vacillating, was noted for dash and determination as a junior officer' (p. 191). Napoleon put it another way, describing Turenne as 'the only general whose boldness had increased with the years and with experience'.[25]

Next in the opinion of both men came perseverance (p. 193), although Napoleon preferred to call it 'firmness of character and the resolution to conquer at any price'.[26] Of course both stipulated that physical as well as moral courage were essential. Clausewitz specifies that natural courage, or indifference to danger, is the more dependable because, 'having become second nature, it will never fail' and it 'leaves the mind calmer' (p. 101). Discussing moral courage, Napoleon once likened it to 'two o'clock in the morning courage'.[27] When distressing news comes to a person at that dismal hour it required a special brand of courage to make tough decisions. Such courage, he contended, is spontaneous rather than conscious, but it enabled a general to exercise his judgment and make decisions despite the unexpected. Clausewitz wrote about the indispensable intellect that 'even in the darkest hour retains some glimmerings of the inner light' and the need for 'courage to follow this faint light' (p. 102). Significantly neither Clausewitz nor Napoleon believed that brilliance per se was as essential as these other qualities. According to Clausewitz determination proceeds from a strong rather than a brilliant mind (p. 103), while Napoleon once reminded his brother Jerome that 'too much intellect is not necessary in war'.[28] They agreed that character was of primary importance and that genius consists in a harmonious combination of all or most of these elements (p. 100). When this happy combination does occur, Napoleon observed, it is a true 'gift from heaven'.[29]

Indeed, one would be hard pressed to point to any significant area where Napoleon and Clausewitz sharply differed. They agreed on the need for meticulous planning, recognizing that the best of plans often fail as a result of what Clausewitz called 'friction' (pp. 119–21) and Napoleon once described as 'a freak of fortune'.[30] Both maintained that superior strength at the decisive point was the essential element in victory at the strategic and the tactical levels[31] (pp. 194–7). Each held that the art of war was simple in concept but often difficult in execution, and each stressed the need for secrecy and speed in operations.[32] Napoleon believed that without fortresses to serve as depots 'one can not wage offensive war'; Clausewitz likewise recognized the need for fortified places in strategic planning[33] (pp. 393–6). These two even advanced similar reasons for discarding tents on campaign – enemy scouts could easily distinguish a line of tents, whereas troops bivouacking in huts or even in the open are less easy to count[34] (p. 273).

If Napoleon, for good reason, showed somewhat greater concern for logistics it is no less true that Clausewitz paid greater attention to the notion that war is an instrument of policy. It should be remarked, however, that when Clausewitz was only a lad of fourteen Napoleon acknowledged the supremacy of policy in his memorandum on the political and military position of French armies on the frontier of Piedmont and Spain. He also served Clausewitz as a useful model when he ultimately came to combine in his person the responsibilities of both the statesman and the strategist, although Frederick probably taught Clausewitz more on this particular subject.

Both stressed the advantages of flexibility. Clausewitz admitted the utility of principles in tactics but saw 'an extreme diversity of factors and relationships' occurring at the level of strategy, policy, and statesmanship. Although Napoleon occasionally gave lip service to the 'principles of the art', he was essentially ambivalent on the subject, asserting that genius acts by inspiration, that what is good in one instance is bad in another, and that when a soldier becomes accustomed to affairs he tends to scorn all theories.[35] Agreeing that military history offered the only way to study war, both men spent the last phase of their lives – Napoleon in exile on St. Helena and Clausewitz at the *Kriegsakademie* – writing about the campaigns of the various Great Captains.

So close were their ideas on fundamental points, in fact, that had Napoleon's *Correspondance* been published at the time Clausewitz wrote his treatise and historical studies, readers might well have concluded that Napoleon furnished him many of the ideas advanced in *On War*. If some of Napoleon's thoughts on military matters were available to Clausewitz in the published *Memoirs*, it is none the less apparent that what Napoleon provided more than anything else was an instructive example.

VII. WHAT CLAUSEWITZ LEARNED FROM FREDERICK AND NAPOLEON

Clausewitz himself helped to instruct posterity when he explained precisely why there had been such significant differences between warfare in the eighteenth century and in his own day. He may in fact have been the first to understand such periodization and the factors responsible for the distinction between limited and absolute war. None other than Hans Delbrück, one of the most noted military historians of the nineteenth century, evidently was inspired by Clausewitz' historical interpretations as revealed in personal letters to Gneisenau. Although Delbrück was often critical of Clausewitz as a military historian, this did not keep him from using essentially the same theme in his monumental *History of the Art of War in the Framework of Political History*, long recognized as 'one of the finest examples of the application of modern science to the heritage of the past'.[36] And by understanding the limiting conditions, the tempo, and the peculiar preconceptions of each age, Clausewitz managed to apply realistic standards to commanders of the past.

> Each period ... would have held to its own theory of war ....
> It follows that the events of every age must be judged in the light
> of its own peculiarities. One cannot, therefore, understand and
> appreciate the commanders of the past until one has placed oneself
> in the situation of their times, not so much by a painstaking study of
> all its details as by an accurate appreciation of its major determining
> features. (p.593)

This distinction is important, particularly since he hoped to expand the thinking of modern soldiers about military operations by scrutinizing the actions of generals in some previous era. Most military writers who started with a set of principles, usually derived from Jomini, and then used examples plucked out of historical context to illustrate the ways these principles had been successfully applied, produced texts that were distorted and oversimplified, requiring little imaginative thought on the part of the reader. (Works by Hamley, MacDougal, or Willison come readily to mind.) Clausewitz however, was able to use both Frederick and Napoleon for instructive purposes because he never regarded them as interchangeable parts. By stressing thought at the strategical level and keeping always in mind any differences between the two ages, he enabled the reader to accept each commander on his own terms.

In the dialogue between Clausewitz and his two Great Captains, the theorist obviously found much to learn. Frederick taught him the virtues of an active defense, Napoleon the necessity of a relentless offensive. Frederick impressed him with his skill in buying time on the defensive, Napoleon with his insistence that time was the one commodity that one could never waste in the attack. Since both were heads of state as well as commanders in chief, they were in a unique position to make strategy an instrument of state policy; they were also unique in that, responsible to no superior, they had more freedom than most to follow their inclinations and choose the bolder course. What each taught Clausewitz about the conduct of military operations as he accompanied them through their campaigns is inestimable.

And finally, through his own critical analysis Clausewitz effectively used Frederick and Napoleon to help teach later generations of soldiers the need for a strategy that would implement policy and the thought process required in the pursuit of what is rather loosely referred to today as 'the operational art'. He has much to say on this subject, most of it probably learned from Napoleon and various of his opponents during the last years of war. Here the advantages of Clausewitz' approach are every bit as valuable today as they were during the heyday of the Prussian General Staff, for reasons best explained by an English commander from the last great European war. When studying military history, the late Field Marshal Wavell explained to a group of British officers half a century ago that what one had to do is to take a particular situation, put himself at the side of the commander, realize the conditions in which the decision was made, and then ask himself how he could have improved upon it. As for the principles of war embodied in the Field Service Regulations,

> For heaven's sake don't treat those as holy writ, like the Ten Commandments, to be learned by heart, and as having by their repetition some magic, like the incantations of savage priests. They are merely a set of common-sense maxims .... The human side of military history ... is not a matter of cold-blooded formulas or diagrams .... To learn that Napoleon in 1796 with 20,000 men beat combined forces of 30,000 by something called 'economy of force' or 'operating on interior lines' is a mere waste of time. If you can understand how a young, unknown man inspired a half-starved, ragged, rather Bolshie crowd; how he filled their bellies; how he out-marched, outwitted, out-bluffed and defeated men who had studied war all their lives and waged it according to the textbooks of the time, you will have learnt something worth knowing.[37]

Wavell contended that one could learn a great deal about the military art from the theoretical study of Great Captains – 'no bad substitute if it is properly done, which it very seldom is ....'

Clausewitz, perhaps reminded of some of his detractors, doubtless would have agreed.

NOTES

1. Carl von Clausewitz, 'Summary of the Instruction given by the Author to His Royal Highness the Crown Prince', in Col. J.J. Graham, trans., *On War*, 3 vols. (London: Routledge & Kegan Paul, 1968), Vol. 3, pp. 178–229; 'Extraits des recits de la captivité', *Correspondance de Napoleon Ier*, 32 vols. (Paris: Henri Plon, 1858–70), Vol. 32, p. 379.
2. Carl von Clausewitz, *On War*, ed. and trans. Michael Howard and Peter Paret (Princeton: Princeton University Press, 1976), pp. 195–6, 275, 290–91, 303. All subsequent references to *On War* are from this edition, and are given in the text.
3. 'Über des Fortschreiten und den Stillstand der Kriegerischen Begebenheiten', as quoted in Arden Buchholz, *Hans Delbrück and the German Military Establishment: War Images in Conflict* (Iowa City: University of Iowa Press, 1985), p. 25. See also, for the ascendancy of Napoleon, *On War*, pp. 515, 592.
4. *Posthumous Works of Frederic II. King of Prussia. Vol. II. The History of the Seven Years War*, trans. Thomas Holcroft, 2 vols. (London: G.G.J. 2nd J. Robinson, 1789), Vol. 1, p. viii.
5. H.A.L. Fisher, *Bonapartism* (Oxford: Oxford University Press, 1961), pp. 113–16.

6. Peter Paret, *Clausewitz and the State* (New York: Oxford University Press, 1976), pp.327–30. The writer is heavily indebted to this incomparable study of the evolution of Clausewitz' military and political thought, which contains a number of passages from works not otherwise available.

7. Baron de Jomini, *Summary of the Art of War, or, A New Analytical Compend of the Principal Combinations of Strategy, of Grand Tactics and of Military Policy* (New York: G.P. Putnam, 1854), pp.18, 198–200, 227–9.

8. See also Clausewitz, *The Campaign of 1812 in Russia* (Westport, CT: Greenwood Press, 1977), p.41. I have made minor stylistic corrections in the translation.

9. *Hinterlassene Werke des Generals Carl von Clausewitz über Krieg und Kriegführung*, 10 vols. (Berlin: Ferdinand Dümmler, 1832–37): 'Die Feldzuge Friedrich des Grossen von 1741–1762', Vol. 10, pp.32–42.

10. Gordon A. Craig, 'Delbrück: The Military History', in Edward Mead Earle (ed.), *Makers of Modern Strategy: Military Thought from Machiavelli to Hitler* (Princeton: Princeton University Press, 1943), pp.272–5; Bucholz, *Delbrück*, pp.30–39.

11. Frederick's view are contained in Jay Luvaas (ed. and trans.), *Frederick the Great and the Art of War* (New York: The Free Press, 1966), pp.23, 273–4, 330.

12. 'Der Feldzug von 1796 in Italien', *Werke*, pp.300–1.

13. Ibid., pp.303–304.

14. Ibid., pp.158, 208, 209, 229–30.

15. Clausewitz, *Campaign in Russia*, pp.252–3.

16. Ibid., pp.80–81.

17. *Clausewitz and the State*, pp.240, 332.

18. F. Loraine Petre, *Napoleon at Bay 1814* (London: Arms 2nd Armour Press, 1977), p.201.

19. Col. Charles C. Chesney, *Waterloo Lectures: A Study of the Campaign of 1815* (London: Longmans Green, 1907), pp.xi–xii, 18–19. Wellington's rejoinder is found in *Supplementary despatches, correspondence, and memoranda of Field Marshal Arthur Duke of Wellington*, ed. by his son, 10 vols. (London: John Murray, 1843), Vol. 10, pp.513–31.

20. Col. Hubert Camon, *Clausewitz* (Paris: R. Chapelot, 1911), pp.vi–vii, 3.

21. Col. Baron Stoffel, *Rapports militaires ecrits de Berlin 1866–1870* (Paris: Garnier Frères, 1871), pp.26–7.

22. Dallas D. Irvine, 'The French Discovery of Clausewitz and Napoleon', *Studies on War: a Military Affairs Reader* (Washington: The Infantry Journal, 1943), pp.32–4.

23. Camon, *Clausewitz*, pp.91–2, 102–6.

24. Ibid., p.70.

25. Napoleon, *Correspondance*, Vol. 31, pp.238–40.

26. Ibid., Vol. 32, pp.182–3.

27. Le Count de Las Cases, *Memoirs of the Life, Exile, and Conversations of the Emperor Napoleon*, 4 vols. (London: Henry Colburn, 1835), Vol. 1, p.251.

28. Napoleon, *Correspondance*, Vol. 10, p.474; Vol. 15, p.178.

29. Gen. Gourgand, *Sainte-Helene, Journal inedit*, 2 vols. (Paris: Flammarion, 1899), Vol. 2, pp.412–24.

30. Napoleon, *Correspondance*, Vol. 10, p.529; Vol. 31, p.417.

31. Ibid., Vol. 17, p.311; Vol. 29, p.331; Vol. 31, pp.360–61.

32. Ibid., Vol. 3, p.263.

33. Ibid., Vol. 13, p.131.

34. Ibid., Vol. 17, p.22; Vol. 31, p.315.

35. Ibid., Vol. 15, p.188; *Journal inedit*, Vol. 2, p.20.

36. Bucholz, *Delbrück*, p.25.

37. Quoted in John Connell, *Wavell: Scholar and Soldier, To June 1941* (London: Collins, 1965), pp.161–2.

Two Letters on Strategy: Clausewitz' Contribution to the Operational Level of War

WALLACE P. FRANZ

I. INTRODUCTION

Two Letters on Strategy by Clausewitz was recently translated for the US Army War College by Peter Paret and Daniel Moran. This work provides us with an opportunity to study Clausewitz' ideas on operational issues in a specific strategic context. The purpose of this article is to discuss in detail several campaign plans and Clausewitz' critique of these plans. Reference will be made to *On War* and to Napoleon's campaigns where appropriate to show the relationship between theory and the practical advice given in *Two Letters*.

Clausewitz' classic work *On War* has been studied by scholars and soldiers for generations. In recent years it has attracted many readers in the US stimulated largely by the publication in 1976 of a newly translated edition by Professors Michael Howard and Peter Paret. Generally readers have concentrated on Clausewitz' philosophy, theory, and political strategic concepts as developed in Books I, II, and III. His views on operations, on the other hand, have been largely neglected both by scholars and soldiers. This situation is especially unfortunate for American army officers in light of the US Army's recognition of the three levels of war, as outlined in *Field Manual 100–5*:

> Strategic, operational, and tactical levels are the broad divisions of activity in preparing for and conducting war.
>
> Military strategy employs the armed forces of a nation to secure the objectives of national policy by applying force or the threat of force. Military strategy sets the fundamental conditions for operations.
>
> The operational level of war uses available military resources to attain strategic goals within a theater of war. Most simply, it is the theory of larger unit operations. It also involves planning and conducting campaigns.[1]

To understand Clausewitz' use of the term 'strategy', it is necessary to look at the concept of levels of war as found in *On War*. Clausewitz gives one of the clearest explanations of these three levels of war when he classifies them according to *time* and *space*. His ideas are expressed in the following quote taken from Book VII, Chapter 8, 'Types of Resistance':

> Since defense in war cannot simply consist of passive endurance, waiting will not be absolute either, but only relative. In terms of space, it relates to the country, the theater of operations, or the position; in terms of time, to the war, the campaign, or the battle. True these are not unalterable units, but the central points of certain areas that overlap and merge with one another. In practice, however, one must often be satisfied with merely arranging things into categories rather than strictly separating them; and those terms, in general usage, have become clearly enough defined to serve as nuclei around which other ideas may conveniently be gathered ....
>
> The concepts characteristic of time – war, campaign and battle – are parallel to those of space – country, theater of operations and position – and so bear the same relation to our subject. (p. 379)[2]

Earlier in Chapter One, 'Attack and Defense', Clausewitz had stated, 'At the strategic level the campaign replaces the engagement and the theater of operations takes the place of the position. *At the next stage* the war as a whole replaces the campaign, and the whole country the theater of operations' (p. 358).

The chart below summarizes Clausewitz' concept of the three levels of war:

Classification	Time	Space	Mass
referred to as 'the next stage' (strategy)*	the war	the country	armies
strategy (operations)*	the campaign	the theater of operations	army
tactics (tactics)*	the battle	the position	division

* The terms in parentheses are used today to describe these levels.

Clausewitz frequently uses the term 'strategy' to represent what we today consider to be the operational level of war. For example, he lists, in Chapter 2 of Book III, the elements of strategy: moral, physical, mathematical, geographical, and statistical (logistics) (p. 183). On the other hand, in Chapter One of Book IV he calls these same items the 'operative' elements of war (p. 225). During the nineteenth century the term 'strategy' generally applied to the maneuver of major formations.

An excellent discussion of the operational level of war appears in Book

V under 'The Army, The Theater of Operations, The Campaign'. Clausewitz says:

> The very nature of the question makes it impossible to give an
> accurate definition of these different factors of space mass, and
> time; but so as not to be misunderstood, we shall try to clarify the
> common usage of these terms, which in most cases we like to follow.
> (p. 280)

1. THEATER OF OPERATIONS [SPACE]

By 'theater of operations' we mean, strictly speaking, a sector of the
total war area which has protected boundaries and so a certain
degree of independence. This protection may consist in fortifications or great natural barriers, or even in a substantial distance
between it and the rest of the war area. A sector of this kind is not
just a part of the whole, but a subordinate entity in itself – depending
on the extent to which changes occurring elsewhere in the war area
affect it not directly but one indirectly. (p. 280)

2. THE ARMY [MASS]

It is easy to define an army by using the concept of 'the theater of
operations' – that is, all the forces located in a given theater. Yet this
obviously does not cover all the common uses of the term. Blucher
and Wellington each commanded a separate army in 1815, even
though they were in the same theater of operations; so supreme
command is another criterion in defining an army. Nonetheless, the
two are closely related: where matters are properly arranged, there
will be only one supreme commander in a single theater. And a
general in control of his own theater of operations will never lack a
suitable degree of independence. (p. 280)

3. THE CAMPAIGN [TIME]

It is true that the term 'campaign' is often used to denote all military
events occurring in the course of a calendar year in all theaters of
operations, but normally and more accurately it denotes the events
occurring in a *single* theater of war. The notion of a single year is
harder to dispose of, for wars are no longer broken into annual
campaigns by long fixed periods in winter quarters. Events in a given
theater of operations tend to group themselves into sections of a
certain magnitude; when, for instance, a catastrophe of more or
less major proportions ceases to produce direct results, and fresh
developments start taking shape. (p. 281)

One of Clausewitz' principal reasons for writing *On War* was to explain how to conduct major operations through war and campaign planning. The following quote from the introduction to Book VIII makes this quite clear:

> We now revert to warfare as a whole, to the discussion of the planning of a war and of a campaign, which means returning to the ideas put forward in Book One.
> The chapters that follow will deal with the problems of war as a whole. They cover its dominant, its most important aspect: pure strategy. (p. 577)

He makes a similar point in an unfinished note about *On War* probably written in 1830: 'The theory of major operations (strategy, as it is called) presents extraordinary difficulties, and it is fair to say that very few people have clear ideas about its details' (p. 70).

Two Letters on Strategy sheds some light on these details by relating them to a particular campaign plan; consequently, most of it has to do with operational questions, in spite of the title. *Two Letters on Strategy* expands on many of the theories developed in Book VI, 'Defense', from *On War*, particularly those that relate to maneuver. Here Clausewitz creates some axioms about strategy:

> that success is always greatest at the point where the victory was gained, and that consequently changing from one line of operations, one direction, to another can best be regarded as a necessary evil, that a turning movement can only be justified by general superiority or by having better lines of communications or retreat than the enemy's; that flank-positions are governed by the same considerations; that every attack loses impetus as it progresses. (p. 71)

The concepts of 'line of operations', 'turning movement', 'lines of communication', and 'flank positions' can be studied in the context of maneuver, which also includes the term, 'base of operations'. The 'base of operations' is the region from which preparatory measures have been taken for the campaign. This region forms the foundation upon which the campaign is built.

During movement, communication with the base of operations must not be interrupted for extended periods of time. 'Lines of communication' (LOCs) extend from the base of operations to a unit. It is over these lines that supplies, maintenance, replacements, and communications flow. Lines of communication are sometimes referred to as 'lines of operations'. However, lines of operations can extend behind the maneuvering forces in the direction of the enemy. These are the routes by which large units move from their bases towards their objectives. These lines of operations are classified (from their positions with respect to the lines of operations of the enemy) as interior or exterior lines; and, from their positions with respect to each other, into convergent and divergent lines. If the lines of operations are within those employed by the enemy, they are known as interior lines; if outside, as exterior lines. If these lines of operations start from points some distance apart, approach one another, and eventually meet, they are known as *convergent* or *concentric* lines of operations. *Divergent* or *eccentric* lines of operations are the reverse of concentric lines; they separate as the units advance and the distance between them widens. (Figure 1) (Cf. *On War*, pp. 341, 345, 367.)

FIGURE 1

INTERIOR AND EXTERIOR LINES
OF OPERATION
A FACTOR OF TIME RATHER THAN SPACE

EXTERIOR LINES

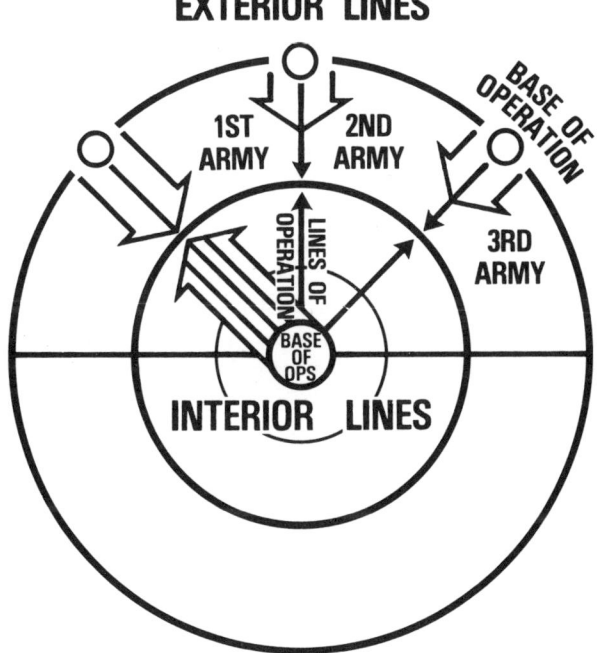

Operations on interior lines allow the concentration against parts of a force operating on exterior lines. This requires the enemy to be so dispersed that his units are too separated to participate in the same action. The enemy can be defeated in detail by containing one of his detachments with relatively small force while using the bulk of one's forces against another enemy detachment. The Napoleonic Campaigns of 1796 and 1814 are excellent examples of this technique.

The Austrians and the Sardinians in 1796 faced the French along the Ligurian Alps. Napoleon concentrated in the area between the Allies north of Savona (Map 1).

He defeated the Austrians at Montenotte, forcing them back along their LOCs and thus creating a gap (1). Containing the Austrians with a detached force, Napoleon moved the bulk of his army against the Sardinians, defeating them in several engagements. With the capture of Mondovi the Sardinians were effectively out of the campaign (2). Napoleon was now free to concentrate against the Austrians again (3), who retreated along their LOCs while their base at Alessandria was threatened by a French detachment (4). The Allies were consistently forced apart by Napoleon's maneuvers.

Napoleon's Marengo campaign (1800) and his Ulm campaign (1805) are examples of the use of concentric lines of operation. (Map 2) In both these examples the French were able to turn the Austrian flank and position themselves between their army and its base. This maneuver generally leads to complete destruction of an army once it is beaten on the battlefield because its line of retreat is cut.

Written for a hypothetical situation in 1827, *Two Letters on Strategy* deals with the planning and conduct of a campaign, based on two problems presented by General Müffling, Chief of the Prussian General Staff, as staff training exercises. Major von Roeder, a Prussian General Staff officer and friend of Clausewitz, asked for his comments on these two operational problems. Roeder worked out his solutions and sent them, along with those of another officer ('M'), to Clausewitz. The relationship of time, distance, and mass in these problems and solutions can only be appreciated through a knowledge of the geography of this theater of operations. The serious reader must refer to the maps included below in order to understand the arguments put forward to Roeder and Clausewitz.

Two Letters on Strategy begins with conditions and assumptions in a conflict between Austria and Prussia as presented in the First Problem. Next, the Staff officer is asked to prepare a memorandum discussing operations in the event that Austria invaded Prussia. Clausewitz then presents his critique of the staff problem as formulated. This critique is followed by 'M's' solution and Clausewitz' comments. Roeder's solution comes next, following by Clausewitz' comments. The same sequence is followed for the Second Problem. The various points of each solution are numbered and addressed by Clausewitz in that order.

Clausewitz begins characteristically by criticizing Müffling's problem for not giving the political background to this hypothetical war. The

MAP 1

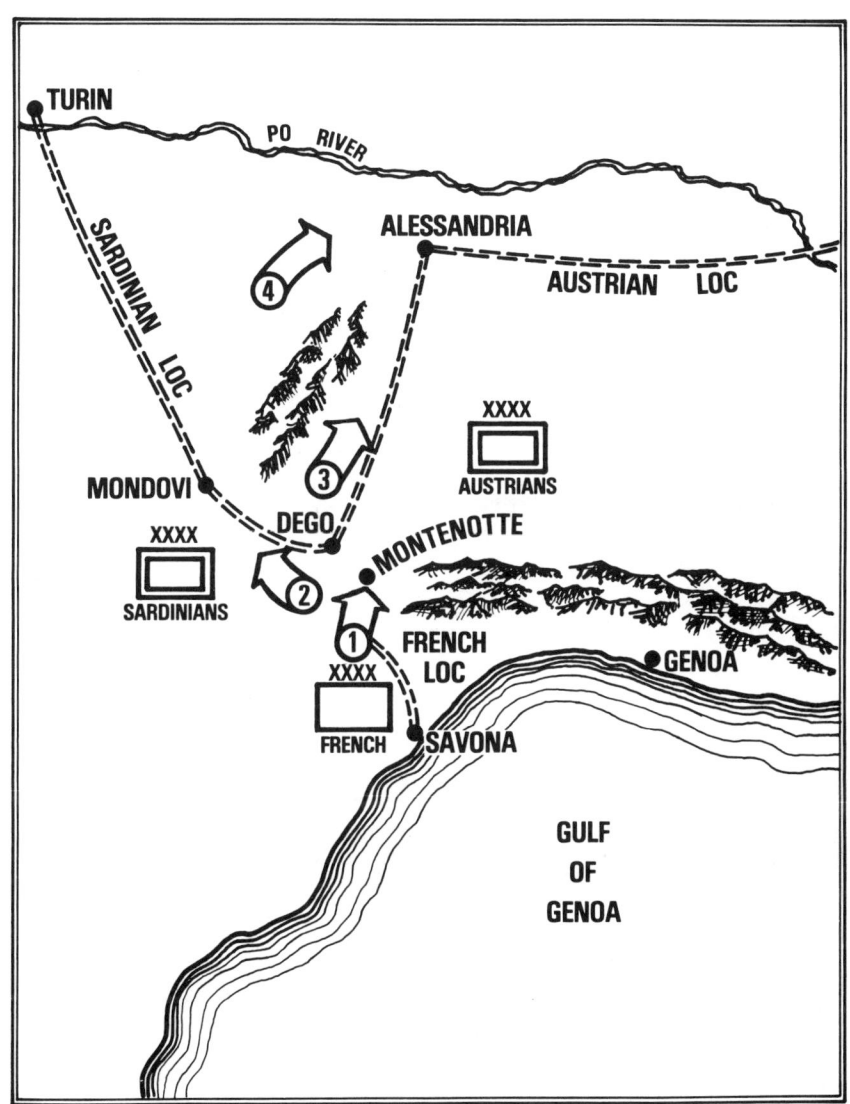

MAP 2

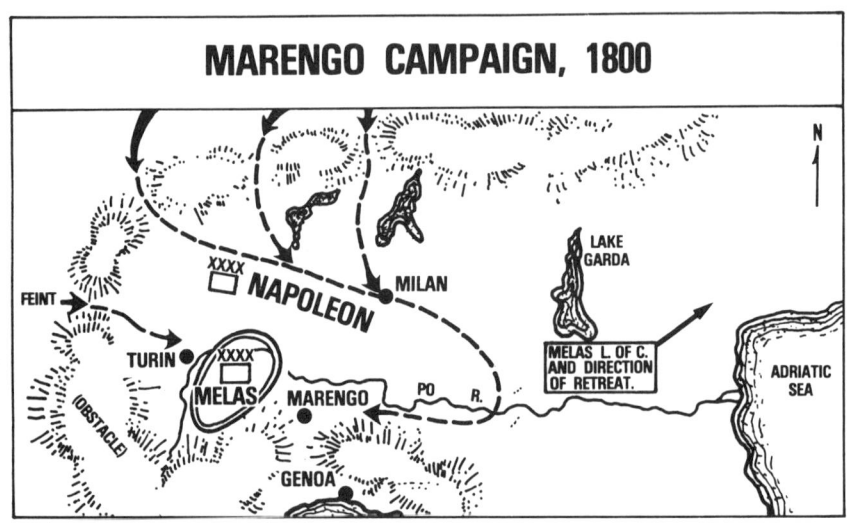

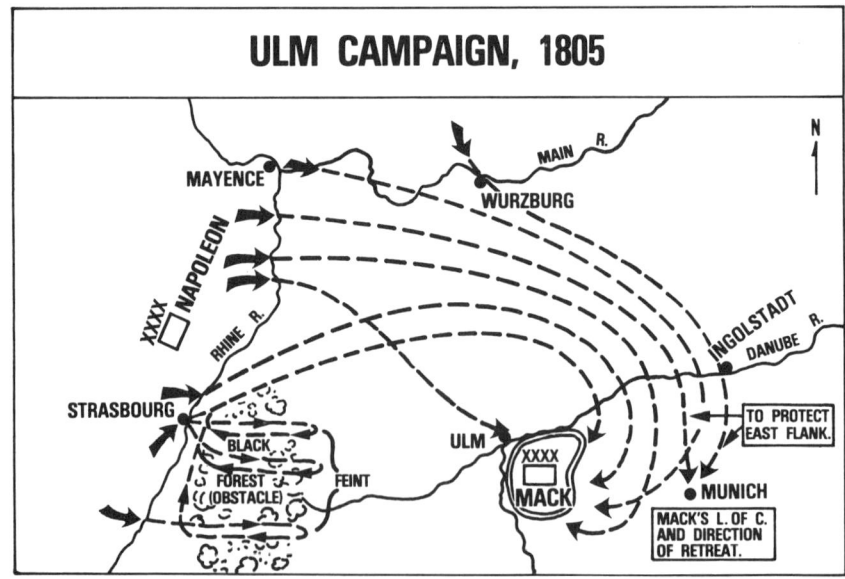

nature of the military effort could only be determined from a more detailed scenario than that presented in this staff problem. The military goals for the belligerents must be given to develop a realistic campaign plan. Another criticism of Müffling's problem is that Austria is attacking with an army no larger than that of the Prussians. In addition, the Austrians must contend with several thousand Prussians garrisoning a number of fortified cities. (Still, in 1866 the role was reversed, and the Prussians, no more numerous than the Austrians, attacked and were victorious at Königgratz.) None the less, Clausewitz does his best to accommodate Roeder's request to discuss solutions to the two problems. In reading Clausewitz' discussion, we must remember that he generally used the term 'strategy' in its normal nineteenth-century denotation, which he himself was instrumental in establishing – that is, the conduct of major operations, rather than the more comprehensive definition found in the Army's *Field Manual 100-5* (where 'strategy' approaches the level of national policy). This paper will study in some detail Clausewitz' discussion of the Second Problem because it is more specific than the First Problem. To assist the reader in following the discussion, the First and Second Problems are reproduced below.

II. THE PROBLEMS

The First Problem

The following conditions should be assumed (Map 3):

Relations between Austria and Prussia are strained. Saxony is allied to Austria.

Austria has assembled her forces in Bohemia, Moravia, and her German territories, and established magazines in Komotau, Aussig, Gabel, Arnau, and Jung-Bunzlau.

Prussia has mobilized the Guards; the 2nd, 3rd, 4th, and 6th Army Corps; and the Silesian Division of the 5th Corps. The fortresses at Erfurt, Magdeburg, Wittenberg, Torgau, Küstrin, Glogau, Schweidnitz, Silberberg, Neisse, and Kosel are supplied for six months.

On 1 June news arrives that the Austrian forces on the Danube have set out for Bohemia. It is certain that Austria will take the offensive once these units have reached their destinations. Austrian strength is assumed to be 130,000 men; Saxon strength, 20,000.

Prussia can put five corps (150,000 men) in the field. An additional half a corps and some reserve formations will garrison these fortresses that are threatened.

Prepare a memorandum discussing the following:

(a) Possible operations by Austria and her ally.

MAP 3

Corps rate of march = 20 km per day.
90 km from Austrian frontier to Prussian border.
25 km from Saxon frontier to Torgau.
☆ Fortress cities.

From *Atlas to Accompany Napoleon as a General* by Yorck von Wartenburg (Department of the Army, West Point, New York, 1958).

(b) Analysis of these in time and space.

(c) Which operation is most dangerous to Prussia?
The overall disposition of Prussian forces, from which each of the Austrian moves can be countered.

(e) A detailed assessment of each possible operation, paying particular attention to the one deemed most dangerous.[3]

The Second Problem

For the purposes of this exercise, the conditions described in the first problem are modified in several respects. First, it is assumed that the Prussian troops will not cross the Saxon border, but must await the Austrian attack on their own soil. They must therefore forego all offensive operations at the start of the campaign, even though, if time permitted, these might prove most advantageous. Furthermore, it is assumed that the entire Austrian force will advance between the Elbe and Spree rivers.

Analyze two possible deployments for the Prussian Army, which consists of five corps of 30,000 men each (Map 4):

(a) Four army corps are stationed between Senftenberg and Spremberg, with the fifth corps at Görlitz:

or

(b) all five corps assemble along the Elbe near Torgau: One corps on the left bank, one corps at Torgau, and three corps on the right bank between the Elbe and Black Elster rivers.

Compare these two deployments.[4]

Many of the situations discussed in *Two Letters* were faced by Napoleon and his enemies just fourteen years earlier. In some respects the position of the French in Saxony was similar to the Austrian deployments in the Second Problem. The Allied armies of Bernadotte and Blücher held dispositions somewhat similar to those of the Prussians in this problem. Clausewitz and Roeder had taken part in this campaign and must have been influenced by this experience in their consideration of Müffling's staff problem. Oddly enough, the only reference to the 1813 campaign in *Two Letters* is Clausewitz' mention of the relationship between Blücher's and Schwarzenburg's armies to Napoleon's central position in Saxony. The area bounded by Berlin, Leipzig, Dresden, and Gorlitz encompasses most of the theater of operations for Napoleon's campaign of 1813, which ended with the Emperor's defeat at Leipzig (Map 5). The most significant geographic feature of this region is the Elbe River, central Europe's major waterway. This river is 500 meters wide in some places between Dresden and Hamburg, and presents a major obstacle to the movement of large formations. Several times in 1813, French armies based on the Elbe advanced on Berlin between the Spree and Elbe rivers.

MAP 4

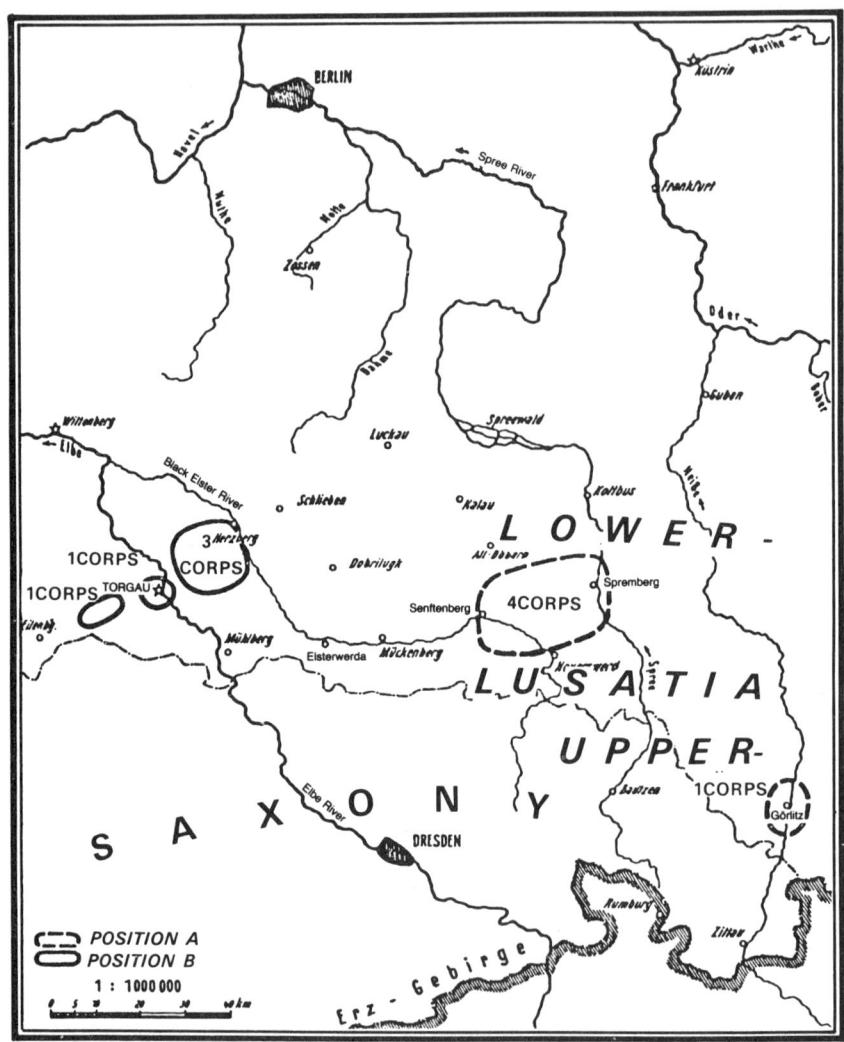

From *Atlas to Accompany Napoleon as a General* by Yorck von Wartenburg (Department of the
Army, West Point, New York, 1958).

The stage is set with both sides fielding the same number of troops. The Austrian army will be concentrated in one formation as it crosses the Saxon frontier and invades Prussia. The Prussian army is not concentrated (see Map 4). Operational skill and circumstances will determine what the balance of forces will be on the battlefield. The essence of the operational art is the deployment of major units to achieve superiority on the battlefield. The problem here requires such a deployment but is complicated by the requirement of maneuvering in the vicinity of large rivers and fortified cities. Roeder has a number of maneuver options available, and Clausewitz cautions him:

> In any strategic problem, but most especially in those that pose *alternatives* (his emphasis.) and ask us to choose between them, I feel the need to *reduce the issue to general principles*, that is to *reveal the relationship between one or the other option and the facts that inevitably result from the nature of the situation* (my emphasis.) In this way, at least, we can recognize the nature of each measure, and its unique characteristics. In the event that we must execute one scheme or the other in real life, we can then decide for ourselves whether the characteristics of one or the other are better suited to our requirements and circumstances.[5]

The general principles referred to above can be found in *On War*. These principles are developed through a discussion of what Clausewitz calls the main factors in strategic effectiveness that benefit the defense. These factors are:

(1) the advantage of terrain
(2) surprise
(3) concentric attack
(4) strengthening the theater of operations, by fortresses, etc.
(5) popular support
(6) the exploitation of moral factors (p. 363).

These factors will benefit Prussia in this hypothetical campaign. Of particular importance is the concept of concentric attack and its effect on maneuver. Eccentric operations provide the opportunity to divide a more numerous enemy and achieve local superiority over one part of his divided force. However, this maneuver is rarely decisive because it is difficult to cut off the defeated enemy. Concentric operations, on the other hand, provide an opportunity to turn or envelop an enemy and prevent his retreat. To employ eccentric operations successfully, one must have the time and space to maneuver; and one must have the initiative. As distances decrease, the operational advantage of eccentric lines changes to the disadvantage of being tactically surrounded; this is what happened to

MAP 4A

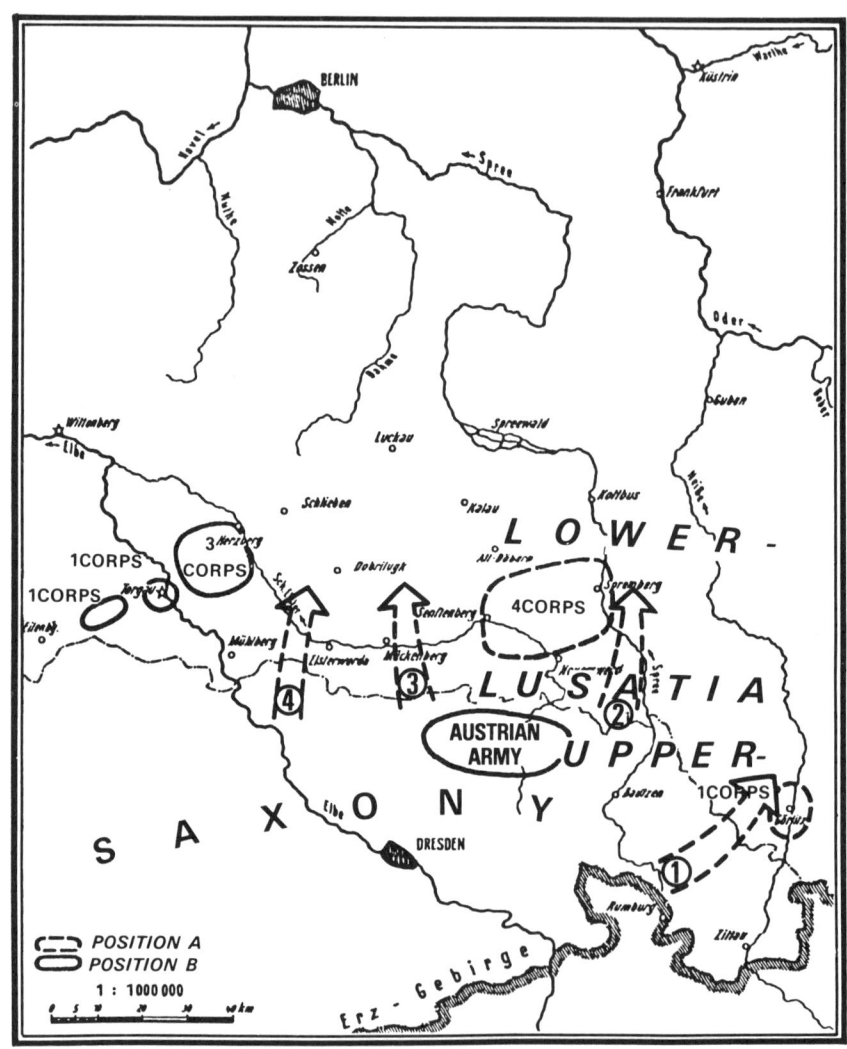

90 KM FROM GORLITZ TO SENFTENBURG – SPREMBURG AREA
40 KM FROM GORLITZ TO THE SPREE RIVER

Napoleon at Leipzig in 1813. Napoleon, when he had the required strength, attempted to employ concentric maneuver in order to destroy his enemy in one battle. Clausewitz discusses the use of concentric maneuver by the defense in his comments on Roeder's solution to the Second Problem.

III. ROEDER'S SOLUTION TO THE SECOND PROBLEM AND CLAUSEWITZ'
     COMMENTS

Part (a) of the Second Problem has the Prussian corps deployed at position A on Map 4. Roeder believed that the Austrians must leave a force to cover Gorlitz and then either bypass the right wing of the Prussian army by crossing the Black Elster River (Sch. Elster on Map 4) in the vicinity of Senftenberg or by crossing below Elsterwerda. He felt that the Prussian corps at Gorlitz would not be defeated because it would avoid engaging a superior force (Map 4A, axis of advance 1).

Clausewitz takes issue with Roeder over leaving a corps at Gorlitz since the Austrians might overwhelm it or choose to mask it with half a corps. Clausewitz suggests it is far safer to unite this corps with those stationed between Senftenberg and Spremberg. He says that just one corps on the flank of the Austrian advance is not strong enough to pose a serious threat to their operation.

Clausewitz had warned Roeder in his discussion of the First Problem about dividing an army in the face of an enemy advance. He makes the point that with the relatively short distance involved (40 km) the Austrians operating on interior lines could defeat the Prussians at Gorlitz before the Prussian main army intervened. In this critique Clausewitz refers to Jomini's term 'operating on exterior lines', what Clausewitz calls an 'enveloping attack'. Clausewitz in *On War* pointed out that an advantage of operating on exterior or convergent lines is that an army directs its efforts toward a common destination and thus concentrates force. Some military theorists believed that the convergent form of maneuver could only be employed by the attacker, and that the attacker must have numerical superiority even to attempt it. Clausewitz held that through skilful deployment the defense could operate on exterior lins. He felt this was possible once the attacker had reached the end of his advance and was forced to halt by the dissipation of his strength; the attacker's lines of communication would then be extended and therefore vulnerable. The theory behind this argument, as developed in *On War*, is that an enveloping attack in strategy is effective only as a threat to the enemy's lines of communication, and these lines tend to become vulnerable as the attacker advances into a hostile country. When the defender goes over to the offense he can use convergent operations to exploit the weakness of

MAP 4B

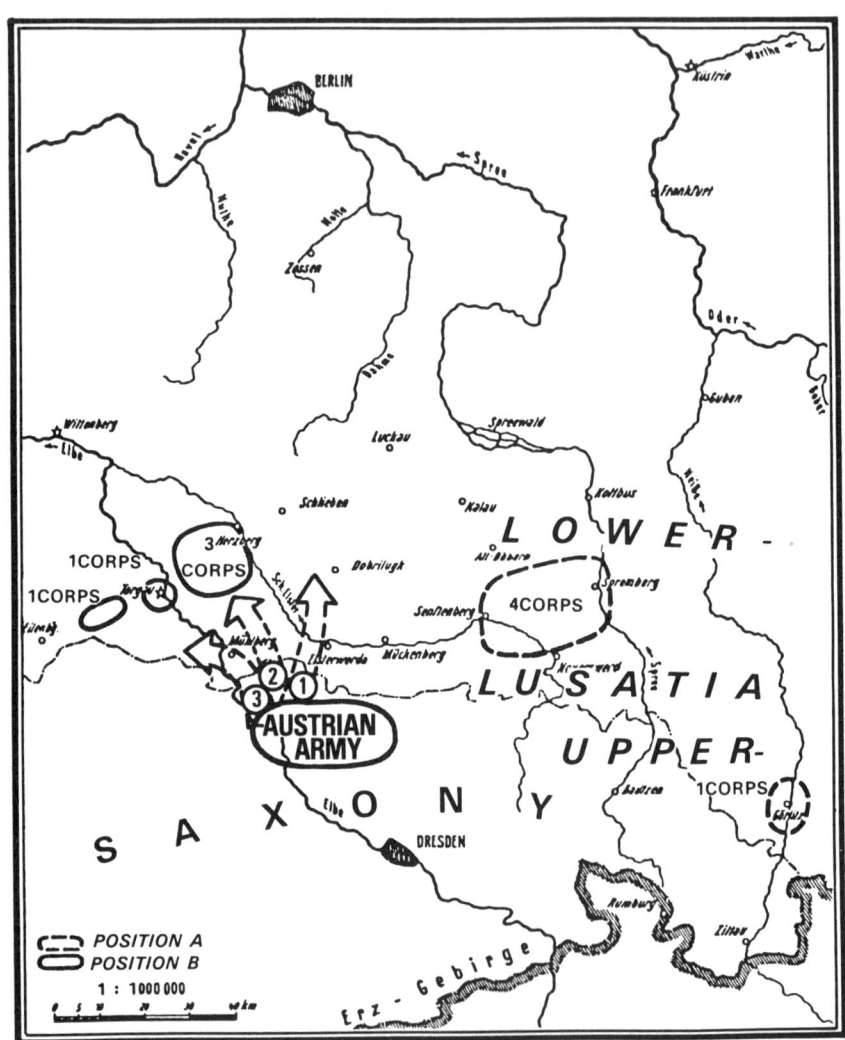

25 KM FROM SAXON FRONTIER TO TORGAU
20 KM BETWEEN THE ELSTER AND THE ELBE NEAR TORGAU
THE PRUSSIAN ARMY IS SPREAD OVER A 40 KM AREA NEAR TORGAU

extended enemy lines of communication. Clausewitz believed that convergent maneuver brought greater success and was more decisive than divergent maneuver but that, on the other hand, it was more risky. The coordination of several detachments is always difficult.

It was too early in the campaign for the Prussians to employ this maneuver against the Austrians. Clausewitz suggested that if Roeder wanted to attack the enemy's communications at this stage of the campaign a force of 5,000 rangers in combination with *Landewehr* and garrison troops might be effective. The absence of this small force would not significantly weaken the Prussian Field Army.

Clausewitz next discusses the terms 'outflanking' and 'bypassing'. Roeder had indicated the Austrians had the option to 'bypass' the main Prussian army of four corps (Map 4A, axis of advance 2, 3, and 4). Clausewitz points out that by 'outflanking' an army we mean to attack it from the flank or rear. 'Bypassing', on the other hand, means ignoring the enemy and continuing the advance. He does not believe the Austrians could *bypass* the Prussian army because this army is too strong to ignore, but they could *outflank* it on the right or on the left. Here we have an example of Clausewitz' correcting an imprecise use of terms such as often leads to misunderstanding and confusion in the implementation of operation orders.

Part (b) of the Second Problem (position B on Map 4) has the Prussian army assembled along the Elbe River near Torgau. Roeder gives the Austrians three viable options: (1) cross the Black Elster River, (2) advance between the Elbe and the Black Elster, or (3) cross to the left bank of the Elbe after leaving Saxony (Map 4B, axis of advance 1, 2, and 3). He believes that the Austrians will most likely advance between the Elbe and the Black Elster.

In this event he sees three courses of action for the Prussian army (Map 5):

(1) Deploy the entire Prussian army of five corps between the Elbe and the Black Elster Rivers;
(2) Deploy before the bridgehead at Torgau;
(3) Concentrate the Prussian army on the left bank of the Elbe near Torgau, giving it the option of avoiding battle. If defeated, the army could cross to right bank at Torgau and retreat to Wittenberg.

Clausewitz begins his answer to Roeder with a general comment on the above options by stating that the Austrians must fight a battle. They must go after the Prussian army. They cannot expect an army of equal size and in its own country to retreat unless beaten in battle. Clausewitz does not believe that the Prussian field army will retreat and uncover Torgau regardless of which axis of advance is employed by the Austrian army.

MAP 5

From *A Military History and Atlas of the Napoleonic Wars* (New York: Praeger).

MAP 6

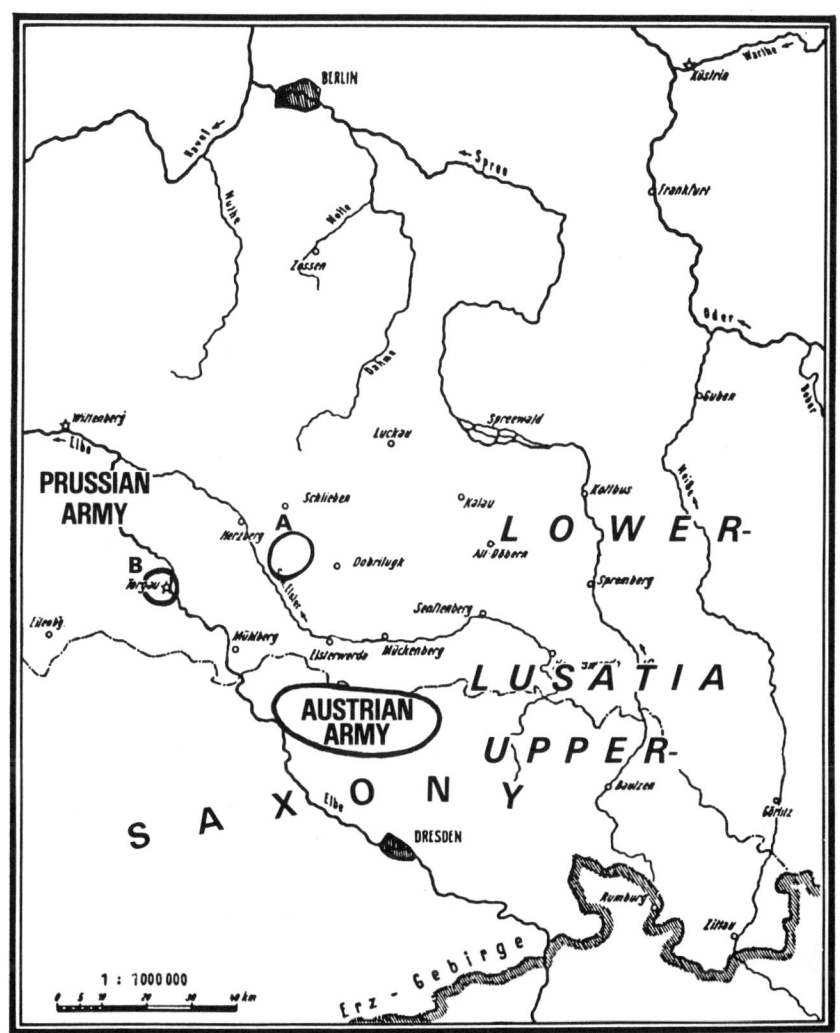

Clausewitz then addresses Roeder's three proposed courses of action for the Prussians:

(1) The Prussian army deployed between the Elbe and Black Elster is hemmed in between two rivers and its movement is restricted accordingly. One must be sensitive to the possibility of a turned flank and of being pinned against one of the rivers. The army should be positioned south of Torgau in order to be able to retreat to Torgau if defeated.

(2) The bridgehead at Torgau is a poor position because the 'front ... – being convex – is very weak ... in general [this] restricts the defender to extreme passivity'.[6]

(3) The Prussian army is concentrated on the left bank of the Elbe; therefore,

(a) The fortress of Wittenberg multiplies the number of options available to the Prussian army because it controls the crossing over the Elbe north of Torgau and allows operations to be conducted on either side of the river;

(b) 'In most cases the strategic value of a position declines markedly when a large river separates the defense from the attacker, since this allows the attacker to divide and maneuver his forces in ways that would not be possible without this barrier.'[7] Clausewitz cautions against repeatedly shifting back and forth over the river because sooner or later part of the army may find itself on the same bank as the attacker's main force;

(c) In summary, there are advantages to 'be obtained by skillful use of the Elbe in combination with the two fortresses, whether to avoid battle for a time, or to give it under favorable circumstances'.[8] (The importance of controlling the Elbe crossings with fortresses such as Torgau, Wittenberg, and Dresden is apparent from Napoleon's statement, made in 1813, 'What is quite clear is that 400,000 men supported by a system of fortresses and with such a stream as the Elbe for their base, cannot be turned.')[9] He goes on to advise not to exaggerate the value of these favorable conditions for, if the opportunities presented are not developed with skill, the advantage of the position will be temporary.

Next Clausewitz summarizes his thoughts on the deployment of the Prussian army either behind the Black Elster or near Torgau (positions A and B, Map 6). He argues that:

If we want to remain realistic, we would have to say that in the event of a major battle, this particular difference would be only a minute factor in the final result. The degree to which both commanders have united their forces for combat, the good planning and skillful conduct of the battle, the perseverance of the commanders, the courage of the troops, their confidence in their leader, the obedience of the subordinate – are these not all factors that have greater significance and that affect the outcome more directly.[10]

He therefore does not believe there is much difference between these two positions. The principal objective of maneuver is to concentrate superior force against the enemy and thus increase the chances of winning the tactical battle. The simple occupation of certain areas because of their supposed strategic significance does not necessarily produce this superiority.

In discussing the location of the Prussian army in the above situations, Clausewitz uses the historical example of the Campaign of 1812, where the Russian army retreated from Moscow to Kaluga rather than to Vladimir (see Map 6). Vladimir is about 150 miles east of Moscow on the road to Gorki, while Kaluga is about 100 miles southwest of Moscow. By placing his army at Kaluga, Kutusov was in a position to threaten Napoleon's line of retreat from Moscow. This maneuver also tended to concentrate Kutusov's army with Russian forces operating south of the Vilna–Smolensk–Moscow line. A move to Vladimir would have continued to drive major Russian armies apart. Clausewitz states that the change in the strategic line of retreat had a decisive influence on the Russian campaign. He does not believe that there is much difference between the Prussian army fighting northeast of the Black Elster or at Torgau because these areas occupy about the same comparative position in relation to the Prussian line of retreat to the north. Neither of these courses of action had the degree of significance that the choice between retreat to Vladimir or Kaluga had for the Russians in 1812.

Roeder proposes a third deployment, not presented as an option in the Second Problem, in the event that Gorlitz is fortified. He proposes to deploy the main Prussian army at Gorlitz. Roeder seems to have a fascination for the use of Gorlitz as a flank position; he takes every opportunity to put Prussian forces into this region. Although Roeder feels that fortifying Gorlitz would combine the advantage of the Prussian dispositions represented on Map 4 as position A and B, Clausewitz does not agree. His discussion centers around the tactical and operational aspects of this flanking position. First, he points out that 'the danger that the army will be forced into an eccentric line of retreat, away from the main part of its home territory, from the center of gravity of the entire military base, constitutes a grave disadvantage of positions of this kind'.[11] Then he explains that to prevent the army's defeat and subsequent retreat, the defensive position at Gorlitz must be tactically very strong. The

MAP 7

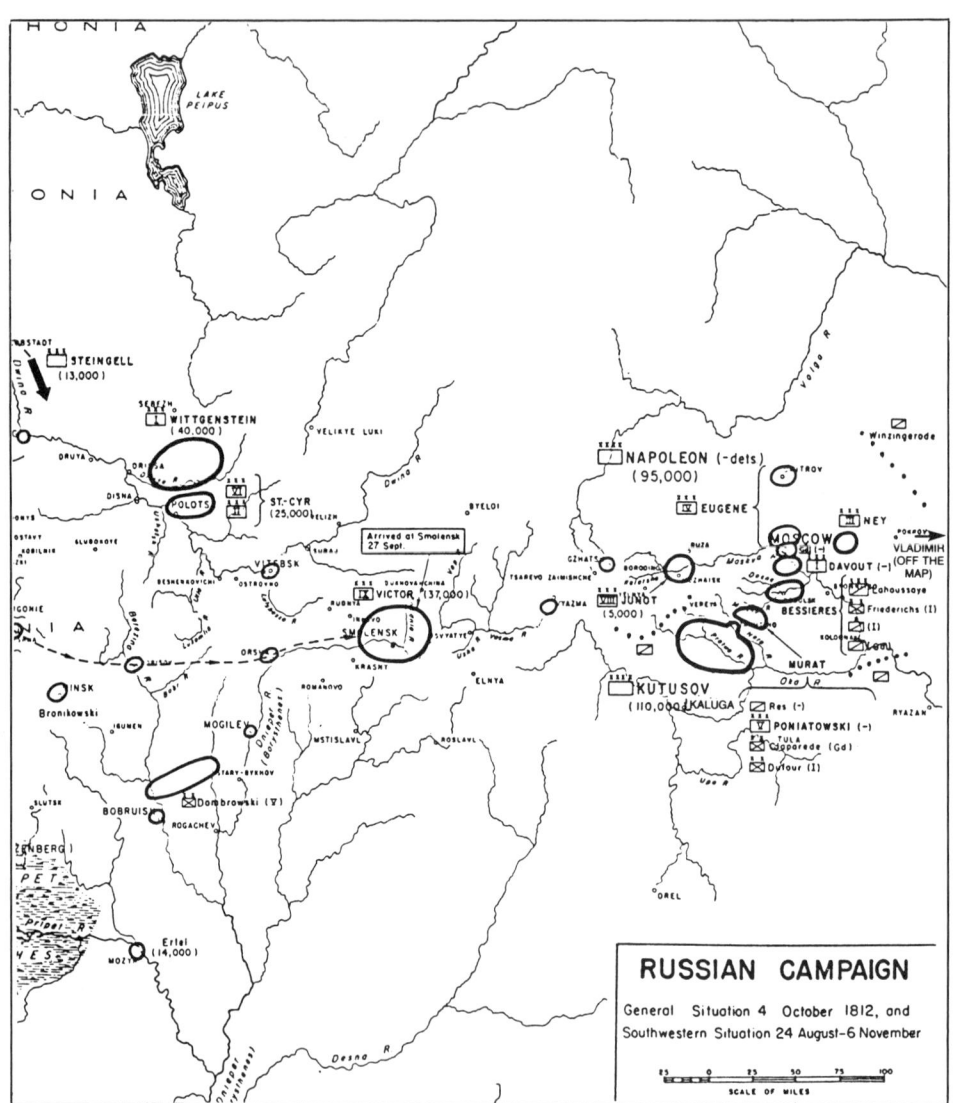

From *A Military History and Atlas of the Napoleonic Wars* (New York: Praeger).

Gorlitz position has operational significance only in that it covers the Prussian territory to its rear in Silesia. The position has little value operationally if the Austrians base themselves on the Elbe River. If the Austrians were to advance along the Elbe River, the Gorlitz position is too far from their lines of communication to pose a threat. While the Prussian army could move to confront the Austrians on the Elbe, as soon as the Prussians leave Gorlitz, they give up the tactical strength that it has provided. There is little value in a tactically strong position unless the enemy is forced to attack it or is immobilized by its operational potential. True, if the Austrians advance along the Spree or Neisse Rivers, they will be forced to deal with the Prussian army at Gorlitz, since a force of this size cannot be ignored. But by placing the Prussian army at Gorlitz, Roeder has countered only one of the most likely Austrian options, thus providing a classic example of a faulty operational decision made in order to take advantage of a tactically strong position. Because a position has tactical strength does not necessarily mean it has operational or strategic significance. While a tactically strong position (fortified) occupied by the entire army may block one enemy axis of advance, if other axes are available to the enemy he can avoid the defender.

In summary, Clausewitz understood the concept of levels of war; he used the term 'strategy' to represent the modern term 'operations', and he viewed campaign planning as involving both eccentric and concentric maneuvers of major formations. His *Two Letters on Strategy* is more than an excellent discussion and critique of a nineteenth century operational maneuver. Clausewitz stresses the importance of the unique characteristics of each situation, reminding us that no hypothetical case can specify all the momentary conditions that give rise to opportunity. Such opportunity is frequently the basis for victory, for campaigns never progress as planned. By making a wise initial deployment of forces, a commander can provide the opportunity for auspicious operations. But action is required to make use of the opportunity, or the advantage of position will soon disappear. These general rubrics make the *Two Letters* as valuable for today's soldiers as they were for Clausewitz' readers in Prussia 150 years ago.

NOTES

1. 'Operations', *FM 100/5* (Washington, DC: Department of the Army, 1982), pp.2–3.
2. All page references to *On War* are given in text, from the revised edition edited and translated by Michael Howard and Peter Paret (Princeton, NJ: Princeton University Press, 1976).
3. Carl von Clausewitz, *Two Letters on Strategy*, ed. and trans. Peter Paret and Daniel Moran (Carlisle, PA: Army War College Foundation, 1984), p.8.

4. Ibid., p.35.
5. Ibid., pp.38–9.
6. Ibid., p.41.
7. Ibid.
8. Ibid., p.42.
9. York von Wartenberg, *Napoleon as a General* (London: Wolseley Series, 1890), Vol. 2, p.282.
10. *Two Letters on Strategy*, p.42.
11. Ibid., p.43.

PART THREE
CLAUSEWITZ MISPERCEIVED

Once again we must remind the reader that, in order to lend clarity, distinction, and emphasis to our ideas, only perfect contrasts, the extremes of the spectrum, have been included in our observations. As an actual occurrence, war generally falls somewhere in between, and is influenced by these extremes only to the extent to which it approaches them.

On War, p. 517.

As so often happens, Clausewitz' disciples carried his teaching to an extreme which their master had not intended.

Misinterpretation has been the common fate of most prophets and thinkers in every sphere. Devout but uncomprehending disciples have been more damaging to the original conception than even its prejudiced and purblind opponents. It must be admitted, however, that Clausewitz invited misinterpretation more than most.

B. H. Liddell Hart, *Strategy*, p. 352.

The most important chapter is the one on Clausewitz, the father of modern war, and instead of attempting to condense his theories, I have quoted liberally from his *On War* for two reasons: because he was the first, and remains one of the few, who grasped that war 'belongs to the province of social life'; and because, although I have met many soldiers, politicians and others who have quoted or criticized his theories, I have come across only three or four who had carefully studied his great work.

J. F. C. Fuller,
The Conduct of War 1789–1961, pp. 12–13.

·

Clausewitz, Fuller and Liddell Hart

JAY LUVAAS

The wars of the French Revolution and Napoleon changed the form, substance, and scope of military operations, unleashed new sources of national energy, and transformed many social and political institutions. A sudden surge of nationalism made possible conscription and even the *levée en masse*, thus causing Clausewitz to think of war in terms of the absolute and forcing Jomini, his formidable rival for the attention of thoughtful soldiers everywhere, at least to acknowledge the dangers inherent in 'attacking an excited nation'. Jomini probably spoke for most professional soldiers when he confessed that as a military man he preferred 'loyal and chivalric war to organized assassination', which may help to explain why he focused his attention on the more traditional aspects of the art of war – strategy, grand tactics, and logistics.[1]

The Great War that engulfed Europe one hundred years after Waterloo was even more convulsive than the Napoleonic Wars, for it was shaped by dramatic developments in the intervening years in communications, transportation, and weapons technology. For the first time mankind was introduced to 'the total mobilization of all the resources of society for a prolonged struggle'.[2] Whether this new 'total war' was what Clausewitz had in mind when he referred to 'absolute war' is another matter, but because his theory seemed to specify the destruction of the enemy and allowed for the possibility that war could approach its 'pure concept with all its rigorous implications',[3] Clausewitz after 1918 was often regarded in an entirely new light.

The Great War forced a fresh look at military problems as serious soldiers everywhere endeavored to modernize and restructure military forces and to assimilate the lessons learned during four years of attrition in the trenches. Unlike the Napoleonic wars, which had produced revolutionary changes in military strategy (in the application of tactics the French armies had found no need to change the drill books issued *before* the wars of the Revolution), the First World War demonstrated the impact of the new technology upon *tactics*, for it was largely the tactical impasse that had produced the trench stalemate of 1914–18. Weapons and tactics had changed more dramatically during the last two years of the war than in all the years since Clausewitz.

The central issue for soldiers in the post-war years was the type of war to anticipate in the future: would it be a war of movement or another four years of attrition in trenches? What would be the size and nature of armies – the mass army or a small, highly trained professional army? What were the capabilities and limitation of air power? And finally, how to use weapons developed specifically to break the trench deadlock – poison gas and the tank?

Of the many military writers who participated in this reassessment, none were more prolific, controversial and influential than Major-General J. F. C. Fuller and Captain B. H. Liddell Hart. Lifelong students of war, both men dedicated their talents to the cause of reform and mechanization. They sought new order in history to provide a meaningful basis for their theories; they attempted to develop a reliable method for deducing scientific principles and for predicting future trends; and they endeavored to synthesize centuries of military experience in order to find signposts that modern armies had missed in the years before the war. Sooner or later in this search each inevitably confronted Clausewitz.

How does a military theorist develop? Almost from the first Clausewitz had shifted back and forth between history and theory.[4] In his instructions for the education of the Crown Prince he had devoted appropriate attention to the theory of combat, but even at this early stage Clausewitz seemed to be preoccupied with strategy. Theory, which came from his careful study of history, also enabled Clausewitz to explain and interpret military operations during the wars of Frederick and Napoleon.

In contrast, both Fuller and Liddell Hart devoted their formative years as theorists to the realm of tactics. Fuller, after publishing a brief work on *Training Soldiers for War* (1914) and a lengthy manuscript about 'Sir John Moore's System of Training', which he wrote in 1915 and published a decade later, next turned his attention to the training and tactics of the new tank corps. Here he was concerned primarily with matters of doctrine, organization, and equipment, and it was not until he had been actively involved at this level for ten years that he began to turn his creative mind to the study of strategy.

Liddell Hart's theories developed along similar lines. As a company officer in the First World War his primary concern had been at the level of small unit tactics. After the war Liddell Hart wrote pieces on battle drill and small arms training and published his military lectures as a small book entitled *The Framework of a Science of Infantry Tactics*. Like Fuller, Liddell Hart waited nearly a decade before he wrote much on the subject of strategy, although manifestly one cannot speculate upon the role of tanks and aircraft in future conflict without framing ideas in some sort of strategical context. Ironically, both Clausewitz and Liddell Hart, who differed so radically on the objectives of military strategy, focused upon Gustavus Adolphus in their early historical writings. Clausewitz' aim was to interpret the strategic policy of Gustavus; for his part, Liddell Hart concentrated on the tactics, organization, and military reforms of the Swedish monarch. The one sought to learn from Gustavus; the other, to use him as a constructive example.[5]

One other difference between Clausewitz and these two foremost theorists of blitzkrieg deserves mention. Clausewitz preferred to treat war as an art rather than a science, the difference being that art had as its object 'creative ability' whereas 'the term "science" should be kept for disciplines such as mathematics or astronomy, whose object is pure knowledge'. Admittedly it is often difficult to separate the two, since 'every theory of art may contain discrete sciences', and 'no science can exist without some element of art', but Clausewitz denied the notion, popular in his own day, that the study of strategy could be made more scientific. Instead Clausewitz argued that 'it is one of the chief functions of a comprehensive theory of war to expose such vagaries'.[6]

In contrast, Fuller believed that

> War is as much a science as all other human activities, and like all other sciences, it is built upon facts, of which there are an innumerable quantity. From these facts may we extract the elements of war and the principles of war and the conditions of war – the circumstances in which the principles must be brought to govern the elements.[7]

In like vein Liddell Hart wrote of pursuing 'objective truth' by establishing means for the 'scientific study of war in its various aspects'.

> There is, doubtless, a science of war [he wrote in 1935]; but we are a long way from discovering it. Apart from the mere technique of utilizing weapons, what passes for 'military science' is hardly more than the interpretation of conventions nurtured by tradition and warped by sentiment, patriotic and professional. Sentiment and science are incompatible, but this truth has yet to be accepted in the military world.[8]

Obviously Fuller and Liddell Hart not only came later than Clausewitz to the study of strategy but approached the subject from a different, 'scientific', direction.

In his booklet on training soldiers for war Captain Fuller indicated that he was familiar enough with Clausewitz to quote him on at least two occasions,[9] but his footnotes reveal that nearly all of his sources were French. Since he failed to document his citations from Clausewitz it could well be that these were derived from French sources as well. This would not be the first time – nor the last – that *On War* has been quoted rather than read. Like so many French soldiers of the day, Fuller did however go back to the ultimate fount of military wisdom, the published *Correspondance* of Napoleon, and from the 22,000 letters and documents contained therein, plus the four volumes that Napoleon had dictated at St. Helena, Captain Fuller deduced six working principles of war that in his judgment had guided Napoleon. Further analysis during the war yielded two additional principles, and after the war these eight principles in a slightly modified form entered the *Field Service Regulations*. Ultimately they crossed the Atlantic to form the basis of US doctrine.[10]

Fuller, who derived many of his insights from a systematic study of Napoleon and his campaigns, was known to friends throughout the army as 'Boney' because of his 'general appearance, stature and feature' and also because he was 'well up in Napoleonic lore' and had all of the maxims at his finger tips.[11] Having studied Napoleon's writings and correspondence, Fuller may well have decided to ignore Clausewitz in his researches into the past. Yet perhaps because Clausewitz also was a student of Napoleon, one can detect early some familiar ideas in writings of Fuller on the subject of strategy. In 1923 Fuller defined the responsibilities of the strategist:

> The first duty of the grand strategist is ... to appreciate the commercial and financial position of his country; to discover what its resources and liabilities are. Secondly, he must understand the moral characteristics of his countrymen, their history, peculiarities, social customs and system of government, for all these quantities and qualities form the pillars of the military arch .... The grand strategist of today must no longer be a mere servant of his ever-changing government, but a student of the permanent characteristics and slowly changing institutions of the nation .... He must, in fact, be a learned historian and a far-seeing philosopher, as well as a skillful strategist .... From the grand strategical point of view, it is just as important to realize the quality of the moral power of a nation, as the quantity of its manpower, or to establish moral communication by instituting ... the will to win throughout the nation and the fighting services.[12]

Like Clausewitz, Fuller believed that the strategist should reflect national policy, and his solution was for the grand strategist '*or generalissimo*' to be a long-standing member of the government, in order to assure that strategy marched in close step with policy. Such Napoleons are made and not born, he argued, and Napoleon himself would have been merely a good general 'had he not simultaneously possessed liberty of action in order to direct his genius according to the necessities of war'. When war comes, 'when Cosmos is dethroned by Chaos ... a nation requires THE MAN, because a study of the history of war ... has proven to us ... that the free untrammelled director in war is the dictator of victory'.[13]

But if Fuller shared Clausewitz' view of the relationship of policy and war, they were far from agreeing on the nature of war itself. Fuller in 1926 described Clausewitz' *On War* as 'little more than a mass of notes, a cloud of flame and smoke'. To describe war as 'a terrible and impassioned drama', to deny the science of war and then to theorize on war *as an art* was, in Fuller's judgment, the language of 'pure military alchemy'.[14]

If any of Fuller's books can be compared with *On War* it would be *The Foundations of the Science of War* (1926). Both works were written 'to teach soldiers how to think'.[15] Fuller's writings on mechanization and his earlier book, *The Reformation of War* (1923), were intended in part to jolt professional soldiers into accepting new ideas, but in this, by far his most serious work, Fuller endeavored to apply the method of science to the study of war. In his mind neither Clausewitz, Jomini, nor any of the other nineteenth-century theorists had succeeded in reducing war to a science. Fuller aimed high, hoping that 'in a small way' he could do for war 'what Copernicus did for astronomy, Newton for physics, and Darwin for natural history'.[16]

Because Clausewitz scoffed at the notion that there could be a science of war and probably also because he had little to say on the subject of technology – a subject dear to the heart of this apostle of mechanization – Fuller ignored the writings of Clausewitz in formulating his own theory of war. He believed that he had discovered certain fundamental laws that could be applied universally, and through which it would be possible to establish a foundation of knowledge about war 'so universal that it may be considered axiomatic to knowledge in all its forms'. If war was indeed a science as Fuller asserted, then truth could be discovered by applying the methods of science based upon analysis, synthesis, and hypothesis, and one could then determine the conditions and therefore the requirements of war in the future.

Clausewitz had asserted that the dominant tendencies in war compared a 'remarkable trinity' comprising blind natural force, the 'play of chance and probability within which the creative spirit is free to roam', and the 'element of subordination, as an instrument of policy, which makes it subject to reason':

> The first of these three aspects mainly concerns the people; the second the commander and his army; the third the government. The passions that are to be kindled in war must already be inherent in the

people; the scope which the play of courage and talent will enjoy in the realm of probability and chance depends on the particular character of the commander and the army; but the political aims are the business of government alone.

A theory that ignored any of these three tendencies or attempted 'to fix an arbitrary relationship between them' would clash with reality and therefore be totally useless.[18]

Fuller based his own system upon a threefold order, maintaining that all knowledge involved a person, an object, and the relationship between the two. Fuller saw the universe and everything in it as an intricate pattern of triads: earth, air, and water; solids, liquids, and gases; mind, body and soul; and so on. Man too, he decided, was organized on a threefold order. The body possesses *structure, control,* and *maintenance.* In *structure* the skeleton provides what Fuller called the stable base, muscles give power of action, and ligaments link the two in close cooperation. In *control* the stable base comes from the senses, the brain furnishes power of action, and the nerves make possible cooperation. In *maintenance* the stomach serves as the stable base, the repair organs give power of action, and the blood links the stomach to all parts of the body in close *cooperation.*[19]

Society was but an extension of this threefold order of man 'in a higher and more complex form'. The military instrument, representing the army, navy, and air force, likewise was built upon structural lines similar to the human organism, providing stability, activity, and cooperation. Like the human body, the military instrument possessed maintenance and control – maintenance meaning the 'link between fighting force and national power', and control provided by the machinery needed for efficient information, decision, and communication within the various fighting services.[20]

The threefold nature of war, according to Fuller, involved movement, weapons, and protection, and in considering the strategical and tactical formations best calculated to unite these elements he decided that artillery should be endowed with a higher power of movement, infantry must be given greater offensive power, and cavalry would have to be more highly protected. To this military scientist, at least, the solution was clear – it lay in the development of armored formations.[21]

Aside from the fact that both Clausewitz and Fuller saw war as comprising a trinity in the one case and a series of threefold orders in the other – a similarity explained perhaps by the fact that both men were somewhat influenced by the German idealistic philosopher Hegel, who also had organized his arguments in a triadic form – there is little evidence that Clausewitz influenced Fuller's *Foundations of the Science of War.* In reaching beyond military history Fuller sought to apply the methods of science, so he drew more upon the writings of Herbert Spencer and William James than those of Clausewitz, who had never attempted to apply modern methods to the study of war. In the pre-1914 era, instead of developing a science of war, 'the Germans were copying von Moltke, the French were trying to discover how to copy Napoleon', and Fuller was not altogether sure what his own army had been doing – probably 'watching these copyists'.[22]

Clausewitz had developed theory to provide the framework for a serious study of wars and campaigns; Fuller wanted to develop a scientific method of analysis that would improve the army's efficiency by imparting useful knowledge. To Clausewitz theory should be study, not doctrine; its role was to guide the *commander* in his self-education. To Fuller it was imperative to study war with the methods of science so that the conditions of the next conflict might be accurately forecast. He wanted an institutional approach, one that would apply intelligently recent developments in technology and other scientific knowledge to prepare the *army* for the next war. Fuller, who once described Clausewitz as 'a general of the agricultural age',[23] was both product and prophet of the machine age. In his book *On Future Warfare* (1928), he never mentioned Clausewitz; there is no obvious reason why he should have.

Fuller does, however, quote approvingly from *On War* in his next book, *The Generalship of U.S. Grant*, although in one inexplicable passage he claims that Napoleon's methods were not understood by soldiers in general and 'by Clausewitz in particular' – which may mean simply that Fuller understood Napoleon from an angle of his own.[24] Clausewitz would have approved, however, the way Fuller accompanied Grant through his campaigns, watching his leadership grow and his strategy take shape. For Fuller endeavored to write 'living history' in which he relied on three basic sources: the official records which he likened to the bones in his threefold order, personal memoirs (the muscles), and his own 'intuitions and deductions' (the nerves). It is curious that Fuller did not use Clausewitz to help present Grant, for Clausewitz in Book III explains and justifies the essential qualities for a strategist – boldness, determination, and success in concentrating superior numbers – the very qualities characteristic of Grant.

In 1930 Fuller was promoted to Major General and placed on half pay. In 1932 he wrote his most detailed and methodical book on armored warfare, and the next year he was retired. By this time he had grown weary of writing about armored warfare, he despaired over his lack of success in convincing the army's leaders, so increasingly he turned his attention to the study of international politics and war. Now Fuller paid somewhat greater attention to Clausewitz, for on this subject *On War* obviously had much to offer. By 1932 Clausewitz impressed Fuller as 'the first great thinker in modern times to review the whole problem of war'. Here again Fuller understood things from his own angle: when Clausewitz described war as 'a political instrument, a continuation of political commerce ... by other means', Fuller undertook to convey the 'inner meaning' of this familiar passage.

> Political commerce – that is, the relations between a government and a people, and a government and other governments – is founded on power, which during peace-time expresses itself in the main morally and intellectually, and during war-time physically. This commerce is therefore threefold in nature, depending upon justice, reason and force. The abolition of force is impossible in a well-ordered society, as impossible as the abolition of justice or reason. To abolish the police is to invite anarchy, and to abolish armies and navies is to do the same in a higher degree. The question is not one of abolition, but of adjustment between justice, reason, and force .... To abolish war, war being looked upon as a thing in itself apart from justice and reason, is ... irrational ... because if by some magician all armies, navies and air forces were removed from this world, war would remain and tomorrow a universal anarchy would prevail.

Thus Fuller drew upon Clausewitz in suggesting that despite the efforts of the League of Nations and the disarmament conference about to assemble in Geneva, war and peace were closely related, and that if war was to be eliminated it could only be by recreating the peace – and 'by drastically changing our social order'.[25] But when one finds Fuller agreeing with Liddell Hart's assertion that Clausewitz had hypnotized soldiers with his theory of absolute warfare, one wonders whether Fuller yet understood Clausewitz – or merely used him.

Fuller returned to this theme in his next work, *War and Western Civilization 1832–1932*. Here his thesis was that war as an expression of mass democracy was becoming increasingly emotional and brutal, while at the same time science had 'delivered into the hands of the masses more and more deadly means of destruction' – two mighty streams which by 1914 had merged to overwhelm the dikes of traditional warfare. Marshal Foch, Fuller wrote, had failed to understand Clausewitz; he also took issue with the notion – popular among readers of Clausewitz – 'that policy is best enforced by destruction, and ... that tactical strength is founded upon numbers', and he relieved his readers of the necessity of reading *On War* by presenting the main ideas:

> War is only a continuation of State policy by other means.
> War is nothing but a duel on an extensive scale ... Let us not hear of generals who conquer without bloodshed .... Destruction of the

enemy's military forces is in reality the object of all combats.
There is only one form of war: To wit, the attack of the enemy.
The best strategy is always to be strong.
The defensive form of War is in itself stronger than the offensive ...
but has a negative object .... The attack is the positive intention, the
defense the negative ....
Only great and general battles can produce great results.
War is divided into preparation and action ....
Everything is very simple in war, but the simplest thing is difficult.

Such in brief 'is the doctrine of Clausewitz, a kind of "Spartanism" which
turns the State into a military machine'. Fuller contended that Clausewitz
believed that the main object of the State is 'to manufacture war-power
instead of merely insuring itself against war'. What Clausewitz really did,
he claimed, was to democratize war; add the spirit of his doctrines to that
of Darwin's *The Origin of Species* and one had the Prussian Military
System; throw in Karl Marx's *Das Kapital* and the Russian Revolutionary
System emerged. All three writers, he noted, based their theories upon
mass struggle, whether in war, in life, or in economics.[26]

By 1936, when he wrote *The First of the League Wars*, Fuller was
concerned about what he called totalitarian warfare – the rationalization
of Clausewitz; the psychology of the moral attack; the organization and
discipline of the modern war state; and the concentration of all powers,
political and military, in the hands of what was in effect a *generalissimo*.
Once again he used Clausewitz rather than studying him, for in tracing
the march of western civilization to the Great War and beyond, Fuller
claimed that *On War* had 'the profoundest influence upon Western
civilization, more profound even than upon the military art'. Whereas
Clausewitz had looked upon war as 'a continuation of political commerce', to the modern totalitarian mind war appeared as its fountain-
head.[27] Convinced that modern civilization was in an advanced state of
decay, Fuller felt an acute need for national discipline and new ideals.
Eventually he embraced fascism and the corporate state as a well-meaning
attempt to seek higher economic, political, and cultural freedom through
coordinated knowledge, order, and authority. Clausewitz had written of
absolute war; Fuller tried to make him appear relevant to modern totalitarian warfare.

The Conduct of War, one of Fuller's last books, contains the mature
reflections on war and policy of this unusual soldier. Examining the
impact of the French, Industrial, and Russian revolutions upon warfare,
Fuller found a unifying theme in Clausewitz' well-known dictum: 'War is
only a continuation of State policy by other means.' Here he refined some
of his earlier theories, softened many of his political views, and claimed

that Hitler and Stalin possessed a surer grasp of what Clausewitz meant by war than did the leaders of the Western democracy, who may have won the war but failed to win the peace.

In this book, which Fuller intended as his final statement on the conduct of war, Clausewitz emerges as though dressed for a masquerade ball. *On War* now appeared as

> a jumble of essays, memoranda, and notes set together in no very precise form. It is prolix, repetitive, full of platitudes and truisms, and in place contradictory and highly involved. It is not, as it is sometimes held to be, a study based on the Napoleonic wars. Instead it is a pseudo-philosophical exposition on war interlarded with valuable common-sense observations.

The previous two-page summary of Clausewitz' basic ideas is expanded to ten, with a section of People's War and the provocative observation that Clausewitz was probably the first to suggest that Russia could only be conquered on her inner front, meaning 'victory through revolution'. Fuller died, however, still convinced that Clausewitz had disregarded Napoleonic Warfare. Of all Clausewitz' blind shots, he concluded, the blindest was that he had 'never grasped that the true aim of war is peace and not victory; therefore that peace should be the ruling idea of policy, and victory only the means toward its achievements'.[28]

Fuller observed that 'the word "peace" barely occurs half a dozen times in *On War*'. He would scarcely say that if he had not read the entire book; on the other hand he would never have written many of his other statements had he read Clausewitz carefully and with an open mind. An admirer once described Fuller as

> a totally unconventional soldier, prolific in ideas, fluent in expression, at daggers drawn with received opinion, authority, and tradition .... His knowledge of literature was wide enough to enable him to condemn most of what was good .... He was a great reader of Shakespeare, whom he admired and understood from an angle of his own, and had dabbled in philosophy, of which he could handle a few elementary statements to the complete confounding and obfuscation of the officers' mess.

Fuller was perhaps too unconventional a soldier ever to come to terms with Clausewitz, which is all the more the pity because he was no less serious in his determination to understand war.

Paradoxically Fuller and Clausewitz had much in common. Both had formulated theory from a detailed analysis of Napoleon or his campaigns. Each was influenced by the spirit of the time and by theoretical methods developed in other and often unrelated fields — the influence of the

German philosophers and also, in the case of Fuller, of exponents of the scientific method. Each excelled in historical synthesis and periodization: Fuller's *Armament and History* (1945) is as masterful in its way as Clausewitz' analysis of the transformation of war following the French Revolution. Clausewitz died before the completion of his great work, while Fuller jumped from one interest to another with such frequency that he produced only a final chapter – his book entitled *The Conduct of War* – instead of a synthesis of his studies on war. Both had strong interest in the relationship of policy and strategy. Each had taught at a higher military college, and, although their techniques differed, each was determined to stretch the thinking of the military reader. Clausewitz would do this through his method of critical analysis; Fuller, by means of the scientific approach to the study of war – and occasionally by being outrageous. Even Fuller did not claim infallibility for his particular theory, insisting only upon the practical need to devise *some* method whereby armed forces could be organized and constructed along scientific lines. Finally, both theorists were highly quotable.

So too was Liddell Hart, one of the most prolific and influential students of war in this or any other century. Liddell Hart, however, was much more in the tradition of Jomini than Clausewitz. His abiding interest was in strategy rather than the nature of war itself. He was as prescriptive as Jomini, and his 'strategy of indirect approach' along with its necessary components was repeatedly offered the reader with the same degree of assurance that Jomini displayed in expounding his 'fundamental principle of all the operations of war'. (This principle consisted in throwing the mass of one's forces upon the decisive points of a theater of war, the enemy's line of communications, or fractions of the hostile army.)[30] Each theorist insisted that his formula was eternal in its application and devoted the better part of a lifetime to persuading readers that this was so. They both liked to coin descriptive words or phrases that conveyed concepts: 'logistics' is apparently a Jomini word, while one finds in Liddell Hart's later writings frequent mention of 'baited gambit', 'alternative objectives', and the 'expanding torrent' method of attack. Jomini and Liddell Hart wrote in measured and lucid prose, in contrast to the energetic, metaphysical, and often contradictory language of Clausewitz and Fuller. Jomini and Liddell Hart (who was born in Paris) seemed to be more closely attuned to French military literature, whereas Fuller, at least in his later years, found German ideas much more to his liking.

In one respect only did Liddell Hart depart from the tradition of Jomini: he was always critical of Napoleon. Clausewitz was almost prophetic when he predicted that it is 'quite possible that at some time in the future, Bonaparte's campaigns and battles will be considered brutalities, almost blunders' by historians and theorists who view battle 'as a kind of evil brought about by mistake' and consequently would praise commanders 'who knew how to conduct a war without bloodshed'.[31] It is not a coincidence that Liddell Hart's first work of a historical nature was entitled *A Greater than Napoleon!*

In his writings on tactics, strategy, and military history, Liddell Hart was driven by one passionate desire – to avoid repetition of the senseless slaughter of 1914–18. His tactical theories centered on the intelligent maneuver of firepower and the sustained exploitation of the breakthrough for infantry and later on the creation of an armored force capable of maneuvering against the enemy's rear; his strategical theories hinged on a strategy of indirect approach aimed at dislocating the enemy's moral, mental, and material balance before attempting to overthrow him on the battlefield; and he used history both to illustrate and confirm his strategical theories. Liddell Hart preferred quality to quantity in things military; he preferred a strategy based upon surprise, mobility, and maneuver; most of all, he vigorously opposed the siege-warfare mentality that characterized the Great War, the 'progressive butchery, politely called "attrition"', which had become the essence of war on the Western front. Another war conducted by similar methods would inevitably mean the breakdown of Western civilization.[32]

Liddell Hart, tracing back the concept that an absolute war could be won only by mass destruction, found it in Napoleon and even more in the 'fallacies' fostered by his disciple Clausewitz. 'He it was who, in the years succeeding Waterloo, analyzed, codified, and deified the Napoleonic method' that contributed directly to the structure of the nation in arms. Although this nation triumphed in the victories of 1866 and 1870, Clausewitz ended 'by bringing his Fatherland into a more impotent and impoverished state even than it was under the iron heel of Napoleon'. Clausewitz' theory, which stressed 'the destruction of the enemy's main forces on the battlefield' as the only true objective in war, was a house built on sand. Clausewitz and his successors, Liddell Hart insisted, were 'false prophets' who preached the 'superficial deduction' that the armed forces themselves constituted the real objective in war.[33] Thus from the first Liddell Hart took a warped and one-sided view of Clausewitz, who seemed to stress mass rather than mobility and the decisive battle above all else.

In his biography of *Foch* Liddell Hart became more specific in his criticisms, asserting that Foch had derived his single-minded views on strategy from Clausewitz.

> The ponderous tomes of Clausewitz are so solid as to cause mental indigestion to any student who swallows them without a long course of preparation. Only a mind developed by years of study and reflec-

tion can dissolve the solid lump into digestible particles. Critical power and a wide knowledge of history are also necessary for producing the juices to counteract the Clausewitzian fermentation.[34]

In not possessing these corrective qualifications Foch (but presumably not Liddell Hart) was handicapped. The path blazed by Clausewitz was too narrow; if absolute war has any meaning 'it is that of a fight until the capacity of one side for further resistance is exhausted'. In modern war only tactical results mattered. Obviously Foch's theory 'was but the reflection of Clausewitz', and while staring ahead along the narrow path, Foch had 'failed to look carefully at the ground beneath his feet'.[35]

Liddell Hart's criticisms of Clausewitz center on what he considered the three dominant theories in *On War*: the theory of absolute warfare, with its corollary of the nation in arms; the theory that one must concentrate first against the main enemy; and the theory that the true objective in war is the enemy's armed forces so that everything is subject to the supreme law of battle. 'Clausewitz, with that tendency to dramatic generalization which obscured his many discerning reflections', was guilty of making too subtle distinctions between ways and means.

> It was an easy step for his less profound disciples to confuse the means with the end and to reach the conclusion that in war every other interest and consideration should be subordinated to the aim of fighting a decisive battle.[36]

Liddell Hart's most extreme views of Clausewitz were expressed in his Lees Knowles Lectures for 1932–33. Calling him 'the Mahdi of Mass', he reiterated his view that Clausewitz had made policy the slave of strategy, that he 'looked only to the end of a war, not beyond war to the subsequent peace', and that his principle of force without limit 'is the negation of statesmanship – and of intelligent strategy'. When Clausewitz wrote that the enemy's armed forces was the only true objective of strategy, he had 'made it a dogma without meaning to do so'. True, Clausewitz had sufficient historical sense to recognize a 'modification in the reality', but his qualifications unfortunately came in later pages 'and were conveyed in a philosophical language that befogged the plain soldier, essentially concrete minded'. Ringing phrases like 'we have only one means in war – the battle', 'the bloody solution of the crisis ...' and 'let us not hear of generals who conquer without bloodshed' blurred the outlines of his theory

> and made it into a mere marching refrain – a Prussian *Marseillaise* – which inflamed the blood and intoxicated the mind .... By making battle appear as the only 'real warlike activity', his gospel deprived strategy of its laurels, reduced the art of war to the mechanics of

mass-slaughter, and incited generals to seek battle at the *first* opportunity, instead of creating an *advantageous* opportunity.[37]

Thus did Liddell Hart challenge what he called the Clausewitzian
concept of 'absolute war' that later emerged as the doctrine 'that the only
right course in war was to pursue an unlimited aim with unlimited
effort'.[38] Not only did he hold Clausewitz responsible for his disciples; he
repeatedly ignored what *On War* had to say about modifications in
practice and the probabilities of real life as opposed to the absolute
required by theory, which in the words of Clausewitz meant that 'without
any inconsistency wars can have all degrees of importance and intensity,
ranging from a war of extermination down to simple armed observation'.[39]

Throughout his life Liddell Hart lived constantly in the shadow of the
Somme. Looking back across the 'no man's land' of the 1914–18 war, he
viewed Clausewitz as being almost as static as the Western front.

> For Clausewitz, in his masterly analysis of the mental and physical
> spheres of war, neglected the material – man's tools. If he there-
> by ensured to his work an enduring permanence, he also, if un-
> wittingly, ensured permanent injury to subsequent generations who
> allowed themselves to forget that the spirit cannot win battles when
> the body has been killed through failure to provide it with up-to-
> date weapons.[40]

More to the point, he could not accept Clausewitz' definition of strategy
as 'the art of the employment of battles as a means to gain the object of the
war'. According to this definition strategy 'intrudes on the sphere of
policy' and at the same time is narrowed to mean the pure utilization of
battle. But even if a decisive battle is the only goal of strategy, as Clausewitz apparently assumed, Liddell Hart would still argue – and did in
practically every book he wrote after 1930 – that the object of strategy
surely was to produce this battle, not by massing for a direct approach,
but by diminishing the possibility of resistance. The correct strategy was
one of indirect approach that exploited the elements of movement and
surprise. Liddell Hart thus preferred to define strategy as 'the art of
distributing and applying military means to fulfil the ends of policy'.[41]

He agreed with Clausewitz on some particulars: his own historical
studies suggested that in most battles 'the loser was the army which was
the first to commit itself to the attack',[42] which Clausewitz had observed
when analyzing the campaigns of Frederick the Great; and in one of
his last books he endorsed what Clausewitz had said on problems of
command and control. Ironically he commented that few soldiers had
ever studied very thoroughly Clausewitz' book, the 'Holy Scriptures' of
the military profession.[43]

Probably Liddell Hart himself should be included in this category, for while there is no doubt that he read *On War* in his formative years, his early conviction that Clausewitz had induced soldiers in the last century to think in terms of preparing armies for the mass slaughter of Armageddon, albeit unwittingly, created a mental deadlock that he never was able to penetrate. His own theory based on a Strategy of Indirect Approach was clearly antithetical in detail and concept to what he had read in *On War*. Quite possibly Liddell Hart's own work habits are a factor here as well, for he was accustomed to concentrating on a given subject until he felt he had assessed it properly and then to put it into his files, to be redeployed intact whenever his mind crossed that portion of the field again. Although he may have consulted Clausewitz occasionally on some particular subject, it is unlikely that he ever reread *On War* – certainly not with an open mind – after his initial exposure in the 1920s. On the other hand, Fuller probably did reread Clausewitz, once his interest shifted from tanks and the science of war to the study of war as a political instrument.

Neither Fuller nor Liddell Hart appear to have been influenced by Clausewitz in formulating his respective theories – quite the contrary. As original thinkers they regarded him as a part of history and not as a source for fresh ideas. Both wrote widely on the subject of history, but often in ways that Clausewitz would have disapproved, particularly in their use of historical examples. (If one presents some historical event 'in order to demonstrate a general truth', Clausewitz had warned, 'care must be taken that every aspect bearing on the truth at issue is fully and circumstantially developed ... before the reader's eyes'.)[44] Clausewitz would have disagreed with Fuller's habit of using someone from history as a peg for his own ideas – which he admitted doing in his fascinating study of Grant – and he would have had little faith in any 'magic formula', such as 'The Strategy of Indirect Approach'. According to Clausewitz, history yields no formulas – that had been Jomini's mistake.

NOTES

1. Baron de Jomini, *Summary of the Art of War, or, A New Analytical Compend of the Principal Combinations of Strategy, of Grand Tactics and of Military Policy* (New York: G. P. Putnam Sons, 1954), pp. 42, 46.
2. Michael Howard, *War in European History* (London: Oxford University Press, 1976), p. 112.
3. Carl von Clausewitz, *On War*, ed. and trans. Michael Howard and Peter Paret (Princeton, NJ: Princeton University Press, 1976), p. 580.
4. Peter Paret, *Clausewitz and the State* (New York: Oxford University Press, 1976), pp. 328–9.
5. Ibid., pp. 85–7; Captain B. H. Liddell Hart, *Great Captains Unveiled* (Boston: Little, Brown

& Co., 1927), pp. 75–152.

6. Clausewitz, *On War*, p. 148.
7. Colonel J. F. C. Fuller, *The Reformation of War* (London: Hutchinson & Co., 1932), p. 25.
8. B. H. Liddell Hart, *Thoughts on War* (London: Faber & Faber, 1944), pp. 16, 24.
9. Captain J. F. C. Fuller, *Training Soldiers for War* (London: Hugh Rees, 1914), pp. 9, 22.
10. Ibid., pp. 41–2; Colonel J. F. C. Fuller, *The Foundations of the Science of War* (London: Hutchinson & Co., 1926), pp. 13–14.
11. Quoted in Captain B. H. Liddell Hart, *The Tanks: The History of the Royal Tank Regiment* (2 vols., New York: Frederick A. Praeger, 1959), Vol. 1, pp. 120–21.
12. Fuller, *Reformation of War*, pp. 218–19.
13. Ibid., p. 227.
14. Fuller, *Foundation of the Science of War*, pp. 20–21, 75.
15. Major-General J. F. C. Fuller, *Memoirs of an Unconventional Soldier* (London: Ivor Nicholson & Watson, 1936), p. 458.
16. Fuller, *Foundations of the Science of War*, p. 18.
17. Ibid., p. 48.
18. Clausewitz, *On War*, p. 89.
19. Fuller, *Foundations of the Science of War*, pp. 55–62.
20. Ibid., pp. 85–92.
21. Ibid., pp. 93–174.
22. Ibid., p. 26.
23. Major-General J. F. C. Fuller, *The Dragon's Teeth: A Study of War and Peace* (London: Constable & Co., 1932), p. 210.
24. Colonel J. F. C. Fuller, *The Generalship of Ulysses S. Grant* (London: John Murray, 1929), pp. 55, 187, 407.
25. Fuller, *Dragon's Teeth*, pp. vi, 66–7.
26. Major-General J. F. C. Fuller, *War and Western Civilization 1832–1932: A Study of War as a Political Instrument and the Expression of Mass Democracy* (London: Duckworth, 1932), pp. 47, 158, 226; *The First of the League Wars: Its Lessons and Omens* (London: Eyre & Spottiswoode, 1936), p. 103.
27. Ibid., pp. 101, 168.
28. Major-General J. F. C. Fuller, *The Conduct of War 1789–1961: A Study of the Impact of the French, Industrial, and Russian Revolutions on War and its Conduct* (New Brunswick, NJ: Rutgers University Press, 1961), pp. 59–76.
29. Quoted in Liddell Hart, *The Tanks*, Vol. 1, p. 120.
30. Jomini, *Summary of the Art of War*, pp. 80–81.
31. Clausewitz, *On War*, pp. 259–60.
32. Captain B. H. Liddell Hart, *Paris or the Future of War* (London: Kegan Paul, Trench, Trubner & Co., 1925), pp. 10, 80–81.
33. Ibid., pp. 16–17; Liddell Hart, *The Remaking of Modern Armies* (London: John Murray, 1927), pp. 103–4.
34. B. H. Liddell Hart, *Foch the Man of Orleans* (2 vols., London: Penguin Books, 1937), p. 33.
35. Ibid., pp. 485, 492, 519.
36. Liddell Hart, *The British War in Warfare* (London: Faber & Faber, 1932), pp. 17–20, 95.
37. Liddell Hart, *The Ghost of Napoleon* (London: Faber & Faber), pp. 120–26.
38. *The Liddell Hart Memoirs 1895–1938* (2 vols., New York: G. P. Putnam Sons, 1965), Vol. 1, p. 280; *Thoughts on War*, p. 43.
39. Clausewitz, *On War*, pp. 78–81.
40. Liddell Hart, *Thoughts on War*, p. 158.
41. Ibid., p. 229.
42. Ibid., p. 293.
43. B. H. Liddell Hart, *Defence of the West: Some Riddles of War and Peace* (London, Cassell & Co., 1950), pp. 293–4.
44. Clausewitz, *On War*, pp. 170–74.

Misperceptions of Clausewitz' *On War* by the German Military

JEHUDA L. WALLACH

> For a whole century Clausewitz, as he feared, was read by men
> who were looking for prescriptions, for ready formulas, and not
> by men who were prepared to learn, to reflect on war.
>
> – Raymond Aron[1]

Although the British military historian Cyril B. Falls regarded Clausewitz as 'the High Priest in the Temple of Mars',[2] and the author of this article maintained in a book, published eighteen years ago, that 'in Germany his [that is, Clausewitz'] work gained general recognition soon after its first publication, and quickly became the "Bible" of the German officers',[3] it is unfortunately true that *On War*, like other sacred texts, has been perverted by its users. The purpose of this article is to examine how Clausewitz was studied, understood, and often misunderstood, by German military thinkers of the late nineteenth and early twentieth centuries. I will first discuss the generalized rejection of Clausewitz by the 'pragmatists', particularly Schlieffen, and then concentrate on two issues on which German thinkers and Clausewitz disagreed: the role of the attack versus the defense and the role of the military leaders versus the politicians.

I. REJECTION OF CLAUSEWITZ BY THE 'PRAGMATISTS'

A. *The Period before the First World War*

The most outstanding feature of Clausewitz' theory is that he does not prescribe a particular course of action to be followed in practice, but asserts that events happen by a lawful process. This, however, naturally irritates many soldiers, who would prefer to be presented with clear-cut instructions. Little wonder, therefore, that as early as 1873 in a supplement to the prestigious *Militär-Wochenblatt* ('Military Weekly') one finds some critical comments mixed with the following appreciation:

> Clausewitz is rightly regarded in the German Army as the principal

military-scientific authority, since he rejected all theories which had tried to perceive the war in a geometrical fashion, either from over-evaluation of the ground or for other narrow-minded reasons; but he has not provided a positive theory .... The endeavor to perceive and prescribe the war and its nature in a scientific way is neglected. The tremendous successes of the wars of 1866 and 1870–71 support this way of viewing things, according to which strict discipline, good weapons, expedient elementary-tactics, good marching orders, rail-ways, practical supply measures and the telegraph decide everything in war. This purely craftsman-like conception, so widely spread in the Army, is the reciprocal consequence of Clausewitz' ingenious work of destruction, the mighty deeds of the last years and the material direction of the present time.[4]

The well-known German expert on Clausewitz, Professor Werner Hahlweg, maintains that the attitude of the German military in the decades between 1871 and 1914 is characterized by a certain ambiva-lence: on the one hand, following Moltke and his disciples, they paid attention primarily to the military theses of *On War*, while they rejected Clausewitz' political postulates or accepted them only conditionally.[5] On the other hand they gradually turned away from Clausewitz, so that in many circles of the Prussian-German Army there appeared a certain ignorance of the true intellectual and political-philosophical foundations of *On War*. The attitude to the problems of war became almost entirely a workmanlike one. The true Clausewitzian demand for a 'contemplative' theory was renounced in order to evolve 'positive doctrines', 'instruc-tions', and 'guidelines' for practical actions in the most limited technical spheres.[6]

Max Jahns, the biographer of Moltke, wrote in 1906 that though the impact of Clausewitz was 'almost of a mystical nature', his works were much less read than one might assume. He added the somewhat indefinite remark, that Clausewitz' 'views nevertheless spread throughout the whole Army' and were 'immeasurably fruitful'.[7]

Count Alfred von Schlieffen, Chief of the General Staff from 1891 until the end of 1905, regarded himself as a disciple of Clausewitz (a view also held by some subsequent German writers).[8] Unlike other military leaders who criticized Clausewitz' 'philosophical conception', he looked at Clausewitz' work as a practical guide for the conduct of war. It probably never entered his mind that he deviated in the slightest from Clausewitz' theory. He wrote in his introduction to the fifth edition of *On War* in 1905: 'He who teaches war in Germany, does this even today consciously or unconsciously, by leaning more or less closely upon Clausewitz, and by drawing from his inexhaustible wealth of thoughts.'

In fact, what Schlieffen really perceived from Clausewitz' theory, as expressed in this introduction, was that

> the permanent merit of the work 'On War' lies, in addition to its high ethical and psychological value, in its emphatic accentuation of the annihilation idea. Clausewitz regarded war as being under 'the sole and highest law of decision by arms'. It seemed to him that 'the destruction of the hostile forces is the most commanding purpose among those which may be pursued by war'. This is the doctrine which led us to Königgrätz and Sedan ...

Whereas Clausewitz presented his reader with the analytical tools to examine the complex phenomena of war, to evaluate its relationship to other social phenomena, and to make a sound estimate of any concrete or hypothetical situation, Schlieffen presented strict rules of 'do' and 'do not'. As one of Schlieffen's most outspoken partisans has expressed it: 'In Count Schlieffen's writings you will never find spacious, theoretical discussions on strategy and tactics nor scientific evolution of theories or maxims, but only life and reality.'[9] Another great admirer of Schlieffen maintained that Schlieffen taught 'applied strategy', as opposed to 'philosophical strategy', clearly appreciating Schlieffen's practical outlook as compared with Clausewitz' 'philosophical' (the latter being a term of abuse in the German military vocabulary).[10]

Nevertheless, most of Schlieffen's supporters and admirers claim that his teachings were in fact firmly rooted in the soil of Clausewitz' theory and of Moltke's extensions, seeking only to adopt these earlier thinkers' ideas to new developments.

There was, however, a minority which was worried by the craftsman-like tendency of the Prussian-German officers' corps. As early as 1912 – still during Schlieffen's lifetime – Friedrich von Bernhardi, a well-known military writer of that time, warned in his book *On War of To-Day*, that narrow-mindedness had taken possession of German military thought. He pointed out the danger that the Germany Army was 'on the high road of becoming slaves to such one-sidedness'.[11] These remarks were without doubt aimed at Schlieffen's military writings, which were widely publicized at that time.

But Bernhardi was then 'a voice crying in the wilderness'. Therefore, one may not be surprised to learn that even the 'Younger' Moltke, a highly intelligent and sophisticated man – also well-versed in philosophy – neglected Clausewitz' theory and went after Schlieffen's more practical teachings. His son, Adam Moltke, remembered in his unpublished memoirs that 'my father gave me, in order to prepare myself for the entrance to the War Academy, the great standard-edition of Schlieffen's "Cannae" and urged me to study if diligently'.[12] That this attitude was not accidental is also indicated by General Groener, who recalled that 'in my military reading, I was more occupied with books of the practical service, than with works on high strategy. I procured Clausewitz' "On War" only in later years.'[13]

B. The First World War

One may state – without running the risk of over-simplification – that the First World War was on both sides of the frontlines void of any strategic ideas. It is therefore amazing that during this war six successive editions of On War were published.[14] From 1915 these editions contained prefaces by the most prominent German and Austrian Generals, in addition to Schlieffen's above-mentioned introduction of 1905.[15] One is struck by the insignificant, or rather nonsensical subject matter of these prefaces. The only point these gentlemen had grasped from Clausewitz' theoretical work was the one and only point Schlieffen stressed in 1905: the idea of annihilation.

Even so clever, intelligent, and educated a soldier as General Hans von Seeckt was as far as Clausewitz was concerned no different from his military colleagues. In a letter to his wife, dated 26 March 1917, Seeckt stated that Clausewitz was insignificant to him. He was quoted too often, so that 'the mentioning of his name alone makes one feel sick'. Seeckt's biographer, Colonel Hans Meier-Welcker, calls this a typical utterance of a German officer – and in particular a Staff officer, for whom Clausewitz' theoretical temperament was senseless.[16]

Indeed, while Clausewitz' impact on the First World War was mainly a negative one, through the disregarding of his theory, Schlieffen's 'shadow hung over the First World War ... and his influence on German military thought can hardly be overestimated', as Hajo Holborn has said.[17]

C. The Inter-War Period

In spite of the German débâcle in the First World War, which might have given the impulse for theoretical contemplation, the general attitude of the German officers towards theory did not change. In a lecture delivered at the Wehrmachtakademie in 1935, a German Staff officer stated that one often quotes theories but seldom reads them, and usually postpones the study of theories until the more leisurely time of retirement. However, until this time is reached, one prefers the role of a 'man of action' and sneers at 'faded theory', believing that war is an art which cannot be taught and learned, but must be an innate quality.[18] After the Second World War Field Marshal von Kleist confessed to Liddell Hart that

> Clausewitz' teaching had fallen into neglect in this generation – even at the time when I was at the War Academy, and on the General

Staff. His phrases were quoted, but his books were not closely studied. He was regarded as a military philosopher, rather than as a practical teacher. The writings of Schlieffen received much greater attention. They seemed more practical.[19]

However, in his critical analysis of the First World War, Leinveber perceived Clausewitz' theoretical contribution to the conduct of this war in the same way as Schlieffen had seen it in the above-mentioned introduction to the fifth edition of *On War*. Therefore Leinveber emphasized that Schlieffen's image of the war of annihilation harmonized with that of Clausewitz.[20]

The same view was also expressed later on, already close to the outbreak of the Second World War, by a retired German General: 'The maxims of "On War", above all the annihilation idea considered as the nature of the war, became the spiritual equipment that constituted the superiority of our leadership in the last great war.'[21]

In spite of the traumatic experience of the lost war, General von Seeckt, now in fact – though not by title – the Commander-in-Chief of the *Reichswehr*, did not change his mind about Clausewitz. On the occasion of Clausewitz' 150th birthday in 1930 von Seeckt still referred to *On War* as 'difficult reading' and as in its diction 'rather obscure and clumsy, following the idiom of the contemporary philosophy'.[22] And some years later he again wrote to his wife that 'regarding Clausewitz I am lacking the profound philosophical training; I am rather an empiricist with the talent to find sometimes a lucky formulation'.[23]

Another German General of the *Reichswehr* period, General Walter Reinhardt, the last Prussian Minister of War of the Imperial era, and later on the holder of many high-ranking appointments in the *Reichswehr* of the Weimar Republic, lectured on Clausewitz. However, he too recognized in Clausewitz' teaching mainly his emphasis on annihilation, ignoring completely the importance he attached to the relationship of policy and war. Reinhardt compared Clausewitz favorably to the French Marshal Foch. He analyzed Foch as striving to shake the enemy's morale, whereas Clausewitz' more realistic thoughts were aimed at killing or capturing the adversary. Reinhardt reasoned that a morally shaken and discouraged warrior might recover and regain his courage, and therefore carry on fighting, while a dead one remains dead. On this point, at least, Reinhardt praised Clausewitz. But on the whole, he considered Clausewitz' theory to be obsolete for a number of reasons, among them the impact of modern firepower, which had completely changed the image of battle; the increased importance of logistics; and the blurring of the division between strategy and tactics. Reinhardt also refuted Clausewitz' concept of the relationship of the defensive and offensive (see section II below). However, his experience in the war did lead him to accept Clausewitz' concept of the diminishing force of the attack, which presents the defense with certain advantages. He also agreed with Clausewitz that a deliberate retreat may serve as a means of resistance, of course provided that it does not turn into a rout.[24] This perception led in fact to one of the operative innovations of the *Reichswehr*: the so-called 'Hinhaltender Widerstand' ('Delaying Resistance').

Whereas most German soldiers of this period, though deviating from Clausewitz' theory, felt obliged to pay lip-service to the great philosopher of war, General Erich Ludendorff was the first German who dared to proclaim an overt and definite break with Clausewitz' teaching: 'All theories of Clausewitz', he wrote, 'have to be thrown overboard'.[25] And 'his work belongs to a past period of World History, and is mostly out of date. One may even get confused by studying it.'[26]

But in actual fact it was Ludendorff who confused the issues by formulating the concept of 'total war', which so many people tended to consider as identical with Clausewitz' 'absolute war'. One should remember, however, that Clausewitz' conception of 'absolute war' was a philosophical ideal type designed logically to reduce war to its essence, and to strip it, for the purpose of theoretical contemplation, of all influences imposed by reality. Ludendorff's 'total war' had nothing in common with Clausewitz' idea and was far from being a philosophical concept. Ludendorff's intellect was simply not fit for philosophy of Clausewitz' kind.[27]

D. *The Nazi-period and the Second World War*

A legend persists that Hitler had studied Clausewitz, and had fully understood *On War*. As early as 1937 the German General von Metzsch wrote in a book with the significant title 'Clausewitz Catechism' that 'the frequent conformity of the two great sons of the German people, Clausewitz and Hitler, is downright amazing. They are a kindred pair (Wahlverwandte).'[28] However, Norbert Kruger has thoroughly investigated Hitler's knowledge of Clausewitz and published his findings.[29] He discovered that Hitler had referred to Clausewitz only once in *Mein Kampf*,[30] never in his famous table-talks[31] during the war, and only once again in his political testament, drawn up on 29 April 1945, the day before he committed suicide.[32] To a group of generals he snapped arrogantly on 23 August 1941: 'My generals know Clausewitz, but they understand nothing about war economy. Moreover, I know Clausewitz, too, and his word: One first has to knock to pieces the hostile field armies, then to occupy the enemy's capital.'[33]

Kruger's conclusion is that Hitler had by no means 'studied' Clausewitz' *On War*, though he probably had heard a lot about the work in the 1920s and something remained in his memory (although very often in a distorted way!). In his private library there was only a small volume of selected writings of Clausewitz. During conversations Hitler quoted occasionally from Clausewitz in order to silence (Kruger uses the German expression 'mundtot zu machen') his opponents and critics. Hahlweg formulated the same perception in other words: Hitler hardly worked his way through Clausewitz in a systematic-critical way, but rather made use of him as a treasure for quotations in the manner of semi-educated people.[34]

These are, of course, hindsights, but in 1940, after the collapse of France, Karl Linnebach, the famous editor and interpreter of Clausewitz in the inter-war period,[35] wrote in a professional periodical:

> We can, as Clausewitz has pointed out, choose different roads in war. We can, for instance, direct our intentions to the aim of doing as much harm as possible to our enemy in the economic field. But that is not the direct road and woe to him whom the God of War finds treading it. This is exactly what happened to our enemies. The *Führer* has forged the sharp sword of the German army and welded the whole German nation together, into one great arm, in which – to use one of Clausewitz' metaphors – the army formed the edge, the people the steel blade. Our enemies, on the other hand, thought that behind their protective wall of concrete and wire entanglements, an elegant rapier would suffice as a weapon. They believed that they could win the war by means of a blockade and without bloodshed. Hoping to avoid a decision by arms and not to be forced to make any sacrifices, the French Government declared at the beginning of this war, that they would be not only sparing, but niggardly with their soldiers' blood.

Linnebach not only held that Hitler had understood Clausewitz, and that the Allies had to pay for not listening to the latter, but also insisted that the Germans 'had drawn the right conclusions from the First World War'.[36]

As late as in 1943 General F. von Cochenhausen maintained in an introduction to an abridged edition of *On War*: 'If one lets Clausewitz' theory affect one's senses and bring them into connection with the political and martial occurrence of the last years, then one will perceive that one's psychical deportment and one's notion of the nature of war has found a perfect embodiment in the *Führer*.'[37]

As we shall see, the Germans' desire to see their Führer as the embodiment of Clausewitz' ideas, combined with their misinterpretation of more ideas, led them to disaster in the Second World War.

II. REJECTION OF THE SUPERIORITY OF THE DEFENSE

Clausewitz' postulate that 'the defensive form of warfare is intrinsically stronger than the offensive'[38] met with fierce opposition by most German soldiers, in spite of his logical explanation of this apparent contradiction. They failed to see that Clausewitz concluded that the defensive is the strongest form of war, not as the consequence of an ethical preference for defense, or lack of offensive spirit, but from a cool calculation of facts:

> If defense is the stronger form of war, yet has a negative object, it follows that it should be used only so long as weakness compels, and be abandoned as soon as we are strong enough to pursue a positive object. When one has used defensive measures successfully, a more favorable balance of strength is usually created; thus, the natural course in war is to begin defensively and end by attacking.[39]

As Raymond Aron has observed, in Germany numerous interpreters made every possible effort to refute Clausewitz' thesis of the greater internal power of the defense.[40] One maintained sadly that he would have been much happier, had the great philosopher of war not written that passage. Colonel von Scherff, the editor of the 1880 edition of *On War*, admitted that Clausewitz' theory concerning defense had divided German military opinion into two hostile camps.[41] A German general exclaimed in despair that the decision to keep on the defensive is the first step on the ladder toward helplessness. German officers simply could not reconcile Clausewitz' concept of the 'application of force to the utmost' with his concept of the defense.

A. *Schlieffen versus Clausewitz*

Hoffman Nickerson[42] perceived the essence of military theory before the First World War in two closely connected ideas: an exaggerated cult of the offensive and a belief in a short war. In promoting both ideas Schlieffen was the leading personality. It is therefore not surprising that he had promulgated the slogan: 'No battle can be won purely by occupying positions, but only by movement.' Little wonder that one of his most devoted followers, von Freytag-Loringhoven, who served under him in the Historical Branch of the Great General Staff, wrote in a 1905 Clausewitz study: 'Only by offensive battles and not by choosing unassailable positions which the Austrian Cunctator[43] used to select so skillfully, and by the little tricks of maneuver, could the final objectives of war be reached.'[44] In all his maneuvers, war games, and exercises Schlieffen had rejected every thought of exchanging offense for defense, even in case of tremendous inferiority. Although putting great emphasis on firepower, he completely overlooked the great advantages of modern long-range and quick-firing weapons for the defender.

The retreat, an essential feature of Clausewitz' concept of strategic defense played but a minor and insignificant part in Schlieffen's teaching. The German military historian Meier-Welcker ventured the opinion that he might have regarded it as too complicated a form of battle.[45] But it rather seems that Schlieffen had his doubts whether the enemy would respond to a retrograde movement and 'enter the trap'. In his critique of the exercise of 1897 he condemned delaying actions:

> This method of occupying positions and breaking off combat may suit a detachment, a division, in some cases an army corps, but cannot be applied to an army, consisting of four to five army corps, which cannot be observed adequately from one point. The commander-in-chief will hardly succeed in recognizing the crucial moment for retreat, even less so, in dispatching the opportune marching-orders to the troops and in ordering the latter to march off in due time.[46]

Schlieffen also never grasped the fact, which Clausewitz recognized, that during the Seven Years' War (1756–63) Frederick the Great was strategically on the defensive. Schlieffen stressed the view that even the inferior, or precisely the inferior, has to attack – always and everywhere (a method which Clausewitz had severely criticized in his campaign studies).[47] Schlieffen's disregard of the defense led, during his term of office, to a complete neglect of any defensive training of the German Army, with grave consequences for the future.

B. *The First World War*

Owing to Schlieffen's tremendous influence on the shaping of the German conduct of the First World War, Clausewitz' warning that 'the line of defense may run from sea to sea or from one neutral country to another'[48] went unheeded. Moreover, this prophecy foreshadowed what actually occurred in the West (from Belfort in the South to Ostend in the North) at the end of 1914 and very soon afterwards in the East (from the Baltic Sea to the Carpathian Mountains). Both sides had missed Clausewitz' warning voice, that 'indeed any attack that does not immediately lead to peace must end on the defensive'.[49]

In fact neither side knew how to handle the problem of defense. They simply were not adjusted to it. Now the penalty for this peacetime omission had to be paid. The field commanders were at pains to make their superiors in the rear realize that the relationship of offensive and defensive had changed in the latter's favor, and that the time for quick and dashing advances was past. Suddenly one had to face the fact that armies of millions of soldiers could not wage a war of movement indefinitely. Defense became the dominant part of the war scenery. Had the German soldiers tried to understand Clausewitz' teaching with regard to defense, they might have been better prepared for the new situation. but inspired by the customary aggressive notion, they would not listen to Clausewitz. Had not even the sober von der Goltz preached the offensive and rejected the defense? In 1883 he wrote:

> Our modern German fighting method aims at bringing on decisive results by a succession of vigorous blows in accordance with our conception of resolute offensive. *An idea of the offensive is tacitly at the bottom of all our theoretical treatises, and, for the most part, of practical exercises also. Temporizing, waiting, and passive defensive, are very unsympathetic to our nature.*[50] (my emphasis)

And in a more advanced part of his book von der Goltz said: 'In this sketch of a battle, we have instinctively described an offensive battle. *What German soldier would do otherwise?*'[51] (my emphasis). In fact, when confronted with the harsh reality of a non-offensive battle, the German soldier hardly knew what to do.

Indeed, as already pointed out, Schlieffen's obsession with offensive and encirclement threw into complete oblivion all knowledge about defense. Nobody had anticipated prolonged position warfare. Even the warning signals from the Far East (the Russo-Japanese War of 1904–5) were ignored or misinterpreted. Bernhardi wrote in 1912 that

> battles lasting for days will probably take place in future only when in the theater of war conditions arise which are similar to those of the Manchurian fields. Such a supposition is, however, not at all likely to be fulfilled. Germany's European adversaries can only act on the offensive, if they wish to achieve anything at all. *The Germans are sure not to defend themselves behind ditches and ramparts. The genius of the German people will save us from that.* A railway net widely ramified in comparison with that of Manchuria, and an ample useful network of roads, afford great freedom of movement in most of the European theaters of war. All these conditions make us rather believe in a war of active operations than in a war of positions, although the spade is held in such high esteem.[52] (my emphasis)

While smiling at such naïveté, one must keep in mind that the 'widely ramified railway net' and the 'ample and useful network of roads' were indeed major factors – in the ability to rush reserves into any spot where a breatkthrough was likely to endanger the ultimate rule of defense.

The famous German expert on defense, General (later Field Marshal) von Leeb, in his book *The Defense* stripped the events of 1914 to their theoretical essentials, and reached the conclusion that the mutual exhaustion at the end of 1914 resulted from not resorting to the more economical strategic, operational, and tactical defense, instead of applying wasteful attack everywhere. This, and the stolid clinging to every inch of captured ground, were considered by Leeb as the main reasons for the deadlock in West and East.[53]

Leeb, then, did agree with Clausewitz, who had derived his concept of flexible defense from his experience in Russian service during Napoleon's invasion of that country. Clausewitz considered this particular mode of defense as the most powerful one: to lure the enemy into pursuit, by means of a retrograde movement, and then to fall upon him from several directions, after he had moved out from his overextended lines further inland. He who acts in accordance with Clausewitz' teaching, creates for himself a new operational basis, on the lines of a war of movement, and has every chance of regaining the ground voluntarily ceded. This approach simply means sacrificing ground in the first phase in order to gain operational opportunity. It is, of course, the very opposite to clinging to every inch of ground, as practiced in the First World War.

It seemed, in fact, but only for a moment, that at the beginning of 1918 General Ludendorff had at least adopted the Clausewitzian concept of flexible defense. 'The Attack in Position Warfare', paragraph 6 of the new Field Service Regulations, issued by Ludendorff on 1 January 1918, read:

> Objective, purpose and conduct of the attack vary according to scale and depth .... Should it be intended to hold the objective permanently, it must offer more favorable conditions for defense than the line from which the attack was originally launched. However, one will frequently achieve the aim of the attack even by withdrawing sooner or later to the line of departure.

But in spite of the convincing success of the German retreat in 1917 (the so-called 'Alberich' movement), Ludendorff refused in the spring offensives of 1918 to adopt a flexible conduct, although the lines reached did by no means offer 'more favorable conditions for the defense'. They rather invited hostile concentric counter-attacks. There was, indeed, no obvious reason why the German High Command should not have restored much earlier to a flexible defense, combined with counter-attacks into the advancing enemy's flanks. The theoretical foundations for these maneuvers could have been learned from Clausewitz.

C. Ludendorff versus Clausewitz

The popular proverb has it that 'a burned child fears the fire'; nevertheless Ludendorff, in spite of his First World War experience, wrote in 1922 that he was unable 'to share the opinion, expressed in *On War*, that the defensive form of war is stronger than the offensive'.[54] And in his book on total war, published thirteen years later, he maintained:

> It is useless talk, to discuss the question, as has so often been done in the past, even by Clausewitz, and as perhaps theorists still do today, whether the offensive or the defense is the stronger form of war, and whether it is not the highest art of conducting war, to let the enemy run against the defenses, and only after the collapse of his assault, to take to the counter-offensive. These are dangerous artificialities which obscure the seriousness and simplicity of the total war .... When attacking, one dwells upon the proud feeling of superior power, those imponderables, that give force to a properly conducted attack, even against an enemy superior in numbers .... The offensive is always the decisive form of battle.[55]

Alas! Nothing learned and nothing forgotten!

D. *Seeckt and the Reichswehr*

Other leaders emerged from the First World War with a more Clausewitzian and flexible view. Although General Seeckt had put Schlieffen's catchword 'operation is movement' at the top of his training orders for the *Reichswehr*, under his command, contrary to the pre-war period, the defensive was not neglected. And his concept of the defense was much more flexible than that unintentionally carried out during the First World War. This is even apparent by a superficial glance into the new regulations 'Truppenführung (T.F.)' (Conduct of Troops) and the terminology created for that purpose. The all-embracing term 'Abwehr' (Defensive)[56] is divided into two main streams: 'Verteidigung' (Defense)[57] in which the defender is determined to wage a decisive battle, and 'hinhaltender Widerstand' (delaying resistance) or 'hinhaltendes Gefecht' (delaying engagement), by means of which the defender is not prepared to accept a decisive battle and avoids it.[58] The latter meant in fact a conscious return to Clausewitz' concept of flexible defense, a step which no German leader had dared to make during four long years of trench warfare. (General Waldemar Erfurth admitted in 1938 that 'the World War had proved that Clausewitz' theory of flexible defense is valid even under the circumstances of position warfare'.)[59]

General Leeb, the German defense expert of the inter-war period, also stressed the importance of flexible defense supported by mechanized troops, the air force, and a high degree of improvisation in erecting obstacles of various kinds. Thus Seeckt and Leeb gave the German Army a lead in the sphere of defense, at a time when most other Armies still remained under the spell of trench warfare, and looked for remedy in concrete and steel (the so-called 'Maginot mentality').

E. Hitler versus Clausewitz

Hitler, siding with the traditional German military opposition to Clausewitz' dictum on defense, explicitly stressed the offensive as superior to the defensive. But after the breakdown of his belated attack on Moscow in the late fall of 1941, he nevertheless had to decide where and *how* to conduct the defensive. The majority of the German generals involved were in favor of the selection of a suitable 'winter-line' and for the adoption of a flexible conduct of defense. But Hitler would not listen to such ideas and prohibited even the slightest retreat. He ordered the strict holding of ground wherever it was. On 21 December 1941, he issued an explicit order: 'Holding on and fighting to the utmost limit. Not yielding a single step voluntarily. Mobile parts of the enemy which have broken in must be annihilated in the rear.'[60] Five days later the *Führer* again ordered that

> in the defensive one must fight to the last for every inch of ground. This is the only way of inflicting bloody losses upon the enemy, weakening his morale and demonstrating the superiority of the German soldier. The yielding of even improvised positions to the enemy without fighting, results, under the present weather conditions, in irrecoverable losses of material and ammunition, and thereby reduces one's own fighting power and allows the enemy to avail himself of increased freedom of action.[61]

The consequences of this policy were, of course, fatal for the troops.

However, there is no doubt that neither theoretical considerations, nor any other considerations connected with the art of war, guided Hitler. His motive was nothing but prestige. He, 'the greatest strategist of all times', as his Minister of Propaganda, Josef Goebbels, had proclaimed him at the peak of his military conquests, could simply not yield captured ground to the enemy. The same phenomenon had happened before with Ludendorff in 1918, when the latter could not decide to renounce ground previously seized. The explanations of both – Ludendorff and Hitler – were identical: retreat would sacrifice valuable war material behind the initial front-line, which could not be removed in time before the withdrawal. Flexible operational conduct of war was replaced by fanatical 'hold on' orders 'to fight to the last man'. These orders, often issued thousands of miles away from the battlefront, and without precise knowledge of the actual situation, resulted nevertheless in an eventual retreat pressed upon the Germans by the adverse circumstances. Dictated by the enemy, instead of being planned beforehand, the retreat resulted in losses of material and of manpower generally heavier than those to be expected in a deliberate retreat. And these losses occurred against the background that the ample space of the Russian theater of war would have allowed a flexible defense in the Clausewitzian style.

In a lengthy document, issued on 8 September 1942, this time in his capacity as C-in-C of the Army, and labelled 'Führer Order About the Principal Task of Defense' an odd mixture of an instruction leaflet and personal reminiscences, rather than an order – Hitler admitted: 'I am reverting consciously to that kind of defense which was applied with success during the serious defense battles of the World War, in particular up to the end of 1916.' He wound up this long-winded document with a strong rejection of a flexible conduct of defense. In an obvious tone of scorn he wrote:

> The so-called *operational evasive movements* (operative *Ausweich-bewegungen*), if not leading into better rearward positions, pre-pared long before hand, will not change the general situation, but rather worsen it .... There was and is, therefore, at all times, only one remedy for the defender inferior in numbers, for the improve-ment of his situation; he must, by holding a well-constructed position, inflict losses upon the assailant to such a degree, that the latter's momentum will not only relax and an equilibrium be created, but also that the material, with which the enemy above all wins his wars, namely his men, will be annihilated. In principle, no C-in-C of an Army Group and certainly not an Army Commander is entitled to initiate a so-called tactical evasive movement without my explicit approval.[62]

It was not Hitler alone who abandoned flexible defense, after its reintroduction into the inter-war German Army by Seeckt and Leeb; the military, too, had a finger in the pie. One finds the following remark in General Halder's private war diary (Halder was then the Chief of the General Staff of the Army): ' "Delaying resistance" to be killed at once!' In a footnote to the printed post-war edition of the diary he explained: 'This form of combat, widely practiced in the 100,000-man Army, should be abolished, because the circumstances have changed, and during the Polish campaign, the toughness of our defensive ("Abwehr") suffered on its account.'[63] It seems that on this point of the superiority of the defense and the need for flexibility, Clausewitz was not only rejected, but sent entirely into oblivion.

III. REJECTION OF THE PRIMACY OF POLICY

I have already written in 'Das Dogma der Vernichtungsschlacht',

Many people who have never read a single word of Clausewitz' teaching, know by heart and quote without hesitation the passage the 'war is merely the continuation of policy by other means.' But only a few know that with this statement they have embarked upon a very controversial subject which constitutes the principal part of von Clausewitz' whole theory. One may even say, that if this component of his teaching were eliminated, the whole structure of his theoretical building would collapse. It seemed so vital to Clausewitz that he mentioned it again and again in various parts of his treatise and examined it many times from various angles. This incessant repetition led Cyril Falls to the unjustified accusation [at least in this author's opinion] that 'he does harp on the same string like a modern director of publicity'.[64] But Clausewitz probably felt that his point would not so easily be understood or accepted by his military compatriots. He learned it the hard way from his sad experience, and would not agree to seeing the problems of war again handled by mere military experts and drillmasters lacking any political orientation and understanding. Moreover, he would of course not know how much would be written on this subject in the future.[65]

Clausewitz defined clearly the division of functions between the statesmen and the generals. In doing so, he made one of his most controversial statements:

The assertion that a major military development, or the plan for one, should be a matter for *purely military* opinion is unacceptable and can be damaging. Nor indeed is it sensible to summon soldiers, as many governments do when they are planning a war, and ask them for *purely military advice*.[66]

It was his firm belief that war and its general outlines had always been determined by the political institutions and not by the military. Therefore, in order to prevent frictions between the politicians and the generals and for the sake of smooth coordination between policy and military actions, Clausewitz suggested, in cases where there was no personal union of the statesman and the soldier, that the commander-in-chief be made a member of the cabinet, so that the cabinet could participate in the principal issues of the commander's action. This clear indication of the primacy of policy over the conduct of war was rejected by the German soldiers. It is the great achievement of Professor Hahlweg of having discovered that commencing with the second edition of *Vom Kriege*, published in 1853, this very statement by Clausewitz was altered deliberately by the editors. Whereas Clausewitz' genuine definition illuminated the problem from the statesman's point of view, the adulterated definition enlarged the powers of the general who was now made a member of the cabinet, so that he could participate in the decision-making process.[67] That means Clausewitz' opinion was turned upside down! Nothing illuminates better the German soldier's rejection of political primacy than this intentional change. As we have seen, they also took issue with Clausewitz' concept of defense, but they never deliberately altered his text on that point. Therefore it is obvious that they could not tolerate the idea of the political agency dominating war, and wished to discourage any discussion of this particular subject.

A. Before the First World War

The 'Elder' Moltke, the victor of Sadowa and Sedan, was, one of the first to deviate from Clausewitz' definition. In an essay on strategy, circulated in 1871, he wrote:

> Policy makes use of war to gain its objectives, it acts with decisive influence at the beginning and the end of the war, in such a way either to increase its claims during the progress of war or to be satisfied with lesser gains. With this uncertainty strategy cannot but always direct its efforts towards the highest goal attainable with the means at its disposal. It thereby serves policy best, and only works for the object of policy, *but is completely independent of policy in its actions*.[68] (my emphasis)

With regard to this view, Raymond Aron remarked sarcastically that Clausewitz could not have approved the doctrine which all German generals would have preferred: freedom of action between the first cannon shot and the peace negotiations.[69] This may, in fact, have been exactly the posture of the German Emperor Wilhelm II, who added a marginal remark to an editorial in the *Frankfurter Zeitung*: 'Policy keeps its mouth shut during war until strategy allows it to speak again.'[70] Although von Moltke accepted the leading role of Bismarck in shaping the objectives of war, even submitting to the Chancellor's political demands in the course of the war, his idea of military autonomy became nevertheless the standard opinion of the German soldiers and, fatefully enough fo Germany, also of the German statesmen!

As early as 1880 Colonel von Scherff had written in his edition of *Vom Kriege* this anti-Clausewitzian comment: 'The interference of policy in the conduct of war leads always to ruin. Policy sets the fashion *how* the house should be built, but it must not interfere with the building process itself.'[71]

Even von der Goltz, who had acquired personal experience in military-diplomatic missions, wrote in 1883: 'It behooves us, therefore, to have a

sharp eye for, and to guard against ... the interference of political considerations with the strategic and tactical decisions.'[72]

Since Clausewitz denied the independent existence of war, he held the
opinion that all great strategical plans are principally of a political nature:
a plan of war emerges from the very existence of the belligerent states and
their relations with others. Therefore he considered it an absurdity to
strive for the separation of the military from the political implications of a
strategical plan. He expressed this clearly in the well-known letter to
Major Roeder, dated 22 December 1827 (that is, before the final formulation of On War):

> War is nothing but a continuation of political endeavor by other
> means. On this opinion I base the whole of strategy, and believe that
> he who refuses to recognize this necessity does not understand what
> really matters. This principle explains the whole history of war and
> without it, all is full of absurdity.[73]

Schlieffen, who typifies the so-called un-political soldier, absorbed in his
profession and impervious to anything outside its narrow scope, had, of
course, different views. (He also expressed a credo of his own about 'the
essential substance of the whole history of war'. But it is surprising that in
his opinion this essence is the attack against the flank.)[74] Little wonder,
then, that Schlieffen would not ask the vital question which Clausewitz
raised: 'How is it possible to draw a plan of campaign for one theater of
war or more, without regard to the political situation of the states and
their constellation to each other?'[75] In shaping his famous plan, Schlieffen
was not bothered by such problems. He provides a case study to support
Clausewitz' opinion, already quoted above, 'that a major military
development or the plan for one, should be a matter for *purely military*
opinion is unacceptable and can be damaging. Nor indeed is it sensible to
summon soldiers ... and ask them for *purely military advice*'[76] (my
emphasis). Indeed, 'the available means' had been given to Schlieffen as
the Chief of General Staff, and he had drawn a 'purely military plan'
without consulting any of the political agencies, and the result was
disaster.

Moreover, contrary to the established practice in other countries, the
Germans never established an institution where statesmen and generals
together discussed war policy. Neither the Chancellor nor the Chief of
the General Staff ever tried to initiate something like a 'Supreme War
Council'. Otto von Moser suspected that the military victories of 1864,
1866, and 1870/71 led the soldiers to believe that the relationship of
policy and war had changed in the latter's favor since Clausewitz' days.[77]
It thus happened that when in July 1914 the crisis emerged, Germany
had nothing but a plan for a military offensive, whose rigid timetable,

uncoordinated with the political agencies, robbed diplomacy of any possible maneuver in the political sphere.

B. The First World War

Bethmann-Hollweg was the German Chancellor at the outbreak of the war. From his memoirs one receives the impression that he did not know Clausewitz and the rights he had granted to the statesmen. Be that as it may, these memoirs show that Bethmann-Hollweg unconditionally surrendered his legitimate position as the leading statesman and consciously yielded to the dictates of the General Staff:

> As with the opening of the war, political measures had to be shaped in accordance with the needs of the campaign plan, which was declared to be unalterable, so too, during the war, the military view of technical possibilities and strategic effects decisively determined the great operations .... The political establishment did not take part in the drawing up of the campaign plan .... On the whole, during my term of office, there was never anything like a war council, in which policy might have interfered with the military pros and cons .... The position which war conceded to the political leadership, vis-à-vis military operations on land and sea, was decided by the things themselves. By no means could the military layman pretend to judge military possibilities, let alone military necessities. I received the impression that it was military necessities that guided the conduct of war. Behind even the most brilliant initiative displayed by the General Staff, was military compulsion. How to solve that compulsion, could only be decided by the military, even on occasions where military and political requirements went hand in hand.[78]

Against the background of the Chancellor's submissive behavior one has to understand the arrogant bearing of the General Staff, as expressed by General Wilhelm Groener at the outbreak of the war:

> We of the General Staff strive with all our deeds to do a good job, so that – shall it depend on us – the German people will live in peace for the next hundred years. Herr Reichskanzler and his clique seem to regard the war as a philosophical idea, and are not disinclined to conclude a dubious peace as early as possible! It is out of question, that we shall not only have to cope with the French but also with Mr. Bethmann [Hollweg] and his Foreign Office.[79]

This was in fact the state of affairs throughout the course of the First World War, as one may learn from the expert testimony of Colonel B. Schwertfeger before the Committee of Inquiry of the Reichstag:

Ludendorff considered the conduct of war, and politics, to be two separate entities, fighting each other with hostility. The conduct of war was full of hope, intending a victorious solution of the bloody conflict, whereas politics and their executives always had the feeling of disaster, if not even a downright malicious will.[80]

When the same Committee took General von Kuhl to task about Ludendorff's discordant relations with the politicians, with reference to Clausewitz' dictum, he answered: 'In spite of the high esteem in which the work 'On War' is held by every soldier, not everything contained in it is still, after a hundred years, unconditionally applicable.'[81]

Ludendorff's superior, Field Marshal von Hindenburg, although sometimes an instructor at the War Academy, seems to have misread (or misunderstood!) Clausewitz' treatise. He wrote in his memoirs:

There is a book 'On War' which is never obsolete. Clausewitz is its author. He knew war and he knew people. We had to listen to him, and if we followed him we would be successful. The reverse meant mischief. *He warned against encroachments of politics upon the conduct of war.*[82] (my emphasis)

And Ludendorff himself explained:

The problem of peace was considered by the OHL[83] as a concern of politics. In that the OHL was in agreement with Clausewitz. It had, however, without jeopardizing the conclusion of peace or prolonging the war, to keep an eye open, lest the peace policy of the Reichskanzler should harm the conduct of war, and to work towards a formulation of frontiers, which based on the war experience, will provide favorable military and economic conditions for the successful execution of a new war. In addition, by the conclusion of peace before the termination of the overall war, one had to guard against direct disadvantages to the conduct of war accruing from the negotiations or conditions.[84]

It is symptomatic of the German war milieu that the more the situation deteriorated, the less cooperation between the civil government and the military authorities could be established. Finally Ludendorff ousted Bethmann Hollweg from the Chancellorship and usurped in fact – though not in title – the role of an omnipotent dictator of Germany.

However, at the very moment it became obvious that Germany was finally forced to give up the war, the military leaders reversed themselves: they claimed that Germany was militarily undefeated; it was the politicians who had lost the war. These leaders wanted to reap the glory for the successes and to leave to the too obedient and submissive politicians the responsibility for the bitter end. This contemptible act of the military found a match in another one: the shifting of the blame for defeat to the homefront – the slanderous legend of the 'stab in the back'.

C. The Inter-War Period

How crucial many Germans considered the problem of the relationship of policy and war, can be learned from the vast number of post-war publications related to this theme.

After the war General Wilhelm Groener, Ludendorff's successor in the OHL during the last months of the war, had second thoughts about the relationship of policy and war. He wrote:

> The standpoint, so often advocated, that the statesman has no say in the operations, but ought simply to wait, until the General reports either victory or defeat or neither, may be considered as having been overcome by the experience of the World War. It would, however, confuse the issue if the statesman should, as it were, now usurp the role of a strategic supreme controller. Yet one should concede him the right, or rather the obligation, of checking whether the presumed results of an operation are compatible with the intentions and objectives of policy.[85]

This extreme change of opinion is no doubt due to the fact that Groener had at that time (1930) already shifted from the military establishment into the political as Minister of Transport and Minister of the Reichswehr in the Weimar Republic.

On the other hand, Bernhardi, whose views before the war were very close to Clausewitz' ideas, returned from the war with a changed mind. In his book *On Future War* he wrote:

> [Diplomacy] must completely yield to the wishes of the Army High Command, and absolutely renounce taking any steps without consultation with the latter …. [In War] the political mistake is followed immediately by military punishment. Statecraft has therefore to restrict itself to paving the way for military success or its exploitation, and in accordance with orders given by the military. … The statesman has to yield to the [military leader] unconditionally, for the coordination of political and military actions is the main point which matters, and the military requirements stipulate the political …. As long as war is waged, and there is no prospect of a suitable peace in sight, only military success should be striven for, and anything else should yield to that endeavor; but if there is any prospect of peace, then similarly, the soldier alone has to decide whether it might be appropriate to achieve it, by increasing the

military effort, or whether it might be advisable to teach it by means of diplomacy, i.e. concessions. *Only the soldier is in a position to judge that.* Germany's calamity can, in the final analysis, be reduced to the fact that these simple rules were not obeyed.[86] (my emphasis)

Ludendorff in his less sophisticated manner actually attempted to rewrite Clausewitz on this point:

The passage: 'War is a mere continuation of policy by other means' ought to run: 'War is foreign politics by other means', and must be complemented by the passage, which will yet be proved to be true: 'As for the rest, overall politics must serve the war.'[87]

And in his book on total war he added a statement to the already quoted passage that all theories of Clausewitz have to be thrown overboard: 'War and politics serve the survival of the people, but war is the highest expression of the racial will to life.'[88] Therefore little wonder, when a certain retired Rittmeister (Captain of Cavalry) Bruno Pochhammer, who edited a popular edition of 'Vom Kriege' in 1937, uttered in his epilogue to his edition that up to the First World War, war could be regarded according to Clausewitz as a means of policy. Nowadays every political measure becomes an expedient subordinated to the all-embracing war.[89]

Even the sober General von Seeckt stated in his essay 'On Catchwords' that he had reservations whether Clausewitz' dictum of 'war as a mere continuation of policy by other means' was still applicable to the present situation.[90] This attitude was, of course, due to Seeckt's negative posture towards the Weimar Republic, which he had agreed to serve only in order to prevent particularistic tendencies from dissolving the Reich.

A different opinion, harmonizing with Clausewitz, was held by General Ludwig Beck, the first Chief of the General Staff of the Army of the Nazi period (1933–38). He stated that among the preliminary conditions for a successful conduct of war, an efficient foreign policy ranks first. This creates the situation under which a state is involved in war and bears the responsibility for it. 'The political purpose of the war must be obvious', he said, 'and must also include in its calculation the final act of every war, the achievement of peace. Only a clearly defined purpose renders it possible to derive from it, and from the available means, a military objective.' One may find historical examples, when a war has been won or lost even before it actually began, and the reason for this has always been the conduct of policy.[91] However, Beck's view did not prevail at the time.

D. The Nazi Era and the Second World War

It is widely believed that Hitler, concentrating in his own hands the conduct of political and of military affairs, had restored in Germany the unity of policy and war. But it was not exactly this kind of unity that Clausewitz had in mind! Hitler was very much influenced by Ludendorff's concept of policy subordinated to the conduct of total war. Though embodying both functions in his own person, he maintained, as the Emperor Wilhelm II did before him, that politics has to keep quiet until victory is reached. But that did not mean that he was prepared to consider the military as responsible partners in the process of decision making. On the contrary! He managed to degrade them to mere receivers and blind executors of orders. Colonel Bernhard von Lossberg, the representative of the Army High Command on Operations Staff OKW,[92] reports in his memoirs that Hitler had ordered strict separation of military and political matters. This was true even at the highest staff level, which ought to have been concerned with the reciprocal aspects of political and military issues. He forbade the use of the term 'military-political situation,' because under the new regime there were no 'military politics'. He declared that any specific matter was either a military issue, and therefore the soldiers' concern, or it was political, to be handled by politicians.[93]

Nevertheless, one has to admit that until the end of the campaign in France, Hitler had in fact acted in accordance with Clausewitz' principle (though with regard to long-range international politics, the wisdom of the partition of Poland and the violation of Danish, Norwegian, Belgian, and Dutch neutrality may be doubted). The partnership of political and military action is clearly indicated in Hitler's personal revision of the directive, dated 30 May 1938, for the attack on Czechoslovakia. The opening sentence read: 'It is my unalterable decision to smash Czechoslovakia by military action in the near future. *It is the business of the political leadership to await or bring about the suitable moment from a political and military point of view*'[94] (my emphasis). Shrewd politics had already paved the way for the annexation of Austria (the 'Anschluss') and later on, owing to the Ribbentrop-Molotov Agreement, for the conquest of Poland. After the overthrow of Poland, the same political agreement with the Soviet Union secured the German rear during the offensive in France.

However, with the decision to attack Russia while an undefeated Great Britain remained behind Germany's back, Hitler had departed from the firm ground of Clausewitz' theory.[95] Policy no longer provided for the victory of arms. Moreover, the more Hitler occupied himself with the day-to-day conduct of military operations and became convinced of his own military genius, the more he gradually renounced any political activity and staked everything on military achievements. Even his minister of Propaganda, Josef Goebbels, was moved to lament in the summer of 1943 in his diary: 'We are doing too much on the military and too little on the political side of war. At this moment, when our military successes are none too great, it would be a good thing if we knew how to make better use of the political instrument.'[96]

A similar idea was expressed after the war by Field Marshal von Kleist, who told Liddell Hart:

> Clausewitz' reflections were fundamentally sound – especially his dictum that war was a continuation of policy by other means. It implied that the political factors were more important than the military ones. The German mistake was to think that a military success would solve political problems. Indeed, under the Nazis we tended to reverse Clausewitz' dictum, and to regard peace as a continuation of war.[97]

Perhaps this was the wisdom of hindsight.

Summarizing the subject of this study, it can be said that it is one thing to hold Clausewitz in high esteem and to idolize him, but a different thing to study him intellectually and intelligently, to try to penetrate into the depth of his thoughts and to digest and absorb his ideas. We have seen that in regard to two issues, the superiority of the defense and the primacy of politics, most German military leaders did the first thing, but that there were very few who attempted the second. Even among these, the majority misperceived his theory, so that fewer still really succeeded in understanding him. However, we did not say that outside Germany the picture was, or is, any different!

To return to the issue raised in Section I of this article, it is always a temptation for the professional military man to embrace a writer for his 'pragmatic' value – or to try to grasp a 'practical' application from a purely theoretical concept (such as absolute war). It is much more difficult to relate a theory to a real-life situation. Yet if Clausewitz' theories had been related to the situation the Germans faced in the First and Second World Wars, the conduct, and possibly the outcome – or at least the analysis of the outcome – could have been very different. Since it is impossible to rewrite history, we need to avoid making their mistake again. Today's military leaders must study Clausewitz for his value in determining the character of wars to come.

NOTES

1. Raymond Aron, *Penser la guerre: Clausewitz* (Paris: Gallimard, 1976). This quotation is translated here from the German edition: *Clausewitz. Den Krieg denken* (Frankfurt am Main: Propyläen, 1980), p.321.
2. Cyril B. Falls, *The Art of War* (London: Oxford University Press, 1961), p.7.
3. Jehuda L. Wallach, *Das Dogma der Vernichtungsschlacht, Die Lehren von Clausewitz and Schlieffen und ihre Wirkung in Zwei Weltkriegen* (Frankfurt: Bernard & Graefe, 1967; Hdtv, 1970), p.13. A revised version of the original English manuscript of this work is to be published in the US: *The Dogma of the Battle of Annihilation: The Theories of Clausewitz and Schlieffen and their Impact on the German Conduct of Two World Wars* (Westport, CT: Glenwood Press, 1986).
4. Quoted in Werner Hahlweg, 'Das Clausewitzbild einst und jetzt', in Carl von Clausewitz, *Vom Kriege* (Bonn: Dümmler, 19th ed., 1980), p.57.
5. Werner Hahlweg, *Carl von Clausewitz. Soldat – Politiker – Denker* (Göttingen: Musterschmidt, 1969), p.105.
6. Ibid., p.107.
7. Quoted ibid., pp.109–10.
8. For example: A.A. Leinveber, *Mit Clausewitz durch die Rätsel und Fragen, Irrungen und Wirrungen des Weltkrieges* (Berlin, 1926), p.169: 'One thing is certain, namely that Schlieffen's ideas about war correspond to the image of an annihilation war, drawn by Clausewitz', or W. Erfurth, *Der Vernichtungssieg* (Berlin, 1939), p.56: 'And thus since Schlieffen the way back to Clausewitz was found'.
9. Wilhelm Groener, *Das Testament des Grafen Schlieffen* (Berlin: Mittler, 1927), p.11.
10. Generalleutnant A.D. von Zoellner, 'Schlieffens Vermächtnis', Sonderheft der Militärwissenschaftlichen *Rundschau* (Berlin: 1938), pp.11–12.
11. Friedrich von Bernhardi, *On War of To-Day* (London: Rees, 1912), Vol. 2, pp.92–3.
12. An unpublished fragmentary manuscript of Adam von Moltke, *Blätter zum Leben, Wirken und Leiden meines Vaters Generaloberst Helmuth von Moltke* (I owe much gratitude to Mrs Eva Schotte-von Moltke, Hamburg, a granddaughter of the 'Younger' von Moltke, who gave me the opportunity to look into this manuscript and allowed me to take notes and quote from it).
13. Wilhelm Groener, *Lebenserinnerungen* (Göttingen: Vandenhoeck & Ruprecht, 1957), p.46.
14. One in 1914, three in 1915, one in 1917, and one in 1918.
15. The prefaces are from Field Marshal Prince Leopold of Bavaria, von Bülow and von Mackensen, Colonel Generals von Kluck, von Einhorn, von Woyrsch, Generals Count von Bothmer, von Beseler, Conrad von Hötzendorf, von Scholz, von Böhm-Ermolli, and from the Prussian Minister of War, Lt. General Wild von Hohenborn.
16. Hans Meier-Welcker, *Seeckt* (Frankfurt am Main: Bernard & Graefe, 1967), p.180.
17. Hajo Holborn, 'Moltke and Schlieffen: The Prussian-German School' in Edward Meade Earle (ed.), *Makers of Modern Strategy* (Princeton, NJ: Princeton University Press, 1952), p.188.
18. Oberstleutnant des Generalstabes Matzky, 'Kritische Untersuchung der Lehren von Douhet, Fuller, Hart und Seeckt', (Vortrag gehalten am 29.11.1935 an der Wehrmachtakademie) – Bundesarchiv/Militararchiv-Freiburg im Breisgau, W10-1/9.
19. Basil H. Liddell Hart, *The Other Side of the Hill* (London: Panther Book, 1956), p.214.
20. Leinveber, p.169.
21. Generalmajor a.D. von Schikfus und Neudorff, 'Clausewitz' in F. von Cochenhausen (ed.), *Führertum* (Berlin: Mittler, 1937), p.346.
22. Generaloberst von Seeckt, *Gedanken eines Soldaten* (Leipzig: v. Hase & Koehler, 1935), p.25.
23. von Seeckt's letter to his wife of 1 April 1936, quoted in Meier-Welcker, p.628.
24. Walter Reinhardt, 'Clausewitz' in Walter Reinhardt, *Wehrkraft und Wehrwille* (Berlin: Mittler, 1932), pp.110–74.
25. 'Alle Theorien von Clausewitz sind über den Haufen zu werfen'. – Erich Ludendorff, *Der totale Krieg* (Munich: Ludendorffs Verlag, 1935), p.10.

26. Ibid., p.3.
27. Cf. Wallach, Ch. 11, 'Ludendorff's "Total War"'.
28. H. von Metzsch, *Clausewitz Katechismus* (Berlin–Charlottenburg: Bucholz & Weisswange, 1937), p.4.
29. Norbert Kruger, 'Adolf Hitlers Clausewitzkenntnis', *Wehrwissenschaftliche Rundschau* 18 (August 1968), pp.467–71.
30. Cf. English translation published in London in 1939, p.544.
31. Cf. *Hitler's Secret Conversations* (New York: Signet Books, 1961).
32. *Kriegstagebuch des OKW* (Frankfurt: Bernard & Graefe, 1961), Vol. 4, p.1668. (Hitler urged his partisans to continue the struggle against the enemies of the Fatherland 'Faithful to the creed of the great Clausewitz'.)
33. Quoted in Kruger, p.470.
34. Hahlweg, 'Das Clausewitzbild', pp.107–8.
35. Karl Linnebach was the editor of the 14th ed. in 1933 and the 15th ed. in 1937 of 'Vom Kriege', which he also provided with an introduction and comments.
36. Karl Linnebach, 'Vom Geheimnis des kriegerischen Erfolges', *Wissen und Wehr* 21 (1940), pp.442–5.
37. Karl von Clausewitz (ed. by F.v. Cochenhausen), *Vom Kriege, Um Veraltetes gekürzte Ausgabe* (Leipzig: Insel, 1943), p.3.
38. Carl von Clausewitz, *On War*, Michael Howard and Peter Paret (eds.), (Princeton, NJ: Princeton University Press, 1976), p.358.
39. Ibid.
40. Aron, 249 (Germand ed.).
41. Carl von Clausewitz, *Vom Kriege* (Berlin: F. Schneider & Co., Königliche Hofbuchhandlung, 1880).
42. Hoffmann Nickerson, *The Armed Horde* (New York: G.P. Putnam Sons, 1940), p.202.
43. He compares the Austrian Field Marshal Daun (1705–1766) with the Roman Consul Fabius 'Cunctator'.
44. Frhr. von Freytag-Loringhoven, *Die Macht der Persönlichkeit im Kriege, Studien nach Clausewitz* (Berlin: Mittler, 1905), p.3.
45. Hans Meier-Welcker, 'Graf Schlieffen' in Werner Hahlweg (ed.), *Klassiker der Kriegskunst* (Darmstadt: Wehr & Wissen Verlagsgesellschaft, 1960), p.349.
46. Alfred von Schlieffen, *Dienstschriften* (Berlin: Mittler, 1937–38), p.45.
47. Cf. Carl von Clausewitz, *Hinterlassene Werke* (Berlin: Dümmler, 1862), Vol. 5, p.367; Vol. 6, p.24.
48. *On War*, p.367.
49. *On War*, p.365.
50. Colmar von der Goltz, *The Nation in Arms* (London: H. Rees, 1906), pp.143–4 passim. The first German ed. was published in 1883.
51. Ibid., p.355.
52. Bernhardi, Vol. 2, p.241.
53. Wilhelm Ritter von Leeb, *Die Abwehr* (Berlin: Mittler, 1938), pp.107–8.
54. Erich Ludendorff, *Kriegführung und Politik* (Berlin: Mittler, 1922), 10n.
55. Erich Ludendorff, *Der Totale Krieg*, pp.77–9, passim.
56. The proper and simple translation of 'Abwehr' is 'warding off'.
57. I am quite aware that it is a futile and arbitrary attempt to try to distinguish in English between 'defensive' and 'defense', but I could not think of a better way of presenting the German distinction between 'Abwehr' and 'Verteidigung'. I am, however, open to appropriate suggestions!
58. For a more detailed explanation of these terms, see: W. Ritter von Leeb.
59. Generalleutnant Waldemar Erfurth, *Die Ueberraschung im Kriege* (Berlin: Mittler, 1938), p.136 (The translation given in the American ed.: *Surprise* (Harrisburg, PA: Military Service Publication Company, 1943), p.186, is inaccurate.)
60. *Kriegstagebuch des OKW*, Vol. 1, p.1085.
61. Ibid., Vol. 2, p.1087.
62. Ibid., Vol. 2, pp.1292–7.
63. 'Hinhaltender Widerstand töten'. – Generaloberst Halder, *Kriegstagebuch* (Stuttgart:

Kohlhammer, 1962), Vol. 1, p.75.

64. Falls, p.14.

65. Wallach, p.19.

66. *On War*, p.607.

67. The German respective versions (*Vom Kriege*, VIII, 1) are: 1st ed.: 'Soll ein Krieg ganz den Absichten der Politik entsprechen, und soll die Politik den Mitteln zum Kriege ganz angemessen sein, so bleibt, wo der Staatsmann und der Soldat nicht in einer Person vereinigt sind, nur ein gutes Mittel übrig, nämlich den obersten Feldherrn zum Mitglied des Kabinetts zu machen, damit dasselbe [that is, the cabinet] Teil an den Hauptmomenten seines Handelns nehme.' The second part of this passage since the 2nd ed. reads: '... damit er [that is, the General] in den wichtigsten Momenten an dessen *Beratung und Beschlüssen teilnehme.*' The English and American translations before the present Princeton ed. were based on the falsified text in use since the German 2nd ed. Cf. *On War*, p.608.

68. *Moltkes Militärische Werke* (Herausgegeben vom Grossen Generalstabe, Kriegsgeschichtliche Abteilung I, Berlin: Mittler, 1892–1912), Vol. 2, part 2, p.291.

69. Aron, p.160 (German ed.).

70. 'Politik hält im Krieg den Mund bis Strategie ihr das Reden wieder gestattet'. Quoted in Otto von Moser, *Die obersten Gewalten im Weltkrieg* (Stuttgart: Belser, 1931), p.10.

71. Cf. note 41 above.

72. Comar, Freiherr von der Goltz, *Jena to Eylau* (London: L. Paul, Trench, Trubner, 1913), pp.75–6. The German ed. was published in 1883.

73. 'Zwei Briefe des Generals von Clausewitz. Gedanken zur Abwehr', *Militärwissenschaftliche Rundschau* (March 1937).

74. Schlieffen's letter to v. Freytag-Loringhoven of 14 Aug., 1912, printed in Generalfeldmarschal Graf Schlieffen (ed. Eberhard Kessel), *Briefe* (Göttingen: Vanderhoeck & Ruprecht, 1958), p.317.

75. Cf. note 73 above.

76. *On War*, p.607. Cf. note 67 above.

77. Moser, p.10.

78. Theobald von Bethmann-Hollweg, *Betrachtungen zum Weltkriege* (Berlin: Hobbing, 1919, 1921), Vol. 2, pp.7–9, passim.

79. Wilhelm Groener, *Lebenserinnerungen*, p.160.

80. Oberst a.D. Bernard Schwertfeger, 'Die politischen und militärischen Verantwortlichkeiten im Verlauf der Offensive 1918', in *Das Werk des Untersuchungsausschusses der Deutschen Verfassungsgebenden Nationalsammlung und des Deutschen Reichstages 1919–1928*, 4. Reihe, 2. Band (1925), p.79.

81. *Untersuchungsausschuss*, 4. Reihe, 3. Band, p.224.

82. Generalfeldmarschall von Hindenburg, *Aus meinem Leben* (Leipzig: Hirzel, 1920), p.101.

83. OHL = Oberste Heeresleitung = Army High command.

84. Ludendorff, *Kriegführung*, pp.104–5.

85. Wilhelm Groener, *Der Feldherr wider Willen* (Berlin: Mittler, 1930), p.164.

86. Friedrich von Bernhardi, *Vom Kriege der Zukunft* (Berlin, 1920), pp.168–70 passim. We do not know whether von Bernhardi was a forerunner of Ludendorff's 'Total War' theory or whether he was already propagating Ludendorff's ideas.

87. Ludendorff, *Kriegführung*, p.23.

88. Ludendorff, *Der totale Krieg*, p.10.

89. General Carl von Clausewitz (völlig neubearbeitete Ausgabe von Bruno Pochhammer, Rittmeister a.D.), *Vom Kriege, Hinterlassenes Werk* (Berlin: Vier Falken Verlag, n.d.), p.632.

90. v. Seeckt, pp.16–17.

91. Ludwig Beck, *Studien* (Stuttgart: Koehler, 1955), pp.60; 63.

92. OKW = Oberkommando der Wehrmacht = High Command of the Armed Forces.

93. Bernhard von Lossberg, *Im Wehrmachtführungsttab* (Hamburg: Molke, 1949), p.33.

94. Michael Freund (ed.), *Geschichte des Zweiten Weltkrieges in Dokumenten* (Freiburg im Breisgau: Herder, 1953), Vol. 1, p.48. The English translation in Alan Bullock, *Hitler. A Study in Tyranny* (Harmondsworth, Middlesex: Penguin Books, 1962), p.447.

95. The decision to attack Russia was also a violation of Clausewitz' precepts. Clausewitz, who

had participated in Napoleon's 1812 attack on Russia – he is mentioned in the second volume of Tolstoy's *War and Peace* – did not blame Napoleon for his decision to attack, but did fault his delay in starting the campaign, his tactics which caused lives to be squandered, and 'his neglect of matters of supply and of his line of retreat. Lastly, he stayed too long in Moscow' (*On War*, p.628). On the point of the dangers to be encountered in Russia, German military leaders were for once in harmony with Clausewitz. Except for General Max Hoffman and General Walter Reinhardt, who felt technology and good organization of a mobile army could overcome the disadvantages of Russian space, they presented a change of dissent – to which Hitler paid no attention whatever.

96. Quoted in Bullock, p.692.
97. Liddell Hart, p.214.

Clausewitz, Ludendorff and Beck: Some Remarks on Clausewitz' Influence on German Military Thinking in the 1930s and 1940s

KLAUS-JÜRGEN MÜLLER

I. INTRODUCTION: WHAT BECK OWED TO CLAUSEWITZ

General Ludwig Beck, Chief of General Staff of the German Army from 1933 to 1938, and later one of the leading personalities of the resistance against Hitler, has often been regarded as Clausewitz' most prominent and important disciple.[1] Some people even call him 'a new Clausewitz', assuming that he developed a modern theory of war based on Clausewitz' ideas.[2]

But although Beck often referred to Clausewitz,[3] it is both misleading and methodologically inaccurate simply to enumerate quotations from Clausewitz, or to show in general what ideas Beck adopted from the great military philosopher. On the one hand, Clausewitz' influence on Beck is more subtle and complex than a superficial reading of Beck's writings might suggest. On the other hand, it was not only Clausewitz who influenced Beck's thinking. Many other intellectual influences, including other military writers, had a greater impact on Beck's thinking than Clausewitz. Moreover, Beck read and assimilated the great Prussian theorist's ideas only to a certain extent.

To draw a direct line of thought from Clausewitz to Beck, therefore, actually represents a considerable distortion of the way Clausewitz was perceived in Germany, both by Beck and by other German thinkers. The following remarks are intended as a limited contribution to the historiographical understanding of Clausewitzian thought in Germany during the 1930s and 1940s.

Beck's understanding of Clausewitz' ideas progressed over time. Obviously, Beck studied Clausewitz intensively only after having resigned from office in August 1938, although he knew Clausewitz superficially before that date. It is striking that before 1938 his references to Clausewitz are infrequent and concerned with peripheral elements of Clausewitz' thinking. For instance, in his famous speech on the 125th anniversary of the War Academy in Berlin, he mentioned Clausewitz' name only three times, no more than he mentioned Schlieffen, and even then rather incidentally. He told his audience that Clausewitz strongly opposed the introduction of 'academic attitudes' in the *Allgemeine Kriegschule*.[4] Then he quoted Clausewitz twice in connection with the combination of intellect and character necessary for a Staff officer.

It is significant that Beck in the War Academy speech, as well as in his tribute to Ludendorff, on the occasion of the First World War general's 70th birthday, refers to Clausewitz primarily in regard to 'moralische Kategorien'. These were the famous 'moral factors' or 'principal moral elements', of which Clausewitz speaks in *On War*. This is quite typical of the way in which Clausewitz was perceived in the inter-war period. Schlieffen, for instance, had drawn these particular lessons from Clausewitz, and Seeckt 'continued to hammer home to the Reichswehr ... the importance of initiative, of the moral forces, of flexibility and self-reliance'.[6] Moral factors, not military–political relations, were the focus of the interest taken in Clausewitz during the inter-war period.

Beck's speech at the War Academy exemplified this rather limited perception of Clausewitz. He simply mentioned Clausewitz – together with Blume, Verdy du Vernois, Goltz, and Bernhardi – when referring to those who had taught at this institution, but he extolled only Schlieffen, 'the great teacher'. Thus, until his resignation in 1938, Beck's attitude towards Clausewitz was a conventional and limited one. Later, he became especially interested in analyzing Clausewitz' ideas about the political–military relationship. Studying Clausewitz, he found the theoretical justification of the attitude he had taken while arguing with Hitler about war and peace in the Czech crisis.[7] Fundamental to his controversy with the Führer was the problem of military–political relations. In his first study written in 1938 he adopted Clausewitz' point of view in asserting: 'Synchronizing the political purpose of war with the means at one's disposal and with the operational objective necessitates the participation of the military high command in formulating foreign policy'[8] (p. 33).

Including the military high command in his planning was exactly what Hitler had not done in 1938. When Beck, referring to Clausewitz, asserts that 'today, the "statesman" and the supreme military commander must work more closely together than ever' (p. 60), he continues his arguments with Hitler on the theoretical level. Thus, he quotes Clausewitz' famous letter to Major von Roeder, 'It is the duty and the right of the strategist to prevent the policy-makers from demanding what is contrary to the very nature of war and from making mistakes in employing the military forces because of ignorance of the efficacy of this instrument.'[9] This was exactly the central point of his controversy with Hitler: the Führer had ordered the military high command in 1938 to embark upon a major war for which the untrained and underequipped army was unprepared. This inappropriate demand was made by a political leader who had not included the strategist, the supreme military leader, in his political decision.

Thus, Beck's deeper and more detailed study of Clausewitz may have resulted from his controversy with Hitler and the need to shore up his own positions not only on peace and war, but also on military–political relations.

This article analyzes two basic problems central to Beck's thinking: first, the relationship between the military and civil authorities, and second, Beck's idea of total war. These two problems continually occupied him during his term as Chief of General Staff and later, during his enforced retirement (1938–44). While dealing with these problems, Beck not only referred to Clausewitz, but also to other military theorists such as Ludendorff, Blume, Moltke, and Seeckt. In particular, he discussed and criticized Ludendorff's ideas by contrasting them with Clausewitz' doctrines. In fact, Beck adopted Clausewitz' ideas as a means of refuting Ludendorff's.

II. THE PROBLEM OF THE MILITARY LEADER'S RELATIONSHIP TO THE POLITICAL LEADER

The complicated problem of the relationship between the military and civil government already occupied Beck's mind at an early stage of his military career. In one of the earliest sources we have, a letter dated 28 November 1918, Beck, confronted with the military defeat and collapse of the German Empire, discusses the role of the military in the state and the political responsibility of the highest-ranking military leaders.[10] He returned again and again to this fundamental problem. He tackled nearly every important question during his military career in the context of the relationship between army (military) and government (civil) control.[11] For him, this dichotomy was, in fact, the focal point of his political thought. He viewed the decisive problem in military–political relations as that of primacy: which ranked superior – the military or the political authority?

In the literature dealing with him, Beck has almost unanimously been regarded as an ardent supporter of the primacy of 'politics';[12] in general, this term is understood as civil control according to the liberal–democratic tradition. In order to support this assumption scholars frequently refer to Beck's famous studies written between 1938 and 1944, specifically to his very critical analyses of Ludendorff's ideas.[13] In his book, *Total War*, published in 1935, Ludendorff had developed the thesis that total war required the supreme military commander to have absolute leadership in every respect.[14] Beck vigorously rejected this idea.

In one of his studies he argues that Ludendorff goes too far in his egocentric demands that politics be subordinated to military strategy and that the supreme military commander in a future war have the right and duty to define policy as well as strategy (p. 32). In contrast to Ludendorff's theory of total war Beck formulates his own theory of 'total politics' and, with reference to Clausewitz conceives 'the legitimate supremacy of politics over warfare' (p. 248). But the relationship between Beck's ideas and Clausewitz' is not easily understood. First we must realize that Beck's concept of political authority is totally different from the well-known principles of liberal–democratic constitutional law, according to which the military is simply an instrument of the civil executive, without any political power of its own. Beck's divergence from this view has often not been sufficiently understood for two reasons: first, because the German word 'Politik' implies two different ideas, and second, because the phases used by Clausewitz and to which Beck refers have frequently been subjected to misinterpretation.[15]

Beck does not, by any means, intend to place the leading political figure above the supreme military commander or to put political leadership on a higher legel than the military. Rather, to Beck the German word 'Politik' means more than 'political leadership', 'civil control', 'government', or 'leading politicians'. Rather, 'Politik' is an abstract, complex term comprising, among other sub-categories, the concept 'war', which in turn contains the military.[16] On this point, Beck entirely follows Clausewitz' idea about war as an extension of politics.

In 1938, Beck quotes the famous formula of the great military philosopher in his study, 'Der Anführer im Kriege': 'War is not an independent phenomenon but the continuation of politics by different means. Consequently, the main lines of every major strategic plan are largely political in nature, and their political character increases the more the plan applies to the entire campaign and to the whole state'[17] (p. 31).

For Beck, following Clausewitz, war is, therefore, a political phenomenon, a special manifestation of politics: because of the political character of war, 'Politik' is the superior entity. As a result – as Beck often wrote – 'politics' has to define and to justify the political aims and objectives of war, from which the military objectives are to be logically deduced.[18] He bases his argument on Clausewitz, quoting *On War*: 'A war plan results directly from the political conditions of the two warring states as well as from their relations to third powers. A plan of campaign results from the war plan, and – frequently – may even be identical with it'[19] (p. 31).

Here, however, it is necessary to point out that Beck uses the word 'Politik' in different ways. Sometimes it *does* mean simply 'political action',[20] sometimes it *is* synonymous with 'the leading politician' or 'political leader(s)' (for example, p. 119). Nevertheless, whenever he discusses the supremacy of politics, he uses the word as a comprehensive concept. Beck refers to 'Politik', for example, as something which has the 'dominant position over all political life in a state'[21] (p. 137). 'Politik' is the sphere in which the supreme military leader *and* the responsible political leader have to act – each in his particular way – but fundamentally together. In 'Der Anführer im Kriege', he argues that the supreme military commander, by necessity, must have a say in foreign policy[22] (p. 242). But this participation in foreign policy does not mean that he is simply to be consulted as a specialist in military affairs – for example, concerning the effectiveness or capabilities of the armed forces – like any other cabinet minister (p. 137). Although some of Beck's formulations might suggest this interpretation, a closer examination of his thoughts shows very clearly that the leading politician and the supreme military commander are to act together *on the same level*. The words Beck chooses to describe and to define this special relationship are significant. The two leaders are 'to exchange their views', the supreme military commander has all military forces 'at his disposal' (p. 122, p. 61), and, quoting General von Seeckt, Beck argues, 'The politician asks the supreme commander: "What are you able to do? What are our opponents able to do?" and the supreme commander in his turn asks: "What do you intend to do? And what are our opponents' aims?" '[23] (p. 122).

And in his study, 'Deutschland in einem kommenden Krieg', he stresses that today the political leader and the supreme military commander 'have to act more closely together than ever before' (pp. 60–61). Beck's view that both leaders rank equally is clearly expressed in his thesis, echoing General von Seeckt, that 'the right of the supreme military commander [is] to contradict the politician, if necessary, and to refuse his demands' (p. 122). In November 1938, he writes in the same context, 'The supreme military commander is not in the politician's service, he is not subordinate to him' (p. 60).

The responsibilities Beck attributes to the supreme commander cover more than sharing power and formulating foreign policy. In the study mentioned above, he clearly states that 'the supreme military commander has the duty and the right ... to extend his strategic deliberations into the field of "politics" '[24] (p. 62). Here again his comprehensive concept of 'politics' is evident: the military and the political leaders work closely together in the waging of war and in deciding strategy.

In accordance with Clausewitz, Beck explains to his readers that, due to the political nature of war, the supreme military commander has to participate in domestic decision-making processes. He must discuss even administrative questions or economic problems, and be especially concerned with 'all questions of national morale' in times of war.

In 'Betrachtungen über den Krieg', written two years later, he makes the point that 'the supreme commander's duties cannot encompass enough and his field of activity cannot be sufficiently broad' if he is not given this wide-ranging power (p. 85, p. 138).

Beck therefore elevates the supreme commander to the sphere he defines as 'Politik', which is a comprehensive abstraction containing war as well as policy. Here the political leader and the supreme commander have to act together, with both the military man and the politician subject to the 'primacy of politics'. Insofar as warfare is subordinate to 'politics', Beck's thinking shows a clear-cut duality; but the cooperation of the two supremely responsible representatives in the political and in the military field requires unity.

Until the very end of his life, Beck supported this comprehensive concept of 'Politik', and consequently the special – and equal – position of the supreme military commander in relation to that of the leading politician. Even in 1944, the year of his death (on the day of the abortive coup d'etat against Hitler), he criticized Marshall Foch, the famous French soldier and Supreme Allied Commander, for always remaining within the narrow limits of his military duties *stricto sensu*.[25] Foch had been unable to rise to the stature of a statesman when necessary, as for instance during the inter-allied debate on the clauses of the Treaty of Versailles. In Beck's view Foch was not aware that as Supreme Allied Commander he carried a twofold responsibility: for waging war as the leading military specialist, and for acting politically – that is, within the comprehensive sphere of 'Politik', together with the supreme political leader – precisely because he is the supreme *military* leader (pp. 283–8). The supreme military leader has to be both a soldier and a political man. Both warfare and policy-making, as derivations from 'Politic', have to be conducted from within the superior sphere of 'Politik'.

In the same way he criticized Foch, Beck blamed the younger Moltke for not having contributed his share to the political decision-making process in 1914. He also refutes Bismarck's view, found in his *Memoirs*, that 'defining and describing the objective of a war as well as advising the monarch during and before a war is and remains a political [that is, not a military] task'. Beck equally opposes the elder Moltke's thesis that 'strategy, although in keeping with politics, is totally independent of it'. He comments laconically, 'Both statements ... are not beyond criticism in every respect' (pp. 120–21).

Thus Beck would appear sympathetic to Clausewitz' view that the ideal leader is a combination of the leading politician and the supreme soldier in one person. His choice of a quotation from Clausewitz is a significant one: 'The first, the supreme, the most far-reaching act of judgment that the statesman and commander has [*sic*] to make is to establish by that test and the kind of war on which he is [*sic*] embarking.'[26] Contrary to the English version, Clausewitz' original German verbs are singular, meaning that 'statesman and commander' is one person. The ideal manifestation of this, for Beck as for Clausewitz, is Frederick the Great (p. 61). But of course, Beck is well aware – as was Clausewitz – that the identity of the supreme political leader and the supreme military commander cannot be a realistic solution any longer because of the growing complexity of political life. 'No human genius is capable of successfully directing a great war in the future both militarily and politically as Frederick the Great or Napoleon once did. The duality of leading politician and supreme military commander is therefore a fact which we have to accept' (p. 61).

In dealing with this problem of the special relationship between military and political supreme leaders, we should note that Beck relies much more on the ideas of the German military theorist General Hermann von Blume than on Clausewitz. Blume, once one of Moltke's lieutenants and then an independent-minded military theorist of great influence, distinguishes between 'war' and 'supreme military commander' in their relation to 'Politik' and 'political leader':

> War is a means of attaining political ends and is, therefore, subordinated to politics. But the supreme military commander (*Feldherr*) has not to serve the politician, is not subordinated to him. Both have to act together, harmoniously and in constant and mutual agreement. Their relationship must be free of every imposing or jealous impulse, of tyrannical or imposing attitude, as well as of all jealous emotions, in order that policy and strategy may be able to coincide and thereby bring war to a successful end. (pp. 60–61, quoting Blume's *Strategie-Krieg und Politik*, 3rd edn. [Berlin: 1912])

Beck fully agrees with Blume that the supreme military leader is *not subordinate* to the leading politician. Military and political problems sometimes require the competence of both (p. 60). There are military problems which have considerable political relevance and political issues with important military implications. Therefore, Blume concludes, the personal relationship of the political leader and the supreme military commander should be based on mutual esteem and mutual education regarding their respective spheres of duties (pp. 73, 123; also p. 62).

Blume convinced Beck to agree with Clausewitz, whom he cites as well: 'Only by the combined intellectual effort of leading politician and supreme military commander is it possible to master the first, the supreme and the most far-reaching act of judgment.'[27] Clausewitz, who lived in a period when the strategist and the absolute monarch was still one person, wrote: 'If war is to be fully consonant with the political objectives, and policy suited to the means available for war, then unless statesman and soldier are combined in one person, the only sound expedient is to make the commander-in-chief a member of the cabinet, so that he may take part in its council and decisions on important occasions.'[28] According to Clausewitz, the war plan results from both leaders' correctly perceiving the nature of the intended war and harmoniously cooperating in the direction and preparation of war.[29]

Referring to Clausewitz as well as to Blume, Beck regards the military commander and the leading politician as factors of equal rank. Thus, in Beck's understanding there is no contradiction between the views of Blume and of Clausewitz. And he, therefore, relies on both theorists in order to prove his view, which he presumes to be in total accord with theirs. This is, however, not at all true. Blume's thesis on the relationship between the supreme military commander and the leading politician considerably differs from that of Clausewitz. As far as I know, until now no one has yet realized the inconsistency of Beck's argumentation in combining Clausewitz' and Blume's points of view.

Indeed, Clausewitz emphatically calls for concordant action from the political and military sectors. The political nature of war requires 'a united and integrated standpoint', but he does *not* regard the supreme political leader and the supreme military commander as equal. Of course, he wanted to make the military leader a member of the cabinet, but the first edition gives his motive: 'so that the cabinet can share in the major aspects of his activities' – that is, simply in order to avoid friction and to preserve a united leadership in conducting the war. Clausewitz firmly believes that the leading politician or the leading political body remains superior to the military commander-in-chief.[30]

According to Blume, however, the relationship between the supreme military commander and the supreme political leader is one of duality and absolute equality. The supreme military commander and the leading politician 'have to act together and in harmony, continuously informing each other, and in mutual agreement, while strictly respecting their different spheres of activity' (p. 61, quoting Blume, *Strategie*).

Beck did not realize the contradiction between these two points of view. He was not able to do so because his perception of Clausewitz was based on a distorted version of the relevant sentence in *On War*. That sentence, referring to the reason the military commander is to be made a member of the cabinet, contains a reversal of emphasis between the first and second editions, as Howard and Paret point out.[31] By using the second version, with the greater importance it attributes to the commander's role, Beck sought to legitimize his own view concerning the absolute equality of the 'statesman' and the supreme military commander. And he combined Clausewitz' with Seeckt's and Blume's ideas in order to refute Ludendorff, who put the military commander above everyone else.[32]

In examining the views of Clausewitz, Beck (and Blume), Ludendorff, and Foch, we recognize that they constitute a fourfold typology. Each perceives the roles of political leader and military leader in a different relationship to each other and to the realm of politics in the largest sense (that is, the realm of national goals). Clausewitz felt that the political leader and the military leader worked together to realize these national goals, but in the last analysis the political leader was superior. Beck and Blume saw the military and political leaders as equal partners, both devoted to the end of politics. Ludendorff relegated the political leader to carrying out the ends of politics, while the military leader was both superior to him and outside the political realm – that is, Ludendorff saw war as having its own goals. And finally, Foch, at least according to Beck, reneged on his responsibility to assist the political leader by removing himself from the realm of politics and taking a subordinate, uninvolved position. Beck, as we have seen, rejected both Ludendorff and Foch. He accepted Clausewitz partly because he mistakenly thought Clausewitz agreed with him and Blume. However, it is worth noting that his thought is close to that of Clausewitz, in that both recognize the supremacy of 'Politik' and the necessity for the political and military leaders to subordinate themselves to it.

Despite the high esteem he had for Ludendorff, Beck criticized him in the letter of 28 November 1918, referred to above, exactly because of his ideas concerning military–political relations.[33] Beck states that he himself had early come to the conclusion that a negotiated peace was necessary for Germany. But, he continues, 'This was quite impossible to do against the will of the "dictator" Ludendorff, for a dictator he was. Nobody was able to topple him, not even the Kaiser.'[34]

Even more outspokenly he criticized Ludendorff in the 1935 radio address broadcast on the occasion of Ludendorff's 70th birthday.[35] Beck mentioned that the hero of the First World War 'very often transgressed the limits set on the authority and the power of a soldier', often behaving with 'grandiose disregard' of the civil authorities. In his address, Beck explained Ludendorff's usurpation of political power by referring to Clausewitz, who, he said, wrote that 'some great emotion must inflame the soul of a supreme commander, be it Caesar's ambition, Hannibal's hatred or Frederick's defiance of a glorious downfall; in this sense, Ludendorff had the same emotion as Prussia's greatest king'.[36] Three years later, however, as we shall see below, he refuted Ludendorff by referring to a different aspect of Clausewitz' thought, this time regarding total war.

Returning to the initial question of Beck's indebtedness of Clausewitz, we can now summarize that his study of Clausewitz – although distorted in one respect – enabled Beck not only to come to a better understanding concerning war and politics, political leadership and military command, but also to free himself from the spell of Ludendorff's ideas. Given the strong influence which Ludendorff exerted on Beck as well as their close personal contact at one time, this intellectual emancipation cannot be underestimated.[37] Moreover, the distorted tradition of Clausewitz' ideas about political relations – the idea that Clausewitz saw military and political leaders as equal partners – enabled Beck to refute even greater authorities such as Moltke and Bismarck on this topic by referring to Clausewitz, Blume, and Seeckt. Considering the sacrosanctity of Moltke and Bismarck in the Germany of those days, particularly in military circles, this was a great achievement.

Even more important to Beck personally was his conviction that in his controversy with Hitler he was not only justified, but well in accordance with the most noble – that is, the Clausewitzian – tradition of German military thinking.[38]

More generally, it can be said that in dealing with the problem of military and political relations Beck opened up a new perspective in the research on Clausewitz. He presented a perception of the great Prussian military philosopher which was quite unfamiliar to his contemporaries in Germany between the wars. In those days, the focus on Clausewitz was almost exclusively on the 'moral forces' he discussed in the third volume of *On War*; what was worse, this narrow interest resulted in an ideological perversion of Clausewitz.[39]

On the question of war and politics, popular thinkers like Schlieffen, Seeckt, Blume, and in particular Ludendorff, carried great weight. It was the intellectual controversy with Ludendorff which brought Beck to a deeper understanding of Clausewitz and made him one of Clausewitz' very few disciples in Germany at that time.

III. BECK'S USE OF CLAUSEWITZ TO REFUTE LUDENDORFF

According to Yehuda Wallach, the well-known Israeli military historian, 'Ludendorff was the first German who dared to reject Clausewitz decisively and in public'.[40] Although not too many Germans, even military men, had read Clausewitz' writings attentively and thoroughly, and although his intellectual influence was always relative to that of other, more popular military theorists, in the realm of German military doctrine and theory he was a sacrosanct prophet.[41]

Ludendorff therefore committed lese majesty or worse when he stated bluntly: 'All theories of Clausewitz are to be rejected.' And he added just as categorically that Clausewitz' writings and ideas 'belong to a far-distant historical epoque and have lost almost all relevance for today; studying his book may even result in confusing the reader's mind'.[42] On the other hand Ludendorff's own influence in the fields of strategy, policy, and military theory in inter-war Germany can hardly be underestimated, although this subject requires more detailed research.

The influence and prestige of 'the greatest of all Generals of the Great War' – as Ludwig Beck once called Ludendorff[43] – was unique because of the role he played, together with Hindenburg, in the first total war in European history. The First World War decisively influenced the ideas of even the independent-minded Ludwig Beck concerning a coming war: 'Since the end of World War I, all intellectual and practical military preparation for war had been dominated by the idea of total war' (p. 53). He therefore was very receptive to the ideas expressed in Ludendorff's book on total war published in 1935.

At that time, Beck had already been in contact with Ludendorff for several years, constantly exchanging letters about mostly military affairs, particularly about the crucial issues of the character of a coming war and military–political relations. Ludendorff himself combined both issues when he wrote to Beck:

> The combined moral, physical and economic forces of a nation constitute its 'military capacity' (*Wehrkraft*). The armed forces are only part of it; they rely on it to defeat the enemy. The representatives of the new German armed forces have to be aware of this interdependency between the military capacity in this sense and the armed forces, and have to provide for it as they do for the armed forces. This is in short the formidable lesson of the Great War. The leaders of the armed forces from the ranks of whom the strategist of the future war will arise, are not allowed to restrict their activities to the purely military sphere. They have to prepare the entire forces of the nation for war, even in times of peace. This is the only way to assure the future victory. (quoted, pp. 53–54)

These ideas about the total mobilization of all national resources organized by the Military High Command had already been adopted by Ludwig Beck when he became Chief of General Staff in October, 1933.[44]

At the inaugural session of the 'Standing Group of the Imperial Defense Committee' in December 1933, Beck, being the Chairman, made a speech concerning committee policy, which reflected Ludendorff's ideas in more than one respect. 'A new war must not find us as unprepared as we were in 1914', he explained to his audience. To Beck a future war would be a total war, as Ludendorff predicted, which would require the total mobilization of all national resources under the planning, organization, and control of the military. To meet these ends all governmental departments should be coordinated by the Military High Command. He then gave orders to the representatives of the different governmental departments present to inquire about the preparations for war already under way within the respective departments.[45]

Coordinating all government departments under the military High Command was ideal, he said later in his studies, especially in 'Der Anführer im Kriege'. Quoting Clausewitz and referring to Ludendorff at the same time, he claimed that 'the limits of the responsibilities and duties of the strategist, the supreme commander of the German armed forces, cannot be defined extensively enough and ... he is not to be excluded from the overall deliberation concerning the conduct of war and war policy' (p. 85). Again echoing Clausewitz he continued that all aspects 'call for careful study. One can win the first decision in a case, and lose it on appeal, and end up having to pay costs as well.'[46] In view of this he deduces that in order to assure the overall preparation for total war, the supreme military commander has to participate in the formulation of foreign policy. Similarly 'the Army's High Command has to have a say in questions concerning general administration, war economy and the morale of the population' (p. 33).

Moreover, Beck adopts Ludendorff's point of view on peace: peace is nothing other than a period of non-war, consequently pre-war or post-war. This conception of war and peace must inevitably result in a complete militarization of the entire nation. In this context it is significant that Beck refers to Ludendorff as well as to Clausewitz with no sense of contradiction.

In retrospect, this linking of Clausewitz's ideas with Ludendorff's with regard to total war, which we find in Beck's studies of 1938, and in his thinking even before that year, seems to be quite illogical and inadequate with respect to both military theorists. This can be explained, however, first by the distorted version of Clausewitz' concept of the relationship between the highest military authority and the leading politician – which we have already referred to in section II of this essay – and second, because Beck dealt here primarily with the problem of the character of a coming war and not with military–political relations. His perception of a future war has therefore to be analyzed, especially since it underwent a remarkable development.

In his speech to the Standing Group of the Committee for Imperial Defense, he already referred to a kind of war quite different from a 'normal' or conventional war. It was evidently a total war – a war in which all national resources had to be mobilized because this war would be a fight for the very existence of the nation. In his studies of 1938, we find the same notion of total war.

Of course, he maintains that the army alone is the decisive factor which will decide a future war for Germany; but he also admits that the Reich can only be defeated by a combination of 'military warfare' and 'economic warfare', in other words, by a total war. This is Ludendorff pure and simple. In accordance with these thoughts Beck states towards the end of 1938 that

> the war to come will be a total war and not a purely military one .... Our prospective enemies will particularly make use of those elements of power against us which they have at their disposal and which are superior to ours.
>
> These elements are time, space, and the inexhaustible resources of their vast empires. At the same time, they will also attempt to increase our shortages and deficiencies in this respect. (pp. 30–31)

He then drew two conclusions: first, the army has to be in charge of the Armed Forces High Command and the organization and control of all operations, because the army alone is able to bring about the decision in what he called the 'Waffenkrieg' ('military warfare'), and, second, 'the primacy of the armed forces has to be the fundamental doctrine for the integration and incorporation of all elements and factors relevant to the conduct of war', which means nothing other than the total mobilization of the nation under military control. He continues, 'The armed forces are only capable of the utmost efficiency if all national capabilities for waging war (*Wehrkraft*) are entirely and from the very beginning at the disposal of the army. This is the basic problem concerning total war' (p. 31).

But in contrast to Ludendorff, Beck did not advocate the inevitable introduction of dictatorship in case of war. Rather he combines this particular idea of war which Ludendorff had in mind with Clausewitz' general doctrine of the political character of war, as expressed in the famous statement: 'War is not an independent phenomenon, but the continuation of politics by different means.'[47]

Thus, as we have seen in section II, he arrives at the conclusion that the supreme military commander has to be of equal rank with the political leader, the 'statesman', and consequently to assume governmental duties and rights, especially of participation in the decision-making process. On the one hand, he rejects Ludendorff's idea of military dictatorship, as the appropriate type of political leadership in the age of total war, by referring to the pseudo-Clausewitzian doctrine of equal rank between the 'statesman' and the supreme military commander. On the other hand, however, he obviously adopted Ludendorff's doctrine of total war insofar as the character of a coming war was concerned, though retaining Clausewitz' belief in the political nature of war. This combination was typical of Beck's thinking in those years. The dual influence of Ludendorff and Clausewitz is reflected quite clearly in the proposals he made for the reorganization of the Military High Command. 'Total War', he wrote, 'is above all a problem of organization to be resolved.' The premises on which he based his argument are the following: 'The armed forces of a nation are like a colossus on feet of clay if they cannot rely on all the elements necessary for total warfare: economy, food supply and morale; these are the essential factors that decide a nation's capability of waging and enduring a modern war' (p. 57). He also calls food supply, economy, and moral strength the 'three pillars ... on which the armed forces rely in time of war .... If one of these pillars becomes weak or even crumbles, the whole structure [of the armed forces] will crumble' (p. 33). He, therefore, demands that the governmental structure be organized to these ends.

Consequently, in the 1938 study, 'Der Anführer im Kriege', he proposes a war cabinet which, on the one hand, differs considerably from Ludendorff's ideas of military dominance and, on the other hand, fits perfectly into the model of harmonious cooperation between two equal leaders that – he thought – Clausewitz had advocated. Had this organizational scheme been realized, the political influence of the military in the Third Reich would have been tremendously strengthened but, seen in retrospect, it is obvious that there was no chance at all of realizing it in Hitler's Germany of 1938.

The main feature of his proposal was that, in times of war, the supreme military commander should become Number Two in the state, the Deputy of the 'Chief of State' who presided over the War Cabinet. It is characteristically Clausewitzian that the Commander-in-Chief and not the Foreign Minister, who likewise is a member of this body, is elevated to this eminence. Beck emphasized the importance of this position: 'As a matter of fact, the supreme military commander (der "Anführer im Kriege") becomes the decisive figure in time of war', particularly because the leading politician (der 'Staatsmann') 'is well advised not to step down from his supreme position while conducting war' (pp. 33–4).

The military predominance in the War Cabinet, moreover, was to be secured by the fact that the commanders of the three services – Army, Navy, and Air Force – were to be permanent members, whereas the Minister of Economy, of Food Supply and of Finance, despite their importance in time of war, were to have only occasional access to the War Cabinet.

The Permanent Secretary of State for War, the General Commissioner for War Economy, and the Minister of Propaganda were to be temporary members. If necessary, all members of the War Cabinet could be excluded from the deliberations and the decision-making process of the statesman and the supreme military commander. Beck also provided for 'the right of the supreme military commander to participate in controlling and directing the domestic administration, the organization of the public food supply, the war economy (finances included), and in controlling and in sustaining the morale of the nation' (pp. 33–4). These guidelines clearly reflect Beck's attempt to realize what he learned from Clausewitz about the harmony and cooperation between military and political leadership, between the supreme military commander and statesman. His model War Cabinet could, he believed, cope with the problems of total war. This plan was not the mere amusement of an old general who, having been chased out of office, lived in his Dahlem town house and needed to pass the time. Beck was still in office when he made the first draft of this power structure.

Of course, the great debate between the General Staff, the Armed Forces High Command, and Göring about what was then called 'Spitzengliederung', the reorganization of the supreme military command, had been already decided[48] when he wrote this study. But four years earlier, while preparing the military and political documents destined to form the basis of a war game on the highest level, he had already drafted a paper on 'The Authority of the Supreme Political and Military Command in Times of War', which provided almost identical guidelines for a War Cabinet.[49] These sources prove that in the 1930s Beck's fundamental ideas had been rather consistent insofar as the problem of total war and the military–political relationship are concerned.

Among the problems raised in conjunction with total war, there was one to which Beck devoted much attention: the securing and sustaining of mass loyalty and national integration. The importance of public morale had been hammered home to Beck's generation of high-ranking military men by the dreadful memories of the 1918 Revolution.

Again and again in his writings, Beck returned to this point, emphasizing the importance of what he called 'die seelische Haltung des Volkes', the spiritual and mental attitude of the people. Here again, he follows Ludendorff, who in his book *Total War* had devoted his second chapter – called 'Die seelische Geschlossenheit des Volkes: die Grundlage des totalen Krieges' – to this topic.

Beck considered 'Moral' (moral, spiritual, and mental strength) a decisive element in total war. Sometimes he speaks of 'seelische Geschlossenheit' (moral strength) or 'seelische Kraft' (perseverance). 'Today the armed forces draw upon the strongest, but also the most vulnerable resources in our nation …. When the nation crumbles and collapses, the armed forces will be carried with it. The lesson of 1918 will remain a formidable warning forever' (p. 57). Thus, writing in 1938, in his study 'Deutschland in einem kommenden Krieg' (Germany in a coming war), Beck echoed Ludendorff's ideas.

Beck frequently deals with the question, 'How to prepare the nation's internal strength sufficiently in peacetime?' The solution he proposes is characteristic of his political thinking as well as of the political situation in Germany at that time. On the one hand, he is convinced of the absolute necessity of charismatic leadership; on the other hand, 'moral strength', in his view, is also created through propaganda and political manipulation of the masses. It is, therefore, logical that the Minister for Propaganda in Beck's model War Cabinet ranks higher than the Ministers of the Interior, Economy, and Finance; they are to be only occasionally allowed to take part in the deliberations of the War Cabinet, whereas the Minister of Propaganda is to be a temporary member.

But what is important in this scheme is that the Minister of Propaganda and the entire apparatus of mass indoctrination and manipulation – the NS Party in particular – are thought to be only instrumental to the leading figures of the War Cabinet, namely the 'statesman' and the supreme military commander. It was obviously out of the question, for Beck, that the Nazi Party should have any chance of monopolizing propaganda and mass indoctrination.

Ludendorff argued that military dictatorship be introduced; military leaders like Keitel and Jodl, fascinated by Hitler as they were, strongly advocated the subordination of the armed forces to the charismatic Führer. For these theorists the Führer's supremacy was the ideal instrument for mass mobilization and ideological indoctrination in the age of total war.[50]

Beck, however, did not accept either solution. Referring to Clausewitz' theory concerning military–political relationships, he advocated the total mobilization and ideological control of the people under the combined direction of the military elite and the leader of the national-socialist mass movement. Once this scheme was adopted, his two main objectives could be accomplished: first, the most effective preparation – both psychological and material – of the nation for total war; second, securing the leading political and social position for the traditional military elite. Thus, although Beck like Ludendorff, conceived of twentieth-century war as 'total war', in defining the most effective organization for total war, he followed neither Ludendorff's extremist militarism nor Hitler's Führer-ideology: his ideal remained the harmonious cooperation between leading politician and supreme military commander proposed by Clausewitz.

The next stage in the evolution of Beck's ideas on war began about 1939–40, when he began turning away from the doctrines of Ludendorff, the strong-willed 'Feldherr' of the Great War. His gradual deviation was, on the one hand, a result of the increasing effect the fatal and destructive character of the modern war raging throughout Europe had upon him. But it is equally obvious that Beck's gradual alienation and, finally, his intellectual rejection of Ludendorff's theories was much more a consequence of his deeper and more intensive study of Clausewitz' ideas. The first indication of this process of intellectual emancipation from Ludendorff can be found in a paper he prepared for the famous 'Mittwochsgesellschaft' and read there on 24 April 1940, 'Betrachtungen über den Krieg' (Reflections on War)[51] (pp. 117–38).

He begins his paper by quoting Clausewitz, whom he calls 'the greatest of all modern military philosophers': 'Nothing is more important in life than finding the right standpoint for seeing and judging events, and then adhering to it. One point and one only yields an integrated view of all phenomena; and only by holding to that point of view can one avoid inconsistency'[52] (p. 118).

Beck is no longer dealing with questions about how best to organize the nation for total war, or how to secure the people's 'internal strength' and 'leadership of the elite'; now the central question is the very nature of war as an abstract concept.

His starting point is Clausewitz' famous sentence: 'War is an act of force to compel the enemy to do our will.'[53] This, he continues, is the political object; force is simply the means. Quoting Clausewitz again, he argues that force is not necessarily the only means 'to compel the enemy to do our will'. Thus he clearly and definitely rejects Ludendorff and implicitly, Hitler also – both because they did not regard war as a political act, as a 'continuation of political intercourse' and because they denied that 'war cannot be divorced from political life'.[54]

For Ludendorff as well as for Hitler, 'War is the supreme manifestation of people's (völkisch) will be life.'[55] For both, war is an end in itself, whereas according to Clausewitz, and his disciple Beck, it is simply a means. Beck implicitly criticizes Ludendorff by arguing that Clausewitz' famous statement, 'War is simply the continuation of political intercourse with the addition of other means',[56] has often been contested in an unfounded and unreasonable way. This statement is undoubtedly aimed at Ludendorff who, in the first chapter of his book on total war, denies that Clausewitz, in asserting that war is an instrument of 'politics', understood the true nature of war. 'War in fact, the 'Feldherr' continues, 'is a struggle of deep ethical significance intended to preserve the life and vitality of a nation'.[57]

In contrast to this point of view, Beck, referring to Clausewitz, maintains the 'ethical limits of war' in saying that war is the 'last resort of foreign policy after all other means prove to be insufficient'. According to Beck, the concept of total war had in reality fatally increased the destructive character of warfare. The partisans of total war were not aware of what Clausewitz had taught, that 'the first and supreme, the most far-reaching act of judgment that the statesman and the commander have to make is to establish ... the kind of war on which they are embarking ... neither mistaking it for, nor trying to turn it into something that is alien to its nature'[58] (pp. 121, 123).

Thus, Beck refers to Clausewitz' doctrine on war, its nature, and the consequent supremacy of 'Politik', in order to refute Ludendorff's theories: 'Ludendorff's postulate cited in his book on total war that "politics" has to serve strategy, can therefore, be easily brushed aside or, at least, reduced to suitable proportion' (pp. 136–7).

Beck then defines more precisely than before what 'total war' means in his view. Total war is not, as Ludendorff maintains, a sort of 'manifest destiny of a nation', – 'the highest manifestation of a people's or a nation's struggle for survival'[59] – it is rather a war that becomes very quickly a 'war of attrition or a war of starvation' (p. 124). Involving economic and psychological warfare as well as military warfare (*Waffenkrieg*), this kind of war, 'in which blockade and attrition are more decisive than purely military operations' will become the war of the future (p. 127). And, according to Beck, the concept of total war has already brought about the reality of total war.

'Total war' as defined by Beck was doubtless contrary to Ludendorff's existentialist view. Beck did, however, still think of a war in which all national resources are to be mobilized. But does this kind of war correspond to what Clausewitz called 'the absolute war'?[60] It was about just this question that Beck had an extensive correspondence with Professor Gerhard Ritter of Freiburg University, well-known historian who, apart from Beck, was the only German scholar doing research on Clausewitz' doctrine of the political relevance of war during those years.[61] In 1935, Professor Ritter had already published an article in the respectable *Historische Zeitschrift*, in which he particularly dealt with Clausewitz' ideas on the political relevance of war. Now he was preparing another article,[62] just when Beck himself began to deal with this subject.

That Beck was much more interested in the general aspects of what Clausewitz had written on this problem than the historian Ritter, might be deduced from what Ritter wrote to the general: 'I myself view Clausewitz much more within the context of his time than you.'[63] Furthermore, Professor Ritter commented upon a draft of a study that Beck had sent him and in which the general had outlined his critical reflections on Ludendorff's theory on total war and his analysis of Clausewitz' thought:

> The conceptual confusion ... results, in my view, from the ambiguity of the concept of 'total war'. You may, in accordance with Clause-

witz, take it to be an 'absolute war' which does not stop until total destruction of the opponent's armed forces is achieved or, on the other hand, you may – against what Clausewitz had had in mind – perceive this concept as a war which becomes an end in itself ... which requires all resources of a nation, and which ... ultimately destroys more than ever can be reconstructed: the whole economic and social structure of a society, not only that of the opponent, but also that of the belligerent party who had embarked upon it. Clausewitz, in contrast to that, talks only about a war between armies, not between societies.[64]

Beck was in fact, more inclined to perceive 'total war' in the second sense which Professor Ritter had mentioned. It was close to what he himself had in mind when, as Chief of General Staff, he had attempted to organize the nation for total war. But when, in 1942, he began to dispute Ludendorff's existentialist view of 'total war', it was necessary, first, to redefine Clausewitz' concept of 'absolute war', bringing it closer to Ludendorff's 'total war' than Ritter had done. And second, Beck had to refer to Clausewitz' doctrine of the political relevance of war.

This was exactly what Beck had already embarked upon some months before he wrote the above-mentioned letter to Professor Ritter. In June 1942, at a meeting of the 'Mittwochsgesellschaft', he read a paper on 'Die Lehre vom totalen Krieg'[65] (pp. 227–58). Whereas, in 1938, he had attempted to combine Ludendorff and Clausewitz and, in 1940, he had only implicitly criticized Ludendorff's doctrines, he now totally rejects the general's point of view; and he does so with direct reference to Clausewitz. In 1938, he called without any hesitation for total mobilization of the nation and of all national resources in view of a coming 'total war'. For him, all this was merely a matter of organizing the nation; at that time he realized neither the inherent dangers nor the political implications. In 1940, he had already, although rather timidly and cautiously, attempted to redefine and to interpret the concept of 'total war' in order to refute Ludendorff implicitly. In 1942, however, he entirely and definitely renounces the concept and even the reality which is designated by the concept.

He begins by explaining Ludendorff's theory of total war as a struggle for national survival. Rather self-critically, he observes: 'Almost all writers who have dealt with the theory of total war have, more or less, adopted Ludendorff's doctrine' (p. 232). But then he immediately embarks upon a fundamental critique of Ludendorff's theory and his method: 'Whoever analyses the problem of the nature of war has to do so on a level higher than that, upon which war is treated merely as a kind of military handicraft' (p. 232).

Proceeding step by step he first criticizes Ludendorff's thesis that total war is an essentially new kind of war inconceivable by Clausewitz. Clausewitz, Beck asserts, 'need not be defended against the charge of not having correctly perceived the new phenomenon of war and of clinging to the obsolete ideas of war' (pp. 235–6). Beck proves that Clausewitz had already realized that there are 'wars waged by both sides to the full extent of their national strength'. But these wars – which Ludendorff would surely have called total wars – are not essentially new ones; it is simply that the act of force (he argues, adopting Clausewitzian terminology) 'has been increased and extended into new areas. New fields of application of force have been found ... but not a new kind of war has been introduced' (p. 237).

He then directly attempts to destroy Ludendorff's concept of total war, arguing that 'we will find the suitable criterion for juding the peculiarity of total war – as Ludendorff says – if we keep in mind what Clausewitz teaches on war in general'. Here Beck quotes the famous phrases of Chapter 1, Book I, of *On War*: 'War is an act of force, and there is no logical limit to the application of that force. Each side, therefore, compels its opponent to follow suit; a reciprocal action is started which must lead in theory to the extremes.'[66] He ends the quotation with Clausewitz' words: 'To introduce the principle of moderation into the theory of war itself would always lead to logical absurdity.'[67]

Arguing against Ludendorff, Beck concludes his exegesis of Clausewitz: 'These quotations prove beyond any doubt that what has been claimed to be characteristic of and essential for total war, namely, the extreme application of force at any time, is nothing other than precisely what is inherent in Clausewitz' concept of war in general' (p. 240).

Beck then emphasizes that Clausewitz speaks of a kind of war that approches the absolute or the abstraction of the concept, and which might be realized 'when the means of war, the force, becomes so dominant, that the political objective seems to vanish'[68] (p. 237). Clausewitz' doctrine of the political character of war is clearly at the very center of Beck's attempt to refute Ludendorff. According to Clausewitz, all wars, 'even those in which politics seem to vanish, are political acts' (p. 241). Ludendorff's theory, however, misses the political nature of war.

The relation between the ends and the means of war has been totally inverted in Ludendorff's theory of total war, and thus perverted. From this inversion result the fatal consequences produced by this kind of war. Beck stresses this point. By arguing along this line, he surely had in mind what happened in Germany and simultaneously in Europe: 'Being without any moderation, total war, due to its very nature, is practically unable to bring results which are politically sound and moderate' (p. 246). For if military strategy, warfare pure and simple, dominates politics, the objectives of war replace the political purpose. Thus Beck refutes Ludendorff and Clausewitzian philosophy. But Beck is far from being content; he carries his argument further, again referring to Clausewitz.

Now he turns to the destructive consequences Ludendorff's theory of total war brings about in reality. First, he argues that

> even preparing total war in peacetime will result in heavy con-
> sequences for a nation .... War preparations will become a 'moloch'
> .... An uncontrolled exploitation of human and material resources
> will result from it, and it will be done all to the good of one single
> object: war .... Thus, all other human activities will be gradually
> spoiled and finally extinguished. All the richness and plurality of
> human life, all free and responsible human activities will be replaced
> by narrow-minded utility. Uniformity of life will become a law;
> intellectual freedom and independent-mindedness, as well as un-
> limited creativity will be confined. Such a political entity can no
> longer be called a state what we define as that political configuration
> known and created during the last thousand years in Europe by
> great nations and also by the German nation. (p. 244)

Here, Beck not only negates Ludendorff, but also disavows his own earlier ideas. He himself as Chief of General Staff in the 1930s had advocated total mobilization in order to secure all national resources for total war. He also, by rejecting Ludendorff, rejects the totalitarian and militaristic Nazi regime and Hitler's style of warfare. In this sense, his intensive study of Clausewitz' ideas provided Beck with an intellectual basis for resistance to Hitler.

Thus it was Clausewitz' ideas that enabled Beck to renounce Luden-dorff's doctrines, to free himself from his earlier fascination by 'the greatest general of the Great War', and, finally, to find the Archimedean point from which he launched his radical criticism of Hitler's state. His study of Clausewitz was, therefore, basic to his criticism of the dreadful and fatal consequences of the doctrine of total war. Beck confirms that total war increases the brutality of warfare to a point hitherto unknown. Obviously aiming at Hitler, he remarks that this brutality results from a preoccupation with the doctrine of total war. 'This doctrine', he argues, 'makes it difficult to contain all those brutal and evil instincts of which Clausewitz has spoken' (pp. 252–3). His conclusion is that 'if we want to overcome the doctrine of total war ... in the final analysis, we need a new ethically based idealism' (p. 258).

IV. CONCLUSION: WHAT BECK MISSED IN CLAUSEWITZ

All this shows very convincingly the impact which Clausewitz' ideas had on the intellectual evolution of the German opposition to Hitler. Professor Ritter was a member of the so-called 'Freiburger Kreis' in which anti-Nazi intellectuals met in order to discuss planning for a post-war Germany liberated from Nazi tyranny. The famous 'Mittwochsgesellschaft', in which Beck twice read his papers on the nature of war, referring to Clausewitz, was also a meeting-place for anti-Nazi elements. Some of its members, including Beck, were deeply involved in the abortive plot of 20 July 1944 and, consequently, lost their lives.[69]

These dissidents obviously found a source of strength and inspiration for their opposition to Hitler in studying Clausewitz. Whereas in those years the great majority of the military writers and military historians tried to exploit Clausewitz' 'moral factors' for ideological indoctrination, Beck and some very few military writers and scholars devoted themselves to studying ideas on the political relevance of war.

Of course, Beck interpreted Clausewitz in a very special way which – as Professor Ritter's comments have shown – was not entirely shared, and we have also to bear in mind that with regard to a major issue, the political–military relationship, he based his arguments on a distorted version of Clausewitz' ideas. Nevertheless, Clausewitz' ideas on the political relevance of war and on the military–political relationship contributed greatly to the development of the anti-Nazis' political philosophy.

But all this is only one side of the coin. Looking at the other side, we may ask why Beck did not carry further his criticism of Ludendorff's ideas and his fundamental opposition to Hitler through referring to Clausewitz' thoughts on the social foundation of politics and of war. To Clausewitz, reality was the empirical basis of theory. And reality can be found in history, for him, in more than 130 important campaigns.[70] But Clausewitz also showed the social background of the wars and the politics which brought about these wars. Clausewitz – as Peter Paret writes –

> did not regard war simply as a craft ..., but as a prism in which all of life was refracted .... War defined that segment of the world which accident of his birth and training had made into the object of his inquiry. It was the part that stood for the whole; and it was his awareness of the whole and the interconnections of all phenomena that was later to enable him to think of war as an act of social intercourse, 'concerned with the living forces and moral forces' with all the political and psychological implications that flow from such a conception.[71]

War as a specific manifestation of political intercourse reflects, thus, society and its peculiarities. Since Clausewitz repeats this idea often in his book, it is strange that Beck did not realize this and did not exploit this idea in order to find a more radical basis for criticizing Hitler's regime. 'War', Clausewitz wrote,

> does not belong to the realm of arts; rather it is a part of a man's social existence. War is a clash between major interests; ... we could more accurately compare it with commerce which is also a conflict of human interests and activities, and it is still closer to politics, which in turn may be considered as a kind of commerce on a larger scale.[72]

This is a rather modern approach to political phenomena – an approach to which modern historiography in Germany, at least, returned only after having confronted the social sciences and neo-marxism[73] – an approach which was not accessible to a man like Beck educated in Wilhelminian Germany.

Nevertheless, it is really strange that even Clausewitz' historical examples did not suggest to Beck the idea of the social origins of a particular regime and of the wars which such a regime was fighting. Clausewitz, for example, when discussing the 'real war' or the 'absolute war', explained to his reader that

> [Warfare] had achieved this state of perfection ... after a short prelude of the French Revolution; Bonaparte brought it swiftly and ruthlessly to that point. War in his hands was waged without respite .... Since Bonaparte ... war again became the concern of the people as a whole, took an entirely different character, or rather closely approached its true character, its absolute perfection. There seemed no end to the resources mobilized; all limits disappeared .... War, untrammeled by any conventional restraints, had broken loose in all its elementary fury. This was due to the people's new share in the great affairs of state.[74]

Here Clausewitz explains very clearly that the character of war as a political phenomenon is directly dependent on 'affairs of state' – that is, on the political character of the state and on its social foundations. Beck could have found that when he was analysing what Clausewitz wrote on the nature of politics. To Clausewitz 'politics' or 'policy' did not mean simple 'foreign policy'. Rather he defined it comprehensively: 'Policy [is the] representative of all interests of the community', the aim of which 'is to unify and reconcile all aspects of internal administration as well as of spiritual values, and whatever else the moral philosopher may care to add. Policy ... is nothing in itself; it is simply the trustee for all these interests.'[75] War, therefore, has to be 'assessed in the light of political factors and conditions'. It 'follows that the transformation of the art of war results from the transformation of politics'.[76]

Reading these statements we can easily apply Clausewitz' ideas on the social background of politics and consequently of war to the phenomenon of 'total war' as it had been manifested in Hitler's 'art' of warfare, and we may wonder why Beck did not realize that Hitler's kind of war was just one manifestation of the character of Hitler's regime. We can assume that Beck's knowledge of Clausewitz' thoughts was perhaps limited; and that he, therefore, had not come across the relevant parts of Book VIII of *On War*; or we may suppose that his selective and defective way of reading Clausewitz resulted from an internal block. After all he had been a general himself, had supported Hitler's regime, and had fervently advocated an overall preparation for total war in an authoritarian state. This authoritarian state had, unfortunately, turned out to be a totalitarian regime. And Beck was, perhaps, still influenced by the idealistic and charismatic interpretation of Clausewitz' ideas in the 1930s.

Be that as it may, in regard to the social background of politics and warfare there are evident shortcomings in Beck's understanding of Clausewitz. But it remains nevertheless true that Beck in refuting Ludendorff and resisting Hitler did resort to Clausewitz' ideas. He was, within his personal limits, ready 'to learn from theory' and to become 'accustomed to ... measuring all his hopes and fears by it, and approximating it *when he can* and *when he must*'.[77]

NOTES

1. See Nicholas Reynolds, *Treason was No Crime: Ludwig Beck, Chief of German General Staff* (London: W. Kimber, 1976), and Klaus-Jürgen Müller, *General Ludwig Beck. Studien und Dokumente zur politisch–militärischen Vorstellungswelt und Tätigkeit des Generalstabschefs des deutschen Heeres 1933–1938* (Boppard am Rhein: H. Boldt, 1980).
2. This point has been put forward by Gert Buchheit, *Ludwig Beck. Ein preussischer General* (Munich: List, 1964) and by Hans Speidel, 'Ludwig Beck', in *Die grossen Deutschen*, Vol. I (Berlin: Ullstein Propyläen, 1956); it has been particularly stressed by Wilhelm Ritter von Schramm in his various articles and books, in particular, 'Generaloberst Beck und der Durchbruch zu einer neuen deutschen Wehrtheorie', in *Aus Politik und Zeitgeschichte* B 8/62.
3. Beck, *Studien*, ed. and intro. by Hans Speidel (Stuttgart: K. F. Koehler, 1955), referred to in the text below by page numbers in parentheses.
4. Müller, *General Beck*, Doc. No. 38.
5. Beck in this context quotes Clausewitz: 'The higher up the chain of command the greater is the need for boldness to be supported by a reflective mind, so that boldness does not degenerate into purposeless bursts of blind passion. Command becomes progressively less a matter of personal sacrifice and increasingly concerned for the safety of other and the common purpose' (p. 484). (See also p. 107: 'We repeat again: strength of character does not consist solely in having powerful feelings, but in maintaining one's balance in spite of them. Even with the violence of emotion, judgment and principle must still function like a ship's compass which records the slightest variations however rough the sea'.) *On War*, ed. and

trans. by Michael Howard and Peter Paret (Princeton, NJ: Princeton University Press, 1976), p.190. All quotations are from this edition.

6. Michael Howard, 'The Influence of Clausewitz', in Clausewitz, *On War*, p.41.

7. See Müller, *General Beck*, Chs. 5 and 6; also Reynolds, *Treason was No Crime*, Ch. 6.

8. Clausewitz, 'Zwei Briefe des Generals von Clausewitz: Gedanken zur Abwehr', special issue of *Militärwissenschaftliche Rundschau* (1937), 6. See also Peter Paret, *Clausewitz and the State* (Oxford: Oxford University Press, 1976), 379ff.

9. Clausewitz, 'Zwei Briefe'.

10. Müller, *General Beck*, Doc. No. 1.

11. Hans Speidel, *Zeitbetrachtungen, Ausgewählte Reden* (Mainz: von Hase & Koehler, 1969), p.155.

12. Buchheit, *Ludwig Beck*, pp.188, 240, 270 and Ritter von Schramm, *Wehrtheorie*, pp.66–8; see also Speidel, Introduction to Ludwig Beck, *Studien*, p.115.

13. Beck, *Studien*, pp.227–58; in his introduction to the *Studien*, the editor, General Speidel, refers only very discreetly to 'die Notwendigkeit des Primates der Politik gegenüber dem Kriege', p.115; Speidel does not speak of the primacy of political control, but of the primacy of 'Politik' (politics).

14. General Erich Ludendorff, *Der totale Krieg* (Munich: Ludendorff Verlag, 1935).

15. See Werner Gembruch, 'Zu Clausewitz' Gedanken über das Verhältnis von Krieg und Politik' in *Wehrwissenschaftliche Rundschau* 9 (1959), pp.619–33, and Werner Hahlweg, 'Das Clausewitz-Bild einst und jetzt'. Vorwort zu *Vom Kriege, hinterlassenes Werk des Generals Carl von Clausewitz, 17 Auflage, vollständige Ausgabe im Urtext mit historisch-kritischer Würdigung von Werner Hahlweg* (Bonn: F. Dümmler, 1966).

16. See my analysis of Beck's use of the concept 'Politik' in Müller, *Beck*, 31ff.

17. See also Paret, *Clausewitz and the State*, 379ff.

18. Beck, *Studien*, pp.30–31, 51, 60–61, 73–4, 77–8, 85, 91–2, 118–27, 137–8, 231–58.

19. Quotation from Clausewitz, 'Zwei Briefe', 6 (Letter to Major von Roeder, 22 Dec. 1827).

20. For example, Beck, *Studien*, p.242: 'Politik und ihre Handhabung durch den Staat' ('state' here is an abstract which does not mean 'politicians' or 'the government', but the relevant factors determining the whole policy of a state).

21. 'Die Politik hat von der Leistungsfähigkeit des Heeres auszugehen.'

22. Beck could also have quoted Clausewitz, *On War*, p.178: 'At that level there is little or no difference between strategy, policy and statesmanship.' Or p.111, 'To bring a war ... to a successful close requires a thorough grasp of national policy. On that level strategy and policy coalesce: the commander in chief is simultaneously a statesman.'

23. Quote is from Hans von Seeckt, *Gedanken eines Soldaten*, rev. edn. (Leipzig and Berlin: 1929), pp.40–41.

24. Beck writes 'the art of war' (*Kriegskunst*), but it is obvious from the context that he had in mind 'the supreme military commander'.

25. 'Foch, unser grosser französicher Gegner, wie ich ihn sehe', Beck, *Studien*, pp.259, 291.

26. Clausewitz, *Vom Kriege*, Vol. 1, p.110; cf. *On War*, p.88.

27. Quoting Clausewitz, *On War*, p.88.

28. Ibid., p.608, incorporating change made in 1853 edn. (fn. 1); cf. Beck's formula, in *Studien*, pp.74–5.

29. 'Harmony' is one of the elements which, according to Clausewitz, constitutes a 'military genius'. In Ch. 3 of Bk. I (p.100) Clausewitz writes, 'Genius consists in a harmonic combination of elements, in which one or the other ability may predominate, but none may be in conflict with the rest'. Beck frequently refers to Clausewitz' concept of 'harmony'.

30. Gembruch, 'Clausewitz' Gedanken', pp.625–30, has convincingly pointed out that what Clausewitz writes on the relationship between military/war and 'politics' is not identical with his views on the relationship between leading politicians and the supreme military commander.

31. *On War*, p.608, n. 1. On this problem see also Hahlweg, 'Das Clausewitzbild', pp.24–5, also p.1121.

32. It is interesting that Beck did not refer to the ambiguous opinion on this problem. In *Gedanken eines Soldaten 155m* Seeckt speaks of the 'political nature of military operations'; on the other hand, he obviously shares Bismarck's view when he writes that the

strategist 'has to submit himself to the directives of the statesman when elaborating a plan of operations for a future war ... or during military operations'.

33. Müller, *General Beck*, Doc. No. 1.

34. Ibid., p.2325.

35. Ibid., Doc. No. 26.

36. Ibid., pp.432–3. Also Clausewitz, *Vom Kriege*, Appendix, p.983. (The appendices are not published in the English edition of *On War*.

37. In his study, 'Deutschland in einem kommenden Krieg', written in November 1938, he quotes a personal letter which Ludendorff had sent him three years before. On the special relationship between Beck and Ludendorff, see Müller, *General Beck*, pp.74–99.

38. The first indication of this may be seen in a memorandum he wrote in May 1937, in which, criticizing some of Hitler's plans in the field of foreign policy, he quotes Clausewitz' famous statement in his letter to Major von Roeder, 'It is the duty and the legitimate right of the art of warfare to prevent "politics" from demanding something which is contrary to the nature of war, [to save] "politics" [from making] mistakes in using the military because of ignorance concerning the use of it'. (For memorandum, see Müller, *General Beck*, Doc. No. 41, p.496.)

39. See Howard, 'The Influence of Clausewitz', in *On War*, p.41, where he stresses the selective perception of Clausewitz' ideas; useful also is P.M. Baldwin, 'Clausewitz in Nazi Germany', in *Journal of Contemporary History*, Vol. 16 (1981), p.5–26. The best survey is still Hahlweg, 'Das Clausewitzbild einst und jetzt'. Excellent also is Yehuda Wallach's *Das Dogma der Vernichtungsschlacht: Die Lehren von Clausewitz and Schlieffen und ihre Wirkung in zwei Weltkriegen* (Frankfurt: Bernard & Graefe Verlag für Wehrwesen, 1967). We need a comprehensive study of German military thinking in the twentieth century.

40. Wallach, *Das Dogma der Vernichtungsschlacht*, p.343.

41. Wallach states that the inter-war period was 'rather the heyday of the Schlieffen orthodoxy' (*Dogma*, p.301; he also stresses the influence of Ludendorff and Seeckt. See also Bernard Brodie, 'In Quest of the Unknown Clausewitz', in *International Security*, Vol. I, No. 3 (1977), 62ff. He also maintains that Clausewitz was generally not well known in German military circles.

42. Ludendorff, *Totaler Krieg*, 3 and 10; see also Wallach, *Dogma*, p.343.

43. Beck, 'Rundfunkansprache vom 9. April 1935 zum 70. Geburtstag des Generals Erich Ludendorff'; in Müller, *General Beck*, Doc. No. 26, 434.

44. After having read Ludendorff's book on total war Beck told one of Ludendorff's representatives in Berlin, 'The book is an extraordinary and brilliant one, idealistically written ... containing ideas characteristic of the eminent and outstanding personality of General Ludendorff'. Letter of Major Holtzbach to Ludendorff, 29 Nov. 1935, in Bundesarchiv, Nachlass Holtzmann, No. 11.

45. *Bundesarchiv–Militärarchiv*: Wi I F 5/701 (5. Sitzung des Arbeitsausschusses des Reichsverteidigungsrates 15 Nov. 1933.)

46. *On War*, p.597.

47. Clausewitz, letter to Major von Roeder, 22 Dec. 1827, in 'Zwei Briefe', *Militärwissenschaftliche Rundschau*. See also similar statements of Clausewitz in *On War*, pp.87, 149, 605.

48. Cf. Müller, *Das Heer und Hitler. Armee und nationalsozialistisches Regime 1933–1940*, (Stuttgart: Deutsche Verlagsanstalt, 1969), 240ff; also *General Beck*, 125ff.

49. Bundesarchiv-Militärarchiv: II H 603.

50. On Keitel and Jodl, see Müller, *Heer und Hitler*, 231ff. See also, on Keitel, Walter Görlitz (ed.), *Verbrecher oder Offizier? Generalfeldmarschall Wilhelm Keitel, Briefe, Dokumente des Chefs OKW* (Göttingen: Musterschmidt, 1961); on Jodl, Louise Jodl, *Jenseits des Endes, Leben und Sterben des Generaloberst Alfred Jodl*, (Vienna, Munich: Molden, 1978).

51. See also *Die Mittwochsgesellschaft. Protokolle aus dem geistigen Deutschland 1932–1944*, ed. and introduced by Klaus Scholder (Berlin: Severin und Siedler, 1982), 237ff. The protocol of the session of the Mittwochsgesellschaft shows Beck's frequent references to Clausewitz.

52. The quotation is from *On War*, p.606.

53. Ibid., p.75.

54. Ibid., p.605.

55. Ludendorff, *Totaler Krieg*, p. 10.
56. Clausewitz, *On War*, p. 605.
57. Ludendorff, *Totaler Krieg*, pp. 6–7.
58. Quotation from Clausewitz, *On War*, p. 88.
59. Ludendorff, *Totaler Krieg*, p. 10.
60. On this point see the informative article of Hans-Ulrich Wehler, 'Vom "Absoluten" zum "Totalen" Krieg oder: Von Clausewitz zu Ludendorff' in *Politische Vierteljahresschrift*, 10, 2/3 (Sept. 1969).
61. On Ritter's studies of Clausewitz see Howard, 'The Influence of Clausewitz', 41 and 41n., and P. M. Baldwin, 'Clausewitz in Nazi Germany', pp. 18–18.
62. Die Lehre Carl von Clausewitz vom politischen Sinn des Krieges', *Historische Zeitschrift*, Vol. 167 (1943), pp. 41–65. Later Ritter integrated this article with minor changes into his book *The Sword and the Scepter* (Coral Gables, FL: University of Miami Press, 1969), Vol. 1, Ch. 3.
63. Letter of 4 November 1942 in *Bundesarchiv-Militärarchiv* N 28/7.
64. Ibid.
65. See also *Die Mittwochsgesellschaft*, pp. 292–4 and Eduard Spranger, 'Generaloberst Beck in der Mittwochsgesellschaft', in *Universitas*, 11 (Stuttgart: 1956), 1: 183–93.
66. *On War*, p. 77.
67. Ibid., p. 76.
68. Beck's quotation is a paraphrase of *On War*, pp. 87–8: 'The more powerful and inspiring the
    motives for war the more they affect the belligerent nations and the fiercer the tensions that precede the outbreak, the closer will war approach its abstract concept, the more important will be the destruction of the enemy, the more closely will the military aims and the political objects of war coincide, and the more military and less political will war appear to be.'
69. See Klaus Scholder, 'Die Geschichte der Mittwochsgesellschaft', in *Die Mittwochsgesellschaft*, pp. 9–48, especially pp. 36–42. Prominent members of the Mittwochsgesellschaft who lost their lives in the aftermath of the July plot were, apart from Beck, Ambassador von Hassell, the Prussian Minister of Finance Popitz, and the well-known economist Jessen.
70. On the relation between reality and theory in Clausewitz' view see Werner Hahlweg, 'Philosophie und Theorie bei Clausewitz' in *Freiheit ohne Krieg: Beiträge zur Strategie-Diskussion der Gegenwart im Spiegel der Theorien von Carl von Clausewitz* (Bonn: F. Dümmler, 1980), pp. 325–32; Erich Vad, *Carl von Clausewitz. Seine Bedeutung heute* (Bonn: Mittler & Sohn, 1984); see also *On War*, p. 170 (regarding historical examples as the best kind of proof in the empirical sciences).
71. Paret, *Clausewitz and the State*, p. 149.
72. *On War*, p. 149.
73. As stressed by Wehler, 'Von "Absoluten" zum "Totalen" Krieg', pp. 94–5.
74. *On War*, pp. 580, 593.
75. Ibid., pp. 606–7.
76. Ibid., pp. 607–10, where Clausewitz before coming to the above-quoted conclusion refers to historical examples:

    It is true that war itself has undergone significant changes in character and methods, changes that have brought it closer to its absolute form. But these changes did not come about because the French government freed itself ... from the harness of policy; they were caused by the new political conditions which the French Revolution created in both France and in Eruope as a whole, conditions that set in motion new means and new forces, and have thus made possible a degree of energy in war that otherwise would have been unconceivable.

77. *On War*, p. 581.

Clausewitz: Some Thoughts on What the Germans Got Right

WILLIAMSON MURRAY

This article largely results from a fall 1984 discussion between the author and Dr Manfred Messerschmidt of the *Militargeschichtliches Forschungsamt*. In response to a suggestion that Clausewitz' influence might explain German military effectiveness at the operational and tactical levels, Dr Messerschmidt demurred, succinctly commenting that few German officers had bothered to read Clausewitz either before or after the First World War. The direct evidence overwhelmingly supports Dr Messerschmidt. On the strategic level, as historians of German military history in the twentieth century have made clear, the German officer corps not only misunderstood, but deliberately inverted Clausewitz' arguments. The depressing litany of German strategic imbecility in both world wars offers little evidence of the German military's having paid the scantest attention to Clausewitz' formulation that

> war is not a mere act of policy but a true political instrument, a continuation of political activity by other means .... War in general, and the commander in any specific instance, is entitled to require that the trend and designs of policy shall not be inconsistent with the means. That, of course, is no small demand; but however much it may affect political aims in a given case, it will never do more than modify them. The political objective is the goal, war is the means of reaching it, and means can never be considered in isolation from their purpose.[1]

The tragedy for Germany on the strategic level was that if the Germans read Clausewitz before the First World War, they read selectively. As Michael Howard suggests: 'Von der Goltz expressed the majority view in refusing to accept [Clausewitz]. It was not that he ignored the political element in the Clausewitzian trinity. He considered it to be no longer relevant.'[2] If the Germans distorted Clausewitz' view of strategy before the war, they gave him even less attention afterwards. The future American General Albert C. Wedemeyer attended the Germany army's *Kriegs-*

akademie in the mid-1930s and submitted a detailed report on his course of instruction.[3] Interestingly, there is virtually no mention of Clausewitz, reflecting the predilection not only of Wedemeyer but also of the German General Staff.

The divorce from Clausewitz' wisdom on political/military relations began with the conflict between Moltke and Bismarck in the nineteenth-century wars of liberation, the 1866 war against Austria, and the 1870–71 war against France. Moltke did not deny the importance of political aims; rather he believed that when war broke out, military concerns became the *dominant* player in national policy:

> 1. Diplomacy avails itself of war to attain its end, crucially influencing the beginnings of a war and its end. It does the latter by reserving to itself the privilege of raising or lowering its demands in the course of the war. In the presence of uncertainty, strategy has no choice but to strive for the highest goal attainable with the means given. The best way in which strategy can cooperate with diplomacy is by working solely for political ends but doing so with *complete* independence of action.
> 2. The course of war is predominantly governed by military considerations, while the exploitation of military success or failure is in turn the province of diplomacy.
> 3. Political elements merit consideration only to the extent that they do not make demands that are militarily improper or impossible.[4]

The clashes between Moltke and Bismarck over strategic policy, particularly during the war against France, were long and harsh. Bismarck was, of course, not about to concede to the military such independence from *his* political control.[5] While Bismarck largely was able to get his way, he had sown the seeds for destruction. His political creation, the new German Empire, possessed no constitutional provisions to ensure civilian control over the military, or even over what we would today term national security policy.

On the other side Moltke's writings clearly suggest confusion between strategy and operations. Indeed, Moltke may have emphasized the operational sphere of war (lying between strategy and tactics as defined by Clausewitz)[6] in German military thought in order to exclude political interference from military operations. Clearly, Moltke believed that during wartime political concerns should be subordinate to military concerns: 'In the case of tactical victory, strategy submits.'[7]

In fairness to Moltke as also to Bismarck, neither man could possibly have foreseen the results of their quarrel. Of course, their quarrel did not prevent the operational success of the Prussian Army, which completely altered the European strategic equation from 1866 to 1871. Unfortunately, Bismarck's successors as Chancellor possessed none of his strength of character; nor did the new emperor possess the slightest inclination to overrule his generals. On the other hand, Moltke's successors were general officers who possessed little depth. If Moltke sometimes confused strategic policy and operational concerns, it is clear that his successors increasingly identified strategy with operations, denying political goals and concerns any influence over military matters, even in peace. The Schlieffen plan, with its wilful disdain for diplomatic and political realities, is only the most obvious of many strategic decisions, made on the basis of pure operational necessity, that contributed to the disasters of 1918 and 1945. In casting its plans for the First World War, for instance, the German general staff in 1906 addressed the potential addition of Great Britain to the anti-German coalition, following the Schlieffen plan's violantion of Belgian neutrality, only by predicting 'that a potential British force of 100,000 men would be "shut up" in Antwerp along with the regular Belgian army'.[8]

This confusion of strategy and operations reached its high point under Erich Ludendorff in the First World War. The Quartermaster-General of the OHL (the army high command) defined his strategical conception for the great March 1918 German 'Michael' offensive thus: 'I object to the word "operation". We will punch a hole into [their line]. For the rest, we shall see. We also did it this way in Russia!'[9] If Ludendorff managed to lower even operational goals to the level of tactics, in his post-First World War writings he might well have changed Clausewitz' definition of the relationship between war and politics to read: peace (or politics) is a continuation of war by other means.

While these depressing facts give us insight into the causes of Germany's tragedy in both world wars, they give virtually no insight into two historical problems: (a) how did the Germans come so close in two great wars, against virtually the rest of the world, to defeating their opponents (and they did defeat the Russians in the First World War and the French in the Second World War); and (b) how did they hold out for so long against numerically superior forces, overwhelming economic resources, and simultaneous pressure from so many directions? This study will suggest that there are elements in Clausewitz' writings that contribute indirectly to excellence in the tactical and operational spheres. That excellence, which marked German military performance in both world wars, provides the answer to how the Germans held out for so long.

Before we turn to Clausewitz and German operational and tactical performance, we must examine the evidence for Dr Messerschmidt's belief that the twentieth-century German officer corps did not read Clausewitz. In late 1949 the great British military writer, B.H. Liddell

Hart, received a letter from Leo Geyer von Schweppenburg in which the panzer general noted:

> During the time of my insight [*sic*], obviously meaning intellectual development], beginning with 1911, when I came to our staff college, up to the finale of the old German army in 1945 when I was responsible as inspector of armored troops, also for their schools, the education of the German general staff was almost entirely based on the authors or strategists as under (unfortunately)
> 1. Schliffen's Cannae
> 2. Frederick the Great
> 3. Napoleon (yes, good old Bonnie, this might be of interests to classics [*sic*])
>
> Although I have not read his book, I want to point to one, called 'defense' of Frh. Ritter von Leeb .... You will be horrified to hear that I have never read Clausewitz or Delbruck or Haushofer. The opinion on Clausewitz in our general staff was that of a theoretician to be read by professors.[10]

The problem in intellectual history has always been to identify the link between cause and effect. In the case of Clausewitz and the German generals, that link is at best indirect and tenuous. One can in fact argue that Clausewitz in his writings was only reflecting the philosophical approach to war of Prussian military reform circles, on which he, as a junior member, had little effect. His only influence on the German approach to war may have been to reinforce the tactical and operational orientation of those few General Staff officers who bothered to read *On War*. On the other hand, we do know that Moltke, who read Clausewitz carefully, was, during his long tenure as Chief of the General Staff, largely responsible for establishing the kind of training that late nineteenth- and twentieth-century General Staff officers received. The conflict between those who detect substantial Clausewitzian influence on the German army's operational approach to war and those who deny such influence may be both irrelevant and academic. Our purpose here is to underline the fact that the twentieth-century German army's approach to war on the operational and tactical planes has been Clausewitzian. The Germany army is perhaps the only army, with the possible exception of the Israeli Defense Force, to have such an approach.

These are two areas where Clausewitz may have exercised considerable influence through those German officers who bothered to examine *On War* in detail. First, his writings reinforced the professionalism of the General Staff officer that the Prussian military reformers Gneisenau and Scharnhorst had effected in response to the shattering defeat of Jena Auerstadt. Second – an indirect, but perhaps easier-to-follow influence

– his comments on operations and the battlefield (even when he is describing nineteenth-century battles) have real relevance to twentieth-century warfare. It is not surprising that Anglo-Americans, who must think first of getting to the battlefield, should concentrate on the strategic and political level of *On War*, while the Prussians and their successors, the Germans, with immediate vulnerabilities on land would gravitate to Clausewitz' thoughts in the operational and tactical sphere.

Interestingly, Clausewitz says little about training and developing professional ethics within an officer corps. Both specifically and generally he comments on those qualities which major command in war demands. Thus, he devotes a whole section of Book I to a brilliant dissection of military genius but makes few specific comments on officership. Nevertheless, Clausewitz clearly states that superior junior officers are an essential element in military performance. He tells his reader that

> in our view even junior positions of command require outstanding intellectual qualities for outstanding achievement, and since the standard rises with every step, it follows that we recognize the abilities that are needed if the second positions in an army are to be filled with distinction. Such officers may appear to be rather simple compared to the polymath scholar, the far-ranging business executive, the statesman; but we should not dismiss the value of their practical intelligence …. Appropriate talent is needed at all levels if distinguished service is to be performed.[11]

Officer quality was indeed basic to the German military in both world wars. In effect, even at the most junior level the Germans preferred no officer to a bad officer.[12]

Not only were the Germans demanding in the selection process for junior officers, they also selected only a small percentage of the best to attend the *Kriegsakademie*. Then, after a demanding two-year curriculum, they honored some of those students with the general staff's crimson stripe. However, the emphasis on intellectual performance at the *Kriegsakademie* was on operational and tactical skills, while strategy fell between the cracks. The intellect and character of these future general staff officers were evaluated, first by their superiors and then by their instructors at the *Kriegsakademie*.[13]

What did the Germans mean by *character*? Perhaps the result of the selection process suggests a definition. First and most important, during the late 1930s, the army high command possessed enough competence and intellectual honesty, albeit within a limited sphere, to recognize major flaws and weaknesses that appeared in the rearmament program and military operations. From the *Anschluss* through the French campaign, it never allowed operational success to serve as a standard of performance.

No matter how stunning the Polish campaign might have appeared to outsiders, most participating units did not come up to the standards of the OKH (*Oberkommando des Heeres*, the army high command). As a result of its dissatisfaction OKH introduced a drastic, thorough training program to correct the perceived deficiencies.[14] Moreover, the German army evaluated combat experiences or maneuvers realistically, depending on an implicit trust that existed between the different levels of command. The OKH, the army group, army, corps, and division commanders (and so on down the line) expected subordinates to give accurate reports on the status and capabilities of their troops. If a unit were substandard, then its commander was expected to say so. (Of course, high headquarters assumed that he would do all in his power to correct those deficiencies.) The higher the level of command, the more critical of performance were the officers and the higher their expectations.[15] Besides its realism and toughness, German military training incorporated past experience and managed to give the German soldier a high sense of unit identification, with a belief that he could depend on the soldier next to him. In this sense, the performance of the army in the late 1930s depended on the *character* of the officers who served.

The second area where Clausewitz' writings jibe with the German approach lies in his sense of the battlefield, so different from the approach of Baron Henri Jomini.[16] Jomini's analysis of eighteenth- and nineteenth-century warfare, which attempted to reduce war to the clarity of a geometric exercise, has influenced much of twentieth-century military thought from Liddell Hart to a multitude of ROTC instructors. All have followed Jomini's efforts to bring order to the chaos of the battlefield by explaining war and battles in terms of clearly elucidated principles. This phenomenon has prevailed in those services dominated by technology; the disciples of Mahan, Trenchard, Douhet, and the Air Corps Tactical School have all seen war with a clarity and precision totally at odds with events at sea and in the air in both world wars. Much twentieth-century military history has been Jominian, as John Keegan so clearly underlined for us in the mid-1970s.[17] This emphasis presents us with the rather sad situation where Michael Shaara's novel *The Killer Angels* may tell us more about what really happened at Gettysburg than most of the historians of that terrible battle.[18]

The Jominian *Weltanschauung* has had an unfortunate impact on the effectiveness of those military services that embraced it. When military doctrine aims at a simplicity and a clarity possessed only by the clean red and blue arrows of post-war military histories, it leaves the landscape littered with smashed aircraft and the burnt-out hulks of tanks, not to mention dead and mutilated human beings. Unfortunately narrowly-educated wartime commanders have often attempted to make reality fit doctrinal preconceptions, for example, the experiences of Eighth Air Force and Bomber Command in the Second World War. In the former case, Eighth Air Force Commanders threw great unescorted formations of B-17s against German fighter defense until their command came close to destruction in the skies over Germany in October 1943.[19] Similarly, Arthur Harris in 1944 nearly destroyed Bomber Command in the Battle of Berlin in his effort to prove that independent 'strategic' bombing could win the war by itself.[20] D. C. T. Bennett, the commander of the Pathfinder force in Bomber Command, has suggested that the best method for avoiding such unwillingness to face reality in the upper levels of command of the air forces would be to make senior air commanders fly on active operations. 'For every Air Vice Marshall lost, the RAF would save 200 air crews.'[21]

This Jominian view of war has spilled over into the area of command and control, where it holds that, despite the spread of military operations over wider and wider areas, advances in technology will allow commanders to cope ever more effectively. Such views, despite the US failure in Vietnam, are unfortunately still alive and well in the American military. The 1980 edition of US Air Force Manual 1-1, the basic doctrinal manual of that service until 1984, suggested that the AWACS (Airborne Warning and Control System) 'allows commanders to comprehend the total air-surface battle'.[22] This belief that a centralized command and control system is the best approach to war, is a basic theme in twentieth-century military history. And for the most part its impact has been unfortunate, whether one recounts military operations on the Somme in 1916 or 'Market Garden' in 1944.

Unfortunately for their enemies, the Germans have generally avoided the Jominian view of military operations in favor of the Clausewitzian one. Above all, *On War* raises the dark, bloody, fearful qualities of combat:

> We are not interested in generals who win victories without bloodshed. The fact that slaughter is a horrifying spectacle must make us take war more seriously, but not provide an excuse for gradually blunting our swords in the name of humanity. Sooner or later someone will come along with a sharp sword and hack off our arms.[23]

Clausewitz' depiction of war not only records its horror but notes the difficulties of acting and thinking under such circumstances. In Chapter 4 of Book I he describes the movement of the novice on to the battlefield. From the first terrifying sounds of battle to the 'sight of men being killed and mutilated', Clausewitz sets out, in a brilliant and still-relevant passage, the fearful impressions that assault the new recruit. 'It is', he tells us, 'an exceptional man who keeps his powers of quick decision intact if he has never been through this experience'. And while exposure to combat may mitigate some of its impact,

> the ordinary man can never achieve a state of perfect unconcern in which his mind can work with normal flexibility. Here again we recognize that ordinary qualities are not enough .... Headlong, dogged, or innate courage, overmastering ambition, or long familiarity with danger – all must be present to a considerable degree if action in this debilitating element is not to fall short of achievements that in the study would appear as nothing out of the ordinary.[24]

Real war has little in common with the clear, concise depictions that appear in military histories, little to do with Jominian clarity: it is blood, and fear, and terror.

Above all, Clausewitz saw that war, like all human endeavors, involved inordinate muddle, confusion, error, short-sightedness, incompetence, and truculence. 'Everything in war is very simple, but the simplest thinking is difficult.' He suggests what separates real war from fantasy:

> Friction is the only concept that more or less corresponds to the factors that distinguish real war from war on paper. The military machine – the army and everything related to it – is basically very simple and therefore seems easy to manage. But we should bear in mind that none of its components is of one piece .... A battalion is made up of individuals, the least important of whom may chance to delay things or somehow make them go wrong. The dangers inseparable from war and the physical exertions war demands can aggravate the problem to such an extent that they must be ranked among its principle causes.[25]

What Clausewitz understood so well was the immense willpower necessary to overcome the inertia of human institutions and the enormous self-discipline necessary to separate the essential from the inessential. As Clausewitz defines character, 'We mean the ability to keep one's head at times of exceptional stress and violent emotion.'[26] Thus, 'in the dreadful presence of suffering and danger, emotion can easily overwhelm intellectual conviction, and in this psychological fog it is so hard to form clear and complete insights ....'[27]

The antidote to psychological terror and resultant inaction is boldness at all levels of command:

> Let us admit that boldness in war even has its own prerogatives. It must be granted a certain power over and above successful calcu-

lations involving space, time, and magnitude of force, for wherever it is superior, it will take advantage of its opponent's weakness. In other words, it is a genuinely creative force .... Whenever boldness encounters timidity, it is likely to be the winner, because timidity in itself implies a loss of equilibrium .... Given the same amount of intelligence, timidity will do a thousand times more damage in war than audacity.[28]

Thus, in the fog, in the fear and terror, and in the frictions of war, the victor is the individual as well as the army that acts with calculated boldness. As Albert C. Wedemeyer in his report to the War Department in 1938 noted, 'The Germans point out, that often a Commander must make an important decision after only a few minutes deliberation and emphasize, that a fair decision given in time for aggressive execution is much better than one wholly right but too late.'[29]

In the twentieth century success in war has depended as much on boldness and initiative as it has depended on material superiority. Centralized systems of command and control have lacked the responsiveness and flexibility to *allow* tactical and operational exploitation of ever-changing battlefield situations. The Dardanelles campaign reveals in graphic detail that timidity at the operational or tactical levels can turn strategic boldness into catastrophic failure. This, the most striking strategic move of the First World War, foundered on lack of operational boldness, the unwillingness of commanders at all levels to act independently, and the strongly centralized command structure. Thus, the colonels at 'Y' Beach awaited instructions that never came, the Anzac troops picnicked on their way to the ridges overlooking the Dardanelles, and General Stopford's troops organized and reorganized themselves for 72 hours at Sulva Bay.[30] As Churchill so aptly noted, 'The terrible ifs accumulate.' The problem today, as in the First World War, is that one cannot act or react in military operations with boldness and flexibility, if one must wait to be told what to do. If that were so in Clausewitz' day, it is even truer today with the expansion in breadth and depth of the modern battlefield.

In August 1914 the German army was no more willing to recognize this reality than were its opponents. In fact, even at the highest level the German commanders displayed an aversion to delegating authority to subordinates. The Chief of the General Staff had delegated control over the Schlieffen plan's right wing to the commander of Second Army, General Karl von Bülow. That general, however, kept so tight a rein over the First Army and its commander, General Alexander von Kluck, that Kluck had to attack the BEF straight ahead at Mons rather than sweeping around the Allied flank.[31]

Nevertheless, from the time of the elder Moltke the Germans did possess at the highest level something that they called 'Auftragstaktik' – 'mission-oriented tactics'. This meant that the overall commander set goals and objectives and provided the means, but allowed his subordinates maximum flexibility in accomplishing their task. In both the Franco-Prussian and the Seven Weeks' War, Moltke allowed subordinate army and even corps commanders great latitude in the conduct of operations. But such decentralization of control went no lower than army or corps commander as, given the nature of the nineteenth-century European battlefield, there was no obvious need for it to do.

In the early years of the First World War under the uninspired leadership of General Erich von Falkenhayn, the Germans fought much as did the other European armies. By 1916 Falkenhayn's efforts to centralize control of the battlefield into his hands came close to ending Germany's war effort. At Verdun he did not even allow the army commander control over his own reserves.[32] While the Germans may have achieved their strategic aim for that battle (to bleed the French white), the costs to the Germans were equally exorbitant. The last stages of the Battle of Verdun saw the opening of the great British offensive along the Somme, during which, on 1 July 1916, Haig and his commanders managed to lose nearly 60,000 men. Few historians have noted that the Germany army lost nearly as many men over the remainder of the battle as did the British, despite the fact that the British were attacking.[33] This reflected Falkenhayn's demand that his troops hold every bit of captured territory to the last man, that they hold the forward edge of the battlefield in great strength, and that they immediately counterattack any British gains. In their deep dug-outs along the Somme, and in numerous pointless counterattacks, German infantry took horrendous casualties. The result was the fall of Falkenhayn and his replacement by Hindenburg and Ludendorff, who became the key player in the dramatic alteration of German defensive doctrine in 1916–17 and of German offensive doctrine in 1917–18.

The new leaders of the army's high command (there was in fact no overall high command of the war) had to face national strategic bankruptcy and to revive an army seriously depleted on the field of battle. The strategic situation was so critical that Ludendorff spent the late summer and early fall worrying whether Denmark or Holland would enter the war on the Allied side. On his visits to the front Ludendorff discovered the poverty of the Germans' tactical and operational approach:

> At the conference in Cambrai [during Ludendorff's first trip to the Western front in 1916] those various matters [i.e., what was happening to the front line troops] were merely touched upon. I got no more than general impressions, but there were enough to show the necessity of altering the plan of fighting and of improving the

army in tactics and in equipment. On the Eastern Front we had for the most part adhered to the old tactical methods and old training which we had learned in the days of peace. Here [in the west] we met with new conditions and it was my duty to adapt to them.[34]

On these visits he demanded a thorough and honest briefing from the chiefs of staff of those units he examined. In line with German tradition, he expected detailed and honest reporting rather than 'favorable report[s] made to order'.[35] Drawing on the experience of the previous two years of battle, the Germans, now under Ludendorff's guidance, set about recasting the army's defensive doctrine.[36] One must stress that Ludendorff did not *direct* but rather coordinated this process, with significant input from the chiefs of staff in the field as well as from *experienced* combat officers who were serving in the front line.

By the end of 1916 the Germans had developed the first modern doctrine of defensive warfare in the era of the machine gun and artillery fire. That doctrine emphasized a lightly-held forward line with successively stronger defensive positions. The heaviest concentration of reserves would lie in the rear areas to counterattack enemy penetrations. The emphasis was on flexibility and elasticity. Intellectually, it rested on a Clausewitzian sense of the messiness of the battlefield. It consequently depended on the initiative of junior officers and battalion commanders. Both conceptualizing and implementing the new defensive doctrine were difficult. For instance, the senior defensive expert on the western front, Fritz von Lossberg, viewed the new doctrine as being too liberal in allowing troops in the front line to pull back, but in *implementing* the new doctrine in Flanders in 1917 was won over.[37]

On the basis of this defensive doctrine and their experience in using an elastic defense in counterattacks, the Germans moved in 1917 to solve the offensive problem of the First World War – not just how to get the soldier across to but *through* the enemy defensive lines. Timothy Lupfer's *The Dynamics of Doctrine* reveals how the Germans went about redefining their offensive doctrine, which depended on the willingness of officers *at all levels* to act independently, according to the situation, without awaiting orders. The new offensive doctrine's emphasis on boldness and forward movement reflected the reality of the modern battlefield, where communications disappear in a maelstrom of artillery fire, where soldiers fight, advance, and die in small groups, and where opportunities occur only fleetingly. As Michael Howard has pointed out in the Princeton edition of Clausewitz' *On War*,

> In the enormous armies of 1900, their communications dependent at best on fragile field-telephones, their size and complexity rendering elaborate maneuver out of the question, commanders-in-chief

could give only the broadest of directions to their subordinates and rely on their intelligence and initiative to carry them out in detail. Junior officers were likely to find themselves isolated on vast battle-fields in a strange, sometimes barely endurable environment, with no recourse save their inner strength to keep them going and their common sense to tell them what to do.[38]

Unfortunately, the German army was alone in recognizing this fact and in developing by the end of the war a doctrine for both offensive and defensive warfare that left decision-making on the tactical level to the common sense, training, and leadership qualities of front-line officers.

Before examining the further development of this doctrine in the post-war period, we must understand that the German army had a fundamentally different approach to doctrine than most other military organizations, one that aimed at providing a *general* tactical and operational framework to guide battlefield commanders. Clausewitz' description of the educative function of theories of war closely parallels the role that doctrine played in the German army. He criticizes rigid prescriptions, saying:

> It is only analytically that these attempts at theory can be called advances in the realm of truth; synthetically, in the rules and regulations they offer, they are absolutely useless.
>
> They aim at fixed values; but in war everything is uncertain, and calculations have to be made with variable quantities.
>
> They direct the inquiry exclusively toward physical quantities, whereas all military action is intertwined with psychological forces and effects.
>
> They consider only unilateral action, whereas war consists of a continuous interaction of opposites.[39]

Thus, doctrine should be descriptive rather than prescriptive, providing a general framework within which one can ask the right questions, rather than offering answers.

> [Theory] is an analytical investigation leading to a close *acquaintance* with the subject; applied to experience ... it leads to thorough *familiarity* with it. The closer it comes to that goal, the more it proceeds from the objective form of a science to the subjective form of a skill, the more effective it will prove.[40]

These doctrinal changes of 1916 and 1917 gave front-line leadership a more realistic basis for conducting offensive and defensive battles. As Timothy Lupfer puts it:

> German doctrine achieved the balance between the demands of

precision for unity of effort and the demands of flexibility for decentralized application. With clearly stated principles, the doctrine provided thorough, consistent guidance for the training, equipping, and organizing of the army. However, this consistency was not rigid, for in the battlefield application, the doctrine provided sufficient flexibility to accommodate the demands of local conditions and the judgement of several commanders.[41]

Above all, the doctrine aimed to accommodate changes as battlefield experience suggested them. The German successes in the spring 1918 offensives underline the degree of superiority that the Germans achieved on the basis of its new doctrine.[42] Yet that operational success underlines their strategic failures. As we have seen, in spring 1918 Ludendorff literally aimed to punch holes in the Allied lines with the strategic purpose of seeing what might turn up. Considering that the Germany army was already scraping the bottom of the manpower barrel, that it could barely assemble 40-plus attack divisions (out of 200) on the western front for its first March offensive, and that numerous American forces were already beginning to arrive, the whole thrust to punch holes in the Allied lines represented strategic insanity.

However, in the preparations for the spring 1918 western offensive the German army, having only in fall 1917 established the new offensive doctrine, began to implement consistent and coherent training for the divisions that would launch the coming attack.[43] A massive, intensive, and thorough program schooled divisional officers first and then worked up the attack divisions. All training was done on the basis of the new offensive doctrine, *Angriff im Stellungskrieg* ('Attack-in-position warfare'). The Germans' skilled performance on the battlefields of both world wars rested on this closely linked doctrine and training.

The army's training, as Clausewitz advocated, aimed at placing maximum pressure on troops and officers. Clausewitz suggests that military spirit results from the interaction of two factors:

> The first is a series of victorious wars, the second, frequent exertions of the army to the utmost limits of its strength. Nothing else will show a soldier the full extent of his capacities. The more a general is accustomed to place heavy demands on his soldiers, the more he can depend on their response. A soldier is just as proud of the hardships he has overcome as of the dangers he has faced.[44]

In another passage in *On War* Clausewitz estimates how important vigorous training is to the preparation of even the common soldier for combat:

> It is immensely important that no soldier, whatever his rank, should

wait for war to expose him to those aspects of active service that
amaze and confuse him when he first comes across them. If he has
met them even once before, they will begin to be familiar to him.
This is true even of physical effort. Exertions must be practical, and
the mind must be made even more familiar with them than the body.
When exceptional efforts are required of him in war, the recruit
is apt to think that they result from mistakes, miscalculations,
and confusions at the top. In consequence, his morale is doubly
depressed. If maneuvers prepare him for [such] exertions, this will
not occur.[45]

The Second World War response of the German army to its victory
in Poland illustrates the close relationship between training, combat
experience, and evolution of doctrine.[46] First of all, despite its overwhelming victory, the OKH was genuinely disappointed with the performance of its troops. The 'after-action' reports suggested all sorts of
weaknesses from doctrinal matters to discipline. Within a month the
General Staff had analyzed those weaknesses in writing *and* had instituted
an army-wide training program to correct them. The training program
required rigorous exercises, conditioning programs, and practice
maneuvers of the whole army.[47] The six months' retraining process
brought the army to a peak of condition by 10 May 1940. Even as late as
the end of April 1940 a senior army commander, *Generaloberst* Fedor
von Bock of Army Group B passed this criticism to his senior commanders:

> In many exercises recently, particularly at the battalion and regi-
> mental level, an inclination to caution and circumspection has
> appeared. Therein lies the danger that on one side German leader-
> ship will pass up opportunities to seize favorable opportunities ...
> while on the other hand the enemy will be allowed time to recognize
> our intention .... Once a commander has decided to attack, so must
> everything that he orders be established that the eyes, heart and
> senses of the troops be directed to the front.[48]

Another element of training is the intellectual preparation of its officer
corps for war. Not surprisingly Clausewitz admits that nothing can really
prepare an officer corps for the reality of combat. 'Peacetime maneuvers',
he suggests:

> are a feeble substitute for the real thing; but even they can give
> an army an advantage over others whose training is confined to
> routine, mechanical drill. To plan maneuvers so that some of the
> elements of friction are involved, which will train officers' judge-

ment, common sense, and resolution is far more worthwhile than inexperienced people might think.[49]

The training of General Staff officers in the post-First World War era suggests why Clausewitz' *Weltanschauung* was so important and useful to the Germans.[50] Ironically, despite the prohibitions of the Treaty of Versailles, the post-First World War German army was taken over lock, stock, and barrel by the General Staff. General Hans von Seeckt played a critical role in the recreation of the German army after the troubles of post-war demobilization, revolution, political turmoil, and Versailles' severe limitations on the army's size. Seeckt ensured that the General Staff would dominate the new army as it had not done even during the last war,[51] by bringing over from the old Imperial Army the whole General Staff. He also ensured that they held the command positions, controlling both the command *and* the staff functions in the new *Reichswehr*. Although a few outstanding non-General Staff combat officers also came over to the army, few rose to positions of authority in the late 1930s and early 1940s. Erwin Rommel was the most notable example of this type of officer, and the uniqueness of his rise to a top command position in the Second World War is suggested by the repetitive notations in post-war memoirs that Rommel did not possess a General Staff background.

General Staff officers in the new *Reichswehr*, men like Leeb, Manstein, Wever, had helped develop German defensive and offensive doctrine on the western front at the end of the First World War. That doctrine had imbued them with a sense of decentralized aggressive military operations, ensuring that the new army would not retreat into happy ignorance of 'the real business of soldiering'. Consequently post-war German doctrine emphasized decentralized, rapid decision-making, as well as other factors such as swift, ruthless exploitation, surprise, the reinforcing of success, and the masking of enemy strong points. The *Reichswehr* was the only military force that consistently recognized the complexity of coordinating firepower and maneuver on the modern battlefield. Everyone – the General Staff and its subordinate officers – absorbed those lessons, not just a few enthusiasts of armored warfare. That explains how so many German officers in the infantry and artillery branches were able to move easily to armored, mechanized warfare in the late 1930s, while officers from similar backgrounds in other armies could not make the transition. German officers understood the principles of exploitation; others did not.

The training of General Staff officers in the inter-war period ensured that new officers, moving up in the army, who lacked combat experience, would absorb this approach to war. When Clausewitz' *On War* appeared in the curriculum of the *Kriegsakademie*, students as well as instructors probably gravitated to the sections that dealt with the psychological aspects of combat, the frictions of war, the qualities demanded of great generals, and the necessity for swift, ruthless boldness. It seems likely that the passages dealing with strategy and the supremacy of policy over military considerations found virtually no audience. Although the training itself, with numerous General Staff rides, field maneuvers with and without troops, and what today are called command post exercises, took up most of the students' time, they did study considerable amounts of military history. Even this portion of their studies emphasized the curriculum's operational concerns.

The interest in hands-on learning suggests what the *Kriegsakademie* wished to achieve in educating its students. The General Staff rides presented students with a wide variety of tactical and operational problems that demanded a quick reaction. The officers were not expected to come up with school-book solutions, nor to exhibit unanimity of thought. Only in a general sense were future General Staff officers taught to think identically; otherwise they were evaluated on boldness, flexibility, capacity to adapt, and steadfastness. As one recent historian of the General Staff during the *Reichswehr* has noted:

> Because General Staff instructors believed that textbook instruction alone could not achieve the objective of flexible response, training stressed certain personal attributes – responsibility, imagination, initiative – which normally did not appear in the course syllabus and instructional materials. Candidates were expected to accept responsibility for their actions willingly, to use their imagination, and to take the initiative. Instructors always challenged the officers to apply their knowledge to practical situations. Clearly trainees were also required to possess a certain kind of stamina because the program was such that only officers who were willing and able to spend long and tedious hours mastering a variety of difficult subjects could succeed ....
>
> Yet how was it possible to develop the characteristics of responsibility, imagination, and initiative in a meaningful, practical way? The answer was never very clear. More often than not the leaders resorted to stressing the even more elusive quality of character, as if it could produce flexible response to tactical problems. As future standard bearers of a proud tradition, General Staff candidates were expected to demonstrate integrity and impeccable personal behavior above all other attributes. Although the third year curriculum included a subject dealing with General Staff duties, there was no formal course on character building as such because character development was expected to result from the personal examples set by the instructors ... and the extremely high standards demanded in course work and personal behavior.[52]

Captain Wedemeyer's final report on his experiences at the *Kriegs-akademie* indicates that the same approach was still in place during the mid-1930s. Student papers on tactical problems did not receive grades; rather they were returned with comments. His instructors made clear that four general points framed any evaluation of student work: '1. *Logical combat thinking. 2. Good tactical judgment. 3. Timely and aggressive application of principles. 4. Seizure and maintenance of the initiative.*' The instruction placed 'a premium on quick logical thinking and decisions, transmitted to the command in clear concise orders for aggressive coordinated action'.[53] The curriculum and the training exercises also aimed to inculcate boldness and decisiveness. As Wedemeyer characterized this emphasis: 'Better a faulty plan or decision permeated with boldness, daring and decisiveness, than a perfect plan enmeshed in uncertainty.'[54]

The *Kriegsakademie* also hoped to achieve a high level of conciseness and clarity in the orders written by future general staff officers. Historically, some generals have possessed a natural ability to express their intentions clearly.[55] But the opposite type has predominated in military organizations. So the *Kriegsakademie* provided substantial training aimed at achieving clarity and conciseness in student writing.

To sum up, as Wedemeyer put it in his final report: 'Invaluable experience, in combat exercises and maneuvers ... contributes to a professional knowledge, that renders cooperative initiative almost axiomatic.'[56]

The German army that invaded Poland in September 1939 reflected the strengths as well as the weakness of its leaders. On the tactical and operational levels it was a flexible, adaptive, and bold instrument of national power.[57] The high command's reaction to individual units' weaknesses suggests an extraordinarily high level of expectation; and the preparation and execution of the invasion of France and the Low Countries in May 1940 shows how quickly the *Wehrmacht* could absorb the lessons of combat and then apply them – boldly – in the next battles.

And yet the German army's performance in the Second World War reflected its ambivalence towards Clausewitz. On one hand, its training of officers and enlisted men, its emphasis on decentralized decision-making, its belief that even a bold error was preferable to delay, its sense of the psychological pressures as well as the fog of war, made its *Welt-anschauung* truly Clausewitzian. Most of its opponents, with their rigid emphasis on carefully controlled operations and cautious preparations, were clearly Jominian. The contrast shows up clearly in the Allies' devastating battlefield disasters during 1939–41.

On the other hand, there were few officers who had any sense of Clausewitz' strategic and political analysis. A few senior officers did see the strategic issues with some clarity, particularly the Chief of the General Staff from 1934–38, *Generaloberst* Ludwig Beck. Beck's memoranda, written in the spring and early summer of 1938, protesting Hitler's aggressive and risky policy of confrontation, stand as a monument to clear-headed strategic analysis.[58] Unfortunately, they were not representative. And with Beck's resignation at the height of the Czech crisis in August 1938, the army and its generals reverted happily to identifying strategy with operations and allowed Hitler to decide what they called the political questions. For example, in July 1938 Beck received a letter from a protege, a bright young General Staff product, General Erich von Manstein. (Soon in the Second World War Manstein would prove to possess one of the best staff minds in the army, as well as being one of its foremost battlefield commanders.) In his long letter Manstein argued that Beck should not resign because his presence ensured that the army high command, the OKH, would continue to dominate strategy, rather than yielding its decision-making power to the armed forces' high command (the OKW, *Oberkommando der Wehrmacht*). Only parenthetically in mid-letter did Manstein turn to the subject that was in fact forcing Beck out of the army: the strategy behind Hitler's confrontation with Europe over the Sudetenland. Hitler, Manstein asserted, 'possessed the final responsibility for national policy and has he not thus far judged the political situation correctly?'[59] The tragedy for Germany was that such slipshod thinking, passing all too often for strategy, helped launch the Second and Third Reichs on two great world wars that Germany had little prospect of winning. Ironically, the tactical and operational skills of the German officer corps then ensured that both wars would last almost to the point of destroying not only Germany but also western civilization. Clausewitz would not have been pleased with what his pupils had wrought.

NOTES

1. Carl von Clausewitz, *On War*, ed. and trans. Michael Howard and Peter Paret (Princeton, NJ: Princeton University Press, 1976), p. 87.
2. Michael Howard, 'The Influence of Clausewitz', in Carl von Clausewitz, op. cit., p. 32.
3. Final report of Captain Albert C. Wedemeyer on his tour at the *Kriegsakademie*, 'German General Staff School', Report 15,999 dated 7–11–38 from the Military Attache, Berlin, 1kb 6/23/39, National Archives.
4. Gerhard Ritter, *The Sword and the Scepter, The Problem Of Militarism in Germany*. Vol. 1, *The Prussian Tradition, 1740–1890* (Coral Gables, FL: University of Miami Press, 1969), pp. 194–5.
5. For a concise, clear formulation of the clash of wills between Bismarck and the generals see Gordon A. Craig, *The Politics of the Prussian Army, 1640–1945* (New York: Oxford University Press, 1964), pp. 202–16.

6. Clausewitz' definition of tactics and strategy: 'According to our classification then, tactics teaches *the use of armed forces in the engagement* [thus combining what we would call the operational and tactical spheres]; strategy, *the use of engagements for the object of war.*' *On War*, p.128.

7. Hajo Holborn, 'Moltke and Schlieffen: The Prussian-German School', in *Makers of Modern Strategy, Military Thought from Machiavelli to Hitler* (Princeton, NJ: Princeton University Press, 1973), p.180.

8. Holger Herwig, 'The Dynamics of Necessity: German Military Policy During the Great War', unpublished paper in the Ohio State Military Effectiveness Project, pp.15–16.

9. Ibid., 40, quoted from Crown Prince Ruprecht of Bavaria, *Mein Kriegstagebuch*, ed. Eugene von Frauenholz (Munich: 1929), Vol. 2, p.322, 372n.

10. Letter from Leo Geyer von Schweppenburg to B.H. Liddell Hart, 3.8.49, Liddell Hart Papers 9/24/61, King's College Library, London.

11. *On War*, p.111.

12. For an excellent examination of the German approach to officership in the Second World War as contrasted to the American approach see Martin van Creveld, *Fighting Power: German and U.S. Army Performance, 1939–1945* (Westport, CT: Greenwood Press, 1982).

13. For a discussion of this emphasis on character see: David N. Spires, *Image and Reality, The Making of the German Officer* (Westport CT: Greenwood Press, 1984).

14. See Williamson Murray, 'The German Response to Victory in Poland: A Case Study in Professionalism', *Armed Forces and Society* (Winter 1981).

15. This observation comes from research in the German military documents of the late 1930s. As one studies the *Erfahrungsberichte* (after-action reports) of the Anschluss, the Sudenten crisis, or the invasion of Poland, one sees an increasingly critical examination of events from the higher level of headquarters. This self-scrutiny strongly contrasts with this author's experience in the United States Air Force in the late 1960s. Neither as a reserve officer, commentator on military doctrine, or graduate instructor of active American military officers did I encounter any indication that self-criticism is encouraged in the American military.

16. See particularly Baron Henri Jomini, *The Art of War*, trans. from the French by G.H. Mendell and W.P.C. Craighill (Philadelphia: J.B. Lippincott, 1862).

17. See John Keegan, *The Face of Battle* (New York: Vintage Books, 1977), Ch. 1.

18. Michael Shaara, *The Killer Angels* (New York: Ballantine Books, 1974).

19. For the most thorough examination of the attempt of 8th Air Force Commanders to prove doctrine correct at terrible cost to their crews see Barry D. Watts, *The Foundations of U.S. Air Doctrine, The Problem of Friction in War* (Maxwell AFB: Air University Press, 1985); and Thomas A. Fabyanic, 'A Critique of U.S. Air War Planning, 1941–1944', (Ph.D. dissertation, St. Louis University, 1973).

20. For the most detailed examination of Bomber Command's operations see Sir Charles Webster and Noble Frankland, *The Strategic Air Offensive Against Germany* (London: HMSO, 1962). On the realities that faced the bomber crews in the Battle of Berlin see Max Hastings, *Bomber Command* (London: Michael Joseph, 1979).

21. Taped interview with D.C.T. Bennett, RAF Staff College Library, Bracknell.

22. Air Force Manual 1-1, 1980, 'Functions and Basic Doctrine of the United States Air Force', pp.2–22.

23. *On War*, p.260.

24. Ibid., pp.113–14.

25. Ibid., p.119.

26. Ibid., p.105.

27. Ibid., p.108.

28. Ibid., pp.190–91.

29. Final report of Captain Albert C. Wedemeyer, p.12.

30. For the best description of the Gallipoli campaign see Alan Moorehead, *Gallipoli* (New York: Harper & Bros., 1956).

31. Bernadotte E. Schmitt and Harold C. Vedeler, *The World in the Crucible, 1914–1919* (New York: Harper & Row, 1984), pp.43–4.

32. For the best discussion of the Battle of Verdun see Alistair Horne, *The Price of Glory: Verdun 1916* (New York: St. Martin's Press, 1962).
33. For an excellent description of the battle on the Somme see A.H. Farrar-Hockley, *The Somme* (London: B.T. Batsford, 1964).
34. Erich von Ludendorff, *Ludendorff's Own Story, August 1914–November 1918*, (New York: Harper & Bros., 1919), Vol. 1, p.324.
35. Ibid., p.24.
36. There are two first-class works on this process: Timothy Lupfer, *The Dynamics of Doctrine: The Changes in German Tactical Doctrine During the First World War* (Leavenworth: Combat Studies Institute, 1981); and G.C. Wynne, *If Germany Attacks, The Battle of Depth in the West* (Westport, CT: Greenwood Press, 1976).
37. Lupfer, *The Dynamics of Doctrine*, p.22.
38. Howard, 'The Influence of Clausewitz', pp.34–5.
39. *On War*, p.136.
40. Ibid., p.141.
41. Lupfer, *The Dynamics of Doctrine*, p.55.
42. For an excellent depiction of the first of these offensives see: Martin Middlebrook, *The Kaiser's Battle, 21 March 1918: The First Day of the German Spring Offensive* (London: Allen Lane Publishers, 1978).
43. Reichsarchiv, *Der Weltkrieg, 1914 bis 1918, Die Kriegführung an der Westfront im Jahre 1918* (Berlin: Reichsarchiv, 1944), Vol. 14, pp.41–2; see also Ludendorff, *Ludendorff's Own Story*, p.200–11.
44. Clausewitz, *On War*, p.189.
45. Ibid., p.189.
46. The following discussion is based on my article: 'The German Response to Victory in Poland: A Case Study in Professionalism', *Armed Forces and Society* (Winter 1981).
47. For discussion of what training in the German army meant in the Second World War the reader should consult, on leadership, Hermann Teske, *Bewegungskrieg* (Heidelberg, 1955); on the individual soldier, Guy Sajer, *The Forgotten Soldier* (New York: Harper & Row, 1971), pp.159–68.
48. Heeresgruppe B, Ia Nr. 2211/40, 28.4.1940, 'Bemerkungen zu den Truppenübungen im Frühjahr, 1940', NARS T-312/752/839741.
49. *On War*, p.122.
50. For the training of the general staff during the period of the Weimar Republic see: Spires, *Image and Reality, The Making of the German Officer*; for the training during the mid-1930s see the Wedemeyer report (a useful, though at times limited, view of what the instructors and curriculum at the *Kriegsakademie* were trying to achieve).
51. Symptomatic of considerable constraints on the authority of the general staff and even of Ludendorff is the fact that they were barely able, in 1918, to persuade the War Ministry to promote the army's *chief* artillery expert, Georg von Bruckmüller, from lieutenant colonel to colonel. Bradley J. Meyer, 'Innovation and Expertise: Some Changes in German Tactical Doctrine during World War II', (MA thesis: Ohio State University, 1981), p.81.
52. Spires, *Image and Reality*, pp.47–8.
53. Final Report of Captain Albert C. Wedemeyer, p.15.
54. Ibid., p.18.
55. As examples of this natural gift, Grant's strategic orders to Sherman (4 April 1864) and to Meade (9 April 1864) are models of clarity. See U.S. Grant, *Personal Memoirs of U.S. Grant*, (New York: Charles L. Webster & Co., 1886), Vol. 2, pp.130–32, 134–7.
56. Final Report of Captain Albert C. Wedemeyer, p.78.
57. As my article in *Armed Forces and Society*, 'The German Response to Victory in Poland: A Case Study in Professionalism' suggests, there were very serious weaknesses in the army that invaded Poland. For a graphic description of those weaknesses, see Heinz Guderian, *Panzer Leader* (New York: Ballantine Books, 1961), pp.50–51.
58. For a discussion of the military balance at the time of Munich see Murray, *The Change in the European Balance of Power*, Ch.7.
59. Bundesarchiv/Militärarchiv, Freiburg, N28/3, Kommandeur der 18. Division, Liegnitz, 21.vii.1938.

Clausewitz and the French 1871–1914

DOUGLAS PORCH

The opening weeks of the Great War held cruel surprises for France. Her army was exposed as poorly trained and indifferently led. Its plan of campaign was desperately flawed. But most of all, perhaps, the doctrine of the offensive which had been preached with evangelical fervor by a generation of French soldiers was revealed to be, to paraphrase Talleyrand, not merely a crime, but an error. 'Offensive spirit' plus 'moral force', so long believed the correct calculus of victory, proved to have neglected an essential element in the equation – defensive firepower. Courage, even of the quasi-celestial variety which many influential French officers believed their soldiers possessed, could not overcome bullets and artillery shells spat out in such quantities that the chances of human survival in the attack were reduced substantially below the level which a betting man might call 'even odds'. The results of this perverse refusal in the years before 1914 to come to terms with modern warfare were utterly predictable for the French – catastrophic casualties and early defeats. These caused contemporaries and historians alike to regard the victory on the Marne of September 1914 with an awe sufficient to qualify it, even in the secular mind, as a miracle.

Responsibility for these miscalculations has been laid at the feet of the French army's 'Clausewitzian school' of military theorists led by Gilbert, Foch, and Cardot.[1] Foch admitted to having immersed himself in Clause-witz before writing his influential *Principes de la guerre*, and, according to J.F.C. Fuller, it was readily apparent: 'When we look back on Foch's offensive *à outrance* we see Clausewitz throughout', wrote the British general. 'His offensives *à outrance* and his battles *aux allures déchaînées* became the doctrine of the French army.'[2] However, Fuller's rather harsh indictment of Clausewitz has since been softened by historians. They see Clausewitz as offering a smorgasbord of principles and aphorisms at which Foch and others nibbled in a very selective way, picking out what suited their preconceptions, and passing over anything which promised to bring on intellectual indigestion, like, for instance, Clausewitz' belief in the superiority of the defensive. Chief among Foch's accusers was Sir Basil

Liddell Hart whose 1932 book on Foch was so critical that it earned the dubious honor once reserved for the more salacious forms of pornography, 'Banned in Paris!' 'Foch acted as an amplifier for Clausewitz' more extreme notes', Liddell Hart wrote. Foch caught only Clausewitz' strident generalizations which he employed as 'proverbial tags', neglecting the nuances. In fact, Liddell Hart suspected that Foch's theories were more a form of psychotherapy designed to strengthen his own will as a commander than a blueprint for applied tactics. But even he concluded that 'Foch's main contribution to the French theory of war was to strengthen its Clausewitzian character'.[3]

Raymond Aron, however, was less convinced that Clausewitz was fairly represented in pre-war French thought. Clausewitz' major contribution as a philosopher was to point up the links between 'moral force' and conflict. In contrast to Jomini and the 'geometric school' which saw war as a sort of complicated quadrille in which the commander who had best mastered the steps would win, Clausewitz held that, 'any theory which ignores moral forces, the human aspects of war, would be useless in reality'.[4] Foch took Clausewitz' espousal of the value of moral force on the battlefield and, by some amazing sleight of hand, reached 'the astonishing conclusion by purely mathematical argument' that an increase in the rate of fire actually favored the offensive.[5] This was pure Fochian *trompe l'oeil*, but it fooled the poor soldiers who were scythed down like so much ripe wheat in the killing fields of northern France. Clausewitz did believe that boldness, a taste for risk, and a thrust in luck were essential qualities in a commander. However, these qualities did not eliminate the need for calculation, for rationality, in the conduct of war. In fact, a close reading of Clausewitz when combined with a knowledge of the developments of firepower in the years before 1914 provides a fairly comprehensive list of the points overlooked by French commanders in the Great War: the need to tailor strategy to one's military strength and political goals; the superiority of the defensive, especially for the weaker side; the value of a strategy of attrition in wearing down the enemy's moral forces; the primacy of politics in the conduct of war. Foch and his successors like Cardot and, above all, Grandmaison, the man who drafted the infantry regulations of 1913 which inscribed the offensive *à tout prix* in staff college stone, drew the wrong lessons from their superficial 'historical' studies of the campaigns of Napoleon and Moltke. They also, ignoring the deadly effects of modern firepower as proven by the wars in South Africa and Manchuria, called for an offensive against the evidence of common sense. If their fervor drowned the protests of more rational men like Antoine Grouard and Emile Mayer, can Clausewitz be held responsible, asks Aron?[6]

Clearly, modern scholarship has concluded that Clausewitz stands blameless for the disasters on the French side in 1914. Rather his 'disciples', especially Foch, have been placed in the dock for masquerading as doctors of military science when, in reality, they were little more than charlatans peddling patent medicine from the back of a wagon. Liddell Hart categorized Foch as 'a professor of the platform rather than the laboratory or the seminar', whose 'doctrine' was little more than a reiteration of simple formulas of suggestion, 'a psychotherapy which ought to be applied to the education of children and to the treatment of the sick'.[7] Indeed, the devastating criticism of Foch's pre-war thought, when combined with the unfavorable verdict more recently passed on his performance as commander-in-chief in 1918,[8] leads one to wonder why the French have not removed the Marshal from the solemn surroundings of Les Invalides and quietly reburied him in an obscure corner of Père Lachaise.

The question, then, is not how the French applied the ideas of Clausewitz, for clearly they did not, at least not in any systematic way. Their reading of him was selective at best, a selectivity which rightly has been condemned by scholars. However, no full explanation has been offered of *why* French theorists were so selective. Indeed, we are virtually led to conclude, at least by inference, that Foch *et al.* must either be mad or short-sighted to the point of criminal negligence. No one has satisfactorily identified the factors which encouraged Clausewitz' popularity in the French army, even in this mangled version – especially in this mangled version!

Why did French theorists believe Clausewitz important? The very selectivity which Foch and others used when quoting Clausewitz may help us to understand the conditions which aided his popularity. It may simply have been, as Liddell Hart obviously believed, that frequent references to Clausewitz gave a spurious appearance of rationality to what were little more than statements of faith.[9] But there is probably more to the relationship between Clausewitz and the French theorists than that. These men obviously believed Clausewitz, or at least parts of his treatise, to be relevant to the French situation at the turn of the century. By condemning the distortions of Clausewitz on the tactical and strategic level by Foch and others, scholars have perhaps overlooked a second aspect of the question.

Clausewitz was, after all, the man who sought to place military activity in its social and political context. French officers believed warfare to be, above all, a manifestation of the social and political organization of the state. It was this article of faith which allowed them to relegate technical considerations like armaments and firepower to the category reserved for 'secondary considerations'. Georges Gilbert, a leading 'Clausewitzian', stated this quite clearly in 1887: 'War is a mode of human activity, like industry and commerce', he wrote. 'Its methods change with the political constitution and are influenced only to a secondary degree by material factors, armaments which are available .... In combat, as in peaceful competition, the nation is all important, for it gives birth to the great social evolution and makes its military or economic action conform to it.'[10] The conditions of French politics and society, and the role of the army in the state, must be critical factors in explaining the receptiveness of French soldiers to selected aspects of Clausewitzian thought. In addition, these factors may give clues as to why the sober and cautious doctrines of Clausewitz were transmogrified in the hands of French theorists into something which resembled a particularly shrill sermon at a fundamentalist revival. Indeed, Foch was not so much a Clausewitzian, or even a neo-Clausewitzian, as a born-again Clausewitzian.

The only scholar to my knowlege who has attempted to explain why Clausewitz' aphorisms fell upon such fertile ground in *belle époque* France is Michael Howard. Professor Howard advances two reasons for Clausewitz' popularity: first, his emphasis on 'moral force' accorded well with the traditions of the French army which antedated the French Revolution and which were reinforced by the colonial experience. Second, the spiritual approach to war fitted well into the atmosphere, the *Zeitgeist*, of early twentieth-century France. French intellectuals, especially on the right, had turned their backs on the Positivism of Comte, Taine, and Renan in favor of the *élan vital* of Bergson.[11]

While these explanations go a substantial way toward providing the answers, they do not tell the full story. (Nor, it must be pointed out, was it Professor Howard's intention to offer a comprehensive explanation of the French experience.) Tradition, of course, is important in determining an army's strategic and tactical doctrine. The *furia francese* and the *arme blanche* were held to be irresistible in some quarters. But should historical memory necessarily take precedence over a rationally contrived doctrine which takes other factors – geography, position, manpower, firepower – into consideration? Also, why were the traditions of the offensive adopted? There were numerous examples of the French fighting successfully on the defensive. For instance, connoisseurs liked to point to Napoleon's defensive campaigns of 1813–14 as among his most brilliant. As for the colonial experience, many of the French army's most spectacular victories (and spectacular defeats!) abroad had been defensive ones. The image of French soldiers holding out against swarms of hostile natives was at least as powerful as the legend of the power of the French bayonet attack. The sieges of Camerone, Tuyen Quang, Bou Denib, or Fez in 1911 were celebrated as evidence of French staying power and will to resist. The Moroccan campaign, the army's last chance before the Great War to gain direct battlefield experience, was won largely by French soldiers fighting on the tactical defensive. If the square survived in the colonies long beyond what should have been its normal lifetime – as late as 1912, Mangin used it at Marrakech – it was because it maximized the advantages of defensive firepower against attacking Moroccans. Nor was it insignificant that the French Foreign Legion adopted Camerone, and not the sweeping offensive victories at Ischeriden, Solferino, or the storming of the Citadel of Bac Ninh, as their *fête du régiment*.

The *Zeitgeist* also provides a confusing, and often contradictory, set of explanations for the popularity of Clausewitz. Historians have detected a shift of mood in pre-war France as the country, seemingly satiated by the excesses of the Dreyfusards and acrimonious debates over church–state relations, after 1905 increasingly turned away from the secular doctrines of Positivism to a Bergsonian spiritualism. The period after 1905 was marked by a renewal of interest in religion and, by 1911, a 'Nationalist Revival' which sought to raise French morale and confidence in the face of the increasing threat of German arms.

That this shift in atmosphere occurred is undeniable. However, it might be dangerous to attach too much importance to its influence on the public mood and, especially, on military theory. Bergson, the religious resurgence, and the 'Nationalist Revival' have been considered right-wing phenomena. However, the best organized and most influential right-wing group, the *Action Française*, remained firmly in the Positivist tradition, seeking to prove the need for Church and Monarchy through rational arguments. (Indeed, Barrès, the leader of the *Action Française*, was an unbeliever.) Nor must one forget that the left, which was firmly Positivist in intellectual orientation, remained in the ascendant and actually increased its power in this period. Eugene Weber has concluded that the Nationalist Revival, while important, was a superficial movement which was most influential among young Parisians, but failed to percolate far down into French society. And hence it did not much influence the Army.[12]

As for the influence of the new spiritualism on military theory, two things must be pointed out: first, that many, indeed most, of the offensive-minded 'Clausewitzian' school – Gilbert, Maillard, and Foch – were constructing their theories, *not* in the atmosphere of Bergsonian spiritualism, but in the dreary days of rational Positivism. Indeed, they seemed to be rowing against the current of the *Zeitgeist*, not with it. Foch was expounding his quasi-mystical theories of the offensive before an audience of spellbound students at the *école de guerre* at the very moment that the spies of General André, the 'Red Donkey', were denouncing him as a priest-ridden reactionary. Second, the contentions of some left-wing historians in the post-war years to the contrary, the offensive and the belief in 'moral force' was not the exclusive domain of the right, against which good republicans argued in vain. It was the left that triumphed with the successful resolution of the Dreyfus affair in 1899. For Dreyfusard officers like Percin and Sarrail, as well as for younger men like Paul Simon and Charles Ebener (whom the victorious left had sent out to the military colleges), offensive superiority was very much part of their ideological baggage. Of course, this is not to say that the *Zeitgeist* did not help to smooth acceptance of the offensive in some quarters in the years before the war. However, the *Zeitgeist* alone cannot satisfactorily explain the triumph of 'moral force' and the doctrine of the offensive in the army before 1914.

If there was an intellectual influence on the acceptance of Clausewitzian 'moral force' in France before the Great War, Liddell Hart has probably come closer to defining what it was than anyone else: 'A psychoanalyst would probably detect a deep-seated inferiority complex', he wrote.[13] While Liddell Hart was speaking exclusively of Foch, his observations might be extended to France as a whole. Although France probably contains more intellectuals per square kilometer than any other nation, their influence has been more critical than creative. In much the same way that German socialists brought up on the analytical writings of Marx, Engels, Bernstein, Kautsky, and Rosa Luxemburg looked down on their French counterparts as 'a scratch lot', so French military writing appeared superficial when held against that of Clausewitz, Moltke, and von der Goltz. This superficiality was in some ways inevitable: most French theorists had to rush out their lectures during their brief tenure at the *école supérieure de guerre*, and did not enjoy the leisure to study and reflect that Clausewitz did at the *Kriegsschule*. It is worth noting that some of the more prophetic French military thinkers, like Grouard and Mayer, retired from the army at a fairly young age. Early retirement both gave them the time, and freed them from the institutional constraints which affected others. Europeans interested in military theory looked for instruction to Clausewitz, Moltke, and von der Goltz, not to Gilbert, Bonnal, and Foch. A combination of lack of time and lack of intellectual depth may have caused French theorists like Foch to fall back on selective formulas and clichés as substitutes for the more profoundly pondered and documented German theories.

Part of the problem too lay with the forum in which French theorists worked – the *école de guerre*. Under the influences of Clausewitz, the Prussians from the early nineteenth century possessed in the *Kriegsakademie* something like a military university. French reformers were seriously handicapped when they attempted to reproduce the Prussian experiment in France. In 1877, General Jules Lewal was given the task of creating a war college from the old general staff school. Although what he produced was superior in every respect to the old system, it fell short of its

German counterpart. Students were recruited by competitive examination in their fifth year of service around the age of 25 or 26. They were put through a rigorous two-year course which emphasized the skills required to be a junior staff officer rather than the imagination and breadth of vision required of future military leaders. Many thought the students too young to make the most of college training.[14] So while Germany possessed a true institution of higher military learning, France organized a vocational school.

The result of this stunted educational system meant that there was no institution capable of formulating a doctrine for the army as a whole. War college instructors were too young (most were only majors) to impose their views on the army even had the general staff and high command been disposed to accept the college as the ultimate authority on tactical and strategic questions. And this they were not disposed to do. General Debeney, who had been professor of infantry tactics at the école de guerre in 1909 when Foch was its commandant, denied that the war college was responsible for the doctrine of the offensive. 'One of the characteristics of the école de guerre's teaching was a great tolerance of opinions', he wrote. 'The four years which preceeded the war were a period of great tolerance during which we concentrated on educating officers and not upon formulating a doctrine.' Colonel de Grandmaison, chief of the third bureau, was responsible for drawing up the controversial 1913 infantry regulations, 'which flew in the face of ideas on the preponderance of firepower taught at école de guerre by Colonel Pétain and so many others', like Colonels Maud'huy, Fayolle, and Debeney.[15] 'In fact, the école de guerre always refused to formulate a doctrine', Debeney continued, pointing out that many of the school's professors were very critical of Grandmaison's 1913 regulations.[16]

Dallas D. Irvine has called the école de guerre after Lewal's departure 'a church without a gospel'.[17] In fact, the same might be said of the army as a whole. French officers blamed their defeat in the Franco-Prussian War on the defensive strategy of Bazaine. Yet, what was to be put in its place? And furthermore, who was to decide? After 1871, the army was confused and divided. The ambiguous political situation of the 1870s when France was a republic ruled by royalists, combined with the fact that too many senior officers of the Imperial army managed to prolong their tenure into the early years of the republic, meant that change could come only slowly, piecemeal, the product of caution and compromise rather than a root-and-branch reform. As the army increased in size and complexity, the command structures were not overhauled, leaving the chain of command looking more like a maze than a neat pyramid. The refusal of republicans to create a true commander-in-chief who might impart firm direction to the forces, and their insistence that authority resided in an ephemeral minister of war, did little to help the army resolve its problems. Consequently, strategic and tactical theory, like much else in the French army, was a mass of confusion – while military school professors like Gilbert and Maillard preached that the 'offensive is the true mode of warfare, it alone leads to victory', the government continued to invest heavily in frontier fortifications as adjuncts to a defensive strategy.[18]

The Dreyfus affair burst upon an army which was still groping for a doctrine. The fifteen or so years before the outbreak of the Great War were not happy ones for the French forces. Hostile politicians delighted in vilifying the officer corps as a citadel of reaction. Of course, there was nothing new in this. But now, the critics belonged to the government, not the opposition. As an official cloud of disfavor drifted over the army, the officers saw their prestige in the nation decline. Petty insults directed at the high command, especially with the arrival of the staunch Dreyfusards Emile Combes and Georges Clémenceau in the Palais Matignon, sapped morale. The 'affaire des fiches' of 1904 – the revelation that war minister André collected through Masonic lodges in garrison towns secret reports on the political and religious views of officers *and of their wives* – offered positive proof that politics and political favoritism had crept into promotion and garrison assignments. Officers resigned in disgust and the number of candidates applying for Saint-Cyr dropped by two-thirds. The decline in the numbers and quality of officer recruits was soon apparent throughout the army.[19]

However, political disfavor was not the only cause of plummeting morale. While the French army was consumed by the political debate of the Dreyfus years, its German rival forged ahead. The French birthrate had stagnated after 1870, so that by the turn of the century, Germany's population was larger by 15 million. France made prodigious efforts to overcome this deficiency in military terms, conscripting 5,620 men for each million inhabitants compared with 4,120 per million in Germany. But in 1903 she was able to muster only 459,000 men and 25,000 officers to 621,000 men and 26,000 officers across the Vosges.[20] With the approach of war, the situation worsened. The 1913 military law voted by the Reichstag gave the German army an almost 2–1 edge over the French, creating places for 42,000 officers and 112,000 NCOs as opposed to 29,000 officers and 48,000 NCOs in France.[21] German numerical superiority was backed up by an advantage in weaponry. In August 1914, Germany counted 4,500 machine guns to 2,500 in France, 6,000 77-millimeter cannon to 3,800 French 75s, and an almost total monopoly in heavy artillery. The long-term projections were even more sobering: by 1932, Germany's military resources were estimated to be 5,400,000 trained men, compared with a maximum of four million in France.[22]

Although French military expenditure accounted for 36 per cent of the national budget, against only 20 per cent in Germany, in real terms the French investment fell far short of the German figure.[23] Klotz, president of the parliamentary army committee, put the 1904 defense figures at 38,256,364 francs compared with the equivalent of almost 100 million in Germany in the same year.[24] General Langlois calculated in 1908 that Germany spent the equivalent of 1,770 francs per soldier while France spent only 914. 'This shows the efforts our eastern neighbors have made to equip and train their army .... Happily, we still have the moral emphasis which we must consider a head start', he said.[25]

Such an obvious disadvantage in manpower and *matériel vis-à-vis* Germany quite naturally sent France in search of allies to offset her deficiencies. In the long term, of course, she was to be successful. But at the time, there was no guaranteed effective help from either Russia or Great Britain to relieve the insecurity of France. The Russian army, badly mauled in the Russo-Japanese War, was not expected to regain its fighting form before 1910. Its leaders who visited France were often more interested in getting to the tables at Deauville or Monte Carlo than in discussing joint strategy, while in St. Petersburg, French generals met a wall of secrecy and evasiveness. French strategists obviously hoped for Russian assistance, but they could not count on it. And even if it came, Russian mobilization was so slow that France would have to bear the full weight of the German army in the initial stages of the conflict.

Relations between French soldiers and their British counterparts were excellent, mainly due to the efforts of Brigadier, later Field Marshal, Henry Wilson, Director of Military Operations from 1910, who drew up the detailed plans which permitted the British Expeditionary Force to intervene effectively in the war's opening weeks. But the British army hardly offered the lifeline which would reassure French soldiers. In the first place, the British government seemed reluctant to mortgage its policies to French action. Immersed in the Irish question, following an 'uncertain' foreign policy, Britain might – so French planners feared – remain aloof from continental events, isolated in her island fastness.[26] If anything, the prospect of British intervention actually complicated French planning, for Joffre and others realized that a premature French strike into Belgium would transform England into an irreconcilable foe. Second, the British army, though highly rated by the French, was small and therefore unlikely to trip the balance in the dramatic initial battle which, it was believed, would decide the outcome of the war. Thus, because British intervention could not be counted upon and because Britain's army was small, French planners did not include the British forces in their lines of battle, continuing to rely on the 'spirit of the offensive' to make up deficiencies in arms and manpower.[27]

To an army in such a state of political confusion and material disarray, a doctrine which preached the superiority of 'moral force' was naturally attractive. Of no group in the French army was this more true than the colonial army. The French army had created a separate colonial force out of the *infanterie de la marine* which, by the turn of the century, counted for ten per cent of French Army strength. However, the influence of the colonial army ran far beyond its numbers. It was the only section of the army which had seen action since 1871, which allowed it to speak with some authority on questions of doctrine. Also, in prestigious men like Joseph Gallieni and, especially, Hubert Lyautey, the colonial army possessed writers who reached a far wider audience than did theorists like Foch.

The actual role of the colonial army in popularizing the offensive in France has perhaps been misunderstood. As has been seen, the colonial army's most spectacular victories had been achieved by employing defensive tactics. Colonial soldiers did not argue for the offensive on the basis of their colonial experience. On the contrary, they argued that colonial warfare taught flexibility, calmness under fire, adaptability to each new situation. They readily admitted that warfare in Africa and Indo-China was not that of Europe. The lessons that colonial warfare held for Europe were not so much in the realm of formal tactics, but in the value of offensive-mindedness, 'moral force', those qualities which allowed Frenchmen to triumph over the adverse conditions encountered abroad.

But moral force also had a second, political, dimension that was bound up with the colonial army's view of France. For soldiers abroad, France was a political and spiritual invalid, deprived of unity by self-inflicted divisions which made a concerted national defense difficult to realize. According to Lyautey, the role of the colonial army was not merely the conquest of colonies, but also the spiritual reconstruction of France. He believed that the colonies, having witnessed the 'continuing, if not growing, worth of *individual* Frenchmen', offered 'an incomparable capital of energy and will which must not be squandered'. Rather, it must be channeled to offset the 'receding influence' of France abroad. Lyautey led a chorus of colonial soldiers who believed it their

> social duty to tear this country from decomposition and ruin. Not by changing the constitution, an empirical and transitory method, but by a violent reaction upon manners, inertias and worries ... react upon metropolitan inertia, establish a continuing and regenerating current of life between France without and France within, which will be a revival for this country.[28]

The Nationalist Revival offered colonial prophets their chance. But the offensive triumphed not because the army was gaining confidence after 1910, but because army confidence and morale had been laid so low.

Grandmaison, who had served in Tonkin, believed that only an infusion of 'moral force' could pull France from her 'decrepitude'.[29] This was especially true for the military organization. The Dreyfus affair had not only divided Frenchmen, it had accentuated the worst features of the metropolitan army: a high command bullied by politicians and terrified of responsibility, a bureaucratized general staff buried in the minutiae of military life, an army organization in shambles leaving troop commanders leaderless in resolving important tactical questions, and finally an understaffed and undertrained body of troops. These problems were virtually unsurmountable in the short term. Only by importing the 'moral force' unleashed in the colonies could Frenchmen hope to meet their stronger enemies on equal terms. 'Moral force' and 'offensive spirit' gained so much credence because they offered a much needed shot of confidence to an army desperate for a doctrine, for guidance, no matter how superficial or illusory, in tactical questions.

Advances in military technology also increased the appeal of Clausewitz' 'moral force', and consequently of the tactical offensive. Such ideas did not flourish, as historians would have it, in ignorance of technological developments. General Fuller accused Foch of being a 'tactically demented Napoleon' and ignoring new developments in weaponry. 'Step by step', he wrote, 'with few variations, he follows Napoleon in the face of magazine rifles and quick-firing artillery as if they were the muskets and cannon of Jena and Friedland'.[30] De la Gorce maintains the French 'ignored the firepower of modern armaments, especially of heavy artillery, and underestimated the effectiveness of defensive tactics'.[31] Liddell Hart said that: 'The new French philosophy, by its preoccupation with the moral element, had become more and more separated from the inseparable material factors.'[32] But it was those very material factors that led to the logical evolution of the offensive. Armaments developments required an almost constant reassessment of tactics. Colonel Langlois believed that,

> The instability of the (tactical) regulation ... results from the instability of our modern conditions. If tactics formerly changed every ten years, according to Napoleon, they change more frequently today, and the regulations must be constantly modified. This is a fact of life. However, the broader the terms in which the regulations are couched, the less the detail, the more durable they will be.[33]

The doctrine of the offensive, based on the superiority of Gallic 'moral force', a faith held by republicans, colonial soldiers, and the traditional right, provided a durable tactical law. The only way to cope with the new technical developments despite poor French resources was to rely on the patriotic audacity, the historic *élan*, of French soldiers.[34]

Increased firepower was the most critical technical development in late nineteenth-century warfare. The modern rifle, machine gun, and cannon compelled military pundits to re-think established tactical theory. Soldiers who once fought successfully in relatively close formation now had to spread out under fire or risk heavy casualties. With a greatly extended battlefield, officers and NCOs could no longer control or keep track of their men in combat. Paul Simon feared that discipline would be the first casualty unless soldiers were fired by patriotic zeal:

> When a company deploys in rank on a 290-meter front ... many will not hear orders. The men will no longer see their leaders. They have no one in front to lead them, no one behind to push them .... Nothing is left to keep them moving foward but the individual will to win .... History testifies that the soldiers who fight best when dispersed are those with the strongest patriotism and will to conquer, and the strongest devotion to their leaders and comrades. Soldiers without these feelings can be led into the attack only in relatively close formation .... The more armaments are developed, the more dispersal becomes necessary and the more individual moral strength is needed.[35]

'Firepower does not weaken the offensive spirit,' General Bazaine-Hayter, commander of the 13th corps, wrote in October 1906. 'Never forget that a defensive battle will seldom bring victory. However powerful weapons become, the victory will go to the offensive which stimulates moral force, disconcerts the enemy and deprives him of his freedom of action.'[36] General Langlois reached the same extraordinary conclusion as Foch: 'The systematic study of history shows that, the more armaments are perfected, the more advantages are offered by the offensive.'[37]

The advantages of morale in the face of modern armaments were held to have been demonstrated in the Russo-Japanese War of 1904–5. The superior moral preparation of the Japanese soldiers had more than compensated for modern Russian armaments. The success of the attacking Japanese discredited those who maintained that in the Boer War the British had suffered by taking the offensive. The Boer's devastating rifle fire not only proved the exceptional Boer marksmanship, but, more important, revealed the sorry state of the British army – professional soldiers led by upper-class officers.[38] 'Tactics ... will depend more on the morale of the nation at the beginning of the war and on the individual energy of the soldier than on the power of armaments', one soldier concluded.[39] Joffre later wrote in his memoires:

> The Russo-Japanese War was dazzling confirmation of General Langlois' view that the Boer War had not discredited the offensive.

Under the direction of Foch, Lanrezac and Bourderiat, the young intellectual elite at the *Ecole de guerre* now threw out the divisive old doctrine [the primacy of the defensive based on Franco-Prussian War experience]. But as always happens when established ideas are challenged, the value of the offensive was exaggerated by this group. People have referred to the 'mystique of the offensive'. This is probably going too far. But it does demonstrate rather well the somewhat irrational character the cult of the offensive took after 1905.[40]

Outmanned and outgunned, France had to look for superiority in other spheres. 'To fight dispersed, a soldier must compensate for the lack of material support by a more solid moral preparation', the Dreyfusard General André wrote.[41] 'We want an army which compensates for numerical weakness with military quality', Adolphe Messimy, Radical Party spokesman on defense stated in 1908.[42] As war minister five years later, his views were unchanged: 'Neither numbers nor miraculous machines will determine victory', he said in 1913. 'This will go to soldiers with valour and "quality" – and by this I mean superior physical and moral endurance, offensive strength.'[43] Patrice Mahon gauged that only drive could beat numbers: 'The truth', he wrote, 'is that the only possible way of overcoming Germany's more efficient mobilization is to confront them with our offensive'.[44] With these substantial material handicaps, France had to oppose mind to Germany's main. '[The Russo-Japanese War] was an impressive demonstration of moral forces', General Négrier wrote.

> Now it is everywhere recognized that with modern armaments the individual worth of the combatant has never been more important. This must comfort our hearts. The character of our soldiers adapts itself marvelously to present requirements. Numbers no longer decide victory .... A certain numerical inferiority does not trouble our soldiers.[45]

For Grandmaison, moral force was more important than endless quibbles about tactics: 'It is more important to develop a conquering state of mind than to cavil about tactics', he concluded.[46]

In the final analysis, Clausewitzian 'moral force' seemed an excellent cure for all of the ills which afflicted the French army – political divisions, deficiencies in armaments, lack of a doctrine. 'Moral force' accorded well with French tradition, both the professional military tradition of the *arme blanche* and the *furia francese*, and that of the patriotic *élan* of the French Revolution. In the divisive atmosphere of the Dreyfus years, 'moral force' offered a rallying point for an army at odds with important groups in

French society, and one at odds with itself. The left could lay claim to it as
a product of the French Revolution triumphant in the Dreyfus affair. For
the right, it was a source summoned up from the depths of *vieille France*.
For the colonial army, it was a unique contribution to the spiritual
reconstruction of France born of the confidence and the sense of mission
spawned by imperial service. So, to answer Aron's, 'But where in 1903,
was the counterpart of the Revolution or the ideas that shook thrones
centuries before?'[47] – they were here: part politics, part imperial confidence, part psychotherapy, part fear. 'Moral force' united left and right,
Dreyfusard and anti-Dreyfusard, colonial and metropolitan.

Nor did the growth of German might dampen enthusiasm for a more
spiritual approach to the study of war. On the contrary, enemy superiority
in manpower and armaments actually encouraged the French to look
elsewhere for sources of military strength. Tradition, both on left
and right, civilian and military, dictated that 'moral force' would be a
necessary substitute for the armaments which France did not have and
was not likely to get. That moral force was associated with the offensive
was not irrational. After all, Clausewitz himself had said that moral force
favoured the offensive, while it could not be brought to bear so effectively
in defense. Theorists like Colonel Hubert Camon could point out that
Clausewitz, by favouring the defensive, was simply being illogical with
himself – how could the great German philosopher say in one breath
that the defensive is the stronger tactic and in the next that only
the offensive will bring victory? As for Clausewitz' advocacy of the
'defensive–offensive' (the defensive to wear down the attacker followed
by an offensive), this, Camon believed, was 'unhealthy' and based upon
an utter misunderstanding of Napoleon's use of 'l'attaque enveloppante'.
Indeed, Camon saw it as his task 'to fortify the reader against (Clausewitz') seductions in favor of the defense'.[48] Camon dismissed Clausewitz'
teachings on tactics as belonging to the least finished portion of his notes.
And what was more, 'Clausewitz did not understand the essential object
of the operational systems of Napoleon's battle, which was the preliminary material and moral disorganization of the adversary'.[49]

Lastly, 'moral force' and the offensive were not the product of a
carefully considered system. Rather, they betrayed the army's lack of any
system of tactical thought. It was the very disorganization and disorienta-
tion of the French army before the Great War which was responsible for
its popularity. The high command, composed largely of timid old men
who had made their careers in the Dreyfus years largely because they
refused to express strong opinions on anything, looked on helplessly as
young, dynamic officers eager for a doctrine, any doctrine, took up the
offensive. The *école de guerre* refused to apply a corrective, taking refuge
in their role as a school of military administration. Staff officers were too

busy making war by shuffling papers to bother with relevant problems of tactics and firepower. In any case, a tactical doctrine was destined to be only half understood and poorly applied in an army which had little occasion to practice it in training or maneuvers. With all of these problems, tactics were left in confusion. Staff training exercises revealed a mass of conflicting tactical theories. The offensive did not filter down to the mass of the forces as a coherent doctrine: 'Only a small nucleus ... was affected by the new ideas', Joffre noted.

> In 1911, the new doctrine had not yet penetrated very far in the mass of the army, but this had begun to move. Tossed about for years between the most extreme theories, led by officers opposed to all innovation, [the army] nevertheless conserved an apathy and indolence which was almost complete .... People probably realized that the offensive was fashionable higher up, and so did their best to 'carry out the offensive' – but in what conditions!⁵⁰

In short, Clausewitz was popular in the French army before 1914 because he was the philosopher who divided Frenchmen the least and because his emphasis on 'moral forces' offered hope to a divided nation and a beleaguered army. 'Moral force' offered a sort of theoretical *union sacrée* which paved the way for the political one of 1914. It papered over serious military defects. The ever-growing strength of the German army, rather than introducing a sobering note of reality, simply increased the atmosphere of fantasy in which war was studied. To admit that France was too weak to face war with Germany was, of course, impossible. The likelihood of war had been growing since 1905. Once French soldiers got over the shock of Tangier and began to reconcile themselves to the possibility, indeed the probability, of a war with Germany, it was unthinkable to back down. 'Moral force' became the substitute for the arms and men which French military leaders did not possess.

NOTES

1. Raymond Aron, *Clausewitz: Philosopher of War* (London: Routledge & Kegan Paul, 1983).
2. J.F.C. Fuller, *The Conduct of War* (London: Eyre Methuen, 1972), p.128.
3. Basil Liddell Hart, *Foch, The Man of Orleans* (Boston: Little, Brown and Co., 1932), pp.25–7.
4. Aron, p.66.
5. Liddell Hart, p.31.
6. Aron, p.264.
7. Liddell Hart, pp.454–55.
8. See Guy Pédroncini, *Petain, général en chef* (Paris: Presses Universitaires de France, 1978).
9. Liddell Hart, p.455.
10. Georges Gilbert, 'Etude sur Clausewitz', *Nouvelle Revue* (1 Aug. 1887), p.540.

11. Michael Howard, *Clausewitz* (Oxford: Oxford University Press, 1983), p.62.
12. Douglas Porch, *The March to the Marne* (Cambridge: Cambridge University Press, 1981), Ch.9.
13. Liddell Hart, p.27.
14. Archives historiques de guerre (henceforth AHG), 7N 3, and General Jean-Marie Pédoya, *L'armée n'est pas commandée* (Paris: Charles-Lavauzelle, 1905), p.14.
15. General Debeney, *La Guerre et les hommes* (Paris: E. Plon, 1937), p.12.
16. Ibid., pp.277–8.
17. Dallas D. Irvine, 'The French Discovery of Clausewitz and Napoleon', *Journal of the American Military Institute*, No. 3 (1942), p.26.
18. Alan Mitchell, *Victors and Vanquished, the German Influence in Army and Church in France after 1870* (Chapel Hill: University of North Carolina Press, 1984), pp.276–7, 112–13, 115–16.
19. Porch, pp.83–5.
20. Paul de la Gorce, *La République et son armée* (Paris: Fayard, 1963), pp.81–3.
21. Archives nationales (henceforth AN), C7257, report by war minister Adolphe Messimy, p.10.
22. Monteilhet, *Les institutions militaires de la France* (Paris: F. Alcan, 1932), pp.277–8.
23. AN, C7257, Messimy report. Messimy includes hidden expenses.
24. L. Klotz, *L'armée en 1906* (Paris: Charles-Lavauzelle, 1906), p.101.
25. *Le Temps*, 15 Nov. 1908.
26. Millerand Papers, Bibliothèque nationale, note 21 Oct. 1912.
27. For an assessment of the prospects of early Russian intervention see, for instance, AHG 7N 1538, report of Col. Janin of the 2e bureau, December 1911: 'Les Russes n'exerceront pas sur les Allemands une action quelconque avant le 30e jour, et cette action ne deviendra sérieuse que bien plus tard. Les défenses de toute nature, la distance permettent aux Allemands, s'ils veulent, de ne laisser de ce côté que des forces actives peu nombreuses ... jusqu'a ce qu'une décision fut intervenue du côté de l'Ouest.'
28. See Hubert Lyautey, 'Du rôle colonial de l'officier', *Revue des Deux Mondes*, 15 Jan. 1900, pp.324–5, 328. Also, same author, *Lettres du Tonkin et de Madagascar, 1894–99* (Paris: A. Colin, 1942), p.489.
29. Col. Louis de Grandmaison, *En territoire militare* (Paris: E. Plon, 1898), pp.265–6.
30. Fuller, p.128.
31. de la Gorce, p.140.
32. Liddell Hart, *A History of the First World War* (London: Cassell, 1972), p.31.
33. *Avenir militaire*, 4 April 1893.
34. On this theme, see John Bowditch, 'The Rationalization of Weakness', in E.M. Earle, *Modern Europe* (Princeton, NJ: Princeton University Press, 1951).
35. P. Simon, *L'instruction des officiers, l'éducation des troupes et la puissance nationale* (Paris: Charles-Lavauzelle, 1905), pp.176, 184–5.
36. AHG, 6N 41, 19 Oct. 1906.
37. H. Langois, 'Le haut commandement', *Revue des deux mondes*, 19 Sept. 1911, 65.
38. Simon, 218.
39. 'Quelques enseignements de la guerre Sud-Africaine', *Revue des deux mondes*, 15 June 1902, 723.
40. Joseph Joffre, *Mémoires* (Paris: E. Plon, 1932), pp.32–3.
41. General Louis André, *Cinq ans au ministère* (Paris: L. Micaud, 1909), 117.
42. AHG, 7N 35.
43. A. Messimy, *Le problème militaire* (Paris: Publications du journal 'le Rappel', 1913), 15.
44. P. Mahon, 'Le service de trois ans', *Revue des deux mondes*, 15 April 1913, 883. .
45. General Négrier, 'Quelques enseignements sur la guerre Russo-Japanaise', *Revue des deux mondes*, 15 June 1906, 333.
46. Grandmaison, *Deux conférences faites aux officiers de l'état-major de l'armée* (Paris: Berger-Levrault, 1911), p.34.
47. Aron, p.248.
48. H. Camon, *Clausewitz* (Paris: R. Chapelot, 1911), pp.2–3.
49. Ibid., pp.249, 267.
50. Joffre, p.33.

Clausewitz Disregarded: Italian Military Thought and Doctrine, 1815–1943

JOHN GOOCH

During the course of the nineteenth century, armies within Europe and far beyond it fell under the influence of Clausewitz' thought. Frequently the dogmas to which they adhered were parodies of the intentions of the author of *Vom Kriege* which had been refracted through the lens of domestic military culture. The result was a grotesque distortion of the philosophical subtlety of a work which was widely misused and widely misunderstood. At a time when so many countries were developing their strategic and tactical delusions, Italy remained immune to Clausewitz. References to his work were few until the middle of the Fascist era, and the first full translation of *Vom Kriege* in Italian only appeared in 1942.

Although uninfluential, Clausewitz' work was not unknown in Italy. Rather, it was discarded as unnecessary and irrelevant: unnecessary because Italian military thought had settled into defined grooves by the late nineteenth century; irrelevant because strategically Italy's chief pre-occupation was with the defense of her land frontiers and her coast-line. Among other things, one defining characteristic of Italian military thought up to 1861 which helped to close the door to Clausewitz was the presence of a strong admixture of socio-political calculation, the product of the competing political forces which sought to determine the shape of a unified Italy. Clausewitz' stress on the social in warfare was nothing new to Italians; but, having shaped an authoritarian parliamentary monarchy after 1861, it represented a problem they regarded as solved.

Despite a high degree of immunity from the kind of distorted Clause-witzian analysis which infused French military doctrine in the years before 1914, Italy too entered the First World War in the grip of offensive tactical doctrines. Her experience in trying to apply them demonstrates one of the most substantial disadvantages of a pragmatically-based doctrinal approach to war. In the years which followed 1918, and especially after the advent of Fascism to power in 1922, a combination of military conservatism and strategic innovation helped keep Italy isolated from *Vom Kriege* until at last the efforts of a lone individual made the work available in its full extent. But by that time it could have no influence upon either thought or policy in the world war which swept away both Fascism and the Italian monarchy.

I. MILITARY HISTORY AND DOCTRINE: 1848–1910

In the years up to 1848, the Piedmontese army was strongly influenced by French military thought. Piedmontese cavalry regulations of 1817 were derived from those of France, and the infantry regulations of 1833 likewise echoed French practice, though in a more formalistic way; emphasis was placed upon shock rather than firepower or movement. In 1838, seven years after her Gallic neighbor, Piedmont adopted a tactical system which laid greater emphasis on the controlled development of the attack and on coordination between the advance guard and the main body. Appropriately, the geometric aspects of warfare were heavily stressed in tactical exercises. As in tactical doctrine, so in strategic thought, France was the model. In his two-volume work *La Guerra* (1839), Andrea Zambrelli sided with Jomini in his interpretation of the Napoleonic military art; other Italian writers who relayed Jominian ideas at this time included Paul Racchia (1832), Joseph Pougni-Guillet (1832), and Sebastiano Vassalli (1847).[1]

However, alongside theories of regular warfare there existed in pre-1848 Italy a second strand of strategic thought. Italian thinkers had shown an early recognition that war could legitimately be considered not simply as a series of technical problems but as an expression of society: this idea had permeated Luigi Blanch's *Della scienza militare considerata nei suoi rapporti colle altre scienze e col sistema sociale* (1832), although it was not explicitly analysed there.[2] This conception of a politicized strategy flowing from the aspirations of separate social groups took root in the political philosophy of the Left, and more particularly in the theory of partisan warfare proclaimed by Mazzini. Mazzinian theory before the war of 1848–49 was based on the proposition that small groups of dedicated patriots could enter enemy territory – or be encouraged to emerge from within the populace – and start an insurrection; once they had seized power, popular bands would then emerge spontaneously to meet the inevitable counter-attack. This democratic theory of warfare received a major setback in the war of 1848–49, when the peasantry played, or were permitted to play, no significant role in the military actions.[3] However, the democratic theory of warfare lived on after the failure of the first war of Risorgimento.

The pre-1848 Sardinian army had been trained and equipped to fight a defensive war against France. Inadequate planning, lack of reserves,

political aims which focused more clearly on Charles Albert's Lombard
ally than upon his Austrian enemy, a complete absence of military objectives, a chaotic command system and inadequate leadership all combined
to cast the long shadow of defeat over what the doyen of Italian military
historians has rightly called 'the war of lost opportunities'.[4] On 25 July
1848 the Piedmontese army was overwhelmed at the battle of Custoza,
and the first round of the contest against Austria came to an end sixteen
days later. Charles Albert unwisely tried again, encouraged by Piedmontese democrats, launching his weakened army against the Austrians
on 20 March 1849. Three days later the Austrian victory at Novara sealed
his fate. On the eve of the battle Charles Albert abdicated in favor of his
son, Victor Emmanuel II, and three days later an armistice ended the war.

Out of the failure of 1848–49 was born a military literature of great
richness and subtlety which carried Italy along on its own path in strategic
thought during the middle years of the nineteenth century. The direct
consequence of unique political circumstances, it analysed and debated
the social and political aims of war in both theoretical and practical terms.
Behind it lay the desire to determine the great objective: the degree to
which Italy should be created as a popular, democratic republic or a
conservative, authoritarian monarchy. Clausewitzian thought may well
have appeared irrelevant to Italians precisely because, when they were
introduced to it, they recognized a pattern of thinking with which – in one
respect – they were already familiar.

The first major contribution to the strategico-political debate which
raged on for the next two decades was Carlo Pisacane's *Guerra com-
battuta in Italia negli anni 1848–49* (1851). Coming from the pen of a
socialist of republican tendencies, the work looked beyond the incompetence of generals and blamed the failure of the war of 1848–49 on the
Piedmontese authorities' dislike of the republican movement and fear of
popular insurrection. Pisacane was equally critical of Mazzinian theories
and of Garibaldi, who had taken a leading part in the defence of the
Roman republic against the French in 1849 and whose tactics he criticized
on the grounds that they were not informed by a 'strategic concept'.
Pisacane argued that mass warfare was necessary at the earliest phase of
an insurrection and urged the creation of a nation-in-arms and of citizen-
soldiers. What Pisacane wanted was the combination of elite and the
mass of the people in a military form which would ensure the creation
of a democratic Italy.[5] Typically, military theory had become deeply
enmeshed in contemporary political problems.

While writers engaged one another over whether the best form of
warfare through which to unite Italy was a popular insurrection sustained
by a regular force, a traditional war fought with regular troops alone, or a
joint war of regulars and volunteer militia, the official tactical manuals

of the years 1848–59 reflected an important change in thinking. The Jominian conception of tactics was still evident in such works as Ulloa's *Dell'arte della guerra* (1851),* but the Regulations on the Secondary Operations of War published in 1855 shifted Italian tactical thinking from the geometric to the topographic. Its tone was set by its early definitions: 'Terrain is all' and 'terrain determines tactics'.[6] Basic ingredients of the attack were mass, surprise, the concentration of force and cover for the flanks. Like the attack, the defense depended on locating the physical key to any position.

The war of 1859, for which the swollen Piedmontese army was once again ill-prepared, was dominated by the bloody battles of Magenta, Solferino and San Martino. Napoleon III operated on the basis of a plan suggested to him by Jomini, and the French army was employed by its leaders in a series of suicidal mass frontal assaults with the objective of getting to close quarters as soon as possible in order to circumvent the superiority of the Austrian Lorenz rifle.[7] All Europe rapidly became a prey to the apparent success of the French tactics of 1859: Prussian maneuvers in 1861 and 1863 featured frontal assaults by battalion columns and the Austrians proved successful with the new technique in the Danish war of 1864.[8] To its own experience and observation of France's successful methods the new Italian army created in 1861 would add a powerful intellectual stimulus with the posthumous publication in 1860 of Carlo De Cristoferis' *Che cosa sia la guerra*.

De Cristoferis, who had fought in the campaign of 1848, attended the French Imperial General Staff School and soldiered with the Anglo-Italian Legion before returning to be killed serving in Garibaldi's forces in 1859, had cómpleted his book in August 1857. The work, which rapidly went through four editions, moved a step away from the Jominian concentration on the mechanics of war. It started from the proposition that there was only one basic military principle which offered a sure guide in all circumstances – the principle of mass. De Cristoferis regarded this neither as a theory nor as a doctrine, but essentially as a method. To put it into operation required neither superior culture nor superior intelligence, but energy of character and determination. In details De Cristoferis was somewhat confusing, arguing for mass 'whether of numbers or of quality'.[9]

One of the key elements of the Clausewitzian 'system' as it was perceived throughout Europe in the second half of the nineteenth century – mass – had been firmly implanted in Italian thought as a consequence of domestic political turmoil and of the struggle by patriots of differing beliefs to shape the future structure of Italy. Nowhere was this more clear than in Carlo Pisacane's posthumous *Ordinamento dell'esercito italiano*, also published in 1860. A convinced socialist, Pisacane had been persuaded to attempt a Mazzinian-style insurrection in southern Italy in 1857 and had been killed in the fiasco that followed his landing at Sapri. His book was essentially a program to introduce a Swiss-style militia army as the middle way between socially-repressive barrack armies and bands of uncoordinated and individualistic partisans. The basic principles of strategy were two: to conduct the mass towards strategic points; and to take possession of these points, deceiving the enemy as to one's own line of march and falling unexpectedly on his line of operations. In tactics as in strategy the work was shot through with Jominian dogmatism; nowhere in Pisacane's work is there any trace of Clausewitzian ideas of total war or absolute war.[10]

The years between 1860 and 1866 were hectic ones for the Italian army as it sought to resolve the problems successively presented by the absorption of the armies of central Italy, the Bourbon army of the kingdom of Naples and – most intractable of all because of the egalitarianism they represented – Garibaldi's armies. Thereafter the prospect of a third round with Austria to gain the Veneto made urgent organizational demands. The consequence was a doctrinal immobility which resulted, according to the most recent commentator, 'more from prudence than from cultural origins'.[11] The war of 1866, with a leadership as confused as that of the war of 1859, produced a catastrophic defeat for the Italian army at the battle of Custoza on 24 June 1866. With Garibaldi doing well against the Austrians in the Trentino, perhaps the only consolation for the regular army was that it was not unique in its record of failure: on 20 July Admiral Persano led the Italian fleet to defeat at the hands of its Austrian rivals at the battle of Lissa.

Among the reforms which followed the war of 1866 were the introduction of a new breech-loading rifle and the creation in 1867 of the *Scuola superiore di guerra* in imitation of the Prussian War Academy; but perhaps most significant were the regulations of 1869. Modelled on the Prussian, they paid more attention to firepower and put more emphasis on individual marksmanship than hitherto; they also stressed mobility, elasticity, and flexibility. They represent an excellent example of the way in which Italian military doctrine developed during the nineteenth century on the basis of pragmatics: to terrain as a commanding tactical factor was now added firepower. Although the shock assault remained the culminating act of battle it was now approached more cautiously than before.[12]

The events of 1870, which made Rome the capital of Italy and completed the program of the early nationalists, had a profound importance for Italy; but there existed no ready consensus as to what had brought the Prussians victory. Liberal reformists and the Left talked in terms of the effectiveness of the Prussian system of conscription and the value of popular energies when correctly harnessed; conservatives highlighted the principles of obedience which characterized the semi-feudal Prussian state; soldiers emphasized the importance of Prussian organization and pointed to the critical influence of the general staff. Enrico Consenz, who was destined to become Italy's first Chief of the General Staff in 1882, believed that the main explanation for Moltke's success lay in the dominating direction which he imparted to the military machine:

> There was sound discipline, a fine body of officers of excellent spirit, intelligent students and practitioners of the art of war; there was knowledge of the country which had to be crossed, there was studied preparation, adapted to the circumstances, there was mutual confidence between everybody, in sum there was a great force of resistance and of character.[13]

The influence of Prussian military organization was to be strongly apparent in the military reforms which followed. The seminal ideas which lay at the heart of Prussian war-making had very much less impact on Italian military thought.

The seal of approval for the Italian organizational reforms of the 1870s which replicated, within limits, the Prussian conscript army was given by Niccola Marselli, the foremost Italian military writer of the age, who has been termed the 'spiritual' father of the Italian army after 1870.[14] Born in Naples in 1832, Marselli had been trained in the old Bourbon army of the kingdom of the Two Sicilies; by 1870 his intellectual power was widely recognized, and his reputation was cemented with a study of the Franco-Prussian war published in 1872. In it, he urged that Italy apply the substance of the Prussian system to herself but not its secondary form: differences in the social and political structures of the two countries made it impossible for Italy to implement a full system of conscription. Marselli argued that the real cause of Prussia's triumph was less her military system than her civilization: 'Without the reform of men, that of institutions is in vain'.[15]

Marselli had visited Germany in 1855 and become acquainted with Hegelianism. Then or at some subsequent time he encountered Clausewitz' *Vom Kriege*, and it was he who first put the great philosopher of war before the Italian public in 1875 with the publication of the two-volume *La guerra e la sua storia*. Marselli acknowledged that Clausewitz was 'the greatest philosopher of war, who had revealed to his fellow-countrymen the true secret of Napoleonic war, who had put in unmistakable terms the supreme importance of tactics, and who had considered moral strength as prominent'.[16] Marselli, however, had become deeply influenced by the current of logical positivism which dominated Italian thought during the latter part of the nineteenth century, and he was therefore not prepared to accept that the human element upon which Clausewitz laid such stress was immune from regulation according to scientific laws. He considered Clausewitz too ready to leave the free action of the mind as unanalyzable when scientific investigation had bypassed this block: 'That which seemed to us yesterday to be arbitrary, today seems determined by causes which make it what it is.'[17] For Marselli it was no longer permissable to say that the moral world, being free, was not susceptible to laws; merely that, for the most part, they were as yet unknown.

In interpreting Clausewitz through what was a distorting mirror, Marselli set out to establish whether particular Clausewitzian norms had a greater or lesser degree of precision and to correct certain definitions. His aim was to enlarge the sphere of calculation and diminish that of chance. Because Marselli believed war to be a science as well as an art, and therefore made up of immutable principles, it was typical of him that he should claim that 'Given a weapon, a stretch of ground and the position of the enemy and you could deduce from them the appropriate tactical course'.[18] In claiming that 'War is and must be dominated by politics', he seemed to accept the basis of Clausewitz' most often misquoted dictum; but he hastened to add that politics ruled in war not like an absolute sovereign but rather like a constitutional queen, respecting the needs of the entity she ruled.

The general principles of strategy proclaimed by Marselli were not original; rather he abstracted them from a variety of sources. From Jomini he took the notion of superiority at the decisive point; from De Cristoferis the idea that victory would be decided by the shock of the mass; from many sources the concept of operating against an enemy's line of retreat. The eclectic nature of the work – which Marselli admitted was one of intuition and of flashes of illumination – meant that it lacked the internal consistency which was necessary to resolve key problems: thus he got locked into a severe tangle over the 'decisive point' and was never able to define it satisfactorily. His aim was to produce

> a *Vom Kriege* of the new positivist era, a re-examined and improved *Vom Kriege*, or at least something which would form the basis of an Italian conception of war which would have an autonomous existence with respect to foreign doctrines.[19]

In this he could be said to have been only too successful.

The lack of a philosophical basis to Italian theories of war is clearly apparent in the history of tactical doctrine up to the First World War. Based as it was on pragmatic considerations, it sent through a series of major changes which can only have confused both trainers and trained. Infantry training regulations went through five different versions between 1868 and 1907 before being dropped in 1914; and cavalry regulations went through seven editions between 1869 and 1914.[20] The first set of regulations on the employment of major tactical units in war since 1870 – the *Norme generali per la divisione di fanteria in combattimento* – published in July 1883 was shot through with a belief in the predominance of firepower and stressed the value of field fortifications; French commentators evidently found it far too defensive-minded, and pointed out that it laid insufficient stress on counter-attacks as the only means by which to produce a favorable result when on the defensive.[21] Two years later it was withdrawn and replaced by general regulations for the employment of infantry, artillery, and cavalry in combat. The new regulations strongly condemned passive resistance in defense and insisted that the defensive could never be considered as anything but a preparation for the offensive.[22]

Mounting concern with 'military science' in these years was stimulated less by any spirit of philosophical enquiry than by the realization that Germany used this science and must be met by it.[23] However, the deficiencies of Italian military thought at the key point of passage from conception to execution can be gauged from the foreword to the 1885 regulations, which stated that they

> must be understood as having the character of mere guides, it being indispensable that the commander retains full freedom of action in choosing the manner of execution which in each concrete case will best lead to the attainment of the object, taking into account the state of the terrain, the order of march, and the various circumstances which can influence the unfolding of an action.[24]

As a recipe to encourage individualism, this could not be bettered. It certainly stood in stark contrast to the contemporary French *Instruction sur le combat*, in which the engagement was rigidly controlled on a minute-by-minute basis.

The regulations of 1883 and 1885 had been prepared under the eye of the first chief of the Italian General Staff, Enrico Cosenz. It is not untypical of the development of Italian military thought that the shift to the offensive which Cosenz oversaw was reversed by a single event – albeit one of stunning magnitude. On 1 March 1896 an Italian army under General Baratieri, outnumbered and out-gunned by its Ethiopian opponents, crashed to defeat at the battle of Adua. Addressing the departing class of the *Scuola di guerra* five months later, its commander, General Pedotti, blamed the defeat on moral indiscipline. Among the undesirable manifestations of this indiscipline were individualism, a tendency to act independently, an excessive desire to distinguish oneself, and a thirst for rewards and decorations.[25]

In fact, Adua provided hostile critics of the idea of the general staff with ideal ammunition against the new institution, not least because two of the four brigade commanders serving under Baratieri, Generals Albertone and Dabormida, who were credited with much of the blame for the disaster, were star products of the *Scuola di guerra*. An Italian tendency to stand aloof from the ideas of Clausewitz was reinforced by the fact that Dabormida had been a disciple of Moltke and had translated *Tactical Themes* into Italian.

In defense of the *Scuola di guerra* it was quickly pointed out that the spirit of initiative and the idea of the *offensive a outrance* were embedded at the heart of the regulations and that both had been given excessive veneration in books, military colleges, and all parts of military life for years.[26] Also General Carlo Corsi, himself a former head of the college, pointed out that commanders of the school had had no part in the compilation of the regulations.[27]

Adua and its aftermath were important for the history of Italian military thought in two respects. First, the supposition that responsibility for the defeat lay with the *Scuola di guerra* and the General Staff weakened those institutions. Thus prospects were diminished for the development of an acknowledged authority which might create and transmit a military doctrine based firmly on a clear philosophical concept of war. Other factors were at work to weaken the military establishment, not least the unwillingness of successive ministers of war to give up their dominating positions within Italian military bureaucracy. Together they ensured that Cosenz' successors never had the power accorded to German, French, or even British Chiefs of the General Staff. Nor did they play any part in the formulation of war policy at cabinet level. It is noteworthy that a rare contemporary citation of Clausewitz – in this case, of his dictum that war develops in the womb of politics – prefaced a list of the requirements for a successful war policy. These requirements included the integration of political aims and military methods, foreseeing and preparing for likely conflicts, and acting with decision.[28] The advice went unheeded.

Second, a widespread acknowledgement that too much dash was the deep deficiency of the Italian officer reinforced a cultural preoccupation with the supposed volatility of the raw material from which Italian armies had to be constructed. Character training was singled out by the commandant of the *Scuola di guerra* at the start of the 1898 course as its most important function, and whenever the army showed a predisposition to become preoccupied with what was termed the 'mechanical' part of a senior officer's duties it was sharply reminded of where its real task lay.[29] A sensitivity to critiques of Italian temperament and military culture published in foreign journals such as *Militar-Wochenblatt* reinforced this trait.[30]

The early years of the twentieth century were confusing ones for the authorities charged with hammering out tactical and strategic doctrine, for no sooner had the Boer war taught the lesson that firepower was the dominant element on the modern battlefield than the Japanese won battles by frontal assault on defended positions.[31] Regulations for the employment of major units in war – *Norme generali per l'impiego tattico delle grandi unita di guerra* – issued in April 1903 demonstrate the complete failure of Clausewitzian concepts to penetrate Italian military thinking. They also demonstrate Italy's avoidance of the neo-Clausewitzian excesses of Foch: the focus is on the mechanics of laying out the march and of such varied actions as retreats, night operations, and mountain operations. Column commanders are cautioned to halt and wait for order when the advance guard has contacted the enemy.[32] The chasm which separated the Italians from Clausewitz was plainly evident in the approbation accorded to Moltke's announcement to Bluntschli, in December 1881, that he could not accept the annihilation of an enemy's military forces as the sole aim in war, but that all his resources – finance, railways, food supplies, even prestige – must be attacked.[33]

New regulations – *Norme generali per l'impiego delle grandi unita di guerra* – were issued provisionally in 1910. A foreword by the then chief of the General Staff, Alberto Pollio, indicates the absence of a philosophical basis for strategic thought – an absence that could all too easily open the way for another Adua:

> In war, either principles which are valid in all cases do not exist or, if they do, they are of such a general kind as to be of very little use in practice because their application is too much influenced by the varying circumstances in which events unwind.[34]

The regulations amounted to a plea for common sense. Pollio acknowledged the importance of offensive spirit but maintained that it must be firmly controlled. Careful treatment was given to the counter-offensive and the defensive as well as the pursuit and the retreat. Finally, in considering the prepared battle, Pollio stated what the target should be: the enemy's lines of communication.[35] The Jominian influence still lived in Italian thought.

II. MILITARY HISTORY AND DOCTRINE: 1914–18

On 27 July 1914, as Italy awoke to the fact that Vienna intended to 'go all the way' over the Serbian crisis, Luigi Cadorna was installed as the fifth chief of the Italian General Staff. He was very aggressively-minded, and has been charged with introducing the following year regulations which reflected an exaggerated faith in frontal attack and which were entirely out of tune with modern warfare.[36] This charge is not entirely fair, for the thrust of Italian military thought had already begun to shift before he came into office. Combat regulations published in 1913 under Pollio, for example, suggested that the new portable modern arms actually favored the attack rather than the defense because their use improved the morale of the common soldier. This mental resilience was held to be stronger in the attacker than in the defender. Successful attacks depended upon the successful combination of movement and firepower up to the moment of the assault, when speed and the *arme blanche* came into their own.[37] This shift in thinking is noticeably less Jominian in tone, for the enemy infantry were now the central object of the attack.

The fact that on the eve of the First World War Italian military thought was slipping into a posture more akin to that of France was less the consequence of a belated absorption of the lessons of Clausewitz and his publicizers than of a changing conception of how the Italian army would be employed in war. Ever since the early 1870s, when the first major strategic appreciations were drawn up, the dominant thread running through Italian policy had been the primacy of the defensive; to this end, vast sums were spent to fortify first the western and then the eastern land frontier, as well as to protect Rome and other major cities. After 1882, when Italy joined Germany and Austria-Hungary to form the Triple Alliance, the possibility of Italian troops operating alongside those of their German ally on the Rhine became the subject of intermittent but continued discussions; however, although this idea was revived in the spring of 1914, planning for it always seems to have been a little half-hearted, and in any case Italian neutrality ended it.[38] The defensive strategic assumptions behind Italy's continental policy acted as a further barrier against the penetration of Clausewitzian ideas: as displayed in late nineteenth-century German operational doctrine, and in the French 'rediscovery' of Clausewitz and Napoleon, the stress on the offensive which apparently dominated *Vom Kriege* was mostly irrelevant to the strategic-political situation in which Italy found herself in the forty years before the outbreak of the First World War.

The extent of the gap between the written word of the regulations and the working suppositions of the high command was clearly in evidence when Pollio led a General Staff ride in 1911 which had as its scenario a joint Swiss–Austrian attack on Italy between Lake Como and Lake Garda. In summing up the results of the war game, Pollio had no doubt that the lessons of this type of campaign offered the best guide to the future employment of the army in war:

> Given the state of development of every country's fixed defenses it is to be expected that any war will begin with repeated attacks upon and defence of reinforced positions around a central point which will have been prepared, or perhaps only studied, in peacetime.[39]

This was a far cry from the sweeping maneuvers which dominated much European military thought and policy in 1914.

Cadorna had been in office scarcely three weeks when he issued new tactical regulations stressing frontal attacks, which were, he claimed, less difficult than they had been made to appear. Then, on 25 February 1915, he produced the infamous *Attaco frontale e ammaestramento tattico*, which laid even heavier stress on the offensive and suggested that it now had a more favorable chance of success than in the past. Although based on the suicidal proposition that the conditions of trench warfare which prevailed on the Western Front were unique and would only replicate themselves on the Italian front in isolated instances and over limited regions, Cadorna's ideas did carry with them a greater element of constraint than had marked previous military doctrine. For the attack to succeed, coordination was essential; accordingly Cadorna de-emphasized 'tactical sense', stressing the importance at all levels of the mechanism of maneuver, for which he demanded careful training.[40]

The sources of Cadorna's theories of war, which were to cost Italy dearly, have never been systematically explored. He was certainly very well informed by both sides about the shape which the war of attrition was assuming in France and Flanders.[41] However, all that he seems to have concluded from this was that stalemate was the consequence of a failure of will. He was far more dogmatic than his predecessor, and far readier to be schematic than the more ductile Pollio. The suggestion that he had whole-heartedly and uncritically accepted French doctrine is difficult to prove.[42] It is equally possible that his regulations were *sui generis*, the produce of a mind which was at once aggressive and impatient. What seems certain is that the hidden hand of Clausewitz was not the fount of the new military thought.

From May 1915 until the battle of Caporetto in October 1917 Italian military thought was in a continual state of flux as it sought to respond to the unexpected conditions on the battlefront. In the first year of the war the high command circulated summaries of French, German and Austro-Hungarian practice in such matters as field works, inviting the recipients to select the parts they deemed most useful to them. Then, with the introduction respectively in April and July 1916 of new criteria for the employment of artillery and infantry, the stress was shifted from conquering enemy positions to destroying the enemy's physical strength, using looser formations in attack and giving light, medium, and heavy artillery separate tasks.[43] A stream of orders went out from Cadorna's headquarters about every aspect of defensive and offensive battle: many contradicted one another, and most were ignored by army commanders who adopted their own tactical practices – as the whole thrust of Italian military doctrine during the latter years of the nineteenth century and the early years of the twentieth century had encouraged them to do.[44]

The shock of Caporetto, at which the Germans unveiled their new penetration tactics, and the pell-mell retreat to the Piave which followed meant that it was not until January 1918 that the new commander-in-chief, General Armando Diaz, could devote himself to the problems posed by deficient Italian doctrine. A circular of 2 January 1918 which went out over his name publicized British and French methods of trench ogranization and invited commanders to apply all possible lessons with the adaptations 'imposed by our organization, which is a little different, and by our less ample means, especially respecting artillery'.[45] Thereafter Diaz began to introduce a series of intelligent reforms based on an accurate analysis of the deficiencies of his predecessor's system: defenses were arrayed in greater depth, artillery was echeloned back according to its range, and much greater use of air in spotting coming attacks by charting the movement of men and supplies behind the lines was enjoined.

The success of the new tactical system was demonstrated in the defense of the Piave against Austrian attack 15–23 June 1918, the result chiefly of intelligent anticipation of enemy moves and of effective use of the artillery.[46] As a direct result of this Diaz circulated on 4 July 1918 *Esperienze della recente battaglia* in which he laid down for the first time the new principles governing successful attack: Violent, rapid, and directed against distant objectives and weak point, it should begin with assaults by select infantry units backed by mobile artillery, to be followed by main enveloping assaults. Specialized assault troops – *Arditi* – had been created in 1917, first as companies and then as separate battalions to spearhead attacks. In September 1918 the Italians introduced what were termed 'T' battalions, which included *Arditi* platoons armed with flame-throwers and other troops heavily armed with automatic rifles, light and heavy machine guns, 37mm cannon, and mortars. These new units played a major role in the successful battle of Vittorio Veneto in November 1918 with which Italy closed the First World War.

III. MILITARY HISTORY AND DOCTRINE: 1918–39

In respect to land warfare during the First World War, Italy had largely been content to sit back and see what others would do. In naval warfare she was equally unadventurous. But in respect to air power, where she had shown the way with innovative use of aerial reconnaissance in the Libyan war of 1911–12, Italian experience during the First World War was to stimulate a powerful and original strategic philosophy. To explain the continued neglect of Clausewitz in Italy in the years following the end of the First World War, Giulio Douhet's imaginative theory of independent air power is of considerable importance.

Douhet had outlined the basis of his theory as early as January 1916: The strength of modern armies was a function of the industrial and commercial capacity of their parent countries, and the first objective of air power should be to 'proceed to the systematic destruction of the enemy nation's means of production, its wealth, its resources, its morale'.[47] Before the war's end others, among them Colonel Pentimalli, were also stressing the importance of air power. And in 1923, the year in which Mussolini signalled his interest in air power by becoming the first High Commissioner for Military and Civil Aviation, one enthusiastic advocate of the new weapon was suggesting its inevitable stimulus to inter-service cooperation:

> A future war will be characterized by the employment on the very vastest scale of the new air power, capable of action over land and over sea; and as the importance of aerial action increases, so the unity of land and sea warfare will be realized.[48]

Douhet argued that air power was the perfect weapon for Italy because it would enable her to bypass her shortage of raw materials, her weak arms industry, and her vulnerable geographical situation. However, the energy invested in the new air arm by the Fascist regime sprang primarily from its publicity value, as well as from pressure from the PNF (Fascist Party) for a thoroughly Fascist branch of the armed forces. Mussolini may have been the more ready to encourage his airmen because Douhet had been one of those who had reassured him of the army's benevolent neutrality on the eve of the march on Rome.

The founder of the Italian air force, Italo Balbo, at first under-secretary of state and then minister at the Air Ministry from 1926–33, was wedded to certain aspects of Douhetism. He recognized that Italy's lack of resources prevented her from developing powerful land forces, and he thought the new theories justified strategic independence. Despite his apparent acceptance of Douhet's writings, he implicitly admitted that no doctrine of air deployment existed: first, by initiating a policy – continued by his successors – of building medium bombers needing fighter escorts rather than the heavy strategic bombers Douhet's theory demanded; and second, by encouraging a rival theorist, Mecozzi, who saw the most effective role for air power as being ground-support operations and who argued for the construction of fighter-bombers.[49]

Douhet's theories were attractive for a variety of reasons, many of which had little or nothing to do with their intrinsic logic. Above all, they were Italian. Their existence and their propagation helped create the belief that, under Fascism, military thought was at least abreast of the times, and therefore had no need to go abroad for enlightenment. Although they were not themselves convinced Douhetists, the officers of the Italian air force did export the new doctrine – with disastrous results. In the search for hard currency, Italy began to train Nationalist China's airmen in 1933, with the result that unprotected Chinese bombers came badly to grief against the Japanese in 1937.[50]

Early post-war developments in Italian military thought did little or nothing to open the way for an exploration of the Clausewitzian roots of European military thought. Pietro Maravigna, in his *Storia dell'arte militare moderna* (1923), claimed that neither the passage of time nor material inventions had had any substantial influence on the 'essence and fundamental regulatory principles of the conduct of war'.[51] However, his claim that aviation had made no significant change other than to improve observation probably did not make his basic proposition any more acceptable to a regime besotted by the dazzling publicity potential of Balbo's new air force. Nor had positivism been dissolved as a barrier to Italian reception of Clausewitzian thought. In *La guerra come scienza positiva ed economica* (1933) – a work which postulated war as one of two branches of the sociology of collective conflict, the other being economics, and which advocated the application to war of utilitarian economic methods – General Giulio Cravero baldly claimed that the possibility existed of 'scientifically systematizing' war.[52]

Air power had its own theories and stood in no need of outside support. On land, the politics of strategic thought acted as an equally impervious barrier to German influence. A major obstacle to innovation during the inter-war years was the traditionalism of most of the army high command, which was tied to the concept of a mass infantry arm and First World War-style attacks. In part this was the consequence of geographical determinism: as an early writer on armored warfare put it, Italy's next war would 'almost certainly begin in the zone of high mountains where the use of tanks is unanimously judged to be impossible or of little use'.[53] In the late 1920s and early 1930s, under Gazzera (war minister 1929–33) and Bonzani (chief of army staff 1929–34), the army was firmly in the hands of men who took an Alpine view and who opposed mechanization, inter-service cooperation, and tactical innovation. When, in 1931, Mussolini encouraged criticism of this dominant strand of thinking his motivation was entirely political – an opportunity for the PNF to relieve pent-up grievances – and included no conviction about the technical validity of the arguments.[54]

In 1933 and 1934 works published by Ottavio Zoppi and Visconti Prasca argued for a war of movement with air and artillery in the main combat roles and fast tanks in use to open the front for cavalry and infantry. These ideas may have owed something to foreign thinkers: at that time the writings of Patton, Fuller, and Liddell Hart were being reviewed and discussed in Italian journals.[55] They owed little or nothing to Clausewitz. Combat regulations published in 1935 reflected this trend in military thought by emphasizing maneuver and the offensive through lightning assaults after surprise air attacks; and in 1936 the outgoing army chief of staff, Baistrocchi, put forward proposals to motorize 12 infantry divisions and three assault brigades. Not too much should be read into these developments, however. Tanks were still regarded as infantry support weapons, and combat experience cast doubt on their general efficacy: at the battle of Dembeguina in December 1935 a detachment of six light tanks had been lost after they – and then the heads of some of their crew – were cut off; and Italian tanks had been effectively repulsed at the battle of Guadalajara in April 1937. The so-called doctrine of the *guerra di rapido corso* ('lightning war') developed after 1936 by General Pariani was specifically designed for combat in North Africa, not northern Italy. The instrument which would put the new style of warfare into operation was to be a mass motorized army, but Italy lacked the industrial base necessary to create it.

The politics of military thought had two important features which help to explain the continuing failure of Clausewitzian ideas to penetrate the Italian military mind at this time. First, military leaders were governed by extreme military conservatism, against which the few innovators fought largely in vain. Machine warfare was opposed by the majority, who still thought in terms of mass warfare and who regarded tanks as elitist: Vallori called armored warfare 'un-Fascist and even un-Italian'.[56] Second and no less important, there remained – even among the 'modernizers' – a deep-seated conviction that non-Italian ideas were irrelevant. Thus Pariani himself could write on the eve of the Second World War:

> Nothing can be more harmful than to adopt the doctrines of others: it would be like pretending that a uniform which gave a magnificent presence to a well-built cuirassier could give the same *bella figura* to an obese pigmy.[57]

IV. CLAUSEWITZ APPEARS IN ITALY

The credit for belatedly bringing Clausewitz to Italy belongs to Colonel Emilio Canevari. In an early work inspired by Pareto, *Il metodo scientifico nello studio della guerra* (1922), Canevari distinguished between 'science' and 'doctrine' of war: the former deepened knowledge of the facts in order to permit the formulation of theories, while the latter aimed to produce solutions to practical problems. This was an important distinction in the theoretical approach to war. In 1930 Canevari followed this with *Clausewitz e la guerra odierna*. The first volume of what was intended to be a two-volume work, this contained a brief sketch of Clausewitz' life, a digest of his ideas and an analysis of his place in European military thought. The second volume was to comprise the first Italian translation of all eight books of *Vom Kriege*.

Canevari claimed that a knowledge of Clausewitz and of those Italian writers who had derived their thought from him – including Marselli and Pollio – had enabled him to understand military history, and that his conviction of the importance of Clausewitzian thought had been confirmed after the war when reading Hindenburg's *Aus meinem Leben* (1920) and Palat's *La philosophie de la Guerre* (1919).[58] He suggested that it was particularly important for Italians to have the ideas of Clausewitz as a basis for the military analysis of method, doctrine and practice because of Italy's situation in Europe and in the world. Unlike his fellow critics, he derided the attempt to re-examine war by gathering what he termed 'fragmentary experiences of the world war or of the period immediately preceding it'; war had changed because the socio-political conditions had changed.[59] In the same year as Canevari's innovative study, the first volume of translated extracts from *Vom Kriege* was published in Italy.[60]

Canevari's pioneering work apparently stimulated no one to follow up the lead he had provided – partly perhaps because the translation which was announced as forming the second part of the work was much delayed. Thus in the preface to a series of four articles summarizing the basis of Clausewitzian thought published in 1939, he remarked that Clausewitz' ideas were still almost completely unknown in Italy. To buttress this he quoted Marshal Giardino who, after reading one of his books, had written 'I have the impression that I never heard talk of this Clausewitz before, either at the *Scuola di guerra* or from the many people who mentioned him ... in vain' [*sic*].[61] Canevari then drew out skillfully and accurately the essential components of the Clausewitzian method and its implications, as is demonstrated in his translation of the central dictum of *Vom Kriege*: 'War is not only a means, it is a political instrument. It is nothing else than the continuation of politics involving the intermixing of other means, and not an independent thing.'[62] Perhaps with an eye to Italy's current political circumstances, he declared that the greatest coefficient of military success resided in 'the will of a government which is strong and determined'.[63]

In laying out the essentials of Clausewitz, Canevari reminded his readers that the wars in which Italy had been engaged in 1848, 1855, 1859 and 1866 had been limited wars but that others – notably the American Civil War, the Franco-Prussian War and the Russo-Turkish War of 1878 – had been closer to Clausewitzian 'total war'. He brought out – as pre-war French commentators had not – the range of methods which could be used to achieve the aim in war, including destruction of the enemy forces to the necessary degree, the occupation of territory, and political activities to weaken the enemy internally and externally; and he anatomized the different types of battle, underlining the fact that, to acquire its special strength, the defensive must at least provisionally renounce the positive aim.[64] In four brief articles, the last of which appeared in June 1939, Canevari had provided an exceptionally penetrating summary of the main concepts of Clausewitz and yet managed to remain true to the master's intentions.

Canevari's efforts to introduce Clausewitz to an Italian audience failed primarily because of the high command's traditionalism. But that failure also owed more than a little to the politics of military policy. In July 1931, with Mussolini's encouragement, General Grazioli published an article in *Nuova Antologia* advocating motorization and mechanization as the way to avoid another war of attrition, and Canevari went into print anonymously to support him. This brought him indirectly to the attention of the military intelligence service SIM, who tried unsuccessfully to identify the author of the book he had written. If this were not enough to put the military traditionalists against him, Canevari got involved in the veiled press campaign run by ex-party secretary Roberto Farinacci in September 1933 as part of a plot to unseat Marshal Badoglio as chief of staff of the armed forces and put Italo Balbo in his place. The move failed and Balbo was hastily whisked off to govern Libya, but Canevari's known sympathies with party plotters can only have stiffened resistance to his writings within the conservative circles which still dominated the army.

Canevari's long-promised translation of *Vom Kriege* – the first in Italian – finally appeared in 1942.[65] The original intention of the authors had been to publish full translations only of Books I, II and VIII and certain chapters of Books III to VI, but they were persuaded to publish an integral edition by the General Staff Historical Office, under whose auspices the work was completed. The only portion customarily reproduced in German editions which was omitted from the first Italian edition was the memorandum on the 'Essential Principles of the Conduct of War' summarizing the lessons given to the crown prince of Prussia in 1812 – on the grounds that the major part of this work was contained within the main body of the text. Apparently little had changed in Italian military thinking; the foreword complains that dogmatic and schematic ideas of tactics and strategy, similar to those propounded by Jomini, Rustow, and Foch, still had wide circulation.[66]

In the same year a selection from all eight books of *Vom Kriege* in 190 pages was published.[67] Doubtless reflecting the uneasy state of Italo-German relations the editor remarked in his introduction: 'That which the critical exclusivism of German authors attributes to a Hegelian influence is instead, indisputably, a product of the thought of Machiavelli.'[68] This conclusion, though no doubt comforting had been reached before, and not by an Italian.[69] In his foreword the editor pointed to the value of Clausewitz' work as lying in his logical thought, his rigorously scientific procedure and his search for the philosophical content of every historical fact, but his closing observation that 'Victory comes from the application of the best rule' suggests that he fundamentally misunderstood *Vom Kriege*. A final and even more abbreviated edition published in 1943 was the last of the four versions of Clausewitz' work to be published in Italian before the end of the Second World War.[70]

The cultural preoccupations of a newly-unified state are among the most important factors explaining Italian insulation from Clausewitzian thought in the nineteenth and early twentieth centuries. As far as relations between army and nation were concerned, the predominant emphasis was on using the opportunity of military service to overcome geographical divisions in Italian society rather than upon creating a ready and effective machine for war; thus conscripts from two separate regions were intermixed in every unit and then posted to a third region. This was so clumsy a system for mobilization purposes that it had to be altered in the 1890s. Much stress was laid by military commentators on the supreme importance of man as the most potent instrument of war;[71] but this did not lead to any significant analysis of the moral factor in war. It was the political rather than the philosophical significance of the moral attributes of men which preoccupied Italians.

Italian traditions of military thought helped to insulate Italy from *Vom Kriege*. A sensitivity to real or imagined national slights helped to foster a strong national pattern of military thinking which precluded Clausewitz. As one critic put it, Italians first considered military questions on the level of general military validity and then skipped over organic or technical issues to concentrate on the financial aspects.[72] Because Italian military thought lacked a solid intellectual foundation, on the eve of the First World war the Italian army had a set of up-dated regulations but no true military doctrine.[73] However, it is perhaps an exculpation of Italian military thinkers that, in 1935, Benedetto Croce chided his fellow philosophers for their 'provincialism' and 'unintelligent specialization' in ignoring Clausewitz. Although undoubtedly more or less antiquated as regarded its technical element, *Vom Kriege*, Croce thought, was still very valuable for the thought it contained.[74]

The absence of a coherent philosophical substructure to Italian military thought was partly a consequence of the way in which the higher levels of the Italian military operated. The General Staff, dating only from 1882, was a small, closed body which was much resented by other officers in the army because of the privileges it enjoyed in respect to promotions and conditions of service. The lack of a General Staff tradition helped allow individual generals' opinions on military matters to carry undue weight – as when Pianell put all his influence behind the argument that forts and permanent fortifications still retained their value despite advances in artillery.[75] For historical, structural and other reasons, no coherent and generally acknowledged 'school of thought' existed in Italy in these years.

After 1922, different factors were at work to continue, albeit along different paths, Italian strategic autonomy. Douhet's uniquely Italian theory of modern warfare – one which soon generated much interest outside Italy – met all the needs of the new state. Politically it conformed to the image of technological adventurousness Fascism liked to project; it also catered to the party's wish that at least one branch of the services should be independent of the monarchy; and strategically it seemed to resolve the problem of Italy's shortage of raw materials. The importance of what may be termed cultural ecology in giving birth to theory was again demonstrated in the 1930s with Pariani's ideas of 'lightning war'. In both cases, the new and home-grown ideas had to stand alongside a powerful conservatism which hindered their full implementation but saw no need to compete – certainly not by borrowing from Germany.

Italy fared no better without Clausewitz than many countries which fell under his influence. She too went to war in 1915 with an offensive doctrine which cost her dearly, although her geographical situation may have exacerbated the difficulty of attacking entrenched troops who were protected by barbed wire and machine guns. No country in Europe, either in 1914 or in 1939, managed to integrate war and politics in the manner prescribed by Clausewitz. Italy entered both wars with armed forces very far from prepared for the contest which her political leaders sought. In 1939, a contemporary critic later stated, the Italian General Staff 'had not the least glimmering of the nature of modern warfare'.[76] Many factors were responsible for that – and many other General Staffs could then be said to have shared the same failings. But, unlike some, the Italian military could not be accused of distorting or perverting Clausewitz. Although ready to adopt some foreign theorists and to cultivate domestic strategic and tactical thinking, Italy persisted in regarding Clausewitzian thought as irrelevant until the eve of Mussolini's fall.

NOTES

1. Piero Pieri, 'Orientamento per lo studio di una storia delle dottrine militare in Italia', *Atti del primo convegno nazionale di storia militare* (Rome: Ministero della Difesa 1969), p. 152; Filippo Stefani, *La storia della dottrina e degli ordinamenti dell'esercito italiano* (Rome: Stato Maggiore Esercito, Ufficio Storico, 1984), Vol. 1, pp. 24, 27–30.
2. Piero Pieri, *Guerra e politica negli scrittori italiani* (Milan, Naples: Ricciardi, 1955), p. 197.

3. Piero Visani, ' "Guerra di popolo" e "Guerra regia" nel Risorgimento', *Politica militare* 4 (1982), 59–60, 66.
4. Piero Pieri, 'La guerra regia nella pianura padana' in E. Rota, ed., *Il 1848 nella storia italiana ed europea* (Milan: 1949), Vol. 1, p.169.
5. Luciano Russi, *Carl Pisacane: Vita e pensiero di un revoluzionario* (Milan: il Saggiatore, 1982), pp.71–84.
6. Quoted by Stefani, Vol. 1, p.98.
7. C. Thoumas, *Les transformations de l'armee francaise* (Paris: Berger Levraulr, 1887), pp.2, 97.
8. Dennis E. Showalter, *Railroads and Rifles: Soldiers, Technology and the Unification of Germany* (Hamden, CT: Archon Books, 1975), p.113.
9. Pieri, 'Orientamento per lo studio', pp.153–5.
10. Pieri, *Guerra e politica*, pp.266–67; Russi, p.117.
11. Stefani, pp.1, 147.
12. Ibid., pp.222, 225, 228.
13. Quoted by Massimo Mazzetti, 'Enrico Cosenz, scrittore militare', *Il pensiero di studiosi di cose militari meridionale: Atti del congresso nazionale* (Rome: Società di Storia Patria di Terra di Lavoro, 1978), pp.103–4.
14. Roberto Battaglia, 'Esercito e unita nazionale', in E. Ragionieri, ed., *Risorgimento e Resistenza* (Rome: 1964), p.46.
15. Niccola Marselli, *Gli avvenimenti del 1870–71* (Turin: Loescher, 1873), Vol. 1, p.144.
16. Niccola Marselli, *La guerra e la sua storia* (Milan: Treves 1881), Vol. 2, p.246.
17. Ibid., pp.79–80.
18. Quoted by Pieri, *Guerra e politica*, p.283.
19. Ibid., p.297.
20. Stefani, Vol. 1, pp.366–7.
21. 'Le Combat de la division en Italie', *Revue militaire de l'etranger*, 15 Feb. 1884, 131–2.
22. 'L'emploi des trois armes dans le combat en Italie', *Revue militaire de l'etranger*, 15 Jan. 1886, 9.
23. 'Le legge di reclutamento e l'istruzione primaria in Italia', *Rivista militare italiana*, 29 (1884), 231–3.
24. Quoted by Stefani, Vol. 1, p.380.
25. 'La scuola di guerra', *L'Italia militare e marina*, 12/13 Aug. 1896; 'Gli avvenimenti d'Africa e la scuola di guerra', *L'Esercito italiano*, 15 Aug. 1896.
26. 'I regolamenti tattici e la battaglia d'Adua' and 'Iniziativa ed offensivita eccessiva', *L'Esercito italiano* 30 Aug. and 2 Sept. 1896; 'Observations sur la bataille d'Adua', *Revue militaire de l'etranger*, Oct. 1896, 325–7.
27. 'La Scuola di Guerra nelle formazioni del comando', *L'Esercito italiano*, 4 Sept. 1896.
28. G. Cantu, *Lezioni di arte militare* (Modena: Società tipogratica modenese, 1903), p.19.
29. 'L'educazione del carattere e la Scuola di guerra' and 'Governo disciplinare', *L'Esercito italiano*, 28 Aug. 1898, 23 Sept. 1908.
30. 'La nostra letteratura militare' and 'Gli ufficiali in Germania e in Italia', *L'Italia militare e marina*, 7/8 Jan. 1901 and 28/29 Aug. 1902.
31. 'Il fuoco e la baionetta', 'Le trincee de battaglia' and 'Divagazioni tattiche ... giapponesi', *L'Italia militare e marina* 15/16 Oct. 1899, 16/17 April 1900 and 18/19 Jan. 1904.
32. Stefani, Vol. 1, pp.404–17.
33. 'Qual' e l'obbiettiva di un esercito in guerra', *L'Italia militare e marina* 2/3 Oct. 1902.
34. Quoted by Stefani, Vol. 1, p.420.
35. Ibid., p.448.
36. Piero Melograni, *Storia politica della Grande Guerra 1915/1918* (Bari: Laterza 1969), pp.34–5.
37. Stefani, Vol. 1, pp.458–65.
38. For a full development of these themes, see John Gooch, *The Road from Porta Pia: Italian Military Policy 1870–1915* (forthcoming).
39. Ufficio storico dello Stato Maggiore dell'Esercito. Relazione del viaggio dei generali 1911, p.119. *Carteggio Campi, Esercitazioni, Manovre*, racc. 44.
40. Stefani, Vol. 1, pp.509–10.

CLAUSEWITZ AND MODERN STRATEGY

41. Giorgio Rochat, 'La preparazione dell'esercito italiano nell' inverno 1914–1915 in relazione alle informazioni disponibili sulla guerra di posizione', *Risorgimento* 13 (1961), 10–32.
42. It is made by Stefani: Stefani, Vol. 1, pp. 520–21.
43. Ibid., pp. 655–8.
44. John Gooch, 'Italy during the First World War', paper delivered at Military Effectiveness Conference, Ohio State University, 8–10 Nov. 1984 (to be published).
45. Quoted by Stefani, Vol. 1, p. 646.
46. Lucio Ceva, *Le forze armate* (Turin: Utet 1981), pp. 146–8.
47. Giulio Douhet, *Diario Critico di Guerra* (Turin: 1921), Vol. 2, pp. 21–2. Quoted by Stephen Harvey, 'The Italian War Effort and the Strategic Bombing of Italy', *History* 70 (Feb. 1985), 33.
48. Romeo Bernotti, *Guerra marittima* (Florence: Carpigiani & Zipoli 1923), p. 303.
49. Massimo Mazzetti, *La politica militare italiana fra le due guerre mondiali (1918–1940)* (Salerno: Beta 1974), p. 116; also Ceva, p. 228.
50. Brian L. Sullivan, 'A Thirst for Glory: Mussolini, the Italian Military and the Fascist Regime, 1922–1936', (Ph.D. dissertation, Columbia University, 1984), pp. 380–81.
51. Virgilio Ilari, 'Il problema epistemologico delle scienze militari', *Strategia globale*, n.s. 2 (1984), 179.
52. Ibid., 174.
53. Mario Gabrielli, *I carri armati* (1923), quoted by J. J. T. Sweet, *Iron Arm: The Mechanization of Mussolini's Army 1920–1940* (Westport, CT: Greenwood Press 1980), p. 56.
54. Sullivan, pp. 277–81.
55. Sweet, p. 88.
56. Mazzetti, *La politica militare*, pp. 138–9.
57. Alberto Pariani, *Le Forze Armate dell'Italia Fascista* (Rome: La Rassegna Italiana 1939), p. 123, quoted by C. De Biase, *Aquila d'Oro*, p. 408.
58. Emilo Canevari, *Clausewitz e la guerra odierna* (Rome: 'La Cardinal Ferrari', 1930), p. ix. It has not been possible to consult the main text of this work as no copy exists in the United Kingdom.
59. Ibid., p. x.
60. *Della guerra: pagina scelte*, trans. A. Beria and W. Muller (Turin: Schioppo, 1930). Until this time, *Vom Kriege* was apparently read in Italy in the French edition of 1886–87: Ilari, 175.
61. Emilo Canevari, 'Clausewitz e la teoria della guerra (1)', *Rassegna di cultura militare*, Feb. 1939, 136.
62. Ibid., 2 March 1939, 258.
63. Ibid., 260.
64. Ibid., 3 April 1939, 341–9.
65. *Della guerra*, trans. General Ambrogio Bollati and Lt.-Col. Emilio Canevari (Rome: Stato Maggiore R. Esercito: Ufficio Storico, 1942).
66. Ibid., p. xl.
67. *Carlo Von Clausewitz: La guerra (Vom Kriege) Pagine scelte*, introd. Oete Blatto (Florence: Le Monnier, 1942).
68. Ibid., p. xi.
69. P. Roques, *Le general de Clausewitz, sa vie et sa theorie de la guerre d'apres des documents inedits* (Paris: 1912), pp. viii–ix.
70. *Pensieri sulla guerra*, trans. G. Cardona (Florence: Sansoni 1943). Since the Second World War, an edition of *La guerra* has been published in Florence (Le Monnier, 1962).
71. 'Guerra alla guerra?' *L'Esercito italiano*, 7 May 1907.
72. 'Del modo di considerare e trattare alcune questioni militari', *L'Italia militare*, 20 Jan. 1881.
73. C. Barbasetti di Prun, 'Dottrina di guerra terrestre', in Pietro Maravigna (ed.), *Un Secolo di Progresso Italiano nelle Scienze Militari* (Rome: Societá italiana per il progresso delle scienze, 1940), p. 497.
74. Benedetto Croce, 'Azione, successo e giudizio. Note in margine al "Vom Kriege" del Clausewitz', in *Ultimi saggi* (Bari: Laterza 1935), pp. 266–79.
75. 'Le conclusioni del Generale Pianell', *L'Esercito italiano*, 1 Feb. 1888.
76. Denis Mack Smith, *Mussolini as War Leader* (Reading: University of Reading, 1973), p. 17.